Bewitched
FOREVER

The Immortal Companion to Television's Most Magical Supernatural Situation Comedy

HERBIE J PILATO

foreword by WILLIAM ASHER

ANNIVERSARY EDITION

TAPESTRY PRESS • IRVING, TEXAS

Tapestry Press
3649 Conflans Road, Suite 103
Irving, TX 75061
972 399-8856
www.tapestrypressinc.com

Printed in Canada.

08 07 06 05 04   5 4 3 2 1

Library of Congress Cataloging-in-Publication Data
Library of Congress Cataloging-in-Publication Data

Pilato, Herbie J.
  Bewitched forever : the immortal companion to television's most magical supernatural situation comedy / Herbie J Pilato ; foreword by William Asher.– Anniversary ed., [3rd ed].
      p. cm.
  Summary: "Contains everything a fan might want to know about the 1960s TV series, Bewitched. It has background information, cast and staff biographies, script summaries, awards, trivia, etc. Includes information on the later Tabitha TV series"–Provided by publisher.
  ISBN 1-930819-40-4 (trade paper : alk. paper)
  1. Bewitched (Television program) I. Title.
  PN1992.77.B48P52 2004
  791.45'72–dc22
                                    2004022367

Cover and book design by David Sims
Cover illustrations by Paul Kreft
Author photo by Sam Companaro

Dedicated to the silent magic named Peace.

"Bewitched is distorted from reality—and nothing is as dull as constant reality."

AGNES MOOREHEAD

Contents

by William Asher

Foreword

I've been *Bewitched* for years.

And there's a good reason for that. I was in love with the show's shining star: Elizabeth Montgomery.

She was my wife, the mother of my children, my coworker, my business associate, and my best friend. She was first and foremost a lady—a lady of grace, of charm, of magic. Her engaging talents were monumental and peerless. Her professionalism, personality, sense of humor, intelligence, and unaffected demeanor were a breath of fresh air.

Bewitched originally ran eight years, and never once did she complain.

She was there for every rehearsal and never once missed a day's work. She appeared in each of the show's 254 episodes.

We went through several cast changes, producers, and writers, and the quality remained high. We could have had *six* Darrins on the show, but we never could have replaced Elizabeth.

She was one of a kind, and the kindest one I ever knew.

Now she's left us, along with Dick York, Dick Sargent, Agnes Moorehead, David White, Paul Lynde, Marion Lorne, Alice Pearce, George Tobias, Maurice Evans, Harry Ackerman, and the several other magical talents from in front of and behind the *Bewitched* scenes. There has never been, nor will there ever be, a gathering of so many great performers on one television program which has brought so much happiness to so many. I'm proud to have known and worked with them all— Elizabeth, of course, in particular.

I believe, like I'm sure many of you do, that there is a purpose for everything, that we are placed on a certain path to complete a specific journey.

Elizabeth and the other members of the show's departed cast and crew reached a distinctive destination in a designated voyage, and it was time to move on.

They have left the physical world that we cling to. Yet, we must take comfort in knowing that the essence of who they were—as with the essence of all of those loved ones we have known who have passed away—continues on another level with a different journey, a vivacity that simultaneously remains each time we channel into *Bewitched*.

This book, then, is aptly titled. It signifies so well the imperishable sense of the show, the eternal hypnotic spell which was cast that one magic night on September 17, 1964, by a good witch named Samantha, played by a beautiful woman named Elizabeth Montgomery, who wasn't a sorceress at all but really an angel in disguise.

Like I said, I've been *Bewitched* for years, and again, as with so many of you, I'll remain *Bewitched* . . . forever.

This Magic Moment

What It Was Like to Meet Samantha
by Herbie J Pilato

I'll never forget the day I first heard Elizabeth Montgomery's voice on my answering machine, trailing off and on the tape, in bits and pieces, with a chipper, near stuttering rhythm. I had been attempting to contact this iconic star of everyone's favorite "wituation comedy" for months. Bill Asher, her former husband and the show's central producer/director, had been playing matchmaker for us, recommending that she speak with me. "You really should talk with Herbie," he told her on more than one occasion. "He is sincerely concerned with this entity known as *Bewitched*."

Consequently, on April 18, 1989 (three days after Elizabeth's 56th birthday), succeeding a long *regular life* working day at the front desk of the Bel-Air Bay Club in Pacific Palisades, California—and following months of leaving messages with her answering service—I came home to my tiny studio apartment in Santa Monica, noticed the flashing light on my machine, pressed *play*, and listened:

"Hi. It's Liz Montgomery. We've been missing each other — Well, you've been missing me. I'm finally back for a while. I will give you a call again. You call me. I'll call you. Hopefully, we'll be in touch. [Pause] This is crazy. [Pause, with a smile in her voice, then adding] Okay, bye-bye."

The *crazy* reference was a nod to the mere fact that I was writing this book and, that upon calling me, she heard on my machine the *Bewitched* theme, punctuated by the nose-twitch xylophone sound from the show's opening credits, pristinely timed with the phone beeper signal to *leave a message*. I can't begin to explain how long it took me to coordinate all that on my machine, but I did it, and when she heard it, she was impressed.

When I finally did meet Elizabeth, of course, it was I who was impressed. I remember driving up to her gated mansion in Beverly Hills, reaching over to the guest-announcement speaker, ringing the bell, and hearing a pleasant, "Hello."

"Hi," I said, "it's Herbie J Pilato."

"Oh, yes. Come on in."

I drove up the long driveway (with four new tires on my 1981 Buick Regal, because I wanted the car to *look nice*), passed a huge tennis court, a well-manicured garden, and closed in on a somewhat disheveled garage that housed a new Rolls Royce with a license plate that had stamped upon it the phrase, *Bent Liz* (as in Bentley). "How funny," I thought, as I read this. It was so in-tune with the amiable personality that I had come to know by then (if only through Lizzie's former *Bewitched* costars and production coworkers).

I soon approached the front door of her home, rang the bell, and she opened the door.

I was stunned. There stood *Elizabeth Montgomery*, the love of my TV life, the woman of my dreams. The idol of my idols. The *mother of all TV characters*.

"Hi," she said forthrightly, and placing her arm straight out in kind, she added, ". . . pleased to meet you." She welcomed me inside, and I followed her into the living room, and then it happened.

I can't believe it happened.

But it happened.

I did something really silly. I tripped over her coffee table. Fortunately, I didn't break my legs, but I at least broke the ice. She giggled like a little girl at my gaffe, we sat down and the first question she asked *me* was, "*Why are you doing this?*"

I went on to explain my *Bewitched* obsession. I can't remember exactly what I said, but I'm sure it went something like this: "Well, the show is really much more than just a sitcom about a witch. She's first and foremost a woman, who happens to be a witch. And she loves this regular mortal guy named Darrin for who he is, and not what he could do for her. And together they prove that any marriage can work, despite their differences, or whatever diverse challenges come their way. That's really what the show is about…prejudice. Looking past differences, and concentrating on what makes people the same."

It was Lizzie who now appeared stunned. She sat back and replied simply with an, "Oh . . . okay," and we became friends. My words were earnest, and she knew it. We went on to have a wonderful two-hour conversation about *Bewitched* and her early life and career, with three more two-hour sessions to follow (one involving a surprise visit from David *Larry Tate* White, her costar from *Bewitched*).

To close our first encounter with a bang, I had prepared a few gifts, making sure to offer them to her after our discussion was complete. I did not want her to feel overwhelmed. I was fully aware of her sensitivity to and fear of the press, due to her having grown up in the public eye as the daughter of famed actor Robert Montgomery.

Consequently, I became the first journalist to whom she granted an in-depth interview in over twenty years.

Upon completion of this monumental conference, I merely said, "I have something for you." I proceeded to take out from my black duffel bag a gold-framed inscription of a letter I wrote to her (that I had ordered in calligraphy), along with a fine-crystal unicorn (poor Bill Asher just got brownies). I knew that Samantha was fond of unicorns. It wasn't until speaking with Richard Baer, one of the *Bewitched* writers, that I learned that Lizzie, also, in real life, took a liking to the mythical creatures. She had collected marble, plastic, glass, and wood unicorns of every shape and size.

"Oh, my," she said, upon seeing the unicorn with which I had gifted her. "Oh, my . . . You know, don't you! You know!!" I once again reached into my bag and pulled out the plaque with the special letter penned upon it. The words explained how I felt. It immortalized all the sentiments I had long-waited to express for years, ending with, "Miss Elizabeth Montgomery, I state in truth and with much conviction, that the world remains blissfully, lovingly and enchantingly *Bewitched* forever, simply due to the fact that YOU are magic."

Upon reading that last phrase (which unbeknownst to me at the time would one day become the title of this book), she turned, as if in slow motion, and wrapped her arms around me. I was under her spell, in person, this time, nearly floating out the front door, upon making my exit. Right before I drove back down the driveway, I turned slightly, and looked at her standing in the doorway, holding the unicorn and the plaque. I could have sworn a mist began to form around her figure, as she stood waving good-bye. It was an incredible sight.

I walked to my car, and began to slowly drive away in a daze. I kept repeating, *I just met Elizabeth Montgomery. I just met Elizabeth Montgomery.* And in what seemed like only seconds, I was back home in Santa Monica (at least fifteen minutes away). Then, just as I opened the door to my apartment, the phone rang.

"Hello," I said, still in a daze.

"Hi, Herbie. It's Lizzie."

I freaked out. "Oh . . . hiiiii," I stuttered, completely clueless as to why she would be phoning me not even a half-hour after our first meeting.

"Just calling to confirm our appointment for next week."

"Uh, uh, uh . . . okay," I continued to stutter. "How about the same time? Four o'clock. That okay with you?"

"Perfect. Oh, how fun. See you then."

I hung up the phone. Was I dreaming? Was I drunk?! Was I alive?!!

I didn't have time for the answers. The phone rang a second time.

"Hi, Herbie, it's Lizzie again."

"Uh . . . hiiii."

"Yeah, I was just wondering," she began to query, ". . . what are the lyrics to that song that I sang as Serena in the episode where I wore the long blonde wig"? (*Hip, Hippie Hooray* was the segment's title.)

"Uh . . . uh . . . uh . . . uh . . . I have to check my notes . . ."

"Oh, okay."

And just before we hung up, I said, "You know something ? . . . I'm really glad you called back."

"You are?"

"Yeah. Remember when I said that I didn't want you to be overwhelmed with the gifts, and everything?"

"Yeah?"

"Well, I was wrong. I think you *should* be overwhelmed . . . in a good way."

"Oh, I am. I am. After you left, I thought to myself, *You know, it really must have been difficult for him to meet me?*"

"Really, you said that to yourself?"

"Yes..I did."

"Wow."

I'll see you next week."

"Okay . . . bye."

Before Elizabeth and I met a second time, I had placed calls into *Bewitched* costars Dick Sargent and David White. I needed to contact them to complete this book, but they refused interviews with me, unless I could confirm Elizabeth's involvement. So I called her one day, and asked if she would speak with them.

"Yes, absolutely," she said. "Do you have their numbers?"

We said good-bye, and about one half-hour later, the phone rang. It was Dick Sargent.

"Hi," he said. "I'm looking to speak with a . . . Herbie . . . is it . . . *Pee-lah-toe*?"

"That's right . . . this is he."

"Yeah. Hi, Herbie. This is Dick Sargent. I just got the strangest phone call from Elizabeth Montgomery, whom I haven't heard from in *years*. She said you're doing some kind of book about *Bewitched*?"

Before I could answer, call-waiting interrupted.

"Hold on, Mr. Sargent. I've got to catch the other line . . . Hello."

"Herbie, it's Lizzie. Did Dick call you?"

"Yes . . . I'm on the line with him, right now."

"Oh, goody," she said, just like a little kid.

I returned to speak with Dick Sargent. We set up an appointment and I hung up the phone. Then it hit me: *I was just on the phone with Darrin and Samantha — at the same time!* This was eerie to me because so much of *Bewitched* had to do with Darrin calling Samantha at home to see if *everything was alright*; if whatever magic madness that had been caused by Endora or the like, had subsided. Then, in some surreal way, I viewed myself as living in an actual episode of *Bewitched*.

More of the blur between fantasy and reality was yet to come.

When I went to meet Lizzie for the second interview, she had mentioned how, at 4:30 PM she was expecting a messenger, and if I would excuse her at that time to retrieve a package that she would be receiving. Sure enough, 4:30 came around, the doorbell rang, and she pardoned herself. About one minute later, she returned and, following behind her, was none other than David White. My jaw dropped. As a matter of fact, Lizzie giggled to David, "Oh, look at his face! Look at his face!!" She couldn't stop laughing. She was so happy that she surprised me.

Again, however, more amazement awaited. As David and I began to chat, Lizzie excused herself once more, this time to fetch us some drinks (an assortment of fruit juices). Then there was a moment of silence in her wake. David looked around the patio, and then intoned, "Beautiful house, isn't it?"

"Yes," I said, still a little bit in awe of the fact that I was visiting with Larry Tate in Samantha's backyard. "Yes it is."

He continued with, "Haven't been in here in fifteen years."

Shortly after, Lizzie returned, sipping orange juice, with grapefruit juice for me, and handing David the same. We went on to share a wonderful afternoon; I couldn't help but believe that I had done a nice thing; that I was responsible for bringing two old friends back together.

When David was ready to leave, Lizzie and I walked him to his car: a Toyota Supra. I joked with him about how that was too youthful a model for someone his age (seventy-something) to drive. He looked at Lizzie and laughed, then road away. As we watched him trail down the long driveway, the same path that introduced me into *the real world of Elizabeth Montgomery*, she turned to me and asked, out of the blue, "Do you like zucchini?"

"Excuse me?"

"*Do you like zucchini?*"

"Yeah . . . I gggguess so."

"Oh, goody."

At that point, she lunged a few feet ahead into her zucchini patch, which was at the center of her circular driveway. She reached down, pulled a huge zucchini from its roots and said, "Here . . . this is for you." Before I could offer a reply, she leapt back into the patch, and picked a second zucchini, this one even larger. "Here," she said, "take another one."

This time *I* was the one who was indeed overwhelmed. Here I was with this legend of television history, picking vegetables from her secret garden.

It was, in a word...*magical*, and a moment in time I obviously will never forget.

Prelude to a Witch

Consider this treatment for a prospective television show for the postmodern, postfeminist era:

A young woman comes from a tight-knit, ethnically exotic family that still observes religious orthodoxy. This woman, in fact, is the family's shining hope, a true believer in the ways of the old world and the most spiritually vibrant practitioner of the family's religious customs.

The woman shocks her family when she chooses to marry outside the faith. In fact, she falls in love with a man with no faith of his own other than the good old American work ethic. He is the consummate American corporate man, and he insists that his betrothed give up the traditional practices of her creed and become a nice corporate wife.

For the good of the relationship, but with misgivings, the woman agrees.

Of course, her family is outraged. More than that, they are deeply hurt that the woman would discard her natural-born talents, especially because they hold the husband in such low regard. He is the embodiment of secular humanism, and they are among the last torchbearers of their increasingly archaic religion. The family has no choice since the woman is determined to please her new husband. Yet, they vow to make life difficult for the newlyweds and try to get the husband to lighten up on his position, if not actually convert.

Therein is the premise underlying each episode of this prospective comedy series. Week after week, the husband will try to succeed in business without the help of his wife's direct

connection to the Greater Spirit. He will be unsuccessful because his wife's family messes things up. As much as the wife tries to keep her word by not letting her natural talents save the day, eventually she must do just that.

The moral of every episode is the same:

- No matter how much one tries to suppress one's natural idiosyncrasies in order to fit into modern society, it will not work.
- Spirituality must always prevail over matters of commerce.
- Love conquers all.

Sound familiar?

Since you are reading this book, you may already realize the unique aspects of *Bewitched*. Debuting in the fall of 1964, the "witch-com" is more popular today than during its initial ABC-TV run.

Bewitched remains progressive without being moralistic. It boasts a brilliant cast of regulars who augment a repertory company of supporting players. The men and women who labored in front of and behind the scenes knew early on that they were blessed with a great premise, and they made the most of it.

Elizabeth Montgomery (who was known to friends and by close associates as *Lizzie*) passed from this life on May 18, 1995, a victim of cancer. She spoke at length about the series for this book, as did other members of the show's cast and production band.

Ms. Montgomery showcased as pleasant a personality as Samantha. She was unassuming, non-threatening, and sweet-natured. Diagnosed with colon cancer just eight weeks before she died (shortly after completing production of her last television film, *Deadline for Murder*—her second turn as true-life Miami crime reporter Edna Buchanan), Elizabeth possessed a personal glow with unassuming demeanor until the end. Hollywood will never again emanate a more down-to-earth star.

In recent years, she had worked with AIDS Project Los Angeles and AmFar, the American Foundation for AIDS Research. She was supportive of her *Bewitched* costar, Dick Sargent (who replaced Dick York as Darrin in 1969) when he announced his homosexuality in 1991, and she even served with him as grand marshal of a 1992 gay parade in Los Angeles.

As Samantha's second husband, Dick Sargent (who succumbed to prostate cancer in July 1994) was involved with the Special Olympics and World Hunger organizations. Overwhelmed with the high statistics of young gay suicides, Sargent dedicated his final years to advocating for equal rights.

Elizabeth's initial TV spouse, Dick York, died on February 21, 1992. He was as caring, generous, and humble in real life as his small-screen male surrogate and *Bewitched* female consort (he referred to his wife, Joan, as "Joey" in the same manner in which Darrin designated Samantha as "Sam").

York provided hours of interviews discussing *Bewitched*. He was upbeat and exhibited an astounding sense of humor, which was courageous considering his extremely poor state of health and economics. He suffered from a severe deterioration of the spine, emphysema, and was hooked up to an oxygen machine. His finances decayed, York lived out his last days in a small cottage in the middle of Michigan's sparse countryside. It was a far cry from his celebrity-filled life as Samantha's inaugural groom.

In the midst of his horrid human condition, York established Acting for Life, an organization dedicated to feeding the homeless.

When he *passed into spirit*, the world lost a master of the acting arena and the human heart.

Each member of the visible, and invisible, *Bewitched* cast continues to make a colossal contribution to the world of entertainment as the show remains enormously popular in syndication.

With commentary from those no longer with us quoted in the past tense, and excerpts from the surviving cast and production team presented in the present tense, this tome was created to honor the entire group of Samantha/Darrin comrades in charm.

Essentially, this spellbound book explores the three forms of *magic* associated with *Bewitched:* first, the *magic appeal* of the sitcom and its stars. Next, the *television magic* required to produce the show; and finally, the *fantasy magic* which was the basis for the program's premise.

Everyone who worked on the show, the actors, the producers, the directors, the writers, the entire cast and crew, had the opportunity to present topics which would not normally have been allowed on a nonfantasy sitcom of the 1960s and early 1970s.

Though *Bewitched* was first and foremost created to produce laughter, it was also essentially a love story about two very different people. The scope was further widened as the series went on to address several social issues. Morality plays within a fantasy orbit were presented years before *All in the Family, Maude,* and the like would attempt to do the same with a reality base.

As Samantha scribe Lila Garrett says about the classic sitcom, "In its own oblique way, *Bewitched* offered a liberal point of view. In that sense, it remains timeless."

Hopefully, *Bewitched Forever* lives up to that notion, inspires you, the reader, to twitch on the light fantastic program, and helps you to unearth, enjoy, and embrace television's most magical, supernatural situation comedy.

Dick York, Elizabeth, and Agnes Moorehead raise their "spirits" to *Bewitched*.

Chapter 1

Welcome to the Magic Show

What would happen if a pretty little witch with a twitch named *Samantha* married a nice young mortal named *Darrin*? That question was successfully answered for eight high-rated television seasons on *Bewitched*.

A triumph of storytelling, special effects, and gimmickry, this magic sitcom originally aired on ABC-TV from September 17, 1964, to July 1, 1972.

The cast was charismatic.

Elizabeth Montgomery was the ideal Samantha; Dick York and Dick Sargent offered a daring dual turn as Darrin; David White was Larry Tate, Darrin's self-absorbed, greedy boss and president of McMann and Tate Advertising; the magnificent Agnes Moorehead was Samantha's feisty mother Endora.

While on ABC, the series collected twenty-two Emmy nominations (five alone for Elizabeth), winning kudos for director William Asher in 1966, and posthumous confirmations for both Alice Pearce as nosy neighbor Gladys Kravitz, also in 1966, and Marion Lorne as the bumbling witch, Aunt Clara, in 1968.

Other performers were Sandra Gould (who stepped in as Mrs. Kravitz when Pearce passed away in 1966), George Tobias (Abner Kravitz), Paul Lynde (the practical-joking warlock Uncle Arthur), Alice Ghostley (the inept magic maid Esmeralda), Bernard Fox (Dr. Bombay, the witch doctor), Irene Vernon and Kasey Rogers (as Larry Tate's supportive wife, Louise, 1964-66 and 1966-72, respectively), Mabel Albertson (as Darrin's nerve-wracked mother, Phyllis Stephens), Robert F. Simon and Roy

I belong to the greatest minority of them all—I'm a witch.

SAMANTHA
"The Battle of Burning Oak"

....

Mabel Albertson (right), as Samantha's mother-in-law, was the perfect rival to Endora (Agnes Moorehead) left.

Elizabeth Montgomery hugs TV father Maurice Evans on the set of "Paris, Witches Style" in 1972.

Roberts (sharing the role of Frank Stephens, Phyllis's husband), and Maurice Evans (Samantha's regal father, also named Maurice), among several others.

The sitcom's debut met a super-receptive audience that was quickly won over by Samantha's magic. In its first season, the series ran second in the ratings only to NBC's *Bonanza* and received a 31.0 Nielsen rating, meaning that 31 percent of the television population tuned in to *Bewitched* for its initial year.

In 1969, the program's combined prime-time and daytime audience (ABC ran it daily from January 1968 to September 1973) totaled fifty-five million viewers, a record for a series in its sixth season. That same year, *Good Housekeeping* magazine named the half-hour comedy "the most agreeable show on the air."

Samantha's adventures averaged a 22.6 rating and a 35 percent audience share for its entire eight-year run on ABC. It was the number-one show on that network for four of those years. Until 1977 (and the surpassing popularity of *Happy Days*), *Bewitched* was the highest rated half-hour prime-time series ever to air.

In syndicated reruns the world over (England, Australia, Germany, and Egypt, just to name a few), Darrin and Samantha continue the trials and tribulations that arise when witch meets mortal, a mixed marriage follows, and they try to live happily ever after.

In the show's pilot segment, *I, Darrin, Take This Witch, Samantha*, she informs him of her supernatural persuasion both after the wedding and during the honeymoon. Each ensuing episode is a new misadventure. Sam tries to adapt her unique ways to the life of an average suburban woman.

Learning to live with witchcraft is one thing, but Endora's petulant dislike for her son-in-law

Though Endora (Agnes Moorehead) may have driven Darrin (Dick York) a little bonkers at times, he never strayed from Samantha's side.

Dick Sargent joined Bewitched in the fall of 1969.

(due to his eagerness to succeed without witch-craft) is the story conflict that carried the sit-com through its extensive run. This dissension, coupled with Samantha and Darrin's love for each other despite differences, is the core of the show's continued appeal.

Satirically, *Bewitched* promotes a positive outlook on the all-American, albeit all-witch American, way of life. Samantha and Darrin are not presented simply as witch and mortal but rather as a caring wife and faithful husband who, as parental figures (they have two super-natural offspring: Tabitha, played by twins Erin and Diane Murphy, and Adam, played by David and Greg Lawrence), take pride in old-fash-ioned and down-to-earth values.

Bewitched proves to be enduring escapist fare with an appeal that extends beyond its supernatural premise and offers a humanistic outlook.

As in contemporary times, the 1960s had its share of turbulence and political tensions. The *Samantha* pilot began production on November 22, 1963, the day President John F. Kennedy was assassinated.

Bewitched premiered less than one year later.

Bill Asher and Elizabeth Montgomery were good friends with the president. Asher had pro-duced Kennedy's famous Madison Square Garden birthday bash at which Marilyn Monroe sang a sultry *Happy Birthday*. He regis-ters the president's passing on *Bewitched*'s first day of rehearsal as a "tough" experience. "Both Liz and I were friends with the president," he says, "but we knew we had to go on."

Elizabeth remembered being in her bedroom getting ready to go to the set and hearing Asher scream from the parlor, "No! It can't be true!"

"For some reason," she said, "I felt it had nothing to do with the family. But it's as if I inherently knew what had happened. The whole thing was very strange, but to keep on working did seem to be the right thing to do. We went ahead and had the first reading of the script. It was very interesting. There wasn't one person who didn't show up. There weren't any phone calls made. It was like everyone on the set just needed to talk with each other."

During the years *Bewitched* was aired, America also lost Senator Robert Kennedy and the Reverend Martin Luther King Jr. to assas-sins; racial tensions were escalating as were the misuse of drugs and sex; and there was conflict in Vietnam.

For many, magic was the only viable solution to the insurrection of the times.

Erin Murphy who, along with twin sister Diane, portrayed Samantha and Darrin's magical preteen daughter, Tabitha, recalls the unhappy era in which *Bewitched* was filmed and the role the show played in relieving certain anxieties: "Elizabeth used to receive phone calls asking her to please stop the war. If you're really a magic lady, then please help stop the fighting."

At the time, Elizabeth herself (who was protesting the war) was deluged with life-threatening communication.

"I used to get calls from people all the time," she confirmed, "who told me that if I didn't stop speaking out against the war, I would be killed."

Suffice it to say, these were not *Wonder Years* at all, but wonderless.

Samantha offered her world of sane fantasy to the insane reality of the television audience. She was beautiful, smart, and filled with magic: everything our world was not. As the American people viewed the weekly escapades of a witch, they could daydream about how much simpler their war-torn lives might be if they had Samantha's magical finesse.

I Dream of Samantha

As a result of its influence and popularity, *Bewitched* inspired several replicas.

I Dream of Jeannie began on NBC-TV in 1965. This fun show, starring Barbara Eden as a genie to Larry Hagman's frantic astronaut master, was most similar to *Bewitched*, right down to the animated opening credit sequence.

While Samantha would manifest her magic with the *twitch* of her nose, Jeannie would do the same with the *blink* of her eyes. On *Bewitched*, Samantha had a mischievous cousin named Serena, played by Elizabeth in makeup and a brunette wig. Likewise, Jeannie acquired a look-alike sister of a Serena-sinister nature, acted by Eden in a black coiffure.

Jeannie's genesis was assuredly Samantha-inspired.

Screen Gems (known today as Sony Pictures Television), which produced *Bewitched*, and ABC's rival network NBC were quite anxious to cash in on the success of ABC's witch-comedy format. So anxious, in fact, that they tried to acquire the services of *Bewitched*'s pilot scripter, Sol Saks, who declined. "I had already created one witch," he says. "I did not wish to do another."

The studio then commissioned novelist (and now miniseries king) Sidney Sheldon to create *I Dream of Jeannie*. Ironically, *Bewitched* executive producer Harry Ackerman (who passed away in December 1990) had introduced Sheldon to Screen Gems executives some years before. He held himself partly responsible for delivering *Jeannie* to her master viewership.

What's more, Bill Asher and Sidney Sheldon worked together on *The Patty Duke Show* and became close friends. "Sidney was very polite about the situation," says Asher of the Samantha/Jeannie connection. "He came to me and said, 'How do you feel if I do a show about a genie?' I told him I didn't care."

Asher's confidence rested with Elizabeth's aforementioned, now famous, unique ability to wriggle her upper lip. As to the birth of Samantha's coveted, quick-twisting nose, Asher knew it had to be something that no one else could do. And the witch-twitch was the answer.

"It was a little nervous thing Liz did without her being aware of it," he says.

When first approached about employing her facial expertise, Elizabeth told Asher, "I don't know what you're talking about. I don't do anything like that."

"It became quite an issue between us," says Asher. "I couldn't believe that she didn't know what I meant. I thought she was trying to avoid doing it. It wasn't until the night before we filmed the pilot that she did it, and I said, 'That's it!'"

Sheldon then wondered with what distinguishing gesture Eden's Jeannie would exercise her magic.

"I don't know," Asher told him. "Maybe you have to marry Barbara to find out!"

Color Copies

CBS jumped on the magic bandwagon in 1970 and introduced *Sabrina, the Teen-Age Witch* to Saturday mornings. *Sabrina* had first appeared in the comic book *Archie's Madhouse* (Number 22; October 10, 1962). She had blonde hair just like Samantha, and while Sam twitched her nose, Sabrina, of all things, tugged her ear to make with the magic. Also, the similarity to the name of Samantha's cousin is apparent.

Other charming carbons include Samantha and Darrin themselves.

The enchanting couple made an animated appearance in an episode of *The Flintstones*, aptly titled *Samantha*. This segment, which was initially broadcast in 1966 and recently released by Hanna-Barbera on video, features the vocal talents of Montgomery and York.

"The network and the studio made us do that," explains Bill Asher. "*Bewitched* and *The Flintstones* were both on ABC, and Columbia had a contract with Hanna-Barbera."

Of her experience working with "Fred and Wilma Flintstone," Elizabeth recalled little. "I just remember going into the voice-over studio," she said, "and having fun with the script."

"It was the 'in' thing to do at the time," added Dick York. "Everyone guested on that show. Liz

and I just decided to go in there and have a great time with it."

York distinctly remembered not getting paid for the job. "Instead of a check," he laughed, "I got a TV."

The *Flintstones-Samantha* pairing, which may still be seen in reruns, involved the Stephenses in caveman garb temporarily moving next door to Bedrock's favorite Stone Age family.

Needless to say, Wilma makes a mild Mrs. Kravitz.

Ain't Nothing Like the Real Thing

As many times as television has tried to repeat the magical formula of *Bewitched*, it rarely manages to duplicate its success.

In May 1989, NBC aired *A Little Bit Strange*, a supernatural sitcom pilot that fizzled. A kind of combination between *Bewitched* and *The Munsters*, with a black cast, *Bit* offered a mom with ESP, a Frankenstein-like son, a vampire cousin, and a young boy warlock who rapped incantations.

Daily Variety magazine explained why *A Little Bit Strange* was even too strange for the fantasy comedy market: "It's a takeoff on the old *Bewitched* series, but the producers seem intent on playing up the gimmickry."

Such a simple reference unravels why *Bewitched* continues to succeed; and how it's distinguished from *A Little Bit Strange* and other fantasy comedy trial and errors.

As Elizabeth spelled it out, "*Bewitched* is not about cleaning up the house with a magic wave, zapping up the toast, or flying around the living room. It's about a very difficult relationship, and people see that. They know there's something else going on besides the magic. When the show is viewed carefully, its other elements may be observed."

One of these other elements is the sitcom's central hidden theme, which is the same as the program's general conflict. In a word, "prejudice." Elizabeth conveyed, "It can get people off on the wrong track at times. As a witch Samantha is an outsider trying to belong, always seeking the approval of Darrin or the mortal world in some indirect way, if not directly. Actually, one of the few things that Endora and Samantha agreed on was that witches were an ousted minority group."

The self-effacing actress did not deem *Bewitched* the message show of the century, but she "always believed there was something in it for everyone.

"As much as I know it is for little kids to watch," she stated, "I also know adults enjoy it as well."

What if the audience, young or old, is indeed looking for a message?

"They'll find it," she affirmed

My Country Witch of Thee

Bewitched speaks to the socially conscious viewer and the patriot watcher.

Many episodes celebrate freedom and equality and condemn prejudice. When great historical figures such as Benjamin Franklin (Fredd Wayne) and George Washington (Will Geer) visit the Stephenses through the magical mishaps of either Marion Lorne's unpolished Aunt Clara or Alice Ghostley's anxiety-ridden witch-maid Esmeralda, they leave behind profound wisdom for Samantha and Darrin—and the audience—to relish.

"An All-Witch-American Family Portrait": Father Darrin (Dick York), Mother "Samantha" (Elizabeth Montgomery), Grandma Endora (Agnes Moorehead), and daughter Tabitha (Erin Murphy).

"I think the show strikes some real chords with the viewers," affirms Bill Asher. "It's concerned with an individual's expression of liberty, people's rights in general, and the restrictions that are placed upon those rights."

Several episodes protest discrimination and hail human unity.

In The "Witches Are Out," Samantha, Aunt Clara, and other immortals (Reta Shaw, Madge Blake) persuade Darrin's client (Shelley Berman) to change the trademark of his Halloween candy from the stereotyped wicked-old-crone-with-warts look to a more flattering guise.

Samantha hopes "Mr. Brinkman" (Shelley Berman) gets the message in "The Witches Are Out."

With "Trick or Treat," and a similar premise, Endora turns Darrin into a werewolf because of his antiwitch comments.

This time, Samantha really lets her mother have it:

"For years, you've complained about how they [mortals] make fun of witches, dressed up as ugly old crones, cackling and pretending to turn people into toads. 'We're not like that,' you said. 'We're civilized, nice people,' you said. But now you're acting just like those ignorant people think a witch acts. Don't you see? You're behaving like all the stereotypes of witches you hate so much. And you've done it to the one person who was willing to believe we were different!"

Endora apologizes to Darrin and Samantha in this "Treat" (she actually says "I'm sorry"). Yet she never seems to learn her lesson and continues to change Darrin throughout the series—as in "To Trick or Treat or Not to Trick or Treat" (another Halloween outing), when she transmutes her son-in-law into one of the old crones to whom her daughter had previously referred.

Bias gets another blast in "Samantha's Thanksgiving to Remember."

Aunt Clara's dysfunctional magic finds herself, Sam, Darrin, Tabitha, and Mrs. Kravitz (who thinks the whole thing is a dream) in seventeenth-century Salem where, Darrin is quick to point out, "They burn witches . . . !" To his surprise, it is he who is accused of witchery. (He's also the one who lights the fire for turkey dinner with a twentieth-century match.)

Samantha delivers this rousing speech on ethnocentrism in the dialect of the day (which Darrin termed as "Pilgrim talk") at her husband's trial:

"Art thou clumsy, 'tis not thy own fault; cry witch. Art thou forgetful, blame not thyself; cry witch. Whatever thy failings, take not the fault upon thyself. 'Tis more a comfort to place it on another. And how do we know we decide who is the witch? 'Tis simple. Does someone speak differently from thee? A sign of witchery. Does he show different mannerisms? Witchery, of course. And should we not find differences in speech and mannerisms to support a charge of witchery, be of good cheer. There are other differences. What of him who looketh different? What of her whose name has a different sound? If one examineth one's neighbors closely, he will find differences enough so that no one is safe from the charge of witchery. Is that what we seek in this new world? Methinks not. The hope of this world lieth in our acceptance of all differences and a recognition of our common humanity."

An encounter with bigotry closer to home is found in "The Battle of Burning Oak." Here Sam and Darrin have a slight brush with the arrogant members of a pretentious private club, and Endora pickets the witch-horror film *Rosemary's Baby* (which Uncle Arthur also opposes at the Cannes Film Festival in "Samantha's Shopping Spree").

Another bias-busting segment (which also happened to be Elizabeth's personal favorite), is "Sisters at Heart," set at Christmastime.

"Heart" involves Darrin's removal from an important toy account because a bigoted client (Parley Baer) mistakes a little girl (who happens to be black) for the Stephenses' daughter. The child, Lisa, (Venetta Rogers), is actually the offspring of McMann and Tate's Keith Wilson (Don Marshall, of *Land of the Giants* fame), and she seeks to become close friends with Tabitha—so close that Tabitha wishes they could be sisters.

While in the park, a mean-spirited playmate tells the two young girls that such a bond is

Elizabeth and Erin Murphy pose with Venetta Rogers in between "spots" from "Sisters at Heart."

impossible; they're different colors. Upset, Tabitha employs *wishcraft* (anything she wishes comes true), and transforms herself and Lisa into sisters.

Sort of.

White polka dots surface on Lisa. Black spots emerge on Tabitha.

Samantha acquires an antidote from Dr. Bombay and speaks with Lisa and Tabitha about true kinship.

"You can be sisters without looking alike," she tells them. "Sisters are girls who share something. Actually, all men are brothers, even if they're girls."

When "Sisters" was completed, Elizabeth thought, "Yeah, this is what I want *Bewitched* to be all about."

"Sisters at Heart" was a special segment for several reasons.

The story was written by students of the fifth period English class at Thomas Jefferson High School in Los Angeles, and that year (1970), an article appeared in *TV Guide* profiling the occasion.

Bewitched writer Barbara Avedon is a veteran of *The Donna Reed Show* and, more recently, *Cagney and Lacey*. She had assisted the students with certain aspects of the story, and, as she recalls, "Sisters at Heart" was her "favorite script of all time."

Avedon had stopped writing for *Bewitched* and everything else when Bill Asher telephoned her and explained how the schoolchildren had written a solid script, which needed only a slight rewrite.

"So I went down to Jefferson High, which was an inner-city school," she explains, "and I was horrified. Locker doors were hanging off their hinges. There wasn't a blade of grass in sight. What was worse is that these kids had been reading on a third-grade level. It was awful. But I walked into their classroom, and when their teacher (Marcella Saunders) asked who had watched *Bewitched* the night before, every hand in the room went up."

Avedon asked them why they liked it.

"Well," said one young man, "it's a mixed marriage. She's a witch and he's human, and she could have anything she wants but doesn't use her powers for selfish reasons—only once in a while to help her husband."

"It was really a wonderful moment," says Avedon, who then read the story the class had penned and was amazed. The script was as good as any that she had seen from established writers. "It just had to be polished up a little," she admits.

So she was honest with the young writers and said, "I don't like to be rewritten, and I don't want to rewrite you. But maybe if we work together, I think we can really create something beautiful." She promised not to make any changes of which they would not approve because she was quite fond of the basic idea. "The one major change I suggested," she reveals, "was that we make a Christmas show, because it was so imbued with the spirit."

After Avedon finished speaking with the class, "They all kind of just sat there stone silent for a minute," she says. "Then one of them stood up and introduced himself. Almost immediately, the other students rose one by one, and the class and I became friends."

Marcella Saunders, who is teaching today, could not say enough good things about this matchless *Bewitched* experience. "We were writing a Christmas story," she recalls, "and we were experiencing a Christmas story. Everyone on the set was pleasant and supportive."

Dick Sargent credited Saunders as the igniting force behind her students' creativity: "She was interested in innovative forms of teaching. These kids, who might have been stuck in the ghetto for the rest of their lives, loved *Bewitched*, and with just a little approval and motivation, came alive on the set. One of them was the assistant director, who had the chance to scream, *Quiet on the set!* It was marvelous. Doing the show gave them, at least for a brief time, a change of pace and scenery, in which they reveled."

The icing on the cake was yet to be spread.

In 1971, "Sisters at Heart" won the Governor's Award at the Emmy ceremony.

Other Social Functions

Bewitched campaigned for UNICEF ("Samantha Twitches for UNICEF"), Samantha supported the proper city councilman ("Red Light, Green Light"). She also stood up for *human* rights again in "Samantha Fights City Hall," in which she saved a neighborhood park from destruction.

It all was, and remains, relevant.

Bewitched appeared to us in the sixties at a time when social upheaval was common and attitudes about marriage and family were being redefined. Its fantasy element offered an escape from everyday life. The humor of absurd situations delighted us over and over. The series wove moral and social values into its illusory tales. It gave us a lovable witch, a happy and committed marriage, and it continues to create wonder in our living rooms.

Elizabeth Montgomery looking yonder during filming of the pilot, "I, Darrin, Take This Witch, Samantha."

Chapter 2

Born in the Sparkle of a Star

television situation comedy is usually created with a particular star in mind for the lead role. With *Bewitched*, stage and film actress Tammy Grimes was originally chosen to play Samantha.

Harry Ackerman explained how Grimes was approached about doing the show, but before production began, the actress informed the executive producer that playwright Noel Coward had asked her to star in *High Spirits*, a Broadway musical directed by Coward and based on his *Blithe Spirit*.

"So we let her out of the contract," Ackerman said. "And it's funny, because I ran into her every two or three years, and she was still kicking herself for not having done the show."

Enter Elizabeth Montgomery and William Asher.

The couple had recently been married, after completing the film *Johnny Cool* (1963, in which she starred and he directed).

"Liz didn't want to work [any more]," Asher recalls, "mostly because it meant separation and shooting locations. But I felt that would have been a great loss because I knew she had a lot to offer the industry. She should have continued working—for herself and for her contribution to the business."

He suggested the possibility of doing a television series with his wife where there would be no degree of separation.

"Liz was all for that," Asher says.

The producer/director then thought of developing his idea for a series about the richest girl in the world, "a real Getty's daughter-type thing."

This project, entitled *The Fun Couple*, centered around a young married surfer twosome named Bob and Ellen. He

We are quicksilver, a fleeting shadow, a distant sound.
Our home has no boundaries beyond which we cannot pass.
We live in music, in a flash of color.
We live on the wind and in a sparkle of a star.

ENDORA
"Be It Ever So Mortgaged"

From left: Dick York, producer/director William Asher, Elizabeth Montgomery, and executive producer Harry Ackerman celebrate the fifth season (1968-1969) of *Bewitched*.

worked at a gas station and was extremely independent. She was extremely wealthy, which proved extremely intimidating.

Asher took *Fun* to Columbia Studios and executive William Dozier (who brought *Batman* to television in 1966). "I think you should talk to Harry Ackerman," Dozier declared. "He's got something in mind that's very similar and that you might like better."

That "something" was *Bewitched.*

Asher said he and Elizabeth "flipped" over the idea, and signed aboard.

As to the original casting nod to Tammy Grimes in the *Bewitched* lead, Elizabeth said she won the role because Grimes turned it down. "I will always be eternally grateful to her for that," she said. "I didn't get the part because I beat out hundreds of women in some huge casting call which was painstakingly narrowed down to me. Tammy said *no*, I said *yes*, and I was simply at the right place at the right time."

Roots Canal

As to who actually gave birth to *Bewitched*, the line of creativity stretches far and wide.

According to Harry Ackerman, he was the man behind the magic woman. "I created *Bewitched* through the instigation of Bill Dozier," he said of the person who was his then Screen Gems superior. Together, they hired Sol Saks (who received screen credit) to write the *Bewitched* pilot.

"Bill Dozier took me to breakfast one morning," Ackerman said, "and asked me if I'd be interested in developing a show about a man who married a witch. I was immediately taken with the idea, and I began typing a treatment that I called *The Witch of Westport*, which ran eight or nine pages. I outlined the characters who would become Samantha, Darrin, and Endora, and I brought it to [Dozier], who was enthusiastic about the project. Then we started to look for writers."

The first person they talked to was George Axelrod, who cowrote the screenplay for *The Manchurian Candidate* (1962) with Richard Condon from Condon's novel. Ackerman had known Axelrod from radio years at CBS in New York. "George was as excited as Bill and I were about the idea," he recalled. But Axelrod later contacted Ackerman and said he was too busy with feature films to do *Bewitched*.

Ackerman was led to meet with another well-known screenwriter named Charles Lederer, who had cowritten the Broadway musical *Kismet*. When Lederer was approached about doing *Bewitched*, cancer had ravaged his health.

Ackerman and Dozier then ventured into television land and hooked up with Sol Saks (who had previously written for Ackerman and CBS on *My Favorite Husband*, 1953-55), and as Ackerman assessed, "Sol ended up writing the pilot."

Though Saks agrees that he wrote the initial *Bewitched* episode, he remembers differently the developing events:

"I met with Harry Ackerman and Bill Dozier, and we talked about different ideas for a comedy series. I then suggested the premise of a witch who lives as a mortal. I wrote the pilot and went on to teach a writers' workshop."

In Sol's *The Craft of Comedy Writing* (*Writer's Digest*, 1985), which features a version of the *Bewitched* pilot script, the author wrote:

"There has been much published and public controversy about who of several were initially responsible for the [*Bewitched*] idea, a contretemps that I carefully stayed out of. I felt the entire question was academic . . . because I was already receiving screen credit."

Ackerman's response?

"The Writer's Guild rules state that whoever writes the pilot [of a particular series] will be credited as its creator. Yes, Sol Saks did write and develop the *Bewitched* pilot, but it was I who had initially introduced the basic concept and story many months before my first meeting with Sol."

Ackerman also confirmed another Guild rule: Any individual who writes the pilot episode of a given series continues to benefit monetarily for his efforts throughout the life of the series, even from episodes that were scripted by other writers.

"I never had any ownership of *Bewitched*," he said. "I was salaried at Screen Gems. But I must say that years later, my agent raised hell [with the studio] for not remunerating me properly for having created the idea. Afterward, we worked out a new deal which paid me $50,000 over and above my salary each year the show was on ABC."

Spirit Move Me

The creator's spot on *Bewitched* was not the only hot seat on the show.

Though William Asher was with the series from the start as its main director, he was essentially a silent producer and was credited as only a production assistant in the program's initial years.

Danny Arnold (who died in August 1995 and who would go on to find fame as creator of *Barney Miller*, ABC, 1975 to 1982), Jerry Davis (who passed away January 1991), and William Froug were credited as producers for the first, second, and third seasons, respectively.

Though Asher was heavily committed to films (including *How To Stuff a Wild Bikini*, 1965, which featured Elizabeth in a cameo role doing the twitch), he was still the central producer of *Bewitched*. He does, however, credit the benefactions of Arnold, Davis, and Froug.

"Each of them made major contributions to the show," he says, "particularly Danny Arnold, with specific regard to writing."

Bewitched story editor Bernard Slade, who wrote seventeen Samantha scripts, confirms Asher's assessment of Arnold's witch input:

"Danny set the tone for the show, and his casting was brilliant. It certainly wasn't by accident that he went on to produce *Barney Miller*, which had impeccable casting. He was just very imaginative and one of the best story people I knew."

As the show evolved, a creative conflict developed when Harry Ackerman suggested that Samantha should become mortal after her first year of marriage to Darrin. Arnold was opposed to the idea and "felt we would have hit a brick wall with that angle. It bypassed the main conflict of the show."

Darrin and Samantha "bump" into each other for the very first time.

Dick York and Elizabeth.

Ackerman's idea proposed that each time Samantha twitched, she would move closer to a permanent mortal transformation because she was practicing witchcraft in a human environment. He felt this would have added an element of suspense to the series.

From Arnold's perspective, the show's conflict was divided into two main categories:

1. The power of a woman versus the ego of a man.
2. A mother's objection to her daughter's marriage to an unsophisticated man.

This dual discord was postulated on *Bewitched* without direct recourse to Samantha's witchcraft and the supernatural premise of the series. The sitcom was allowed to concentrate more closely on the relationship between the characters. Samantha remained a witch, and Darrin never formally granted her free use of her powers on a regular basis.

Spell a Cast

Beyond its basic premise and the casting of Elizabeth, there were other decisions to be made during the genesis of *Bewitched*.

For one, who would play Darrin?

Before Dick York won the role, Richard Crenna (a good friend of Bill Asher's) was a distinct possibility, and according to Dick Sargent, the "second Darrin" had actually been cast as Sam's mortal love for the pilot, years before he replaced York in 1969.

By the time Sargent was contacted, he had signed with Universal to do a television show called *Broadside* for ABC [1964-65], with Kathleen Nolan and Edward Andrews.

Sargent did not mean to denigrate York, but he said he was "the first person they saw, read, and liked for the role." Before he did finally appear on *Bewitched*, ironically, Sargent had portrayed the twin brother to initial *Bewitched* lead choice Tammy Grimes in her series, *The Tammy Grimes Show.*

Her character's name?

Tamantha, with a T.

Still, as Dick York reported, he was the first Darrin at which viewers guffawed:

"I went and met with Elizabeth. Someone handed us a script. We did a quick run-through. We went through it again in front of Bill Asher and Harry Ackerman. When we finished, I hopped on Liz's lap, turned to them and said, 'Hey, aren't we cute together? You have to hire us!' And I got the job. That's how I got all my acting jobs. I figured they'd either hire me or they wouldn't. So I would never pull any stops and just go for it."

Though Sol Saks thought York's animated face was a plus, the *Bewitched* pilot scripter says that, after the pilot was completed, there was serious speculation as to whether or not York was "good-looking enough."

Bill Asher, however, doesn't recall any such discussion. "Dick [York] was just too perfect for the part," he says. "We had to hire him."

"What made it work," Elizabeth added, "is that you didn't have Cary Grant, which, don't get me wrong, would have been lovely. But Darrin didn't need to be exquisite-looking for Samantha to have married him. That was the whole point. She could have zapped up the most gorgeous guy in the world, straight out of *GQ*, but she didn't. She loved Darrin in particular and despite the way he looked, talked, or thought. There was so much more going on between them besides any physical attraction they had for one another."

Next in line to cast after Darrin was Endora, who was referred to as just plain "Mother" in the original pilot script.

Right from the start, Endora tried to convince Samantha to change her mind about Darrin, as displayed in this scene from the show's pilot.

Harry Ackerman had suggested Agnes Moorehead.

Everyone in Hollywood had perceived Moorehead as a highly dramatic actress. Yet Ackerman had worked with her in radio days on *The Phil Baker Show*, for which he was the assistant director. Baker had regularly employed her as a comedian positioned in the audience (then called a "stooge"), and, as Ackerman recalled, "She was quite funny."

Elizabeth, on the other hand, remembered meeting Moorehead in Bloomingdale's department store in New York, and says it was she who offered the veteran actress the role of a magic lifetime. She heard this "voice," turned around, and there, in the ribbon department, was "this incredible redheaded lady with a rather large hat on her head" [made of pink tulle]. She looked like a serving of cotton candy," said Elizabeth. "I had never seen anything like it."

One actress then questioned aloud the identity of the other.

Upon learning it was Moorehead, Elizabeth marched on up to her soon-to-be TV relative and asked if she would ever consider doing a television series.

"Probably," Moorehead replied, and "probably not."

Sounds good to me, Elizabeth thought, and ran to find Asher.

"I found 'Mother,'" she told him.

"That's nice," Asher responded casually. "Where is she, and why don't you invite her to dinner? We haven't seen her in a while."

"Not *my* mother," Elizabeth laughed. "'Mother', as in *Bewitched*."

It didn't take too much to persuade Asher to hire Agnes.

He remembered working with the famed red-topped star in the NBC-TV remake of *The Wizard of Oz*, in which Agnes played—what else?—the Wicked Witch of the West.

Moorehead, however, reluctantly agreed to do the *Bewitched* pilot. As she told a reporter in 1965: "It was absolutely ridiculous the way it happened. First they offered me an enormous amount of money to make the pilot of the series." She then read the script and said to herself, *Why not? This series is so way-out, so totally devoid of commercial possibilities, it couldn't possibly sell.*

So she did the pilot, pocketed the money, and went on the road to do a one-woman show. She completely forgot about it until she returned to California. She then received a call from the producer. *Bewitched*, he said, has been sold. All Moorehead could think of was, "Oh, how dreadful!"

Though Moorehead initially shuddered when *Bewitched* received the green light, she came to love the series. "Aggie confessed to me once," Elizabeth recalled, "that she was hoping *Bewitched* was going to be a terrible flop so that she wouldn't have to be stuck in it."

Lizzie joked with her and said, "Now, that's a wonderful attitude." Yet Moorehead also let her TV daughter know "how happy she was to be a part of" the show.

Grounded Pilots

There were several characters created by Sol Saks, Bill Asher, and Danny Arnold who did not appear in the *Bewitched* pilot.

Darrin's sister and Samantha's father, for example, were written out of the first *Bewitched* script due to a lack of time. According to Saks, who created each of these characters, this was an unfortunate development. Sam's dad was eventually written into the show, but Darrin's sibling was not.

"That's too bad," Saks says. "She would have been a good character, someone on his side."

Fortunately, more members of Darrin's family, such as his parents, Frank and Phyllis Stephens (who were also created during the pilot's formation), did appear as the show continued.

"We always knew we'd use them," says Bill Asher, "so we just kept them on the back burner until it was the right time for them to show up."

A Magic Melody

According to technically oriented production notes, several people were responsible for creating the sitcom's theme and general music content as well as its opening tuneful credit sequence.

Don Kirshner (of NBC's 1970s precursor to MTV, *Don Kirshner's Rock Concert*) was the show's musical consultant; Warren Barker, Van Alexander, Pete Carpenter, and Jimmie Haskell coordinated the general music on the series; Howard Greenfield and Jack Keller wrote the opening theme.

At one point the Broadway tune *Bewitched, Bothered and Bewildered*, from the classic stage musical *Pal Joey* (1940), was to be employed as the theme.

"Everyone was really excited about that," recalled Danny Arnold, "and though Columbia did own the rights to *Joey*, the studio wanted to use an original song."

Elizabeth was disappointed. "I thought the one we used served its purpose," she said. "It was lilty and nice, but *Bewitched, Bothered and Bewildered* is so pretty. I really wish we could have used it, mostly because the lyrics were so wonderful."

Though lyrics were also written for the Greenfield/Keller theme, they were not employed when the show hit the screen.

Harry Ackerman thought it would have been too much activity for the audience to follow. "I wanted them to be able to read the credits and see the animation," he revealed. "Listening to the theme's words might have almost become a chore. I was quite thrilled with the animation. It was a different way to go. It kind of tipped off the fact that Samantha had supernatural powers."

Elizabeth, however, was never fully satisfied with the cartoon image of Samantha and Darrin. She thought it was "cute but too simple," and wanted something snappier. "I always looked at it as a great animated storyboard,"

she said, "that could have been developed into something more sophisticated. It just never looked as good as it could have. I was hoping for something along the lines of what they did with *Who Framed Roger Rabbit?* If not, then at least *Bambi* or *Snow White*."

The Last Wave

There was one final conceptual adjustment to make.

Elizabeth and Bill were about to have their first child, William Jr.

Would Samantha and Darrin be expecting as well?

Asher had experienced a similar predicament on *I Love Lucy* (for which he directed several segments), when Lucille Ball became pregnant with Desi Arnaz Jr. After much discussion, it was decided that the TV *Lucy* would be giving birth to "Little Ricky," to counteract the real-life expectancy.

On *Bewitched*, a decision was made to shoot around Elizabeth's ballooning condition. That is, only close-ups, over-the-shoulder angles, and long shots with Liz were employed. Later, when Elizabeth went on to have two other children in real life, Tabitha and Adam were written into the show.

As to the birth of *Bewitched* and its ensuing soaring popularity, it was a sure thing to come. Samantha's series was the first television program to use magic in a modern, suburban world. It was a test, an unconventional stab at entertaining America. Each carefully cast actor worked with writers, directors, and producers to create a convincing picture of an unreal world.

Happily, the cooperative effort continues to delight us into old age.

Nancy Kovak (far right) on the set of the pilot, directed by William Asher (far left).

Chapter 3

This Witch for Hire, on Fire

Bewitched was not without its controversies on the way from the finished pilot to full sponsorship and a place on ABC's schedule. Even today, network executives would be leery of programming a series with themes of witchcraft or satanism.

Imagine how cautious a network had to be in the sixties.

It may come as some surprise, then, that it was a sponsor which finally prodded ABC executives to add *Bewitched* to the schedule.

Quaker Oats sought to promote its products on ABC and chose to back *Bewitched*. Yet ABC President Tom Moore was concerned that the show's supernatural themes would offend viewers in the Bible Belt.

"My network will lose all the South and the Midwest," Moore told Bill Asher.

"Tom," Asher retorted, "this is all made up. It's only a TV show."

"If it's only a TV show," Moore returned, "then the audience won't believe it or watch it anyway."

Because ABC waffled on picking up *Bewitched*, the show was offered to CBS executive James Aubrey, who wanted the series for his network. Ultimately, Tom Moore was pressured into picking up the series despite his own discomfort, and ultimately the show enjoyed the shared sponsorship of Quaker Oats and Chevrolet.

When it comes to controversy, network executives have changed little in thirty years. *Bewitched* associates, however, were careful not to interject the darker elements of the

When we had Samantha in bed with Larry,
and Darrin in bed with Louise
. . . that was
about as racy as we got on the show.

RICHARD MICHAELS
Bewitched *director/associate producer on "Mixed Doubles" in which a spell causes Darrin and Larry to mistake each wife for the other*

Sam and Endora are boiling mad in "Sam's Hot Bed Warmer."

Not only was Samantha a good wife, she was a good mother, first to Tabitha (pictured) and later to young Adam.

supernatural into the show. As producer Jerry Davis affirmed, "We were very conscious not to cross those lines."

Associate producer Richard Michaels directed fifty-four episodes of the series. He believes there were never any intentional evil elements to *Bewitched*. "We were all having too much fun to concern ourselves with such an angle," he says. "If people drew such conclusions, they did so on their own accord. I mean, we're talking about a comedy here. We had people like Marion Lorne and Paul Lynde, for Pete's sake."

"The only objections I've come across," comments Sol Saks, "were through a radio show I did promoting my book. Before I did this one show, the station manager asked me not to mention anything about *Bewitched* because the station was very family-oriented. I thought this was a little silly, as *Bewitched* has been the most financially successful work of my career, not to mention that I included the series pilot script in my book.

"But I found out later that it's the belief of some very conservative people that witches are considered very evil creatures. The truth of the matter is that there have always been bad witches and good witches, such as *Cinderella*'s godmother. I just couldn't understand how they were picking on little innocent Samantha."

Shortly before his passing, Dick York had also experienced some flack by way of static radio receptions over Samantha's allegedly bad attitude.

York was doing a show for the homeless. A listener called in and said he or she wouldn't allow his or her children to watch *Bewitched* because it was sacrilegious. "I respected that response," York said, "but I felt the assumption was a bit off the mark. I never thought of

Samantha or any of the other witches on the show as evil. The show was about how much two people loved each other, no matter how different they were."

When a television program is as popular as *Bewitched*, there is bound to be a wide range of viewer contact, with varying perspectives and opinions to debate. Yet labeling the show as unfit for family viewing seems, as Dick York relayed, "a bit off the mark," especially since there was never any conscious aim to stir up a rumpus. In the long and short of it, *Bewitched* offered high entertainment values, and continues to bring television viewers the world over hours of joy.

Proof in the Pudding

Samantha and Darrin displayed many traditional beliefs.

The Stephenses honored Sunday as a day of rest in several episodes.

In "Nobody but a Frog Knows How To Live," Sam says a silent prayer that two opposing characters not run into each other.

In "Double, Double, Toil and Trouble," she helps out a church function, while she's actually inside a church in "Love Is Blind."

As previously discussed, *Bewitched* spoke heartwarmingly in several episodes that addressed universal respect, especially holiday segments.

In "A Vision of Sugar Plums," the Stephenses take an orphan (Billy Mumy of *Lost in Space* and now *Babylon 5* fame) who hates Christmas to see Santa Claus (Cecil Kellaway) at the North Pole.

The bearded one tells the child: "We all grow older, and our eyes get weaker, but what we've seen with our hearts remains forever a thing of joy and beauty."

And later: "Remember—the real happiness of Christmas isn't found in what we get, but in what we give."

Agnes of God

If *Bewitched* had ever intended to slur any church or religion, Agnes Moorehead would have put a stop to it. The daughter of a Presbyterian minister, Moorehead was a strong-willed, opinionated Christian woman. As author James Robert Parish reported in his book, *Good Dames* (A. S. Barnes and Company, 1974), Agnes once said: "My life has been ruled by my beliefs (working for the glory of God) and in matters of belief I am a fundamentalist."

David White was Moorehead's *Bewitched* costar, contemporary, and often a sparring partner on and off the screen. As he recalled,

Agnes Moorehead as Sister Cluny in MGM's *The Singing Nun* (1966).

Agnes Moorehead as she appeared in a campy episode of TV's classic *Night Gallery*.

dressing room, and that's when I came to realize that she was a deeply pious woman. Very nice and obviously talented, but extremely spiritual."

In fact, Moorehead had initially questioned the seer-allure of *Bewitched* when she signed to do the pilot. "How could witchcraft appeal to the general public?" she asked.

Ironically, Vernon believes Moorehead's conservative religious views and personal spiritual energy enforced the redhead's theatrical talents and allowed her to play Endora with "flair and conviction."

It may be appropriate to add here that Agnes appeared in the films *The Left Hand of God* (1955), *All That Heaven Allows* (1956), and *The Singing Nun* (1966); and tutored the late Jeffrey Hunter (Captain Pike in the original *Star Trek* pilot, entitled *The Cage*) as Jesus in the 1961 version of *King of Kings*.

So Let It Be Written, So Let It Not Be Done

There were some restrictions, though not spiritual in nature, that were placed upon *Bewitched* religiously.

McMann and Tate had every possible kind of advertising account, from "Tinker Bell Diapers" and Halloween candy to truck transmissions. Yet *Bewitched* was not allowed to employ certain names as clients of the firm.

Bewitched writer Richard Baer, who penned twenty-three episodes, explains: "We had a very good research department. If a writer created a particular name, and that name turned out to be a real person in the advertising business, we would have to have it changed. It was unfortunate because one of the best ways for a writer to think up a good-sounding name is to reference the real people they know or at least know of."

the actress was "extremely religious. We never got into an actual debate over the matter," White said, but if he said something of which she did not approve, Moorehead would tell White, "You'd better be careful, David. God is watching." To which he would reply, "Then may I be struck by lightning. And just to be safe," he recalled, "a couple of people who may have been standing around me at the time would carefully move away."

Irene Vernon, who portrayed White's first on-screen wife, Louise Tate, became friends with Agnes. While Vernon confirms the veteran performer's strong beliefs, she also discusses Moorehead's other side:

"Agnes did quote God a lot, but there were so many other aspects of her personality that she made you feel that you could talk with her about anything. On occasion, I would be invited to her

Baer's predicament was minor compared to what Bill Asher was confronted with regarding the show's censorship blues. There was one Samantha script having to do with greed and the auto industry, which was not filmed because Chevrolet was the sponsor.

In the never-mended story, Darrin was promoting a new car while Endora showcased how such behavior was another example of his insincerity as an adman. She believed there to be no real necessity for mortals to purchase brand-new automobiles. At one point in the unfilmed script, Endora protests: "You make people buy things that they don't really want or need." A strong position, similar to those of which she took in several other episodes that did make it to the air.

Endora continuously and insistently berated Darrin's profession. As Asher recalls, she was always making false claims about products that her son-in-law never used or would never think of using. Yet these other opinions were not stated as directly, nor was there even the slightest chance of offending one of the show's sponsors.

Still, Asher was disappointed at not being able to complete the "auto" show.

"I thought it was a good idea," he says, "and that it taught a great lesson. People don't have to buy new cars every year. They only do it because their neighbors up the street do and because they're overloaded with commercials that are very convincing. If no one bought a car for, say, a year, it wouldn't affect anyone's life. People who would buy cars for their kids coming of age would simply choose a used car with a couple of years on the road. There's nothing wrong with that. It doesn't have to, nor should it have to, be a new car."

Other developments in this unproduced *Bewitched* script blew a spark plug at Chevrolet. In the story, Endora places a spell on the entire country, prohibiting anyone from buying a new car for the entire year. Consequently, the economy begins to deteriorate. The Chevy people were, as Asher recalls, "not too happy."

The "auto" script aside, Asher was surprised that *Bewitched* got away with as much as it did, regarding the advertising business.

The Smoldering Pot

Despite Bill Asher's experience with the *lost Bewitched* script, the show somehow managed to produce and air material which may have been considered disputable.

In "Business, Italian Style," Darrin needs to learn Italian for proper client negotiations with "Chef Romani Foods." Endora casts a spell on him, and essentially transforms him into an Italian. Such a happenstance prompts Samantha to say things like, *Oh, Ma Ma!* and *Mamma Mia!*

Through the course of this segment, Darrin understands the Italian language so well that he has forgotten English, which he has to rediscover with his wife's assistance. One of the first lines he utters upon relearning his native tongue, is broken English, heavily accented with Italian. When he meets Mr. Romani (Fred Roberto), he says: "I-am-a-hoppy-to-a-make-a-your-a-cuaint-a-nence."

Samantha reacts with embarrassment, and Darrin replies:

"I'm-a-doin'-the-best-I-can."

Sam insists that her mother remove the spell from her afflicted husband. It's a slow road, as Endora offers sarcasm in mock-response to Darrin:

"I'm-a-doin'-the-best-I-can."

Samantha was a kindhearted, gift-bearing witch.

Elizabeth defended the funny and innocent dialogue of this and other *Bewitched* segments:

"We were always careful not to overstep the bounds of good taste, and not to get anyone too upset. I guess it would have had to depend on whom we were offending, but it would have to have been something really terrible. If we received letters from Italians saying, 'How dare you make fun of our people?' it would have been one thing. But we never received anything like that."

Of his foreign-speaking part in "Business, Italian Style," Dick York said he loved saying "I-am-a-hoppy-to-a-make-a-your-a-cuaint-a-nence," and he didn't feel he offended anyone.

Bernard Slade was story editor on *Bewitched* during its first two seasons and, in 1970, went on to create *The Partridge Family*. He expands on the *Bewitched* language barriers:

"At the staff meetings, if someone ever objected to a story, it really wasn't because of censorship, but rather because they did not like the idea itself. When writers would come in, they would generally pitch maybe six or seven plots. Sometimes we used them, and sometimes we didn't, or maybe we had already used them before. If someone came in with a risqué idea, which never happened, the network would not have objected anyway, because they had much less control over their television shows in the days of *Bewitched*."

In fact, when the *Bewitched* pilot was made, it was sold to ABC as a finished product, which allowed for very little editorial impact from the network. Despite the lack of censorship on the show's plot issues, the *Bewitched* writers stayed well within the bounds of mainstream American standards of good taste.

The series presented a broad array of characters, none of whom was employed as a stereotype. Though the cast and production team occasionally received negative feedback from viewers who took the witchcraft a little too seriously, the *Bewitched* band was delighted with the wide range of viewers they were able to reach and please.

Elizabeth Montgomery added dimensions to *Bewitched* with her "animated" twitch.

Chapter 4

The Twitch Dimension

Several *Bewitched* episodes showcase Samantha's loss or lack of powers. This was instigated by some rare witches' disease or metaphysical presence such as Endora or the Witches Council, both of whom strongly objected to Samantha's mortal bonding. These storylines contributed to the show's substance.

Often, Samantha being left without witchcraft to function as a mortal was the result of a miscast spell. There were times, too, when she chose to forfeit her powers. In such cases, the mortal audience related more easily to her on a human level and it further endeared her to them.

Bill Asher knew that the magical aspects of *Bewitched* would not hold up on their own. "In the beginning," he explains, "the audience would think it was cute and funny that Samantha could twitch her nose, but if it was done too often, the gimmickry would lose appeal. And at first, Liz was having trouble holding back Samantha's witch-twitch."

Asher believed Elizabeth was somewhat uncomfortable with the fact Sam would always wait to zap or hex some obnoxious character. She would say, "Samantha's a wimp!" Asher would tell her, "No, she's not. She's a hero. She's *Shane.*"

The director was referring to the 1953 film of the same name starring Alan Ladd as a retired gunslinger who hangs up his guns. The character goes through severe humiliation and insult as his townspeople taunt and challenge him to draw his weapons.

Asher screened the movie for Elizabeth and told her: "Sam doesn't twitch her nose until the audience wants her to."

I happen to think cooking on a stove is a lot more fun than using witchcraft. I also enjoy taking care of my husband and children in the everyday mortal way.

SAMANTHA
from "Darrin, the Warlock"

Samantha takes a (the) "stand" in "Samantha for the Defense."

Of the Shane-Samantha correlation, Elizabeth decided that it made "absolute perfect sense." "If you have a weapon," she construed, "be it a gun, witchcraft, or a sharp-tongued wit, you recognize it as something that you can rely on. But your principles are such that you do not pull out the big guns unless you really have to.

"There was a certain dignity to Samantha's decision to hold back on her power just as there was for Shane to control his fast draw. It had to do with Samantha's promise to herself and to Darrin of not using witchcraft, her own self-expectations, and living up to those expectations. A kind of exaggerated promises-you-can't-quite-keep-except-only-sometimes type thing.

"And the feeling that maybe if Samantha does help, then getting caught at something she wasn't supposed to do wasn't so bad after all, because the end result was positive. The guns shouldn't be pulled off the wall indiscriminately because someone could get hurt. It also just implies good manners-something we're all brought up with-that you simply don't take advantage of other people."

A good example of Samantha's heroic, Shane-like ethics occurs in an episode from the third season, "Samantha for the Defense," which is the conclusion of a two-part story involving a surprise visit from Benjamin Franklin (Fredd Wayne), compliments of Aunt Clara's wayward wizardry.

In the court of "Defense," Franklin is accused of stealing a classic fire engine from the town's firehouse and is brought to court on charges of grand theft. Assistant D.A. Chuck Hawkins (Mike Road) feels Franklin is a publicity stunt planted by McMann and Tate. So he insults Franklin, thinking him only an actor in disguise. Such a development incites Samantha to whisper to Darrin:

"I wish I could put a hex on him."

Darrin holds her back.

Finally, Hawkins calls Sam to the bench as a witness.

By now she, along with the audience, has had enough of his inconsiderate behavior. With a long-held twitch, she immobilizes the D.A.'s jaw, and presents a plaque that she had earlier removed from the engine.

It reads:

"Benjamin Franklin Memorial Fire Engine."

The courtroom extols her as she states:

"A man can't be accused of stealing his own property."

In "Defense," and other episodes involving repugnant characters (as with "Disappearing Samantha," involving a witch-hunter) our favorite witch withholds her powers with discretion, as would any average mortal when pushed to the limit.

After Elizabeth understood her character's affinity with Shane, as an actress she felt more comfortable with her TV counterpart's apprehensive manifestations of magic.

Accordingly, Samantha retained her self-respect. She was endeared to the audience, and the witch-twitch became something eagerly anticipated by the audience.

The Big Witcher

Bewitched was the sum of its parts and never relied on any one specific element of its premise but rather on the rigid structure and format from which it was initially conceived.

Bill Asher expands on the program's original idea as he explains the boundaries in which it remained: "The story I was after all the time, and the one we usually would use, would be one that would work without witchcraft. There was always the danger of ruining the premise and characterizations with too much magic. I always felt that the audience really didn't care about the magic but rather the relationships and interactions between the characters. Darrin loved Samantha enough to stay with her regardless of how bad the situation was. It would have been worse without her. Samantha's love for Darrin was so potent, she was willing to give up her heritage to be his wife."

Asher feels it's important to remember that Samantha could have had anything or anyone that she wanted. Yet, she chose not to take the easy way out. He thinks that, on a subconscious level, the audience picked up on this development. They would view Darrin and Sam and say, "Hey, they're not going for the easy way out.

They want to earn their way. If Samantha doesn't think life as a mortal is so horrendous, I guess I don't have it so bad after all."

Elizabeth believed that Sam and Darrin's marriage was "the one thing that witchcraft couldn't do anything about, one way or the other."

"Sam's feelings for Darrin," she said, "were so real and honest that even though she could have gone and zapped him into being madly in love with her, it would have been a hollow victory. He would have only been under a spell."

According to Elizabeth, when it came to Samantha's love for Darrin, Sam knew exactly how she felt. If there was any question as to how he felt about her, Elizabeth said Sam would have experienced the same shadows of doubt voiced by the average mortal woman: "Has he found someone else? Have I done something wrong? Is there anything I could do right?"

Sweet Justice

Samantha/Darrin dialogue from "Charlie Harper, Winner," and "One Touch of Midas" illustrates succinctly their mutual love.

In Winner, Samantha conjures up a fur coat to impress Daphne (Joanna Moore), the snobbish wife of Darrin's overachieving college chum, Charlie Harper (Angus Duncan). After Darrin gets wind of this, he confronts Samantha:

Sam: Darrin, what was I to do? Daphne was being so patronizing. She practically called you a loser.

Darrin: So to prove what a winner I was, you gave yourself a mink coat!

Sam: I'm sorry, darling. She could have said anything in the world about me, but I didn't want her to knock you. Don't you understand?

Darrin expressed his true love for Samantha because of the "fuzz" in "one Touch of Midas."

Darrin: Perfectly. I'm enough of a breadwinner to provide you with the necessities, but when it comes to the luxuries I want to give you, I can't compete with your witchcraft. I can't give you anything that you can't zap up yourself.

Sam: Darrin, please let me explain-

Darrin: Explain what? I think everything is all too clear.

Later, Samantha ends up giving the coat to Daphne, who so fell in love with the fur that she offered to purchase it from the Stephenses.

Sam: Daphne, you don't understand. I want you to have the coat.

Daphne: You're giving it to me?

Sam: Charlie told me how much you admired it, so I want you to have it.

Charlie: That's a marvelous coat, Samantha. This is worth a great deal of money. You can't do that.

Daphne: You can't give away anything this valuable.

Sam: Oh yes, you can, Daphne, when you value something else a great deal more.

Daphne: More than this? Oh, you're kidding.

Sam: No, I'm not. I don't think I've been as serious or meant anything as much in my life.

Meanwhile, Darrin is watching from the side. On hearing these last lines from Samantha, he walks over and hugs her, speaking her name softly.

In "Midas," Endora manufactures mayhem with a toy doll she bespells, which will make Darrin a rich man. Unaware of her plan, Darrin confesses to Samantha that he'll now be able to give her the things he's always wanted to but could never afford.

Darrin: Honey, it's just that I've always wanted the best for you and Tabitha. When we were married, you made a big sacrifice for me. [He tickles her nose]

Sam: But-

Darrin: Now you did. You gave up, you know what. And I realize I'm probably overdoing it, but this money is my chance to give you all the things you could have had.

Sam: Darrin, all the money in the world couldn't buy what we already have.

Darrin: I know that, Sam. Just let me have the joy of overdoing it for a little while.

Sam: Uhm? That may be the nicest thing you ever said to me.

Of the "Winner" and "Midas" segments, Dick York said:

"When these moments occurred, the show was no longer just a sitcom."

As such, Samantha and Darrin endured trials and tribulations that were universal. With "Winner" and "Midas," and several other episodes, they were a young married couple who worked at their marriage. They occasionally doubted each other, but they always reaffirmed their love and commitment. It was the power of Samantha's human qualities that allowed Bewitched to transcend its time and make her the most adored witch in television history.

Actress Nancy Kovak played Darrin's ex-fianceé Sheila Sommers, who wanted Samantha out of the picture as much as Endora sought to get rid of Darrin.

Kovak exposes a comforting alternative view of the Darrin/Samantha relationship and how it was the major key to *Bewitched*'s success:

"Samantha lovingly touched everyone in the audience by devotion to Darrin. She was forgiven the slight use of her witchcraft because she was supportive of him. I used to watch the episodes for that very same reason. I was unmarried [today, she's the wife of orchestra maestro Zubin Mehta] and probably wanted to be. I liked to watch how different couples got along. That may sound awfully simplistic, but I think everyone is looking for a promise in the world. And by giving up her extravagant powers to be with Darrin, Samantha bespeaks that promise."

It is this unconditional, mutual support between Darrin and Samantha, and between the show and its audience, that invariably defines *Bewitched* as a love story. With this perspective, it may be seen how imperative it was to minimize the magic, particularly where Samantha was concerned.

Nancy Kovak's *Bewitched* characters (here, Miss Vinita from "Serena Strikes Again") were bent on separating Samantha and Darrin. In real life, Kovak loved to see the Stephenses together.

Nancy Kovak Mehta

Bill Asher sensed the viewer would hold Samantha in higher regard when she regulated her powers. "We were dealing with witchcraft," he says, "with someone who could do anything and get out of any situation. That's such a powerful weapon that you can only respect the person if they don't use it. That's how Samantha gained respect-by not using her powers in the face of all kinds of embarrassing situations."

Sam, of course, would twitch the eggs sunny-side up or fly to her husband's side in dire need, but she was just too nice a witch to hurt anyone's feelings or to use her powers for personal gain. To maintain the balance and appeal of the show's fantasy element, the majority of the witchcraft was saved for other supernatural characters such as Endora and Aunt Clara.

Yet, even their metaphysical manifestations were carefully monitored.

There were certain developments that Asher would never allow to transpire on the show. For example, the witches had the ability to bring someone back from the past. "We would do this only in an extreme emergency," Asher says, "or by mistake."

Cases in point: Clara zapping up Leonardo DaVinci (John Abbott) in "Samantha's Davinci's Dilemma" and Uncle Arthur popping up Julius Caesar (Jay Robinson) in "Samantha's Caesar Salad."

"If they were able to have used that power correctly," Asher explains, "then we would have had to do a show in which President Kennedy or Martin Luther King Jr. would have been brought back. And that would have been too heavy."

The show's magical characters also had the power to see the future and read minds, but Asher chose not to have these supernatural characteristics developed:

"Those were things that I thought the witches didn't care about. They didn't have those kinds of needs or that kind of ego. Why would they develop a skill they wouldn't use? It's as if someone had the talent to be a great pianist, but they never developed their ability. What good would it be? Reading someone's mind is like opening their mail. You don't intrude upon a person's privacy. That's just rude."

Elizabeth concurred. If there was any dialogue such as, "I know what you're thinking," she felt it would have taken away from the mystery of the show and the relationship between Darrin and Sam.

"It's like knowing what sex your baby is going to be before it's born," the actress explained. "You go through nine months of labor, anticipating the birth. It happens, and then you say, 'Oh, I knew it was going to be a boy.'"

Beyond the show's witchly provisions, and after Bill Asher defined the rules for the cast, crew, and himself, he had his own "quiet little fun." Like making sure most of the witches' names ended with an a or its phonic sound, such as with Samantha, Endora, Aunt Clara, Esmeralda, Hepzibah, and Tichebah.

He thought, I'll just keep this one to myself.

B Is for Best

If Bill Asher were to choose a favorite episode of *Bewitched*, it would be "A Is for Aardvark," from the first year.

That episode, he says, was definitive of the series. "In 'Aardvark,' Darrin sprains his ankle, and Sam gives him the power of witchcraft to make his life easier while he recuperates. He goes wild with the power but soon realizes that if you can have things without working for them, then they're not worth having. We repeated this theme on the show many times."

This is why Asher would allow Endora to ridicule Samantha for scrubbing the floor or cooking dinner. Sam would defend herself by saying something like, "Oh, Mother, you just don't know what it's like to set the table or prepare a meal for your husband and have him appreciate it."

Asher "never wanted to get too sticky about it," so he would have Darrin come home and say something like, "What's for dinner? Pork chops? I hate pork chops." "But the sense of morality was still there," Asher says.

Unconditional Power

From the onset, Samantha promised love, honor, and no witchcraft to Darrin. She loved him for who he was and not for what he could do for her. Because whatever he could do or buy for her, she could zap, pop, or twitch something up that was better.

She vowed never to defy, doubt, or betray him in any serious way—to be faithful always. She consistently offered him love, support, and devotion unless, through circumstances beyond her control, one of her spells backfired

Samantha and Darrin talk about what really matters in life in "A is for Aardvark," which is considered to be the definitive *Bewitched* episode.

or she fell ill with some personality-altering witch affliction.

What's more, Samantha was well aware of her near-unlimited powers.

She could have rid herself of any annoyance or problematic situation at will. She chose, instead, to deal on a mortal basis with any conflict and employed her secret abilities only as a last resort.

A hypnotic Elizabeth Montgomery.

Chapter 5

Some Enchanting Woman

Elizabeth Montgomery did not believe her being cast as Samantha helped or hindered the popularity of *Bewitched*. "Whether or not it was me or someone else from the beginning really doesn't matter," she said. *"Bewitched* told too wonderful a story for it not to succeed."

Born in Los Angeles, Elizabeth was the daughter of the late and famed actor Robert Montgomery and Broadway/film star Elizabeth Allen. She enjoyed a privileged childhood and upbringing. Her parents were wealthy, established, and respected in the entertainment industry and various social and political arenas.

Elizabeth's school vacations were usually spent with her parents in England where her father produced films. She was educated at several highly regarded halls of academia, including the Westlake School for Girls in Beverly Hills, California, the Spence School in New York, and the American Academy of Dramatic Arts (also in New York), which Agnes Moorehead had also attended.

Elizabeth brought a well-adjusted, levelheaded personality to *Bewitched* coupled with a great deal of charm. Had she developed an arrogant personality, which could have easily occurred because of her heritage, that insolence would have filtered into Samantha, and *Bewitched* would have bombed.

Instead, she made everyone like and believe in witches, because she made witches likable and believable.

The late E. W. Swackhamer directed eight episodes of *Bewitched* (and countless other classic TV shows) and gave his analysis of Montgomery's portrayal of Samantha: "There are not

Hers was a remarkable performance. I've never seen an actress more suited to a role. She was to Bewitched *what Jean Stapleton was to* All in the Family; *perfect for the part. As an actress, she lent credibility, warmth, energy, and a great positive view of life.*

LILA GARRETT
Bewitched *writer, regarding Elizabeth Montgomery*

many actresses who can get away with playing a witch week after week and bring to it the sense of realism that Elizabeth did. She was extremely professional and had a lot of talent. She'd make scenes work that I thought were impossible."

"In many of the animal shows that we did," adds Richard Baer, "she'd talk and react as if she was really communicating with them. This, I believe, was a very difficult thing to do. Yet there wasn't any question as to whether she could pull it off."

Baer remembers asking Elizabeth if she ever grew tired of playing Samantha.

"Oh, no," she told him. "I love it. I find new things to do with the role and professional challenges every week."

Years later, Montgomery still envisioned comedy as more challenging than drama. She proposed that if you have ten people in a room, and someone comes in and proclaims, "I just saw a dog get hit by a car," those same ten individuals will respond to the incident in the exact way (with "Oh, no! That's horrible!").

Yet if someone entered that identical room and proceeded to tell those same ten people a joke, then that person will receive ten different reactions. "Some may think it's moderately humorous," she said. "Some may believe it's very funny, and others may feel it's not funny at all."

"So with humor," she continued, "you're not always hitting the same emotional chords with people as you might with drama. Therein lies the challenge. That's why I love acting, and why I loved doing *Bewitched*. I enjoyed playing Samantha because I liked her sense of humor, and I knew the audience would love the humor of her situation and perceive it in any way they chose. I also respected Samantha's incredible

amount of discipline. She certainly possessed more than I ever did."

My Favorite Wituations

Besides "Sisters at Heart," Elizabeth had several favorite *Bewitched* episodes:

"I liked the two we did with Henry VIII ("How Not To Lose Your Head to Henry VIII," Parts 1 and 2). I liked most of the ones we did with Serena. They were fun, especially when she sang ("Hippie, Hippie Hooray" and "Serena Stops the Show"). I loved all the shows we did with Aunt Clara, mainly because of Marion Lorne. She was so very special. She used to prove such a challenge to move from one place to another.

"I also loved all the *double* shows we did ("Double Tate," "Accidental Twins," "Which Witch Is Which?," and several others). I think the audience enjoyed seeing how other people behave as they shouldn't behave."

Montgomery's other favorite Samantha segments included:

- "The Crone of Cawdor" ("That was really different.")
- "Three Men and a Witch on a Horse" (Elizabeth enjoyed the races.)
- "Samantha's Curious Cravings" ("I love it when Samantha's standing there eating the head of lettuce.")
- "Samantha Goes South for a Spell" ("Isabel Sanford was wonderful.")
- "My, What Big Ears You Have" ("Those ears!")
- "Long Live the Queen" ("I enjoyed playing dress-up.")
- "Weep No More My Willow," in which Samantha was bewitched and bouncing between crying then laughing ("*That* was a challenge.")

You Two, Serena

If Elizabeth was ever compelled to try other theatrics on *Bewitched*, she would don a black wig, raise her skirt a tad higher, and voila! Samantha's jaunty, man-crazy cousin, Serena, would appear.

In opposition to Samantha, Serena was a whole new ball of crystal. She was a free spirit with a quick temper who would not think twice about turning Darrin into a gorilla or his mother into a cat.

"I was a little bogged down that Samantha was so nice all the time," she admitted. "So Serena just kind of became my alter ego. I could have a smidgen more fun playing her than Sam."

"Serena was somewhat of a chameleon," Bill Asher says. "She changed over the years, from a deep-voiced sultress to a hippie, and in the last three seasons, kind of kooky. But we tried to give her the attitude of the time. She would show up in the guise of whatever was hot at the moment. But she was always a flirt."

The Serena idea was generated in "Which Witch Is Which" and "That Was My Wife," both from the first season.

In "Wife," Larry thinks that Darrin is fooling around with another woman, but Mr. Tate is unaware that this other woman is Samantha in a raven headdress.

In "Which," Endora transforms herself into a Samantha-clone.

Yet there are additional details of Serena's parturition.

When Elizabeth was growing up, she had a cousin named Panda who was always playfully starting trouble, but Montgomery would receive the blame.

Serena's beauty mark changed over the years. Here she wears a heart.

She remembered it as "just kid stuff. We'd wear the same clothes and have a great time confusing adults," she recalled. "I would walk up to someone and start a conversation, leave, and then Panda would show up and start talking. It was an ESP type of thing."

Starting with "Serena Stops the Show," Pandora Spocks was credited on screen as the actress who played Serena. Yet this listing was not a reference to Elizabeth's cousin. It was a play on words that alluded to the ancient Greek myth of Pandora, the evil being created by Hephaestus. When she opened her jar or, as in some versions, her box, she loosed on the world all the ills and failings of mankind.

At one point, someone asked Elizabeth: "Why don't you just use the name *Pandora*

Box?" She replied with just the right amount of decorum, "I don't think so. Pandora Spocks is somewhat more subtle, and a lot funnier."

Surprisingly, the Pandora credit led many fans to believe that Serena was actually portrayed by an actress other than Montgomery.

There were even those on the *Bewitched* set who were sometimes confused, such as the late Jerry Davis.

He recalled what happened one day during the filming of "And Then There Were Three," when the Serena character emerged for the first time:

"I noticed this rather hot-looking brunette on stage. I walked over and started to flirt with her. I remember wondering, 'Now, how am I going to get this lady to go to dinner with me?' But before I had a chance to ask her, she picked the time, the place, and the day we were going to go out. Then it dawned on me who this woman was. Elizabeth had the time of her life putting me on for twenty minutes."

There were other times when Elizabeth was

Serena's mod and blond look from "Hippie, Hippie Hooray."

just as mischievous on the set as Serena was on the show.

Marvin Miller was assistant director on *Bewitched* for its first five seasons. He says, "Lizzie was like a little kid," and remembers one pregnant moment, when she reveled in self-deprecation: "We needed her for a particular scene, but she wasn't anywhere to be found. I searched the entire set. I even went to the ladies' room and screamed *Lizzie! Lizzie!* from outside the door. And still nothing. I was just about to ask Melody [Thomas, Elizabeth's stand-in] to go inside, when I heard this little giggle coming from Lizzie's dressing room. There she was, underneath the makeup table, covered with a blanket, hardly able to come out from under there because she was so pregnant."

Elizabeth recalled it well, with a few alterations. "I wasn't just pregnant," she said, "I was pre-e-e-e-egnant. I had to look twelve months. No one could believe that I was able to fit under that table. The space was no larger than two feet wide. All I could see from underneath were Marvin's legs. Then I flashed back to when I was a little girl, hiding from parents in my dad's bathroom. They were yelling all over the place, looking for me, just like Marvin was. I remember thinking, *Ha, ha. They can't find me.* When my dad came into the room, all I could see were his legs as I was hiding behind the loo. So, years later, when I was under the makeup table on the *Bewitched* set, and Marvin came looking for me, all I could think of was, *My, my. Things change but remain the same.*"

As much laughter as Elizabeth caused on the Samantha stage, Dick Sargent noted how impossible it was to break *her* up—though he did succeed finally. Each time his back would be toward the camera, he would lip-synch, "Oh, shit,

Samantha!" and Elizabeth would always laugh.

The heartiest *Bewitched* chortle Elizabeth ever chuckled, she said, happened one cold day at the races, within the confines of the Santa Anita horse track in Southern California at which, as an avid equestrian bookmaker, she frequented:

"It was freezing," she said, "and I went into the ladies' room to freshen up. These two women walked in, and one turned to the other and said, 'Boy! It's colder than a witches' ti-,' and when she saw me, she stopped dead in her tracks and said, 'Oh, excuse me.'

"Well, I laughed so hard. I just couldn't believe it. When I left the ladies' room, I was still laughing. I started to tell everyone I saw what this one woman had said. I told the headwaiter and maitre d' at the track restaurant. I went around the entire room. I even told the bartender. I'm sure that poor woman was just chagrined about the whole thing. Everyone else, including me, thought it was hysterical."

Bad Vibrations

Of her *Bewitched*-related, general public encounters, Elizabeth said, in her most innocent way, that most of the time people were "nice." Different generations of little kids watch the show, so it was "really neat."

The only time she felt uncomfortable was when some parent forced a child, against the child's will, to "say hello to Elizabeth Montgomery." This inevitably happened at least once a year, and, for her, it was "heartbreaking."

For example, one day Elizabeth was shopping. A woman, with her preteen daughter in tow, approached the *Bewitched* star and began a scene.

"You come over here and say hi to Miss Montgomery," the mother ordered the little girl.

"No," the child responded. "No. I don't want to."

The entire time, the mother is professing to Elizabeth how much her offspring wants to meet Samantha.

"If that's true," Elizabeth wondered, "why is she yelling to the contrary?"

"She's just shy," the mother replied. "I told her that if she didn't say hello to you, you would turn her into a toad."

On hearing this, Elizabeth became furious.

"You told her *what*? How dare you say such a thing? No wonder she's scared to death!"

The woman grew angry and scuffed away.

Other snubs have been more show business oriented but no more entertaining.

The Academy of Television Arts and Sciences nominated Elizabeth Montgomery nine times for the Emmy award: five times for *Bewitched*, once for an episode of *The Untouchables* (entitled "The Rusty Heller Story," which also featured David White), and three times for various TV movies, including the groundbreaking 1974 film, *A Case of Rape*, which is one of the ten highest-rated small-screen films ever aired. *Rape* was also one of the first TV-issue movies ever made, one of which addressed the topic of spousal abuse ten years before Farrah Fawcett did with *The Burning Bed* (NBC, 1985).

Still, Elizabeth had never attained the heralded TV prize.

Was she disappointed? No.

She thought it was funny, and figured she was in good company, citing Susan Lucci (Erica Kane on the daytime serial *All My Children*) who had been nominated several times, but at that time had never won an Emmy:

"Maybe the two of us should work together," she laughed, "do something really brilliant, and then both lose. That would be extremely comical."

Other television performers who have never won an Emmy endorsement for their work include such veterans as Jackie Gleason, Bob Newhart, Leonard Nimoy, and *Murder, She Wrote*'s class actress, Angela Lansbury.

Bewitched associate producer/director Richard Michaels offers this opinion:

"Even though the Emmy is a major form of acknowledgment in the industry, it's not the only one in the world. Audiences adore Elizabeth just as much as they did in the

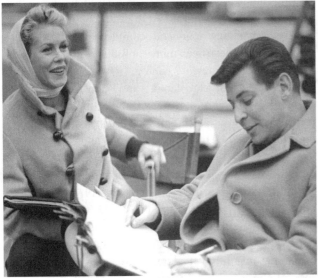

Elizabeth and director/associate producer Richard Michaels relax between scenes.

1960s, and no one will ever forget her or the show.

"When people find out that I worked on the show, especially little kids who weren't even born when the show first aired, the first question I hear is, 'What was Elizabeth really like?' or 'How did she twitch her nose?'

"This, more than anything, is a definite form of acknowledgment. It proves her main-

stay in television history. She knew she wasn't an actress solely by definition. She was a person and a very complete person at that.

"She was the darling of the *Bewitched* crew, and she was equally admired on every picture she made. She took care of everyone on the set, and she made sure each person had everything they needed. She was just as friendly with the gofer as she was with the director. She immediately disarmed people, and not everyone is like that, especially in the entertainment business. She was a dream."

Bewitched director R. Robert Rosenbaum concurs with Michaels, as he recalls Elizabeth as "a very caring person on the set. She was probably the most loved actor in our business. It was fun working on the show, and she helped make that happen, and the whole crew really did adore her. She was sincerely interested in everyone and everyone's family. The show itself grew to become a family. We all had wonderful relationships, professionally and socially. It was a love company, and she and Bill enhanced that.

"I feel very pleased with my years on *Bewitched*. I enjoyed doing the show and going to work. It was probably one of the best jobs I ever had because Liz and everyone there made it fun."

Rosenbaum, then head of production for Lorimar Television (which cranked out for ABC hits such as *Full House* and *Family Matters*), admits that working on *Bewitched* produced the regular TV show stress, but those on the show helped to alleviate that pressure.

"Today," he says, "you're in a different business. There's more of a corporate structure and different patterns and routines are followed. The industry is larger than it was during the

Elizabeth gazes off as director R. Robert Rosenbaum and Agnes Moorehead fidget with a prop from the show's fifth season.

time of *Bewitched*, and today's television stars are rarely as modest as Elizabeth was."

According to Bernard Slade, Elizabeth was and remains the main ingredient in the success of *Bewitched*. "She was never an overly gregarious woman to be around, but most enchanting. And that transfers to the screen."

Son Screen

One day, Elizabeth's "screen transfer" became a little confusing for her firstborn, Billy Asher Jr.

Circa 1968, when *Bewitched* was broadcast on ABC's Thursday night schedule at 8:00 P.M.,

little Billy was watching his mom on TV. At one point, Samantha popped out in a scene. It just so happened that on Thursdays the *Bewitched* associates also worked late, and Elizabeth didn't arrive home until around 8:15 or 8:30 P.M. So this one Thursday evening, just as Samantha twitched away in TV-land, Elizabeth walked through the door in real life.

Billy Jr. was startled.

"Jeez, Mommy," he said, "you really are a witch."

"No, honey," Elizabeth had to explain, "I just play one on TV."

Later on, Billy Asher grew to have the same

demeanor as his mom. As with Elizabeth, the younger Asher has never been one to boast about position or money, and he chooses not to walk around declaring his heritage. If people find out he is the offspring of Elizabeth Montomgery, so be it. If not, so be that as well.

One night a friend of Billy's was visiting his house. The acquaintance was unaware of Billy's background. The two were sitting in the living room. In walked Elizabeth to retrieve a magazine. Billy's buddy said, "Oh my gosh. It's Elizabeth Montgomery." "Naw," Billy replied casually, "that's just my mom."

Billy Jr. and his siblings, Robert and Rebecca, knew how fortunate they were to have Elizabeth Montgomery for a mother, as was the case with the *Bewitched* cast and crew, who had her as a coworker.

"We were the luckiest people in the world to have someone as warmhearted and appealing as Elizabeth Montgomery," Harry Ackerman concluded. "No one could twitch her nose like she did. Believe me, we all tried."

"She has a quality," Agnes Moorehead once declared about her TV daughter. "Charm, warmth, intelligence—she plays herself."

Elizabeth Montgomery's Samantha made you believe she could talk to the animals.

When two Darrins meet.

Chapter 6

A Tale of Two Darrins

T he history of having two Darrins on *Bewitched* began to formulate while the first Darrin (Dick York) was filming *They Came to Cordura* with Gary Cooper in 1959.

York and several other *Cordura* actors were acting in a scene that required them to lift a railroad handcar. At one point, the director yelled *Cut!*, and everyone but York let go. The car fell on him, wrenching his spine and tearing the muscles around it. His pain continued on *Bewitched*, later escalated, and he was replaced by Dick Sargent in 1969.

William Asher toyed with the idea of having Endora change Darrin's facial characteristics, but, upon thinking that it would have created a wall between Endora and Samantha, the tampering attempt was aborted.

"Samantha would never have put up with that," stated Elizabeth. "It wouldn't have been fair to the characters or the actors, and the audience would have hated it."

Of the York-Sargent exchange, Elizabeth maintained the replacement of performers as a common occurrence on television serials and in the theater:

"Audiences aren't stupid. They're certainly a lot smarter than any network executives give them credit for. We presented our case as if to say, 'Look, guys—we know you're out there watching. So bear with us. We're going through some changes, but hang in there because it's gonna work.'

"And it did. We were just fortunate enough to have had Dick Sargent and fortunate that he was available."

I could zap up mink coats all day long, but I could never zap up another Darrin Stephens.

SAMANTHA
"Charlie Harper, Winner"

Dick York, however, felt they should have changed the Darrin character completely, that Darrin should have been killed off, or that he and Samantha should have received a divorce.

"That would have been contrary to what the show was all about," Bill Asher responds. "How could you break up a love story and start it with someone else? It just wouldn't have worked. Darrin had to be so special that he'd be the only mortal that any witch, specifically Samantha, could be involved with. We just couldn't mess that up."

Obviously, Dick Sargent was happy the *Bewitched* troupe went the way they did.

Of Sargent's initial audition for the pilot, before York tried out, Harry Ackerman noted:

"We were very interested in pursuing him for the part of Darrin, but his contract with Universal prohibited him from being cast."

Prior to the commencement of the Sargent era on *Bewitched*, York felt he could have finished the run of the series. "All I wanted," he said, in reference to the end of the 1968–69 season, "was that summer to rest up."

York missed fourteen episodes, twelve of which were due to his back ailment. "The other two," he claimed, "I missed because my father had passed away, and Bill was gracious enough to allow me the time off."

A Third Darrin?

When Dick York was unable to portray Darrin, and before Dick Sargent was formally cast as his replacement, David White's Larry Tate would end up speaking or reacting to the magic with which Darrin would have confronted.

"We compensated," clarified Elizabeth. "It was an adjustment. At the same time, it introduced an additional element for Samantha. It allowed her to play off of someone other than Darrin in a very safe, platonic, and nonthreatening way."

A unique aspect of the York/Sargent exchange was that it permitted the flexibility to remake York episodes with Sargent.

For example, "Junior Executive" had York's Darrin shrunk to adolescence, while a similar spell was put upon Sargent's Darrin in "Out of the Mouths of Babes."

"When you produce 254 scripts," Bill Asher explains, "you're constrained to remake episodes no matter what you're doing. You can't help but dig back and rework old scripts. There's a limit to the situations you can come up with and still be able to maintain your premise. Without developing a whole new way to go, you're bound to travel the same ground."

Of York's health and the show's future at the time, Asher says the ailing actor was heroic, yet a decision had to be made: "Dick was able to hang on through the back injuries. But it became a real tough problem. In the third season, he began to miss episodes. At first, we were ahead enough in shooting to afford to take off a couple of weeks if Dick couldn't do the show, but then it became pretty consistent. So we would always keep one script without Darrin in order to keep going.

"We would shoot a tag [designated final scene] with him, just so his presence was there, or have him on a trip to Chicago, or just have someone make him disappear. The show's premise allowed us that luxury."

Richard Michaels believes that these non-Darrin episodes were not as conceptual as the rest. "The show was about Samantha *and* Darrin's marriage," he states. "Without Darrin, the central conflict was gone. It still would have worked with just Elizabeth, but the main format would have had to be changed."

"Darrin was the main protagonist who served as a counterpoint character to Samantha and the rest of the witches on the show," adds writer Bernie Kahn, who with then-wife and literary partner Lila Garrett penned several episodes of the show. "Once you removed him, you removed the show's central discord. You would have just had a show about witches and warlocks."

Darrin of York Style

Dick York felt tagged as the neurotic, hyperactive Darrin. He wanted him to stop being "so damned mad at Samantha all the time." He mused, "Why should he come home and start raising hell every day?" And he was finding such a philosophy doubly difficult to justify as an actor and as a human being.

"I knew when I would come home from a long day's shooting on the show," York explained, "I wouldn't want to start ragging on my wife that, 'Oh, boy, honey. What a day I had today,' and proceed to tell her all about my job, then condemn her because she didn't follow my prescription for life.

"So I thought it was terribly selfish of Darrin to do that to Samantha."

York said that if he were Samantha he would have told Darrin to "lay off or I'll zap you one."

Though the actor disagreed with Darrin's overtly contrary behavior, he felt the character had his more tender moments, as when Tabitha was born in "And Then There Were Three."

Both York and Agnes Moorehead had tears in their eyes while shooting "Three," and that's when York believed that Endora felt at least a pint of love, pride, and mutual respect, when it came to Darrin.

Dick York

At this point, York also believed: "No matter what Endora did to Darrin, he would always jump right back on his feet. Endora was beginning to realize just how much Darrin really loved his daughter."

York applied several guidelines and subtexts to his Darrin interpretation.

He listed what he thought were the character's beliefs in his relationship to Samantha:

1. I don't care what your mother does to me, I just want to be with you.
2. I don't expect you to be perfect, I just want you to be yourself.
3. I love you, and I want you to know how much I care.

"Darrin had to work hard for everything he got in life," York decided. "He had witches, neighbors, and even his own parents to deal with, but he didn't care. All he wanted to do was be with Samantha."

"As a conventional husband trying to succeed," writer Richard Baer perceives about Darrin, "he was a square. He didn't want his wife to use her witchcraft because he didn't want to be embarrassed."

"That wasn't it at all," York argued. "Darrin didn't want Sam to use her powers because he didn't want anyone else to find out about her or anyone else to have her. He wanted her all to himself."

An example of how fearful Darrin was of anyone's discovery of Samantha's true identity is found in "I Confess," from the fourth season.

Here, Darrin is displeased when Sam discourages a drunk with witchcraft. He declares his wife should disclose to the whole world that she is a witch. Knowing Darrin doesn't mean what he says, Samantha employs a dream spell and showcases what life would be like if everyone knew her secret.

In the dream, the government wants to use Samantha's magic as America's main defense weapon, and Larry seeks Samantha's power to control the world. Darrin then awakens, and changes his mind about the desire to reveal his wife's shrouded abilities.

Sam asks him what made him change his mind.

"I slept on it," he replies.

"'I Confess' says it all," York reported. "The comedy in that episode was brought out in a dramatic and effective way."

York believed timing was the essence of what fuels an acting scene, dramatic or comedic. Yet, he had mixed feelings about whether or not such a technique could be learned.

"I can always explain how I do a scene," he said, "but not while I'm doing it. Though I do admit it's easier to cry on cue than it is to laugh."

York's Darrin laughed a lot in "Weep No More My Willow," from the show's fifth year.

In "Weep," Samantha accidentally falls under a healing spell that Dr. Bombay intends for her ill willow tree on the front lawn. Whenever the wind blows, Sam cries. The more Dr. Bombay tries to right his wrong, the worse things get. Whenever the breeze misses the trees, Sam weeps uncontrollably.

Later, when Darrin comes home from work, he finds Samantha laughing out of control in the living room with Larry who's there because he thinks his two best friends are experiencing a marital rift.

Darrin is confused. When he called earlier, Sam was crying. Now, she's laughing, and it's contagious because Larry is laughing, too. Darrin doesn't know what to think but ends up jesting along with his wife and his boss as well because of the miscast spell.

How was all that handled on the set?

"It was ludicrous," York said, uh, with a laugh. "It got way out of hand. We were laughing about something we were told not to laugh about, and that made it funnier. We also shot that scene at the end of the day. We were all beat, and that made it worse. But it made the scene work."

David White recalled "Weep's" laugh segment and credited York's professionalism and strong theatrical background for allowing this spot and other *Bewitched* scenes to function.

White focused in on one scene between Larry and Darrin from "Dangerous Diaper Dan," which he thought flowed particularly well due to York's talents.

"Dangerous" involved Larry and Darrin visiting their favorite bar where they believe a martini is bugged with a microphoned pimiento placed by a rival ad agency. White decided, while filming, that he would take the pimiento out of the glass and flatten it on the bar. This move was completely improvised and a surprise to York, but as White explained:

"Dick just went right along with me. He was marvelous to work with. Most of the scenes we did at the office were a lot of fun to do. That was our environment. We were most comfortable there, and whatever techniques we tried at the office always worked."

Although many of Dick York's days on *Bewitched* were filled with grueling hours of physical pain because of his back ailment, he enjoyed his role as Darrin and never complained.

There were days, he said, when he had to memorize five and a half pages of a client's presentation, "and every single line had to be recited word for word. If it wasn't, we'd keep shooting until it was. Yes, it was a lot of work, but that's the kind of stuff of which actors are made. I was always prepared to do a scene a thousand times if I had to, to get it right."

York's tough background contributed to his strong work ethic. He grew up in a poverty-stricken area of Chicago, lost his baby brother to malnutrition and continued to suffer numerous health problems throughout his life. His hardened upbringing contributed to his solid work values, which then bled into his portrayal of Darrin, much like Elizabeth Montgomery's amiable disposition transferred to Samantha.

York went on to discuss his theatrical theory:

"I think actors who experience a deep sense of loss find it easier to relate to both the dramatic and comedic aspects of life. One of the toughest things to do during a dramatic scene is to know just how far to take the tears. It's important not to go overboard and have the character feel sorry for himself. As an actor, you can't fall to pieces. You're supposed to make the audience do that. Knowing when and where to draw the line is the actor's job.

"I believe I played Darrin as hard and as best as I could. When the pain became too great, I went as far as I could. When I wasn't able to give one hundred percent, I left."

Though Dick York felt that had he been granted more time to recuperate, and thus would have been able to finish the run of the series, he wanted everyone to know that he was happy to do the show.

"I couldn't have played Darrin," he proclaimed, "unless I loved the part."

Dick Sargent

Sargent's Savoir Dar(e)

How did Dick Sargent feel about being labeled the "kinder, gentler Darrin"?

"To tell you the truth," he said, "I think there was a stronger sense of warmth between Samantha and Darrin when I did the show. Liz and I were more kissy-kissy."

Like Dick York, however, Dick Sargent did object to some of Darrin's harsh behavior. "Darrin was a pain in the neck," he admitted. "He could really be unlikable. He was the *no-man* on the show. As much as he said *no* to Samantha's witchcraft, he was still unable to put his foot down completely and prohibit Samantha from using her powers. Yet, he had to at least try to stop her, however unlikable that made him to the audience.

"If Darrin didn't object to Samantha's witchcraft, then the show would have been about people who can get anything they want [as in Bill Asher's initial *Fun Couple* idea]. So in a strange way, Darrin was almost the moral backbone for the show."

Many *Bewitched* fans believe that Sargent's portrayal of Darrin *was* more laid-back than Dick York's. But Sargent's comedic prowess was equally as distinguished, as in "The Phrase Is Familiar," from his first season as Sam's main man.

In "Phrase," Endora tries to help Darrin in advertising by casting a spell that has him speaking in clichés. After Larry hears a few of these idiotic idioms, he becomes infuriated with Darrin and threatens trouble if he isn't more clever in dealing with an upcoming account.

Endora later alters the spell: Darrin's clauses are fewer, but those he does state he acts out. At a dinner meeting, he expounds: "I wish I could see eye-to-eye with you," and his eyes cross; then, "I'm keeping my ear to the ground," and he proceeds to throw himself to the floor, placing his ear on the carpet. He excuses himself from dinner, blurting out, "I

better shake a leg," at which time one of his lower limbs vibrates. Finally, he says, "I'll just bow out," and continues to do so literally.

"Phrase" is a genuinely merry episode and features some of Sargent's most wonderful moments of physical comedy. The whole cast glimmers in support of him, producing memorable performances by all.

As Sargent recalled, the comedy in "Phrase" was based on the truth presented by the show's scribes:

"I acted out the way it was written. I've always described comedy as having a third eye. You can't see it and feel if it's right while you're doing it. You can hear the timing and sense the look of the scene's physicality, checking on what body postures work, but can you really measure if it's funnier to sit halfway down, all the way down, or just fall down? I'm not too sure.

"But *Bewitched* was so well written, Darrin remained consistent whether it was Dick York or myself in the role. Most of what I did as an actor was in the scripts. They were just so damn good. Darrin's motivations were already put there by the writers. All I had to do was find reasons as to why Darrin would do the things he'd do."

Sargent pointed to the old cliché, "Why does an actor open a door? Because it's in the script. But the actor has to find a way and a reason to open that door," he said. "Sometimes, actors go beyond that into method acting [calling upon real-life experiences of people similar to an actor's role], but if the basic explanation of what a character should be doing is in the script, then all the actor has to worry about is personally interpreting that meaning.

"On *Bewitched*, that was a very easy thing to do. Darrin was well defined. It wasn't long before I realized that he would be either angry, furious, dismayed, or horrified when it came to Samantha and her magic."

As with Dick York, David White had much praise for Sargent:

"There was an incredible amount of dry humor that Dick brought to the role," White said. "He created a persona that was his and his alone. He played that type of arid comedy very well. The way he would deliver a line with a certain subtlety. He knew when to hold back and exactly when to zing it to Endora with the right amount of punch."

Like Dick York and many of the *Bewitched* cast, Dick Sargent had performed in dramatic parts as well.

"Drama is really only the dark side of comedy," Sargent decided. "Mostly because I am a comedic actor, I am also able to do drama. Dramatic actors can't always turn around and do comedy. It doesn't always work the other way around. But as actors get older, they usually get better, or at least more versatile."

Sargent hardly ever viewed his own performances.

"I hate watching myself," he revealed. "It's always painful."

If, perchance, he did take a peek, Sargent would ask himself, "Now why did I walk like that? Why did I turn like that? Why did I just say that?"

Yet, filming *Bewitched* was one of the happiest times in his life, "if not the happiest," he claimed.

The actor enjoyed working on various films for months at a time, but *"Bewitched* was three straight years of pure delight." Of his stint as Darrin, Sargent said there was never a moment when he woke up and thought, *Oh no, I have to go to work today.*

Still, the performer admitted to being somewhat nervous during his initial few appearances on the show. In fact, the first episode he filmed, "Samantha's Better Halves," ironically involved having two Darrins and contained dialogue that both he and Elizabeth deemed inappropriate.

In "Halves," Endora splits Darrin into two people: one business, the other all fun and games. When Sam begs her mother to put Darrin back together, she exclaims:

"I want only one Darrin!"

"I was kind of uncomfortable with that," Sargent said, "but I never thought it was a good episode anyway."

"Halves" was shelved as Sargent's premiere segment, replaced with "Samantha and the Beanstalk" and later aired as a flashback episode for a time when viewers became more familiar with the second Mr. Stephens.

Sargent admitted that there were certain aspects of the series that he, as an actor, had to figure out—specifically, and critically, the relationship between Darrin and Endora, with whom he could not have acted superior in any way. He recalled with a grin one time in which he behaved in a most un-Darrin-like manner, nearly prompting Bill Asher to speak with him as a father would advise a young son.

"He almost took me by the hand," Sargent remembered, "and walked me around the set, and said, 'No, Dick. Now Darrin wouldn't act like that.' I felt like I was five years old."

Following his introduction to the cast and the show's theatrical procedures and rules, Sargent understood his character's bottom line. "I knew that Darrin truly loved Samantha," he said, "and that he would always be by her side no matter what happened."

Witch Way To Go?

Dick York and Dick Sargent's respective Darrin portrayals suggested a question:

Was there a change in the direction of the series or in the chemistry of the Darrin character or between any of the *Bewitched* actors when Samantha changed husbands?

Marvin Miller, the show's assistant director, does not feel the series or the Darrin part altered course, but he does believe that York's interpretation was "more neurotic" than Sargent's.

The late Ed Jurist, who took over as story editor after Bernard Slade left, agreed that both actors were funny in the role but that Sargent had a "calmer air" about him.

Elizabeth, on the other hand, didn't think the situation was all that black and white.

"They overlapped fairly well," she said. "When Darrin needed to be strong-willed or strong-tempered, Dick Sargent compared equally to Dick York. They were both fantastic on the show. Each brought his own uniqueness to Darrin. By the time Dick Sargent came on the show, Darrin's and Samantha's relationship was five years old. Darrin's objections to witchcraft would have mellowed anyway, whether it was Dick Sargent or Dick York.

"Darrin was becoming a more easygoing presence. The show's situation almost became funnier. He would lapse into this kind of complacency and maybe into something that he just might enjoy for a minute or two. It was almost as if Darrin grew as the relationship developed. He didn't have to be on his guard as much. So when he was suddenly confronted by witchcraft, the newness of the marriage was gone. It wasn't as shocking an experience as it was in the show's first season.

"By the final year, he wasn't quite the nervous wreck he was when he first found out about Samantha. He was still against her using her powers, but the objection may not have been as harsh as it was in the past."

If some do feel there was a change in the series, associate producer/director Richard Michaels thinks it was very subtle.

"Darrin was insulted and manipulated in exactly the same way by Endora," he says "and was loved equally by Samantha, whether it was Dick York or Dick Sargent playing Darrin. The truth of the matter is that one day Liz as Samantha came on the set and said, 'Hi, sweetheart!' to Dick York's Darrin, and the next day came on the set and said, 'Hi, sweetheart!' to Dick Sargent's Darrin. As long as we all kept that straight, we were fine."

Either way, Elizabeth perceived Samantha's witch/mortal marital union as challenging for both Darrins. "It was difficult," she said. "Who would have gone through or put up with the stuff that Darrin did? It had to be a very laborious thing for him to be married to this woman who could have anything she wanted. Yet, the marriage lasted eight years, and how many of those do you find, especially with a mother-in-law like Endora?"

It may be comforting for *Bewitched* viewers to know that there was little competition and only mutual praise between Dick York and Dick Sargent.

"Dick's a marvelous actor," York remarked of Sargent. "He had a job to do, and he did it well."

Said Sargent of York: "He was excellent as Darrin."

Therefore, Elizabeth remains the main attraction of *Bewitched*, and Dick York and Dick Sargent continue to be the show's dynamic double feature.

Chapter 7

Mother and the Son of a Gun

Larry: "Hello, Endora."
Endora (curtly): "Mr. Tate."

A generic greeting between the two.

Had it not been for the theatrical expertise of Agnes Moorehead, perhaps Endora would have been considered too severe a television character and labeled unlikable by the audience. As *Bewitched* continued, she evolved gradually from Darrin's central nemesis to a mischievous prankster with just a touch of evil. Whenever she incorporeally interfered with Darrin's personality, or his looks, or his life in general, and she wasn't anywhere to be found, Samantha would simply shout for Mother! to appear.

David White's parody of the credit-grabbing, mildly deranged Larry Tate, who constantly put the client's wishes ahead of Darrin's (or whoever was in the room at the time), might have proved just as off-putting if it had not been for White's ace acting. Larry would heartily approve of Darrin's latest campaign slogan by affectionately calling him a son of a gun, and giving a soft punch on the shoulder. Yet, he was essentially describing himself. It was so typically Larry to fire Darrin over the most easily forgivable mistake.

Moorehead and White raised their television personas beyond the basic nature of their on-screen characters and added dimensions that were jovial and welcomed by the audience.

What Moorehead Knew Best

Bewitched scripter Lila Garrett talks about Agnes Moorehead's role as a stunning but outlandish mom:

In a rare moment, Endora defends Darrin to Hepzibah, queen of the witches in "To Go or Not to Go, That is the Question,"

"I think Aggie's interpretation of Endora really did speak to and for all the mothers in the audience who wanted their daughters to marry the perfect man. They were a little annoyed at times to see a woman like Samantha, who was that capable, insisting on staying home all the time."

"She was Everyman's mother-in-law," adds Richard Michaels. "Every man in the world has a certain mother-in-law image in his mind, and where Samantha was concerned, Endora came with the marriage. It was a package deal."

The late Jerry Davis thought Moorehead was an "especially gifted actress, a queen mother in her social life." He remembered attending elegant parties given by the actress and "a sort of very elite theater group from which she sprang. She was very kind, and I loved her, but she had that nice bitchy exterior that worked brilliantly for the show."

Active in all entertainment media, Moorehead gained the largest audience of her forty-five-year, four-time Oscar-nominated career, on *Bewitched*. She was gratified that the show was loved by an audience of both fans and advertisers, even though she could not confess to complete satisfaction with it and the Endora character in the beginning.

"There are so many things I'd like to do with the role," she once said, "but there isn't time to polish in television." In another interview, she relayed her discord about TV: "This is the treadmill. Mad, hectic. No time to relax. Every second counts. The treadmill's a marvelous living-[but] I'm not the treadmill type."

"That was Aggie's big debate on the set," recalled Dick York. "When do we get to act?" York remembered Moorehead asking constantly. "She was trained in the theater, so the fast pace of television acting would get to her at times."

A reporter from Moorehead's hometown newspaper, the *Cleveland Plain Dealer*, asked her if it was fun to do *Bewitched*.

"No," she responded. "I can't say that. In TV, there simply isn't time to have fun; people have the impression that actors in television, particularly on comedy shows, sit around having a ball. Nonsense. It's the hardest medium an actor can work in."

Still, *Bewitched* writer Richard Baer believes Moorehead luxuriated herself on the series. "Though she'd never admit it," he says, "I think she really enjoyed sitting on the mantelpiece in chiffon gowns."

Bewitched director R. Robert Rosenbaum had tremendous respect for Agnes.

"She took direction better than anyone," he says, "and she was fabulous. For her to listen to a little nudnick like me [an assistant

Endora and Samantha share an intimate moment in "If They Never Met."

director turned director], I thought, was a fantastic thing. But she would just do it, act exactly the way I explained it. She was one of the great ladies of our business. She took two to three hours in makeup every morning, and was never, never late. She was always ready on the set, and she always knew her lines. She was very prepared and did not respect someone else who didn't come as well prepared as she. The show survived due to her talents, and due to the chemistry between her and Elizabeth."

I Like My Mother, I Like My Daughter

Contrary to speculation by the press, Agnes and Elizabeth were close friends who held each other in solid mutual regard.

"She knew I loved her dearly," Elizabeth recalled, "and there really was so much communication between us. It's like we actually had a mother-daughter relationship."

One scene from "Long Live the Queen" attests to Samantha's kinship with Endora and symbolizes the bond Moorehead shared with Montgomery and between all those on the Sam set.

In "Queen," which opened the fourth season, Endora glows with glory as her daughter is crowned Queen of the Witches. Knowing how happy she's made Endora, Samantha, in return, flashes that wide, closed-lipped smile that came to be her second most popular facial trademark, next to her nose twitch.

Elizabeth commented on the scene:

"There always seemed to be this animosity between Endora and Samantha because of Darrin. So at times we tried to establish how much the two of them really cared about one another and how close they really were. That scene is a testament to how they felt about each other and how close Aggie and I were. There'd be times when I would look at her in the very same way that Samantha looked at Endora. It may not have been for more than a second's time, but it somehow confirmed that something had mutually gone right for the two of us on a professional or personal level. It's like many times after Aggie and I would complete a scene, we'd kind of look at each other and say, 'Yeah, that went well.' It's nice when that kind of communication takes place between actors on a set. And it's funny because she once told me, 'You know, I'm very proud of you.' I just looked at her, and gave her this big ol' hug."

Hugging was the farthest thing from Marvin Miller's mind when he first met Moorehead. "I'll never forget that moment," he says, as if recalling the day he reached puberty. It was his first day on the set, and he had to meet Agnes at 5:30 A.M. in makeup. Miller arrived there at about 5:20, and Moorehead was already in the chair. When he

introduced himself and wondered if she would care for breakfast, Miller says the actress replied with this kind of stony, "No. No, thank you."

Moorehead was then fully made-up, and the two went down to her stage dressing room, of which the actress had two (one on the set, the other, above it).

Soon, it was 4:30 in the afternoon. *Bewitched* was filming all day, and Moorehead was not used in any scenes. R. Robert Rosenbaum (then assistant director) walked over to Miller (then second assistant), and asked, "Would you please go and tell Aggie that we won't be able to use her today?"

"I panicked," Miller says with a chuckle. "I can't express the fear that statement instilled in me. Here I was, having to tell this great actress that after two hours in makeup and after a full day of not using her one bit, that we wouldn't be needing her at all! Somehow I found the courage to knock on her door, timidly."

"Yeeessss," Moorehead replied in an *Addams Family*-"Lurch"-style deep voice.

"I opened the door," Miller continues, "and just stood there, looking at her, speechless for a second or two." Then he thought, Let's try to be funny.

"But no words came out of my mouth," he says today.

Finally, the young assistant director told Moorehead: "You know, it's a terrible shame to have been all made up and let it go to waste. Why don't you go upstairs and we'll go over your lines, because they won't-they won't-they won't be able to use you today."

As Miller recalls, the veteran actress looked at him with that famous Moorehead glare, and he started to shake a little when her face became somewhat expressionless.

Suddenly, he saw this twinkle in her eye, and she said, "Oh. It's going to be another one of those days."

With an "I guess so," Miller was gone.

He and Agnes eventually became good friends, and as he expresses, "Behind her stony demeanor was a very warm and wonderful lady. But that first day, I must have lost five pounds before I got to her dressing room."

Bewitched semi-regular Bernie Kopell, who played various roles on the show and made several appearances as the witch apothecary (and is also best known as "Doc" on *The Love Boat*), shares a similar stunning experience of working with Agnes:

"She was very complimentary of my work on *Bewitched*, and I was thrilled. I remembered seeing her in *Don Juan in Hell* on Broadway. I was blown away by her performance. She was the only female in the cast, and in one scene everyone was dressed in formal clothes. The men in black tie. There was Agnes, with her stunning red hair, decorated in this beautiful dress.

"That picture of her stuck in my mind every time I did *Bewitched*. She was such an overwhelming presence on that Broadway stage. Years later, to work with someone like her, and to have someone with that much charisma and talent praise your work, was a very wonderful thing."

When Irene Vernon, the first Louise Tate, was reminded of Moorehead, she recalled the generous amount of theatrical and personal advice that Endora's real-life counterpart would dispense.

"No matter what happens in life," Agnes would say to Irene, "feel it, live it to the fullest, and continue working. Be it good, bad, or indifferent, always work. You will get some good out of it, and you will learn and grow as a human being and as an actress."

"You know something," Vernon contended, "she was right."

Agnes Moorehead may not have admitted to having fun on *Bewitched*, nor may she have been the most approachable person, but as the late *Bewitched* director E. W. Swackhamer contended, she had a sense of humor about her person.

"She didn't mind making fun of herself. It was somehow flattering. At the same time, she was humorless, in a strange way. You'd tell her a joke, and three days later, she'd laugh."

Yet, when it came time to portray Endora, Swackhamer thought she said to herself, Listen, this is nonsense, but I know what I'm doing. I'm a witch, so's my daughter, and this is the way it is. "She never fooled around with the part. It was more like, 'Boom! I'm Endora!'"

The White in Larry's Eyes

Like Agnes Moorehead, *Bewitched* costar David White was a pro whose theatrical background included television, film, and the stage.

He came to *Bewitched* after a brief meeting in New York with first-season producer Danny Arnold. The two hit it off immediately. When Arnold was scheduled to fly to Florida to shoot a TV pilot entitled *Beachfront*, which he wrote with Sam Wolfe (who created television's *Have Gun, Will Travel*), he asked David if he would be interested in acting in it.

White approved and was cast as the heavy in *Beachfront*, alongside star Keef Brasselle, best known for his performance in the *Eddie Cantor Story*, released theatrically in 1953.

While viewing the *Beachfront* dailies, Arnold asked White for his opinion of the show.

Samantha and Darrin are shocked when Larry gets greedy once he learns Sam's secret in this "surrender" scene from "I Confess."

As David remembered it wasn't much, and he told him so.

Yet, David did not think Arnold needed to hear his opinion.

"I think Danny just wanted to see if I would tell the truth," White said.

Honest enough to work with again.

Years later, when casting *Bewitched*, Arnold remembered White's frank response, and David received the nod to play Larry Tate.

"I got the part because I was an honest man," White said. "And that's how Larry and I were different. I'm not two-faced, and he was. I had more integrity than Larry ever had. I was smarter and had a deeper sense of values. I had to diminish who I was to play Larry, whom I viewed as a very insecure person who only had a certain brilliance in certain areas. He was smart enough to hire people who possessed the skills he did not—like Darrin."

As White saw it, Larry wasn't a creative man at all. He was a businessman, and a reasonably good one under Darrin's guidance. Which is why, whenever Larry fired Darrin (which was often) he would always question himself. He knew he was cutting off his nose to spite his face and that he would have to think again and hire Darrin back.

Yet Larry was no dummy.

He was quick and sharp and the ultimate chameleon. One who could whiz back and forth and contradict himself in the same sentence if he thought he was about to lose a client or even notice an ensuing frown on a client's face.

White pointed out that had Larry been brilliant, he would have expanded his employees at McMann and Tate. His ego was tremendously large, but his self-esteem wasn't great enough to push him further. If so, White said, Larry "would have had his own advertising agency instead of just being partners with McMann."

White believed Larry was interesting to portray, a character of whom he did not stand in judgment, and he was extremely protective of his TV alter ego.

White expounded on the comedic theatrics previously addressed by Elizabeth, Dick York, and Dick Sargent:

"I wasn't born to play Larry. I had to create him. He was a make-believe character of his own truth slated in a comedy series. When playing humor and farce, you take that truth and stretch it as far as it will go. But not any farther.

"When I was playing Larry, though he was a funny character, I never tried to be funny. To me, acting has to do with fulfilling the needs of the character you're playing, not the actor who's playing him. Although the one thing the actor and the character have in common is that both have needs."

Whereas some may label Larry a "heavy," White maintained that Larry was a man who displayed how far he would reach to shield his wants. "A real heavy," he said, "is a man who doesn't have any moral structure whatsoever; one who ends up cheating or even killing someone. Larry was selfish, but he was never that extreme. If anything, he was still a little kid who never matured."

On hearing the latter assessment, some viewers may be reminded of the *Bewitched* episode entitled "Serena's Youth Pill," in which Sam's cousin reverses Larry's aging process. He returns to his youth, red hair and all.

During the filming of "Pill," there was some discussion of whether or not Larry's hair should remain white, just for laughs. Though such a decision was vetoed, in view of the show's integrity, David's white locks caused some on/off-screen, off-color humor.

Whenever Elizabeth played Serena in a scene with Larry, she would refer to him as cotton top, which bothered David slightly.

"The way I feel is this," he noted: "Some jokes should not be taken too far. Once, maybe twice, but after awhile it gets to be too much."

Whenever anyone on the set would jive with him about the nickname, David responded by saying his hair was prematurely gray. In the long run, he was able to laugh at himself, indefinitely, after all.

When Serena would come on to Larry, David thought it was harmless, but according to him, in the beginning, Larry was quite the flirt himself.

"If they had not toned down that aspect of his personality," the actor said, "he would have been presented as a totally rotten character."

Unlike Dick Sargent, David frequently viewed his *Bewitched* performances, for two reasons:

1. If he thought it was a good script, well done on all accounts, with regard to acting, writing and directing.

2. On the rare occasion when it was not a good script, he just wanted to see how it turned out.

Three of David's favorite Sam segments were "The Moment of Truth;" "Bewitched, Bothered and Infuriated" (both from the third season); and "Toys in Babeland."

"Truth" had to do with Samantha salvaging the courage to tell Darrin that Tabitha was a witch while preventing the Tates from seeing her daughter's hocus-pocus as they visit one night for dinner.

"Larry and Louise really got to interact in that one," White said. "They were able to show some honest affection for each other."

At one point during "Truth," Samantha tries to supernaturally induce Larry into believing that he's drunk so that the Tates may exit before they observe Tabitha make with the magic. Sam and Darrin even ask Larry to take a sobriety test of sorts in their living room. Larry agrees. When he begins to walk a straight line, Sam twitches him to fall into Louise's arms, where the now-ruffled Larry faintly asks his wife a question:

"Louise," he states melodramatically, "is that you?"

On this development, the Tates decide to go home.

In "Bothered," Aunt Clara conjures up the wrong newspaper from the past, where Sam and Darrin are led, thinking they will prevent Larry from breaking his leg.

The problem?

The Tates are on their second honeymoon, and the Stephenses are unwelcome pests.

"That was a great episode for many reasons," David stated. "First, it centered around the regular cast. And second, Larry and Louise spent a good amount of time together on screen, which didn't happen too often."

David's favorite *Bewitched* scene, however, transpired in "Toys," which has Tabitha bringing her toys to life. Larry ends up having a drink with her toy soldier at a bar. Darrin tries to convince Larry that he's mixing with the wrong company.

"Larry," the young adman says, "he's a doll!"

To which an oblivious Mr. Tate replies, "Well, make up your mind, Darrin. Do you like him or not?"

"Now that's funny," responded White. "Like every scene in the show, we played it for real, which added to the humor."

Besides "Truth," "Bothered," and "Toys," the episodes David most enjoyed were the show's seventh season visits to Salem, Massachusetts.

"I had a lot of fun with those," he admitted. "I had never been to Boston, to Salem, or to the House of Seven Gables [featured in "The Salem Saga" and "Samantha's Old Salem Trip"]. It was different for me."

What was it specifically about the House of Seven Gables?

"People must have been smaller when the place was built," he mused, "because I remember almost hitting my nose on the doorways. I had to bend over [going] from one room to the next."

David's coworkers adored him.

"Larry Tate was a rude character," explained director E. W. Swackhamer. "But David's ability as an actor took the edge off the character and made him likable."

"I always loved watching him," Elizabeth said. "He was so funny. Half the time I really don't think he knew just how funny he was. Fortunately, everyone else did."

With an ironic nod to the witches' anthem quoted in the show, Bill Asher concluded that "David's performance was like quicksilver."

Larry catches the spirit of Christmas as he revels in Darrin and Samantha's "holiday decorations" on the front lawn in "Santa Comes for a Visit and Stays and Stays."

A gaunt (or should that be "gutted") Uncle Arthur sings "Dry Bones" in "Samantha's Power Failure."

Chapter 8

This and Other Worldlies

The cast of *Bewitched* was ever in transition. Many characters left and several new roles were created. The theatrical evolution enhanced the mortal/supernatural conflict on the show. The world of Samantha and Darrin opened up to include funny and zany relatives and friends; witches and warlocks faced off against human neighbors, clients, and random historical figures who were plucked from their familiar eras.

A team of supporting players was essential in keeping the audience captivated week after week, year after year. They were a talented group of actors who had a bundle of laughs playing real and fanciful parts.

Very rarely, if ever, did we settle for anything less than we initially desired for any role or character on Bewitched. *The size of the role or the actor's work history was not a concern. We were always after the quality of talent.*

ELIZABETH MONTGOMERY

Several Super Naturals

Samantha's unearthly family and friends who made frequent visits to the Stephens household were portrayed with unique verve by a lively bunch of actors.

First, there was Aunt Clara, played by the obliging Marion Lorne.

Lorne's Clara was an odd egg. High-spirited and experienced, she was inefficient and unskilled. But pick on her?

No way. Not when Samantha was around.

As Sam's adored aunt, Clara was the first baby-sitter Samantha called upon when Darrin begged for someone other than Endora. No matter how many times Clara's powers failed, Samantha came to her defense.

Aunt Clara's in the can in "Alias Darrin Stephens."

In "The Trial and Error of Aunt Clara," Endora and the Witches Council set out to have Clara stripped of her witchhood. Samantha pleaded that Clara's kind of love was rare. Such emotion did not sit well with Judge Bean (Arthur Malet), and just as he was to despell Clara, a surprising turn of events took place.

Darrin came home early. Shortly before he arrived within view of his altered living room, which had been transformed into a witchly court, Clara waved her arms, and, as she declared, everyone disappeared.

Darrin's nerves and his marriage to Samantha had been saved.

These occurrences resulted in two important developments.

1. Clara proved to the Witches Council that when push came to shove, she was ready and powerfully prepared.

2. This sequence of events sealed the special bond between Clara and Samantha.

As Sam loved Clara, Elizabeth loved Marion. "She was a blast to be around," Montgomery beamed. "When Aunt Clara would hit those walls [as she'd attempt to walk through them], it was a riot. We would hear this shriek on the set; Marion's hearing aid conflicted with the stage microphones."

Elizabeth remembered an even more humorous mechanical interference with Marion that happened one night at the famed Beverly Hills Hotel: "She called me from her room and insisted I come to see her. When I finally got there, she was awfully nervous. She kept on saying, 'I did it! I did it!' She told me that I was the only one who would understand."

Apparently, Marion thought she had attained some form of magical surge. She was unaware that her bracelets had created an electrical current that somehow transferred on the same frequency as the television set in her room. "Everytime her arm would move," Elizabeth recalled, "the bracelets would clink and the channels would change. I wasn't about to tell her what was really going on. She was walking on air."

Despite this airy story, Elizabeth confirmed Marion's intelligence: "She was a very smart lady and a brilliant performer who knew exactly what she was doing as Aunt Clara."

Lorne chose to have Clara stammer, which became the character's trademark; that and the fact that Clara used to collect doorknobs (as did Lorne).

Once, early on in the series, producer Jerry Davis remembered Lorne stumbling through her lines and taking a lot of time to spurt them out. Finally, he said, "Honey, don't worry about

replace their regular housekeeper (ironically named Esmeralda).

Ghostley was not, however, initially pegged to play pretty maids in a row.

When Alice Pearce passed away, Ghostley was offered the role of Mrs. Kravitz.

She declined because Pearce had been a friend of hers whom she had known from New York. The two had worked together in many of the same clubs, including the popular Blue Angel. "So when they called me to play Gladys," Ghostley says, "I said no. I guess I was superstitious about replacing her."

Ghostley had also worked with Marion Lorne in *The Graduate*, released theatrically in 1967. Because the two had not known each

Alice Ghostley was Esmeralda to a tee.

other socially, Ghostley agreed to play an Aunt Clara-like character.

William Asher could not have been more satisfied with the end result.

"I was very happy Alice decided to come aboard," he says. "I always wanted her on the show."

Once there, Ghostley's Esmeralda cornered a mishap magical market of her own.

Besides the fading, the witchly maid's other dysfunctional wizardry included sneezing or hiccuping up some kind of catastrophe by mistake.

As Ghostley relates, "Esmeralda would sometimes take the long way around a situation, but she had powers that would cause excitement one way or the other. There were certain aspects of her personality, her shyness for one, that made her very lonely. She was very amiable and wanted to be part of everything, but her bashful nature stopped her from joining in. At the same time, this made her more a human-witch than a witch-witch."

Ghostley joined *Bewitched* in the show's sixth season, 1969 to 1970, the same time Dick Sargent debuted as Darrin. As new kids on the block, the two became close friends (a bond which lasted until Sargent's death in 1994). Like Sargent, Ghostley found it difficult to watch herself on *Bewitched*.

"It's always hard for me to critique myself," she admits.

Still, the actress has two favorite *Bewitched* segments: "Samantha's Magic Mirror," and "Samantha's Not-So-Leaning Tower of Pisa."

"Mirror" concerns Esmeralda's rendezvous with an old warlock boyfriend and a bout with extreme anxiety. To boost her maid's ego in other areas, Samantha zaps the hall mirror into presenting a beautiful likeness of Esmeralda each time she gazes upon it.

"I loved that," Alice says, "because Esmeralda had the chance to express varied emotions. It gave the audience a chance to know other sides of her, to understand why she was so shy."

Alice favors "Mirror" also because of the presence of guest star Tom Bosley, who is best known for his regular roles from TV's *Happy Days* and *Father Dowling Mysteries* and with whom Ghostley had previously performed. "We had known each other from the early days of television," Ghostley recalls. "We had been friends for a long time, and it was nice to have worked with him again."

Alice favors the "Pisa" segment for more comedic reasons.

In this outing, we learn of Esmeralda's ties. She's the reason why Italy's famous Tower of Pisa bends. Centuries before, during its construction, Esmeralda was working for *Bonano Pisano* (Robert Casper), the structure's designer and architect. Upon ordering his lunch, the nervous witch accidentally incants a sandwich to appear, "And make it *lean*," she reverberates.

Instead, the Tower obliges.

Years after this episode premiered, Ghostley journeyed to Italy for the first time and made an assessment:

"I just looked at that thing and thought, 'Wow! It's so large and powerful, not even I could move it.' The reality of the situation set in."

Though Esmeralda's nerves were shot, and though she may have believed Pisa's tower unstable, Ghostley's popularity remains on solid ground. The comedic thespian continues to win rave reviews and applause in all areas of performance.

Some years after *Bewitched*, Alice played orphan housemother *Miss Hannigan* in a musical stage version of *Annie*, based on the comic strip *Little Orphan Annie*. In heavy makeup and gaudy costumes, Ghostley was almost unrecognizable.

Except to *Bewitched* fans—especially the young ones.

"The kids didn't care how I was made up," Alice explains. "All they wanted to see was Esmeralda. I was in that show for over two years, and after each matinee, they'd be standing outside the theater waiting to see me, screaming, *Esmeralda! Esmeralda!*"

In later years, Ghostley won accolades, and an Emmy nomination, for her role as the dippy *Bernice Clifton* on TV's *Designing Women*. After the show's taping, the studio audience would rally around her then as well. And just in case her loyalty to *Bewitched* was ever in doubt, she would nostalgically endorse each autograph with *Best Witches, Alice Ghostley.*

Playing Dr. Bombay! Playing Dr. Bombay!

As with Alice Ghostley and Paul Lynde, Bernard Fox appeared in an early episode of *Bewitched* before establishing a regular part in the series.

In "Disappearing Samantha," the actor portrayed Osgood Rightmire, a mortal debunker of witches. Ironically, his future recurring role as Dr. Bombay would possess an opposite personality and objective as Samantha's family physician of witchery.

Upon detection of a magical medical problem, Samantha would alert the good doctor via the metaphysical continuum with this poetic yelp:

"Calling Dr. Bombay! Calling Dr. Bombay.

Emergency! Emergency! Come right away!"

Dr. Bombay, as played by English actor Fox, would then appear, sometimes in just a towel.

"You've interrupted my bah-th," he would say.

Because they were not human, witches did not have ordinary prescriptions or cures for their ills. To relieve a given witch experiencing a dry spell or to right some witchery gone wrong, Dr. Bombay would attempt to diagnose the faulty sorcery with the appropriate incantation.

Dr. Bombay pulls no bull in this photo, which was actually used (to slide under Samantha's door) in "Okay, Who's the Wise Witch?"

At times this required the assistance of one of his many attractive witch-nurses or supernaturally induced medicinal mechanisms.

If all else failed, Bombay would try to cover his mistakes with poor attempts at humor. He would comfort himself with a *Ha-Ha! Ha-Ha!*, followed by dead silence from those who did not share in his joyful exertion.

Consequently, Dr. Bombay was labeled a quack on many an occasion.

Bernard Fox offers an analysis of the warlock Darrin used to call a witch doctor and who Uncle Arthur said (in "Super Arthur") had "the bedside manner of an orangutan":

"I never wanted him to be a run-of-the-mill character. I based him on a commanding officer I encountered while serving in the naval transit camp in what was then Ceylon. This elderly gentleman had, in civilian life, been a veterinary surgeon of the old school and was hard of hearing. He assumed everyone else was also, so he constantly yelled at everybody.

"Some twenty years later, when I came to play Dr. Bombay, I was searching for something more colorful than the everyday doctor, and that officer came to mind."

As Elizabeth explained, William Asher and the *Bewitched* writing staff enjoyed creating situations for Bombay, as much as Fox delighted in playing him: "Dr. Bombay was so outrageously odd. And we were always on the lookout to present unique characters and actors. One of the neat things about Bernie [Fox] was that he would come up with all these really weird kinds of sides to Dr. Bombay."

"All the characters on the show were unique," Fox says. "The success of *Bewitched* is largely due to all the talented people on and behind the screen. Agnes Moorehead and

Maurice Evans are perfect examples of that. They were two highly trained performers of the theater. You rarely find such talent in the business."

Next to Bombay, Fox is probably best known to television viewers for his role as Colonel Crittenden on *Hogan's Heroes*.

"I tried to play them all energetically," the actor remembers.

The hardest part of playing Dr. Bombay, he says, was the character's long, breathless constructions and incantations:

"They were a difficult study. I usually have a good head for names, titles, and lines when I'm working, but Bombay's dialogue was complicated."

One of Fox's favorite pieces of *Bewitched* dialogue comes from "Make Love, Not Hate," when Sam and Bombay patter away:

Bombay: "Where's the clam dip?"
Sam: "In the kitchen sink."
Bombay: "I may join him. I could do with a swim."

During the filming of "Make Love," numerous puns on dip and swim abounded on the set. At one point, Fox was required to squeeze a lemon into the clam dip, which expanded its comic proportions on the set between Fox and Elizabeth:

"Having found the dip," Fox recalls, "I proceeded to squeeze the lemon, and a tiny squirt shot out from one side, straight into Elizabeth's eye. She reacted instantly, and we both thought it funny. But something was technically wrong, so we had to have another take. Elizabeth said, 'Bet you can't do it again.' But it did happen again and even on the third take, and so there it is on film for posterity."

Fox's fondest *Bewitched* recollection is of a cast and crew Christmas party:

"My wife and I were invited, of course, and my eighty-year-old mother was visiting from England. So we took her along. Mother, an actress herself, wasn't too thrilled with the idea, as she evidently envisioned herself sitting off to one side like a bump on a log and being totally ignored.

"The first one to sit down to chat with her was Elizabeth, then Bill Asher wandered over, and soon she was the center of a chatty, happy group. Mabel Albertson [Phyllis Stephens], a terrific talent, was playing the piano like the expert nightclub performer she had been. The group then moved over to her, and in no time at all, my mother was singing songs from the old musicals like *Desert Song*, *Rose Marie*, etc., and having a ball.

"My mother left for England a few days later, and because of doctor's orders was never able to visit us again. But she took with her a warm and wonderful memory of that night, for which I never cease to thank Elizabeth, Bill, the cast, the crew, and all the delightful people that I met and worked with on *Bewitched*."

Double, Double Toil as Tabitha

Twins Heidi and Laura Gentry began "doubling" as the infant Tabitha on *Bewitched* at the start of the second season (1965–66), for approximately $27 per day.

Slightly older babies were then required, and the Gentry girls were replaced by Tamar and Julie Young. This new set of twins remained on hand for the rest of the show's sophomore year, earning approximately $75 a day (their roles were somewhat more circumscribed).

In May 1966, twins Erin and Diane Murphy

auditioned for the Tabitha role and started on the series a day before their second birthday. From the beginning, the twins looked different, but they both appeared in the role.

"We were fraternal," Erin explains. "We looked as much alike as two kids who were the same age with the same color hair. We didn't even have to be twins, and they could have used us the way they did [Erin was employed for the close-ups; Diane for the long-shots]. After the fourth season, however, Erin played the part, and Diane acted as her double.

On the set, the sisters had a private tutor for three hours every day. That was the law then, and it still is.

The law was another reason twins were

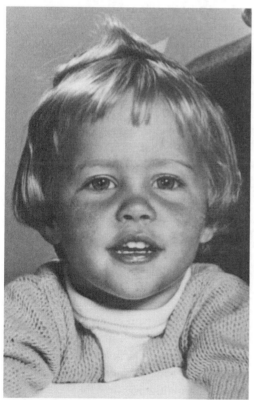
There she is . . . little Tabitha.

chosen to play Samantha's twitchy daughter. Child actors are allowed only a certain amount of airtime on television and film. Having twin actors means the workload for each child is cut in half. Such rules were enforced on ABC's later hit, *Full House*, where Mary Kate and Ashley Olsen played little daughter Michelle to Bob Saget's Danny.

Despite all the legalities, Erin says, "Being on the show was a lot of fun."

Even when it didn't look like fun, as in the episode entitled "Tabitha's Very Own Samantha." Here, Tabitha creates her "very own mommy," one she doesn't have to share with anyone, specifically her brother Adam (played by the Murphy's coworking twins David and Greg Lawrence).

Throughout the segment, Tabitha is seen wearing a Band-Aid on her chin because she tried flying at too young an age. In reality, Erin fell in her real-life kitchen at home because, as she says, "I was a klutz. I was excited because we were having ice cream sundaes, and then I fell on my face." The *Bewitched* writers decided later to reference Erin's bandage to flying.

As Erin continues to say, in that same episode her sister Diane was employed as an extra and rode a pony "and received hazard pay."

Both Erin and Diane loved being around the show's special effects.

"I remember seeing hooked wires all over the place," says Erin, "and not understanding why they were there, but everybody explained it to me."

Overall, Erin and Diane's time on *Bewitched* was pleasurable, though Diane's theatrical goals differed from her sister's:

"Everyone was really great. I enjoyed working on it while I was doing it, but I realized later that acting was not something I would be inter-

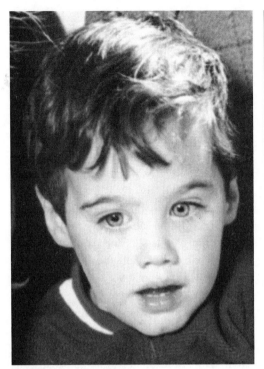

There he is . . . little Adam.

ested in pursuing as a career. We called our TV parents 'Darrin Daddy' and 'Mantha Mommy' to distinguish them from our real parents. In the beginning, we couldn't pronounce Samantha, so that's when we just kind of shortened it.

"I remember Elizabeth used to like to eat coffee ice cream with honey on it, which Erin and I called the 'Mantha Mommy Special.' Her dressing room door was covered with autographs, and I was real excited when she let me sign it. I wrote a big *D*, but my mother said I shouldn't take up too much room, so I wrote the rest of my name inside the *D*."

Erin and Diane enjoyed all of the episodes which featured other children, like "Samantha and the Beanstalk," or when Tabitha's adventures in school were featured, as in "Tabitha's First Day at School." It was in "Beanstalk" that Erin met child star Johnny Whitaker.

"He was my first date," Erin reveals. "And it was really funny because we later appeared on *Good Morning, America* in a show about former child actors, and we mentioned how we first met on *Bewitched*."

Up and Adams

Like Erin and Diane Murphy, David and Greg Lawrence were brought into the *Bewitched* fold and offered a double play as one of Samantha and Darrin's children. And it's all because of actress Barbara Feldon.

Yes, Barbara Feldon.

Feldon, best known for her role as Agent 99 on the 1960s spy-com *Get Smart*, became pregnant, and a future *Smart* script called for her to give birth to twins. An enterprising talent agent, who had no six-month-old twins as clients, began calling pediatricians in an effort to locate potential candidates. When she reached Dr. David Rottapel, a pediatrician in Sherman Oaks, California, he said, "I don't have six-month-old twins. But I have absolutely gorgeous, small-for-their-age, nine-month-old twins. Let me call their mother for permission to give you their names."

As fate would have it, *Get Smart* was canceled. But having seen pictures of David and Greg Lawrence, the agent knew she had a winning combination with which to work.

The twins were soon in demand for commercials. David and Greg achieved a 100 percent batting average, landing every role for which they auditioned.

Bewitched was no exception.

After an exhaustive search and a look at sets of twins throughout the state of California, the producers decided to go with the Lawrence twins, not only because of their dark hair, blue eyes, rosy cheeks, cleft chins, and great smiles, but because they had the same quizzical quirk in their right eyebrows that Elizabeth had.

The boys enjoyed working on the show and even fought over whose turn it was to be in a scene. Although they found Agnes Moorehead's Endora a bit intimidating, their favorite was Grandpapa, Maurice Evans, who, according to the boys' mother, "was a truly warm and loving gentleman."

Though Elizabeth was generally very busy on the set, she still found time to play with the boys. One day she suddenly grabbed David, threw herself on the floor, and began bouncing him on her knees, much to the chagrin of wardrobe mistress Vi Alford, since Elizabeth was in a shimmering white pleated skirt for the next scene, and the floor was filthy.

Viewers would be hard pressed to detect it, but both David and Greg had ear infections and raging fevers during the filming of their biggest episode, "Adam, Warlock or Washout." They were troupers, however, and refused to quit until shooting was completed, probably because they found it such fun to be wired to fly; a feeling that was not totally shared by their mother.

When the final season of *Bewitched* ended, the Lawrence twins' parents made the decision to retire them from show business. And though both David and Greg say today that they would return to acting, if asked, they agreed with their parents' decision to allow them to grow up as just regular kids.

"If an acting career is meant to be, let it be their own decision," says their mother.

Strangely enough, the young men, who are adopted, discovered at age fourteen that their natural father was an actor of extraordinary fame and celebrity. It's anyone's guess as to how things might have turned out had they been raised by him.

The elegant grace of the late Maurice Evans complemented the sophistication of Agnes Moorehead.

Mr. Majestic

There is no better way to close a section on the central supporting supernaturals of *Bewitched* than with a profile of the classically trained and very charismatic actor Maurice Evans and his portrayal of Samantha's father, also named Maurice.

Though Evans and his television counterpart shared first names, Evans preferred the proper British pronunciation, *Morris*, while his TV self demanded that his name be pronounced

Mor-EECE. All of this led to some behind-the-scenes humor during the filming of "Samantha's Good News."

In *"News,"* Maurice makes Endora jealous by hiring a beautiful witch-secretary. She seeks emotional revenge by enlisting the assistance of warlock John Van Millwood, played by the late Murray Matheson. When Van Millwood refers to Evans's character as *Morris*, Maurice cringes, emphasizing the pronunciation of his name. None of this, however, matters to Samantha, who knows her father only as Daddy.

Beyond the pronunciation of their first name, Maurice Evans and his warlock persona also shared a penchant for all things Shakespearean, but this is where the similarities between the two ended. Evans himself was nowhere near as threatening as Samantha's father, who proved to be an even stronger adversary for Darrin than Endora.

"He was charming and gallant," Elizabeth said of Evans, who passed away in 1989. "And he had a marvelous sense of humor. One night some friends and I went out to dinner. When the waiter came over to take our order, Maurice gestured toward me and said, 'My daughter will have a glass of champagne,' and everyone just roared."

The one aspect of Evans's personality that made him perfect for Maurice, according to Elizabeth, was that he did not look flamboyant. "He wasn't six feet four," she said. "But whatever he lacked physically, he made up for with his huge talents as an actor."

Fright master Vincent Price and Cesar Romero (the Latin lover of early films, also best known as the small-screen Joker from TV's *Batman*) were once considered for the role of Sam's papa.

"Either one of them would have been bliss," Elizabeth said. "I even wanted my father to do it [he said no], but I thought it was tremendously beneficial that Evans could play Maurice with so much demonstrative strength."

Maurice Evans balanced a sophisticated sense of style with Maurice in much the same way that Agnes Moorehead played Endora; an impression his life and career nearly demanded.

Of his tenure on *Bewitched*, Evans wrote in his autobiography:

"I have special reason to be grateful to have been cast as Samantha's father in *Bewitched* since, apart from the enjoyment of working with Elizabeth Montgomery and her merry gang of witches and warlocks, it put me for the first time on more than a nodding acquaintance with my grandnephews and -nieces. Up until then their uncle Maurice's career in America was to them a topic of yawning dimensions, but as I began to appear regularly in the show, they became eager to get to know me, insisting that I enlighten them on the magic tricks that made *Bewitched* so much more than just another domestic comedy.

"I was voted in as a regular member of Samantha's household, and, although it involved commuting constantly between New York and Hollywood in the 1960s, it was a thoroughly enjoyable experience."

Bewitched director E. W. Swackhamer thought it was just as pleasurable to work with Evans. "He was a remarkable actor who never turned any part down," the director said. "It didn't have to be *Hamlet* or *Macbeth*. That's the way most English actors are. If you go to direct a project over in England, you get the most incredible people that walk into a casting office. You end up pinching yourself as if to say,

'You mean I can really get these guys to work with me?' Even if they're starring on the stage in some major production, they'll come in and do small parts for you. Acting is acting to them. America doesn't have that attitude, unhappily. But Maurice did. He was like that totally. He would come up with the most incredible ideas and give himself over completely to a role."

Bewitched producer/writer Jerry Davis had done a film with Maurice called *Kind Lady* in 1951, in which Evans played the villain. When he came on *Bewitched,* Davis said, "It was a nice reunion for us. I never had anything but a pleasant relationship with the man."

Human Resources

"Comedy is all about reaction," said story editor Ed Jurist, "and the human characters on *Bewitched,* whether they knew it or not, were reacting to the very unnatural phenomena that were presented to them."

In addition to the principal mortals on *Bewitched,* the sitcom was filtered with a fine cast of additional characters, such as Darrin and Samantha's neighbors, Abner and Gladys Kravitz. George Tobias played the passive Abner to spastic Gladys, interpreted by Alice Pearce (1964 to 1966) and Sandra Gould (1966 to 1972).

No one reacted more to Samantha's unnatural phenomena than Mrs. Kravitz.

Gladys and Abner lived across the street from the Stephenses at 1168 Morning Glory Circle. Mrs. Kravitz was convinced from the onset that Samantha was "different," though she could never prove it.

Abner didn't help matters. He never listened to her.

Explains Richard Baer:

Abner (George Tobias) captured the attention of his "second wife" (Sandra Gould).

Alice Pearce's "Mrs. Kravitz" beams in "Samantha, the Dressmaker."

"Mrs. Kravitz accepted what she had seen, however strange, and would run back to the house and tell Abner, who just wanted to read the newspaper or watch the ball game. He would always tell his wife when she would complain about what she had seen to take a pill and relax. She would try, but she would see an elephant on the roof or something."

Such evidence would disappear when Gladys ran to Abner to spread the news.

"Abner," she would scream, "you're not going to believe this," and, assuredly, he would not.

Mr. Kravitz would then advise his wife to take a nap, which he usually did himself.

Gladys was thought of as an airhead by her husband or any public or government official whom she would bring in to confront Samantha's secret. Yet, she may also be viewed as probably one of the smartest and most aware mortals on the show.

Think about it: Did Larry, in all the years he knew Darrin and Samantha, ever suspect Sam or any of his employee's families to be anything but regular people?

Granted, Samantha made such perceptions difficult because of her beauty and nonwitchly charms. Yet, other than a chosen few dream sequences or spellbinding situations, Larry remained pretty much in the dark about what was really going on with the Stephenses.

On the other hand, nosy housewife Gladys, whom many defined as weird, proved otherwise. Because she lived across the street from Sam and Darrin, she was more accessible to what was really going on in the neighborhood.

Abner lived in the same house, but he never suspected a thing.

Gladys was constantly being made the fool by, and in front of, her husband.

Yet, who was zooming whom?

Played variedly by Alice Pearce and Sandra Gould, Gladys's traits remained consistent, and her perceptions, keen.

Marvin Miller offers his take on the Pearce/Gould distinctions:

"Alice had that scream of hers that made her Gladys almost most maniacal. I think that made you feel more sorry for her. Sandra played it down more, but was still more defiantly opposed to Samantha's witchcraft. When Alice would get scared, you really believed Mrs. Kravitz was going to pieces, whereas Sandy offered a more shocked reaction."

Pearce, who died of cancer while still working on the show, told *TV-Radio Mirror* in 1965:

"When I first heard that I was going to play a character called Gladys Kravitz, I couldn't understand how they could invent such a nutty name. Well, the day before I was to report on the set of *Bewitched* for the first time, I came down with one of those minor upsets, and I needed a doctor real fast. A friend recommended someone. His name? Dr. Kravitz."

It was quite a coincidence that bode well for *Bewitched* and Pearce, who went on to tell the *Mirror*:

"I'm playing someone who's going over big with kids. They stop me and want to know if I can wiggle my nose like Liz Montgomery. And they like my snooping and poking around. The more frenzied my reactions are, and the louder my eeks get, the better."

As Harry Ackerman recalled, Pearce was offered the part of Gladys without auditioning since he, Bill Asher, and Danny Arnold were familiar with her work, and because she got along splendidly with the other members of the cast. "She never admitted the onslaught of cancer," Ackerman said, "although it was painfully obvious to all of us that she was losing weight rapidly. Actually, she worked almost up to the day she died."

Prior to *Bewitched*, Pearce auditioned for the part of Grandmama Addams on *The Addams Family*, but she was too young, and the part was given to Blossom Rock. Only a few years before this audition transpired, Pearce told an interviewer, "Playing strange, sweet oddballs is exactly my cup of tea."

Pearce also commented on her unique appearance, which was partly caused by slipping from a swing during a visit to Brussels as a child.

"Look at me," she said, "I'm a chinless wonder. If I'd sustained no accident as a kid, if I had developed an ordinary chin, today I'd probably be just another starving, middle-aged actress."

When Sandra Gould replaced Pearce, she did not feel obligated to imitate Alice's Gladys interpretation.

"I couldn't," she explained. "That would have been unfair to myself and to Alice's memory. I knew I couldn't change the character. That was left up to the writers and producers. All I knew was that I had a part to play, and that it was my job as an actress to play out that part."

George Tobias was supportive, as he and Gould had been friends before *Bewitched*. "I was what they called a 'stage child,'" Gould revealed. "I started in the theater when I was nine years old, and that's when I met George. He, Orson Welles, and [fellow actor] Eddie O'Brien were friends. They took care of *the kid*, which was me. It was the funniest thing in the world when I grew up to play George's wife, because he was something like twenty years older than I."

"I'd probably be better for the part now than I was then," Gould said with a laugh. "I wasn't asked to age or anything like that for the part, and they didn't do anything to George either. But if you watch the show closely, I do think George looks a lot older than I do."

Harry Ackerman had met George Tobias at Warner Bros. Studio, where the future Mr.

Mary Grace Canfield in 1991.

Kravitz was featured in such films as *Yankee Doodle Dandy* in 1942, and *Air Force* in 1943. "I believe he thought doing a semiregular role on a TV show was a bit of a comedown for him," Ackerman said. "But I also believe he was still grateful to have the part.

"He was in his mid-sixties when I approached him, and work was few and far between for him at the time. And Abner was such a different role for him to play. He was always used to much tougher and more physical roles. By the time he came to *Bewitched*, he was more suited to character roles, which is exactly what Abner was."

The Canfield Kravitz

Between Alice Pearce passing away and Sandra Gould's Gladys entrance, Mary Grace Canfield, later a supporting actress on TV's *Green Acres* (for which a TV reunion was directed by Bill Asher), was given the role of *Harriet Kravitz*, Abner's sister. When Alice Ghostley turned down the role of Gladys, the *Bewitched* associates were unexpectedly thrown for a loop. More time was needed to find a proper replacement for Pearce.

In the meantime, Canfield was hired for three episodes and referred to as *Miss Kravitz*.

"I got the part without reading for it," she remembers, "and once we began the show, it was not an easy time. The entire set was in mourning because of Alice's death."

Shortly thereafter, Gould came aboard as Abner's spouse, and the *Bewitched* stage lights brightened up a bit.

Twin Louises

After Irene Vernon left *Bewitched* to pursue a career in real estate, Kasey Rogers took over the role of Louise Tate, Larry's wife, for the show's final six years.

Was Vernon's Louise interpretation as different from Kasey's as Dick York's Darrin was from Dick Sargent's? Or as unique as Gladys Kravitz personas provided by Alice Pearce and Sandra Gould?

David White, Larry's real-life counterpart, had the answer:

"You had to look at Larry and see whom he would marry. He would marry someone who would further his career, who would schedule dinner parties, who was, more or less, in control. To that extent, I think Irene Vernon's Louise was

Irene Vernon played the first Mrs. Tate.

Kasey Rogers was Louise No. 2.

more along those lines. She was colder in the role than Kasey, which worked better for the character. But Kasey was more animated in the role, which worked better for the show."

"It Shouldn't Happen to a Dog" was the first episode that featured Irene Vernon as Louise. Here, Mrs. Tate was simply one of the guests invited to a dinner party thrown by Sam and Darrin. Vernon had one or two lines but nothing more.

"I never had a clear picture of who she was," the actress said. "She always seemed to be groping. So that's how I played her. Though I do think Louise was the antithesis of how Larry saw her and what he thought she was. I remember Danny [Arnold] saying that he didn't want Louise to be the bossy, nagging wife; he wanted her to be attractively sweet and an understanding partner for Larry. That's the person I tried to present on screen."

Irene felt there was little comedy for her to have drawn from. She believed Elizabeth was the show's center comedian, and since many of Vernon's scenes were with her, Montgomery should have received the laughs.

"When two actors are doing a scene together," Vernon explained, "they should be able to play off each other well and not try to out-act one another and contribute to each other's performance."

Expounding on David White's comedic techniques, Irene added, "If two actors are trying to be funnier than each other, or trying to be funny, period, then the scene they're working on won't fall into place."

Kasey Rogers says she played Louise "as they wrote it," but confesses that it did take her a couple of episodes before she properly shrieked her first *Larry!* the verbal exclamation that became a staple of the Louise character.

"I don't even think I knew what I was doing," Kasey reveals about Louise's manic yelp, "but people still come up to me and ask if I would please do the 'Larry' scream."

When Rogers first auditioned for Louise, her hair was red and of medium length.

"They asked me if I would mind wearing a black wig," she recalls, so as to make the transition from Vernon to Rogers less jolting for the viewer. By the end of the fifth season, which was Kasey's third year with the show, she asked if she could stop donning the dark headlocks.

"Sure," William Asher replied. "But why did you start wearing it in the first place?"

All these years later, Kasey's view of Louise and *Bewitched* remained untethered.

"Louise," she says, "I love you. And thank you for allowing me to be party to *Bewitched*."

Irene Vernon loved playing in the sitcom as well, though she does not regret leaving it for a successful career in real estate.

"I'm saner," she said, because of the acting exit. "But the show was a wonderful experience. It taught me about life and myself, and in that sense it really was magical."

The Other Mr. and Mrs. Stephens

As previously mentioned, not much of Darrin's family was revealed on *Bewitched*, as it was thought best if he was the primary mortal on the show.

Other than Uncle Albert (Henry Hunter) in "A Bum Raps," and Cousin Helen (Louise Glenn) in "A Prince of a Guy", the only relatives of Darrin's who were regulars were his parents, Frank and Phyllis Stephens. Phyllis was played by stage, film, and television great Mabel Albertson (sister of actor Jack [*Chico and the*

Roy Roberts, Mabel Albertson

Robert F. Simon was the first to portray Darrin's dad.

Man] Albertson, and mother-in-law to Cloris [*The Mary Tyler Moore Show*] Leachman).

As Samantha had two Darrins, Darrin had two dads; the role of Frank was played by veteran professionals Robert F. Simon and Roy Roberts.

Dick York may have been replaced by Dick Sargent as Darrin because of health problems, but the reasons for the Simon/Roberts exchange were quite different.

Bill Asher explains:

"We were operating on the theory of actor availability and character necessity. There were times when we couldn't get either Robert or Roy, so we had to switch from time to time. We were allowed to do that because neither was under contract with the show."

Both Roberts and Simon have passed on, but before his death, Simon offered an analysis of his role, which was eerily similar to Dick Sargent's assessment of Darrin. "The show was so well written," Simon said, "that the characters literally spoke for themselves."

On working with Albertson, Simon added:

"Both Mabel and Aggie [Moorehead] were hard to know. They were both very strong-willed women. They were kind enough, but they both wanted power over everyone in their life. I always try to stay clear of women, if not anyone, like that. But they both certainly were clever performers."

When Elizabeth would view the two of them together, she would just sit back, enjoy Albertson/Moorehead, and say, "Okay, well, let's just see how this turns out," because she said Albertson was just as iron-willed as Moorehead.

According to Elizabeth, whoever was directing Albertson would say, "Now, Mabel, relax a little bit, come down in your performance a couple of notches."

"She was great that way," said Elizabeth. "She was never afraid to go too far with her acting."

David White, who directed Mabel in "Samantha's Double Mother Trouble," attested to Elizabeth's summation of Albertson's talents:

"Mabel was always ready and willing to try anything. When I gave her instruction, she listened carefully and adhered to my guidelines. Just to have the chance to work with Mabel made it all worthwhile."

William Asher praised the work of Simon and Roberts but made one thing clear:

"As long as we had Mabel Albertson, we were fine. She was the key to the conflict that we needed where Darrin's parents were concerned. She was the one who was overreactive, who was more apt to jump to conclusions and make assumptions of her own.

"Whereas Mr. Stephens was thought of as a very easygoing kind of guy, Phyllis was the typical mother-in-law, always looking to find a dirty house, and one who would offer the humorous opposition to Endora. We could have done a show [and they did] without Darrin's father, but we could not have done it without his mother."

"There are certain aspects of a show that you can't mess around with," Asher decides, "and replacing Mabel was one of them."

A Galaxy of Guests

Besides those performers already mentioned, *Bewitched* also featured several highly regarded thespians in semiregular, recurring, and guest-star parts. Each offered a theatrical expertise of his or her own.

Mercedes McCambridge (with regular guest star Steve Franken) as "Carlotta" in "Darrin Gone and Forgotten."

Steve Franken

Dick Wilson (TV's "Mr. Whipple") was a bum in many *Bewitched* episodes.

The guest list included many classic TV legends:

Dick Wilson (otherwise best known as *Mr. Whipple* from the Charmin TV commercials) as the show's resident drunk; Charles Lane (*Petticoat Junction*) was a frequent client of Darrin's and school principal for Tabitha; Bernie Kopell (*The Love Boat*) as the warlock apothecary; Steve Franken (*Dobie Gillis*) as a probing mortal detective and later Sam's cousin Henry; Julie Newmar (*Batman*) was a cat-witch; Henry Gibson (*Laugh-In*) was an evil imp; and Sara Seegar (*Dennis the Menace*) played various McMann and Tate-related roles.

Besides the show's stalwarts such as Ruth McDevitt, Reta Shaw, Madge Blake, and Jane Connell, such familiar faces as Nancy Kovak, David Huddleston, and Parley Baer appeared with Samantha, as did big-screen personas such as Mercedes McCambridge, Cesar Romero, Peter Lawford, Charles Ruggles, Estelle Winwood, and Richard Dreyfuss.

Dreyfuss, in fact, made his acting debut on *Bewitched*, as did Adam West, Raquel Welch, Peggy Lipton (*The Mod Squad* and *Twin Peaks*), Bill Daily (*I Dream of Jeannie*), and *Star Trek*kers James Doohan and Grace Lee Whitney.

A list of child actors premiered their talents on the show: Johnnie Whitaker (*Family Affair*), Billy Mumy (*Lost in Space*), Maureen McCormick (*The Brady Bunch*), and Danny Bonaduce (*The Partridge Family*), the latter three of whom made two Sam segments each.

Bewitched guest star Henry Gibson, who appeared in "Samantha's French Pastry" (as Napoleon) and "If the Shoe Pinches" (as a leprechaun), describes how the visiting cast of actors was treated on the set:

"Although the shooting days were very long, this was not the usual half-hour ball game. I felt not unlike a guest artist invited to play at a concert by virtuoso performers under the baton of Bill Asher, a very wise and energetic conductor who knew his orchestra like the back of his hand."

Gibson is unaware of the several dozen times his *Bewitched* episodes have run, but he is constantly reminded of the show's enormous impact, such as his experience during the filming of *Switching Channels*, a theatrical film with Burt Reynolds and Kathleen Turner, which was released in 1988, nearly twenty years after Gibson's Irish elf gig on *Bewitched*.

One night Gibson and a few other *Switching* cast members were having dinner. A very dignified woman stopped by their table as she was exiting the restaurant.

"I know you," she said.

Gene Blakey's "Dave" counseled Darrin in many *Bewitched* outings.

Henry Gibson

Henry Gibson's "Napoleon" appears in "Samantha's French Pastry."

A fellow actor playfully took his cue and replied, "We all think we know him."

The actor then went on to banter off a list of film credits, some of which Gibson says were "good" and "not so great."

"No, I haven't seen any of those," the woman responded as she turned to leave.

Suddenly, she stopped, turned around, came back to the table and said to Gibson, who played the wicked elf in "If the Shoe Pinches," "You're the leprechaun. That's who you are."

A Guest by Any Other Name

J. Edward McKinley played a record nine clients on *Bewitched*, beginning with "Long Live the Queen." Jack Collins and Charles Lane were runners-up with seven clients in eight appearances each.

Sara Seegar was a client's wife seven times in a total of eleven appearances. Richard X.

Slattery appeared nine times but only played one client (in "Samantha's Magic Sitter").

Bernie Kopell appeared in nine episodes.

Gene Blakely (who died in 1987) played Darrin's best pal Dave a total of eight times.

Paul Barselow was a bartender in eight segments. Jean Blake and Bernie Kuby were on seven shows, as was Steve Franken.

John Fiedler, Ronald Long, Cliff Norton, Jane Connell, and Herb Voland were in six segments apiece.

Jill Foster played Darrin's secretary, Betty, and other such roles ten times. Jean Blake, Irene Byatt, Samantha Scott, Ann Dorn, Susan Hathaway, and Marcia Wallace (*The Bob Newhart Show*) also played Betty.

Bernie Kuby was a waiter four times.

Dick Wilson appeared on the show seventeen times, a record for any nonregular, and more than several semiregulars. In fifteen of his appearances, Wilson played various drunks, but in "Ho, Ho the Clown," he was a client; in "George Washington Zapped Here," Part 2, he was a neighbor; and in "Samantha's Wedding Present," he was a lush again, but with a heart of gold.

Sara Seegar was runner-up to Wilson with eleven appearances, seven as a wife, three as a guest, and once as a client.

J. Edward McKinley and Jill Foster were next with ten appearances each.

Ten episodes have no guest stars at all, employing only regulars.

"Is It Magic or Imagination?" was written by the late Arthur Julian, who played clients in four episodes, and Hogersdorf the butcher, whom Sam zaps to make Mr. Kravitz jealous in "Splitsville."

Bernie Kopell guested on consecutive single shows ("A Bunny for Tabitha,"

Bernie Kopell (*That Girl*, *Get Smart*, and *The Love Boat*) guested in several segments of *Bewitched*.

"Samantha's Secret Spell"), as did Cliff Norton ("Cousin Serena Strikes Again", Part 2; "One Touch of Midas"), Jud Stank ("Darrin on a Pedestal," "Paul Revere Rides Again"), and Allen Jenkins ("Darrin Goes Ape," "Money Happy Returns").

J. Edward McKinley was in three shows in four weeks, as was Cliff Norton, Ron Masak (later of *Murder, She Wrote*) and Allen Jenkins, while Ysable MacClosky guested three times in five weeks and four segments in ten weeks; Noam Pitlik appeared in three shows in six weeks.

As to the employment of the same guest actor more than once, Bill Asher says:

"If I like an actor's style, or know of his talents, I never have any qualms about using him or her again and again. Some producers do. I don't."

"You see some shows," Elizabeth said, "and you say, 'Now why didn't they take a little more time with the recurring roles or guest players?'

Then you realize that the actors were cast because they were from some corporate office and considered the better choice because they had a name.

"I don't agree with that philosophy, and we never used it on *Bewitched*. We always went with the best possible people, conceding to their abilities as actors and capabilities with the roles being cast."

"I thought every performer on the show was extraordinary," she concluded.

William Asher (left) and guest star, Robert Brown, on the set of "Darrin on a Pedestal."

Samantha, a wacked-out dodo bird (Janos Prohaska), and Darrin in "Samantha's Witchcraft Blows a Fuse."

Chapter 9

Assorted Arts and Witch Crafts

One of the most amazing things I learned while filming Bewitched *is that at any given moment, the crew is infinitely more important than any actress or actor working on a television show.*

ELIZABETH MONTGOMERY

The magic behind the magic was vital to the success of *Bewitched*.

"Technically," says Bill Asher, "*Bewitched* was a tough show to direct. In the early years I made sure I directed all the episodes that were more magic-oriented because I knew how to move things along more readily. There were also times when we were enough ahead of schedule as well as the air date that I was allowed to shuffle random scenes for different episodes out of sequence."

In the event that Asher could not finish shows, he would arrange time at the end of the third day (the series shot in four) to complete scenes that took place in the Stephens house with the regular cast members and would assign the rest to the assistant director. After the last frame was filmed, he would edit all the scenes together and fit them in.

"Today you can't do that," he says. "At times, we would have one of those thirteen-page days when the sides [dialogue between actors] would just fly by. But we more or less maintained a balance."

The optical illusions on *Bewitched* took a long time to devise and film.

Around 1970, while half-hour comedies like *The Odd Couple* were allocated a show-by-show budget of $90,000, each thirty-minute *Bewitched* episode cost approximately $115,000. Such a figure may not seem expensive by contemporary standards (*Star Trek: Voyager* costs about $1.5 million an episode), but during Samantha's original run, it was a high figure.

"At first," recalls story editor Bernard Slade, "we really didn't use any extravagant special effects. It wasn't as if we were doing *Star Wars*. We kept things simple because we felt the magic was not all-powerful. We wanted to keep it within the boundaries of believability."

In the later years, Bill Asher says the budget increased as the show developed. "That just meant we worked harder," he says. "We did the same amount of dialogue as *The Donna Reed Show* or *Father Knows Best*, but we had to correlate the magic, which took some doing. After a while, we had it down to a science."

There were several individuals who brought these special effects to life. After veteran Willis Cook oversaw the *Bewitched* pilot (and went on to other projects), Screen Gems brought in Richard Albain, who worked on features for Columbia, including *Bell, Book and Candle* (1959).

When Albain left to work with Sidney Sheldon on *I Dream of Jeannie*, Marlow Newkirk, Hal Bigger, Terry Saunders, John Bendowski, and Roy Maples lent their assistance through the years.

Albain describes the intricacies of the work:

"We'd receive a script two or three days in advance of rehearsal, and then go over it in a production meeting with the rest of the cast and crew, noting changes to be made. Then an hour or two before we went to shoot the gag, Bill, or whoever was directing, would come over and give his okay, or say something like, 'I'd like this [prop] to do this or I'd like this [prop] to float over here.'"

If it was an overly involved special effects sequence, Albain says the gag would have to be positioned in advance. "We would all work around it until it came time to shoot," he remembers.

Endora "pops" out.

Hocus Focus

There were several camera tricks that were employed on the show, but the most frequently used sight gag was the appearance or disappearance of various witches and warlocks on the show. For this effect, the graphic camera was used.

Dick Albain elaborates:

"We'd get an angle on whoever was about to pop in or out and then mark the lens where the character would swing his arms or whatever. Then someone would mark the other camera in the same way. We'd stop tape [filming] at the proper time on one camera, and keep another one on to give the illusion of someone disappearing."

When objects appeared or disappeared from the hand of Samantha or anyone else, that person would freeze and hold the mark. Albain would then come on the set and take the object away. When the episode was viewed, the object would appear to vanish.

To make it look as if there were particular people or objects levitating in midair, Albain used an old diving board and crane that Columbia had discarded. He situated the board between the catwalks in the ceiling on the set, where there was a six-foot clearance. He would then secure special wires and strings from up above.

Play Misty for Me

As Dick Albain recalls, other effects such as the puff-smoke technique proved challenging:

"At first they wanted Samantha to pop in and out in a puff of smoke, called a *screen explosion*. So I developed the idea. When they did the pilot, they used black powder, and they put three or four feet of it in front of the camera, which would black out the whole screen after somebody blew on it.

"Then I thought of building a trough to put at Samantha's feet at such an angle that it would deflect the heat. This way the smoke and the heat would blow far from the camera and Elizabeth, keeping her cool and the camera

Carlotta (Mercedes McCambridge) and Juke (Steve Franken) cause problems for Sam in "Darrin, Gone and Forgotten," which employed fog sequences.

from exploding. When she would pretend to disappear, we would just puff her out. The director would cut, and Elizabeth would change her clothes or whatever and be ready for the next shot."

Another foggy technique was the dry-ice or mist effect, employed in many of the Salem and Witch Convention segments from the seventh season. This procedure was used to create a cloudlike look in "A Good Turn Never Goes Unpunished," in which the Stephenses argue, and Samantha is forced to retreat with Tabitha and Endora—literally—to Cloud Nine.

This method was also used in "Darrin Gone and Forgotten," in which Sam flies to the abode of witch Carlotta (Mercedes McCambridge) up yonder to plead for the release of Darrin, whom the not-so-nice witch has displaced.

To produce the heavenly effect, carbon dioxide was solidified into a white, icelike substance. This, in block form, is called dry ice. It was extensively employed as a coolant. Permitted to warm, the dry ice gradually dehumidified and gave off clouds of vapors as it returned to its original gaslike form.

Dry ice was not costly, and it was kept on hand so it could be manipulated easily, as in "Gone" and other segments. The only essential precaution was to avoid prolonged skin contact.

During the filming of "Samantha and the Beanstalk," Elizabeth found that dry ice made it difficult for her to breathe. "I was pregnant at the time," she recollected, "and I was more apt to queasiness around that stuff. But I didn't realize how strong those vapors could be. It was real scary."

To a less harmful extent, small pieces of dry ice were used in many of the *Bewitched* episodes involving Dr. Bombay's potions. Minute amounts would be dropped into a test tube or a glass of water, and the result was a bubbling or swirling white steam.

Other Systems of Sorcery

To showcase Samantha and Endora's flying (as in "If They Never Met," where the two travel back in time), a process adopting multiple wind supplements was employed, localizing the bewitching breezes as much as possible.

When mass confusion had to be created in Sam's house (as when High Priestess Hepzibah, played by Jane Connell, arrived in "To Go or Not To Go"), apparatuses capable of various speeds and larger wind machines were utilized so that props could fly all about.

When Bernie Kopell's apothecary from the witch world was seen in his laboratory, it was covered with cobwebs. A novel instrument empowering a rubber solution to trickle onto a revolving fan blade helped to produce the meshy look. The pitched substance was usually spun over extended black cotton threads. To add more to this effect, the crew would dust the webs with a substance called *Fuller's earth*, which made the webs more visible.

When ghosts and apparitions would partially appear or disappear on the show (as in "McTavish" or "The Ghost Who Made a Spectre of Himself"), the spirit-actor in question would be placed in front of either a black or a blue background, and the chroma-key effect would be put to use. As a result, any body part or piece of clothing that was supposed to disappear would be cloaked in the same black or blue material in order for headless torsos and bodiless arms and legs to appear. This technique was used extensively with Alice Ghostley's Esmeralda who, as explained earlier, had a tendency to fade from view.

Every once in a while, when Samantha and Endora wove a magic spell or spoke an incantation, a gleaming light effect would be added to the projected scene. Here, glitter, stardust, and other glimmering agents, patterned with sequins or something similar, would be employed. Occasionally, metallic dust was used for sparkling coiffures, as on Elizabeth's hair just before Samantha was crowned Queen of the Witches.

When dream sequences were needed on the series ("I Confess"), the ripple reflection effect was applied. This commonly used process involved having a machine hold a receptacle of water. It was held in a crisply centralized light stream, as its image was projected on a nearby surface that the camera then filmed.

When the Stephenses' home was being rocked by whatever angry supernatural force of the moment, an effect called "tilting the picture" was employed.

"Tilting" was created by having various mirrored lens attachments handy to enable the special effects people to rotate the picture. By superimposing a regular scene on a tilted one, the illusion of a slanted frame is easily created.

This process was extensively employed on the *Batman* TV series. It was also used on the original *Star Trek* series whenever the *Enterprise* was under attack by an alien vessel, and the crew would be seen swaying from side to side on the bridge.

Pop a Prop

Certain props used on *Bewitched* almost had a life of their own.

One such prop was the mobile chair with the collapsible legs from "Sam's Spooky Chair."

Samantha handles a prop and the situation in "The Trial and Error of Aunt Clara."

Doorknobs with broomsticks.

Maurice's special whistle prop from "The Trial and Error of Aunt Clara."

Elizabeth said there was "an absolutely wonderful propman named Fairchild, who would 'doze off' quite often on the set. He had this habit of going off to a corner and resting. Well, when we had that chair built, we had to be very careful about where we placed it when we weren't using it, because everyone had this vision of him walking over to the chair and sitting down and having him collapse in it."

Kasey Rogers (the second Louise Tate) also recalls two wonderful props that she was allowed to have and hold after the filming of an episode.

The segment "Mona Sammi" involved Larry and Louise admiring a portrait they assumed to be Samantha. But it's really her Grandaunt Cornelia.

The Stephenses convince their friends that Darrin is the artist. Louise then asks him to paint a portrait of her, leading Sam to zap her husband into a true artist.

Just as Darrin is about to complete a perfect likeness of Louise, Endora rezaps him to create a hideous image.

Kasey got to keep both portraits.

"I still have this fantasy of having the pretty picture hanging on my den wall at the beginning of a party," she laughs, "only to turn it around and have the ugly one on the other side by the end of the party."

In "Birdies, Bogeys, and Baxter," Samantha and Endora cast a spell on Darrin, which makes him a superior golfer while he and Larry are on the course with a client. A golf pro was brought in to substitute for Dick York during the sequences showcasing Darrin's newfound abilities.

As York recalled, the golf pro was having a bad day:

"He couldn't get one of those balls to hit the green. It was the funniest thing in the world. We had to keep on fixing the shoot. Then I gave it a shot myself. I damn near hit some of the golfers on the other side of the green. Everyone joked that if they'd known I could do that, they never would have hired the other guy."

Besides that prop-fly golf ball, another York-related prop also had an "air" about it. You might even say it was the "fly of the party," or at least of "No Zip in My Zap."

Here, Darrin thinks Samantha has transformed herself into a fly to spy on his meeting with a client, who also just happens to be an old girlfriend.

York recalled filming the scene with the fly:

"It was one of the grossest days on the show. The prop guys took the wings off this poor little fly and placed him right on my nose."

The portrait props of Kasey Rogers's Louise from "Mona Sammi."

Endora is taken for a ride.

Animal Attack-Tion

Bewitched assistant director Marvin Miller relates a few other instances where much larger creatures were used.

Like the time Bill Asher asked him to stand between Marion (Aunt Clara) Lorne and an ostrich, a creature which tends to be temperamental.

"What do you mean?" Miller wondered about Asher's request.

"Marion's afraid to be too close to the ostrich," Asher replied.

"Well," Miller said, "I'm not too happy about it either."

The only way to motivate the animal to move was to flag it down, and, as Miller says, "You had to be careful. It usually takes two people to ride them out."

Miller's other creature conflict transpired early on in the series, on the set "It Shouldn't Happen to a Dog," in which Samantha transformed a client (Jack Warden) of Darrin's into a canine.

Miller remembered a day out at the Columbia Studios ranch where he questioned the acting dog's trainer about a certain scene. They were ready to start filming, and Miller asked if the dog was ready.

"Oh yeah," the trainer replied. "No problem."

As it turned out, the dog was supposed to be level with the ground, run up to a car and then place his paws on the hood. As Miller describes it:

"We later found out that the hood was hot and the dog was smarter than the trainer. He wouldn't put his paws up there. It delayed

Steve Franken with then-pregnant wife Julie and their friend from the set of "A Gazebo Never Forgets."

shooting for quite some time that day. That's when I learned that whenever I heard an animal trainer say, 'No problem,' I'd get nervous. I knew there would be a problem."

Miller recalls additional animal scenes gone awry, including a penguin with a severe lack of self-control who, as the *Bewitched* associate puts it, "left droppings all over the place"; and a pink elephant (employed in "A Gazebo Never Forgets").

Of the latter, Miller says: "We had to get that elephant to go up the stairway in Samantha's house. But he was just too big and too wide, and the steps couldn't hold him."

Dick Sargent remembered a few animal actors who were difficult to work with in "The House That Uncle Arthur Built," which involved the employment of chimpanzees:

"Liz and I were very nervous about having them on the set. There were ten or twelve of them running around the living room, and we weren't exactly sure of what they were going to do next. They had real big mouths and teeth, and rumor had it that they got vicious after seven years of age. And those monkeys were way past that stage."

Side by Side

One of the central audiovisual techniques employed on *Bewitched* was the split-screen effect, showcasing Samantha and Serena in the same frame. Director Richard Michaels discusses how this effect was achieved with the assistance of Elizabeth's stand-in, Melody Thomas.

"The first thing we would do was to secure two cameras in identical positions, with angles situated on Elizabeth and Melody. We then would shoot the over-the-shoulder shots with Elizabeth as Samantha and Melody as Serena before we did the master shots of Elizabeth as Serena and Melody as Samantha, because Elizabeth used heavy makeup and a wig as Serena, while Melody used only the black wig.

"Next, we'd do the sound track with Elizabeth as Samantha and Melody as Serena, and then vice versa. How it sounded really didn't matter as much as how long it took to record it. We could perfect the sound quality and character distinction later on when editing."

Melody's voice-overs of both Samantha and Serena (which was employed for timing purposes during filming) were edited out. Only Elizabeth's voice performances were edited in during an additional dubbing session.

The Sound of a Muse

Many of the special effects on *Bewitched* would not have been as effective had it not been for the whimsical sound effects which accompanied them.

For example, the tinkling tone behind Samantha's witch twitch was accomplished by a xylophone.

And what would Samantha and Endora's pop-ins and pop-outs have done without the play-along *ping* pitch of approximately one-half second of a symphony?

"Like everything else we did on the show," said Dick Sargent, "we tried to go for the gold. Bill Asher and Liz were behind the production 100 percent in every aspect. And the sound effects did not escape the detailed standard of quality that Bill demanded."

What a witch would wear in the cold.

One Darrin's professional look.

Larry, "Mr. Hitchcock" (Cesar Romero), and Samantha make like models in "Salem, Here We Come."

Four of the many magic guises of Endora.

The Witch-Drobe and Mortal-Wear Department

Byron Munson, who passed away in 1989, was the head of the wardrobe department for *Bewitched* and most of Columbia's shows at the time. His assistant was Vi Alford, who is also now gone.

Byron, who was allotted a thirty-five-hundred-dollar budget for each *Bewitched* episode, explained the costume procedure he employed for dressing Sam, Darrin, et al.:

"I arrived early on the set and stayed late. On Monday morning, we'd have a meeting. I would sit there with the script in front of me, listening to whatever any of the other departments had to say. I then went around to each of the actor's scripts and penciled next to their dialogue what they were to wear for which scenes."

Munson would also periodically shop for dresses and suits, which was a lot cheaper than making or renting them.

When Munson did decide to rent, he had an associate with whom he worked at Western Costumes, which remains a major Los Angeles firm that is used by the entertainment industry and the general public. As soon as he finished a breakdown of the script, he would send a copy to his Western colleague, who would then read it and get a feel for what Munson required. After a time, Munson said his associate "got pretty good at interpreting what each show called for."

Munson employed Western for several of the period-related *Bewitched* segments, including visits with George Washington, Caesar, and Ben Franklin. Munson also requested Western costumes for various visits with Santa Claus and Mary, the Good Fairy, and magical trips into Tabitha's storybooks

Mother and daughter fantasy fashions.

("Samantha and the Beanstalk," "Hansel and Gretel in Samanthaland").

Munson also made specific designs for the show, including Samantha's and Endora's witches' gowns, both of which encompassed different designs during the years.

Make-Believe Makeup and Hairstyles

The *Bewitched* makeup and hair department was supervised by Ben Lane, who was head of the division for Columbia and assisted by Rolf Miller,

who was nominated for his work on Elizabeth and Dick Sargent in "Samantha's Old Man."

Lane was with the show from the beginning, working on the initial screen tests and pilot, and then stayed the entire eight years. He created all the face fashions for the entire cast of characters. Everything from Endora's severe eye shadow to Darrin's skin-colored, oversized ears ("My, What Big Ears You Have").

The show's hairstyles were created by a woman credited as "Peanuts," whose real name was Lillian Hokum Ugrin. Others of the hair set

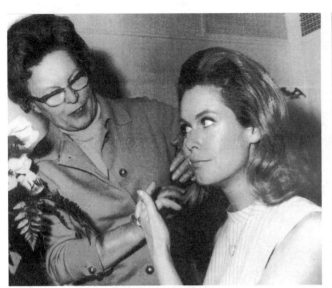

Stylist Vi Alford helps Elizabeth with her hair.

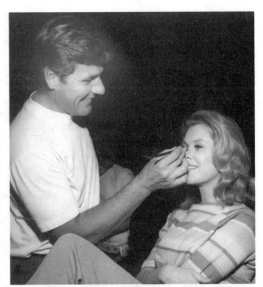

Makeup man Rolf Miller with Elizabeth behind the scenes of "Samantha's Secret Saucer."

included a man named Cosmo, who made an on-screen appearance in "One Touch of Midas," as Darrin's stylist, also named Cosmo.

Other follicle facades were Endora's famous bouffant, Serena's black wigs and long blonde hair ("Hippie, Hippie Hooray"), and Samantha's season-to-season fashions (which Elizabeth requested), and various wig formations (as with Queen Victoria in Aunt Clara's "Victoria Victory").

The show's makeup routine varied from segment to segment, depending on whom or what Endora decided to turn Darrin into, or who or what came into the Stephenses' lives.

The most difficult part of filming *Bewitched*, however, remained staging the special effects,

as was initially assessed at the beginning of this chapter.

Dick York offered a memory from "Be It Ever So Mortgaged," in which Sam and Darrin move into their home on Morning Glory Circle, and which also summarizes the entire "effectual" *Bewitched* experience:

"There were times when I would get a line perfect, and the magic was off. I remember once having to wait almost twelve hours for the crew to shift the furniture in the living room as it was zapped in and out, in and out, because Sam and Endora were choosing which sofa and chairs looked best in the living room. But when push came to shove, we were all masters of making the magic work."

Elizabeth and Dick Sargent in Rolf Miller's Emmy-nominated aging makeup from "Samantha's Old Man."

Endora's distinctive high hair.

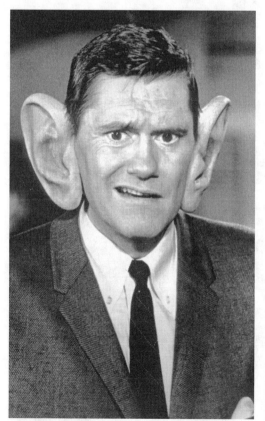

Dick York's Darrin has "big" problems in "My, What Big Ears You Have."

Jane Connell's queenly appearance from "To Go or Not to Go, That is the Question."

Reheating potions and popularity.

Chapter 10

Remixing the Magic Formula

Several elements contributed to the successful summation of *Bewitched*.

The show was created week after week with care and dedication, which explains why most contemporary shows pale in comparison to the series, and why it's still screened—and widely accepted—in syndication.

When *Bewitched* first materialized in the 1960s, it showcased a great deal of compassion and humanity for a series about nonmortals. It wasn't extremely conservative, reactionary, or broadly comedic.

When Samantha initially began to twitch, the majority of television characters were lovable and flawless people. Rarely would a three-dimensional person show up in a situation comedy. To address an audience, television types had to be likable and never really cry or display intense emotion. There were good guys and bad guys but hardly any in between.

On *Bewitched*, the producers, directors, and actors were able to make the witches and warlocks more dimensional because they were not human beings.

In Bill Asher's quintessential episode, "A Is for Aardvark," Samantha cries real tears when Darrin presents her with a watch inscribed "I Love You Every Second."

In "School Days, School Daze," she grows increasingly angry with her daughter's mortal teacher (Maudie Pickett), who invades the Stephens household one too many times seeking an explanation for Tabitha's Endora-induced genius.

Bewitched is one of the pantheon of classical American TV shows created before the medium itself lost its innocence. We seemed to have lost the formula.

Now all we have is a medium that is only bothering and bewildering.

PROFESSOR ARTHUR ASA BERGER
San Francisco State University,
author of The TV Guided American

Paul Lynde's Uncle Arthur was outlandish and irresponsible each time he showed up; Serena was somewhat wild and loose; Endora was ungenerous and grudging. Each was permitted to stray from the norm and to do the outrageous, because they were party to an outside world, a bewitched world.

Endora exhibited emotional distaste for Darrin every week and flaunted traits that most human beings consider unappealing. Her conduct was considered inappropriate by Samantha and Darrin. Yet she was given the stamp of approval by the audience. In keeping with the programming philosophy of the times, Endora was a *bad* good witch.

"I think fantasy shows like *Bewitched*," said Harry Ackerman, "filled a great gap in television in the 1960s. I also think that the networks were much too quick to wipe out the *Bewitched*-type of programming and to replace it almost immediately with *All in the Family* and comparatively realistic shows."

To the viewer's satisfaction, Samantha controlled her witchcraft and twitching only on occasion and in an emergency. She remained a witch without succumbing to what Bernard Fox's Dr. Bombay might have termed *primary mortalitis*. As a result, she continues to enjoy her immortal success in television. Had she become human, *Bewitched* would have obviously no longer been a show about a witch in a mortal's world, and Samantha's reign as *Queen of the Witches* would have been curtailed.

Reality Bites

When CBS programmed *All in the Family* opposite *Bewitched* in its last season (1971-72), Samantha held her own against Archie Bunker, and the magic sitcom was renewed for three more years.

Elizabeth Montgomery, however, had decided to leave the party while it was still popping and move on to other projects.

Yet the mark of Samantha, as in *z* for *zap*, has been ingrained in the psyche of the general television-viewing, music-listening, and movie-going public.

Bewitched entered national syndication in September of 1973 via Screen Gems and was renewed in 1988 via barter with Dancer Fitzgerald and Sample of New York. The show appears in hundreds of markets, most of which are in the United States.

In the fall of 1989, cable's Nickelodeon network, Nick At Nite, began showing the first two black-and-white seasons, which had not been seen in more than a decade.

Other cable networks televise the show weekdays, as do independent stations and networks around the world. Samantha can be seen as much as four times a day in places like New York City, Chicago, Los Angeles, and Phoenix.

There are thousands of female mortals around the world who were named after little Tabitha ('born' on January 13, 1966) and Samantha.

Several comedians, including Rosie O'Donnell and Ellen Degeneres, perform monologues about *Bewitched*, while funny girl Claudia Sherman even has tattooed on her ankle an animated image of Samantha.

Classic TV shows like *My Favorite Martian* (created by *Bewitched* writer John L. Greene), *Alice* (of which several episodes were directed by William Asher), *Newhart*, *The Golden Girls*, and *Cheers* have each made many references to Samantha and company.

The Nanny, Roseanne, Frasier, Dave's World, and *Saturday Night Live* have alluded to *Bewitched*. ABC's 1989–1993 groundbreaking drama, *Life Goes On*, featured a Larry Tate-like adman named Jerry Berkson (vigorously played by Ray Buktenica).

On a more direct television line, in the fall of 1996, ABC somewhat duplicated its *Bewitched* success with *Sabrina, the Teenage Witch*, starring Melissa Joan Hart (from Nickelodeon's *Clarissa Explains It All for You*). *Sabrina* was a live-action version of the animated series (based on the *Archie* comic book character).

Yet ABC has found from past, post-*Bewitched*, Sam-similar tryouts, that "wituation comedies" do not necessarily attract audiences.

In 1977, the Alphabet network tried to clone *Bewitched* itself, with the defunct *Tabitha* series. They tried again in 1989 with *Free Spirit*, which featured a witch named Winnie Goodwin (played by Corinne Bohrer), who was the housekeeper for a divorced father (Franc Luz), and his three children (Paul Scherrer, Alyson Hannigan, Edan Gross). The last *Spirit* spell was cast after only three months on the air.

Syndicated supernatural sitcoms reminiscent of *Bewitched* have done better, at least for two seasons or so. *Small Wonder, Out of This World*, and *Down to Earth* (with Dick Sargent) appeared in later years, while NBC's once-big hit, *Alf*, featured Mrs. Ochmonek (played by Liz [*Seinfeld*] Sheridan, a good friend of Elizabeth Montgomery), a nosy neighbor in the vein of Mrs. Kravitz.

Even more spooky is the relationship between *Bewitched* and the ABC-originated series, *Who's the Boss. Boss* stars Tony Danza as housekeeper Tony Micelli to Judith Light's Angela, who owns her own advertising agency.

Angela refers to her mother Mona, played by Katherine Helmond, in much the same manner that Samantha referred to Endora. Helmond's hair is Agnes Moorehead–red, and Mona is just as interfering as Endora was (though Mona sides with Tony and not her daughter Angela). What's more, Danza's TV daughter (played by Alyssa Milano) is named Samantha, while the front door to Angela's house is a replica of Samantha's door on *Bewitched*.

More still, *Boss* was filmed on the very same lot (then ABC Studios, now Sunset-Gower Studios) in Hollywood as *Bewitched*, owned by the same company (Columbia), and aired on the same network.

Somebody put a spell on somebody.

Bewitched fan Steve Randisi outside **Bewitched** house at Warner Brothers ranch studio facilities, circa 1977.

The central producer of *Bewitched*, Bill Asher, and his then wife and Samantha-star, Elizabeth Montgomery.

The real-life **McMann, Tate & Stevens** stationery.

On the big screen, the theatrical films *Big* (1988), in which a young boy suddenly becomes a man (played by Tom Hanks), and *Bill and Ted's Excellent Adventure* (1989), which involves historical figures visiting the present, both employed plot devices that were first used on *Bewitched,* while *The Witches of Eastwick* (1987), *Warlock* (1991), *Wayne's World* (1992), and *Pulp Fiction* (1995) made forthright references to *Bewitched.*

Of musical note, the rock band Red Kross recorded its own version of the Boyce and Hart composition, *Blow You a Kiss in the Wind,* which was sung by Elizabeth Montgomery as Serena in *Serena Stops the Show*. There's also a rock band in Los Angeles which named itself *The Larry Tate Experience.*

Even Edie Brickell, of the *New Bohemians* band (and wife to Paul Simon) once stated in *Rolling Stone*, "All I ever really wanted was to have a job like Darrin Stephens on *Bewitched*— where you could be creative all the time."

Advertising man Craig Winner of Los Angeles took his *Bewitched* inspiration one step further and opened McMann, Tate, and *Stevens* Advertising, Inc., adding and slightly altering the spelling of Darrin's last name (with a *v* instead of a *ph*). "I always wanted to be an advertising man like Darrin," says Winner. "So I made my dream come true. I'm successful due to a lot of hard work, and the inspiration I received from *Bewitched.*"

Does the actual ad business differ from the way it's portrayed on *Bewitched*?

"The pace is just as hectic," Winner avows, "and there's just as much on-the-spot decision making and slogan creating at my company as there was on the show." Yet, he admits to one major distinction between Darrin and himself:

"I'm not married to a witch."

The Message Behind the Magic

In 1990, an article entitled "She Worship" (by Iran Lacuna) appeared in the *Los Angeles Times*. It had some interesting things to say about how real witches are viewed.

"For some," Lacuna wrote, "goddess worship is merging as the latest wave in the evolution of women's rights. If feminism first took on economic issues in the 1960s and the 1970s and then moved on to questions about family life in the eighties, then the nineties are seeing women grappling with a more elusive target."

With regard to *Bewitched*, similar comments are made by two of the show's associates: guest star Bernie Kopell and writer Barbara Avedon.

"Women love to be liberated," professes Kopell. "They love to have great powers. Whether Darrin realizes this or not, Samantha motivated his life, something he possibly felt impotent to do."

Avedon believes people in the 1960s watched *Bewitched* and said, "Yes, it's right. Samantha shouldn't use her powers. The audience might have felt," continues Avedon, "that if she did, they would have had to relinquish their strengths as well and give in to society and just go along with the crowd.

"Every woman does for the man in her life," Avedon goes on to say. "I think, in a sense, Darrin was the voice of society. The one who would say, 'Sam, what have you been up to?' It wasn't the outside world that was telling her not to fly her child to school, it was absolutely within her relationship with Darrin that she held herself back. Not because she wanted to live the mortal life as a challenge in and of itself, but because she chose to live the mortal way because she loved Darrin.

"Samantha and Darrin's marriage even may have been the basic metaphor for the male-female relationship of the 1960s, when women really kept their own strengths hidden with the prescribed boundaries of marriage."

Does this mean there is a message behind the magic of *Bewitched* after all?

"If I can't write a message into the script I'm working on," Avedon replies, "then I don't go up to the plate. If a story doesn't teach some kind of lesson, then it's not worth writing. If it's written totally as a message, then it should be sent as a telegram. If it's delivered with drama or comedy or hopefully both, and it says something, too, then that's art. Though without the message it's not art."

Bewitched director E. W. Swackhamer offered an opposing view:

"Television is supposed to take your mind off what happens during the day, not necessarily teach you something. If that's what viewers want, they certainly have that opportunity with public television and A&E [the Arts and Entertainment network], but basically situation comedy should be fun, escapist fare and make you feel good."

"Television comedy is a great medium to get things across," adds Marvin Miller. "But I don't think that many of the episodes we did on *Bewitched* had any hidden themes. Elizabeth was pretty clear and upfront about what she said and did as Samantha.

"When you're a star, and you have a hit show, then of course you'll have a forum where it's easier to discuss matters that are important to you, to have people listen to your perspective. Maybe the audience might not even like the politics of the subject matter, but they're going to listen to whatever is said because they like and respect the actor who's saying it. The actor has made himself or herself accessible to the viewer.

"Whereas if I [a person behind the scenes] got up and spoke on the air about a topic, no one would know who I was, and they wouldn't care or listen to what I had to say."

There were times when Elizabeth would have preferred to have been more political on *Bewitched*. But it was a comedy, and as she stated, "There were certain parameters we could not have passed."

"Television is a very strange medium," concludes Miller. "For people to welcome shows into their homes, they have to feel comfortable with the performer on the screen. That's why some actors make it on TV, and some don't. They may succeed in the theater or in motion pictures as it is more of a physical choice and effort to see a play or a film, but if the audience isn't comfortable with them in their living rooms, the actors or actresses can forget it."

Star Power

The ongoing success of *Bewitched* subliminally rests mainly with its star power.

Elizabeth's Samantha is quite attractive, and as *Bewitched* writer John L. Greene (creator of *My Favorite Martian*) relayed, "You can just see the intelligence in her eyes."

Though she may not have always seemed so, Samantha was an independent woman; it was her decision to surrender her sorcery for the mortal life. For such behavior to have been accepted by viewers of the 1960s, the female lead in a series would had to have been a supernatural woman.

Notwithstanding, Elizabeth was the first female sex symbol of the television generation. She arrived on the tube long before *Charlie's Angels* and Suzanne Somers combed the hairwaves. *Angels* and shows like *Three's Company* were popular strictly because of the frosted locks, right amount of jiggle, and constant displays and mentions of the unmentionables of their female stars. Ditto for the '90s babes on *Baywatch*.

Elizabeth's Samantha needed no such ploys.

People continue to fall in love with how she works inside.

The fact that she's elegant to watch on the outside is an added benefit, not her central attraction.

The trouping of Dick York and Dick Sargent on *Bewitched* also proves advantageous to viewers. Their idiosyncratic interpretations of Darrin almost allow the series to be screened as two different shows, which contributes to its long-lasting appeal.

Of the other actors who shared the same role on *Bewitched*, associate producer/director Richard Michaels says they could not have hired another actor to play Aunt Clara [Marion Lorne] the way they replaced Dick York with

Bewitched **assistant director Marvin Miller in 1989**

Dick Sargent as Darrin. That's why an entirely new character was created with Esmeralda for Alice Ghostley.

"Darrin was a critical character," Michaels explains, "and we really didn't want to tinker with the basis of the show and replace a central lead character. With Aunt Clara and Esmeralda, the disappearance of a bumbling aunt and the appearance of a bumbling maid were acceptable because both were not as central to the show's basic premise as was Darrin."

On the viewer's double vision of Alice Pearce/Sandra Gould as Gladys Kravitz, Michaels says they were either going to stipend someone new to play Gladys after Alice Pearce had passed away or move new neighbors to replace the Kravitzes altogether. They opted for the former due to the fact that Gladys's interplay with Abner was too funny and too essential to the show's format.

Regarding Irene Vernon and Kasey Rogers as Louise Tate, Michaels reveals:

"We couldn't have Larry just marry someone else. The character of Louise softened his persona. For him to get a divorce or even become a widower would have made him less appealing and too bitter. It was just cleaner to hire Kasey after Irene left."

With each of these replacement cases, it should be noted that none was ever a question of recasting because of an actor's unacceptable performance. The decision to replace an actor was made because of the performer's death (Marion Lorne, Alice Pearce), illness (Dick York), personal decision to leave (Irene Vernon), or scheduling conflicts (Robert F. Simon, Roy Roberts).

The high performance caliber of David White and Agnes Moorehead cannot go without final mention in analyzing the everlasting

Agnes Moorehead and Paul Lynde meet with a smile off-screen.

appeal of *Bewitched*.

White's Larry Tate may have been conniving and manipulative, but it was David's endearing nature and spirited theatrics which softened Larry's son-of-a-gun arm punches to Darrin.

"He was an artist of the double take," Dick York said of White. "No one could have played Larry Tate like David. Nobody."

It was Moorehead's Shakespearean deliveries of Endora's spells and incantations which continue to endear both individuals to the viewer. Moorehead's stance was elegant. With her eyes piercing and glistening, she hypnotized the audience each time she swayed her neck and felicitously waved her arms from side to side, hexing, zapping, and metamorphosing Darrin on a weekly basis.

Bewitched **guest actors Fritz Feld (left) and Dick Wilson reunite.**

Such antics were tainted with a dash of witchly evil that was camouflaged due to Moorehead's impeccable professional training. Of her lasting reputation, writer Bernie Kahn says she was "brilliant, a forerunner who added a great deal of class to Endora. She was ahead of her time. Just as much as the show was."

Key Ingredients

It's important to remember that *Bewitched* succeeded (and still flourishes) because:

1. It was funny, and
2. Because of Samantha's sound mortal perspective and priorities. Her magic abilities, and the show's general fantasy premise never outshined the series with overkill.

The sitcom's stories never tampered with the internal rationalism of its own imaginative realm (there was logic within the illogic). The dialogue was masterfully structured to give life to its characters; there was no mistaking Darrin for Larry Tate or Samantha for Endora.

"Everyone took the show very seriously," reveals Bernard Slade, the show's first and second season story editor. While penning for Samantha, Slade also wrote for the sitcom, *My Living Doll*, which starred Julie Newmar as a mechanical woman.

"So there I was," the writer recalls with a laugh, "a grown man writing about a witch and a robot, sitting in rooms with other grown men debating things like, 'Would a witch really say that?'"

The late Ed Jurist, who took over for Slade as story editor, was also amused by how seriously he and his colleagues viewed the series.

"I remember working in Palm Springs one season with Bill Asher. We were discussing the life of a frog [for "Nobody but a Frog Knows How To Live"], and I recall thinking, "If anyone overheard this conversation, they would think we were nuts."

Richard Baer, too, remembers thinking "Who's crazy here?" in considering the *Bewitched* dos and don'ts. "Uncle Arthur couldn't pop out of the kitchen cabinet. It would have to be a book, and this book could never have been an encyclopedia. It had to be *Swiss Family Robinson*."

As to the employment of lyrical spells on the show, Baer states, "I used to love writing those incantations. I would steal from Kipling all the time. It was our job to take something natural and make it supernatural."

Make that *super-popular*, which Dick York believed *Bewitched* to be, "because it was about faith and trust. It was first shown in the proper time," he said, "when we needed to return to innocence and sanity. It was the way things should have been after World War II and the announcement of democracy."

"If there's ever something to fear in life," York concluded, "and if you believe in miracles, then *Bewitched* makes you believe in magic."

Bewitched, Again?

Could it ever be time again for a new *Bewitched* series?

Even with Elizabeth Montgomery, Dick York, Dick Sargent, Agnes Moorehead, David White, and a host of other *Bewitched* stars now gone?

Elizabeth had been approached several times about returning to the role of Samantha in an updated TV show but declined.

Why?

"I don't see any reason to do that," she replied. "Once you have completed a project, you should move on. I am very proud of *Bewitched*, and I seriously doubt that whatever type of reunion could be made would ever top what we did on the series or even come close."

Elizabeth was extremely fond of *Bewitched* and its firm adherence to structure:

"One of the great advantages of our format was that it opened itself up to many ideas. We were allowed to take it in any direction we wanted as long as we stayed within the ground rules. And we did."

Despite Elizabeth's stated position, at one point (circa 1988) there was to be a new *Bewitched* series, and there was talk of a feature film, and TV's original Samantha was allegedly interested in appearing in both.

The updated tube seer-series was to be called *Bewitched Again* and was set to film in London. Elizabeth was to have emerged as Sam in only the first episode, in a cameo

Bernard Fox and Erin Murphy at TV Collectors Show in 1995.

capacity, to introduce a new weekly witch.

There would have been one major difference between Samantha and the new small-screen conjurer: The updated sorceress would have been given free reign to use her powers by her mortal love, a plot device that may have spelled an early cancellation.

The idea of a feature film has since been granted a green light. Production began in 2004 on *Bewitched*, starring Nicole Kidman, Will Ferrell, Michael Caine, and Shirley MacLaine, cowritten by Nora and Delia Ephron and directed by Nora Ephron. In this film adaptation, scheduled for release in summer 2005, a beautiful young witch named Isabel (Kidman), determined to live without witchcraft, transports herself to Hollywood in search of true romance. There, she meets Jack (Ferrell), a handsome, but bumbling actor. With her sights set on him, Isabel casts a spell to open up Jack's heart to love, as madcap adventures of mortals and witches ensue.

Maurice Evans, Agnes Moorehead, Elizabeth Montgomery, Erin Murphy, and Dick Sargent.

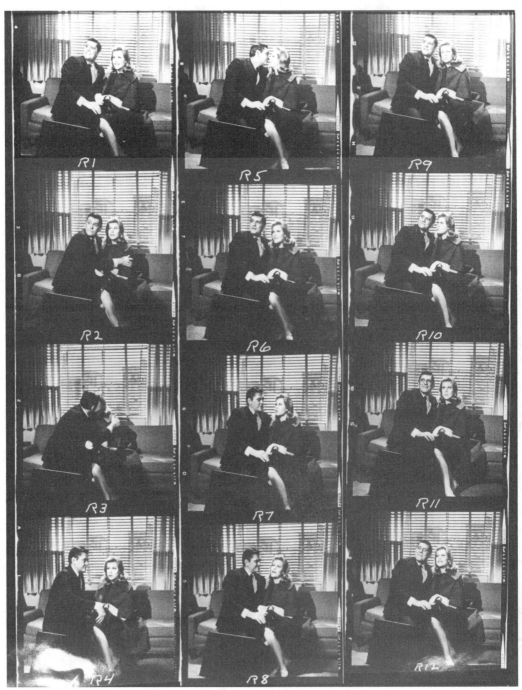

Let the reruns begin

Chapter 11

Seasons of the Sam-Witch

Bewitched Broadcast History

ABC .... September 17, 1964, to July 1, 1972

ABC (Daytime) .... January 1, 1968, to September 9, 1973

ABC Saturday Morning .... 1971 to 1973

Original ABC Schedule (Eastern Time)

Thursday 9:00 P.M., September 17, 1964, to January 5, 1967

Thursday 8:30 P.M., January 12, 1967, to September 9, 1971

Wednesday 8:00 P.M., September 15, 1971, to January 5, 1972

Saturday 8:00 P.M., January 15, 1972 to July 1, 1972

Original ABC Nielsen Ratings

Season	Rank	Audience Share
1964 to 1965	#2	31.0
1965 to 1966	#7	25.9
1966 to 1967	#8	23.4
1967 to 1968	#11	23.5
1968 to 1969	#12	23.3
1969 to 1970	#25	20.6
1970 to 1971	—	15.4
1971 to 1972	—	10.4

Unofficial *Bewitched* Theme Lyrics

written by
HERBIE J PILATO

My pretty witch spells the moonlight sky,
Twinkles the stars as she zips by.

Her charm is enchanting,
Her appeal, incantageous,
Ever inspiring.
A supernatural sensation,
She's so startling.

I'm captured by her smile.
Magically raptured all the while.
I can't believe what I see and hear.
Music sounds as she disappears.

(Instrumental)

Yes, she's got me hypnotized.
Me-ta-phy-sically, I'm undenied.
And whenever my hands are tied.
She loosens up the bind.

But with the twitch of her nose,
Or the snap of her finger,
Samantha flies by my side.
Lo and behold,
I am bewitched.
Lo and behold,
I am bewitched.

Emmy Amulets and Nominations

1965 to 1966

Outstanding Comedy Series
Bewitched (ABC)
The Dick Van Dyke Show (CBS)
Batman (ABC)
Get Smart (NBC)
Hogan's Heroes (CBS)

Outstanding Continued Performance by an Actress in a Leading Role in a Comedy
Elizabeth Montgomery, *Bewitched*
Mary Tyler Moore, *The Dick Van Dyke Show* *
Lucille Ball, *The Lucy Show* (CBS)

Outstanding Performance by an Actress in a Supporting Role in a Comedy
Alice Pearce, *Bewitched* *
Agnes Moorehead, *Bewitched*
Rose Marie, *The Dick Van Dyke Show*

Outstanding Directorial Achievement in a Comedy
William Asher, *Bewitched*
Paul Bogart, *Get Smart*
Jerry Paris, *The Dick Van Dyke Show*

1966 to 1967

Outstanding Comedy Series
Bewitched
The Monkees (NBC)*
The Andy Griffith Show (CBS)
Hogan's Heroes

Outstanding Continued Performance by an Actress in a Leading Role in a Comedy
Elizabeth Montgomery, *Bewitched*
Agnes Moorehead, *Bewitched*
Lucille Ball, *The Lucy Show* *
Marlo Thomas, *That Girl* (ABC)

Outstanding Performance by an Actress in a Supporting Role in a Comedy
Marion Lorne, *Bewitched*
Frances Bavier, *The Andy Griffith Show* *
Nancy Kulp, *The Beverly Hillbillies* (CBS)

Outstanding Directorial Achievement in a Comedy
William Asher, *Bewitched*
James Frawley, *The Monkees* *

1967 to 1968

Outstanding Comedy Series
Bewitched
Get Smart *
Family Affair (CBS)
Hogan's Heroes
The Lucy Show

Outstanding Performance by an Actor in a Leading Role in a Comedy Series
Dick York, *Bewitched*
Don Adams, *Get Smart* *
Richard Benjamin, *He And She* (CBS)
Sebastian Cabot, *Family Affair*
Brian Keith, *Family Affair*

* Emmy recipient

Outstanding Continued Performance by an Actress in a Leading Role in a Comedy
Elizabeth Montgomery, *Bewitched*
Lucille Ball, *The Lucy Show* *
Barbara Feldon, *Get Smart*
Paula Prentiss, *He And She*
Marlo Thomas, *That Girl*

Outstanding Performance by an Actress in a Supporting Role in a Comedy
Marion Lorne, *Bewitched* *
Agnes Moorehead, *Bewitched*
Marge Redmond, *The Flying Nun* (ABC)
Nita Talbot, *Hogan's Heroes*

1968 to 1969

Outstanding Comedy Series
Bewitched
Get Smart *
Family Affair
The Ghost and Mrs. Muir (NBC)
Julia (NBC)

Outstanding Continued Performance by an Actress in a Leading Role in a Comedy
Elizabeth Montgomery, *Bewitched*
Hope Lange, *The Ghost and Mrs. Muir* *
Diahann Carroll, *Julia*
Barbara Feldon, *Get Smart*

Outstanding Performance by an Actress in a Supporting Role in a Series
Agnes Moorehead, *Bewitched*
Barbara Anderson, *Ironside* (NBC)
Susan St. James, *The Name of the Game* *
    (NBC)

1969 to 1970

Outstanding Continued Performance by an Actress in a Leading Role in a Comedy
Elizabeth Montgomery, *Bewitched*
Hope Lange, *The Ghost and Mrs. Muir* *
Marlo Thomas, *That Girl*

Outstanding Performance by an Actress in a Supporting Role in a Comedy
Agnes Moorehead, *Bewitched*
Karen Valentine, *Room 222* (ABC) *
Lurene Tuttle, *Julia*

1970 to 1971

Outstanding Performance by an Actress in a Supporting Role in a Comedy
Agnes Moorehead, *Bewitched*
Valerie Harper, *The Mary Tyler Moore Show*
    (CBS) *
Karen Valentine, *Room 222*

Outstanding Achievement in Makeup (A Single Program of a Series or Special)
Rolf Miller, *Bewitched* *[*"Samantha's Old Man"*]*
Robert Dawn, *Mission: Impossible*
    ["Catafalque"*]* (CBS) *
Marie Roche, *Hamlet, Hallmark Hall Of Fame*
    (NBC)
Perc Westmore, Harry C. Blake, *The Bill Cosby Show* *[The Third Bill Cosby Show]* (CBS)

ALSO
The *Bewitched* episode, "Sisters at Heart," received the Governor's Award at the 1971 Emmy Award Ceremony.

General Credit Listing

Samantha/Serena, Elizabeth Montgomery (254 episodes as Samantha/24 as Serena)

Darrin (1964 to 1969), Dick York (116 episodes)

Darrin (1969 to 1972), Dick Sargent (84)

Endora, Agnes Moorehead (144)

Larry Tate, David White (166)

Gladys Kravitz (1964 to 1966), Alice Pearce (28)

Gladys Kravitz (1966 to 1972), Sandra Gould (29)

Abner Kravitz, George Tobias (53)

Louise Tate (1964 to 1966), Irene Vernon (13)

Louise Tate (1966 to 1972), Kasey Rogers (33)

Maurice, Maurice Evans (12)

Aunt Clara (1964 to 1968), Marion Lorne (28)

Uncle Arthur (1965 to 1972), Paul Lynde (10; 1 as Harold Harold)

Dr. Bombay (1967 to 1972), Bernard Fox (18; 1 as Osgood Rightmire)

Esmeralda (1969 to 1972), Alice Ghostley (15; 1 as Naomi)

Phyllis Stephens, Mabel Albertson (19 episodes)

Frank Stephens (alternate), Robert F. Simon (6 episodes)

Frank Stephens (alternate), Roy Roberts (7 episodes)

Tabitha (1966 to 1972), Erin Murphy/Diane Murphy (100 alternate episodes/scenes)

Adam, David Lawrence/Greg Lawrence, (17 alternate episodes/scenes)

Executive Producer/Creative Consultant (1964 to 1972), Harry Ackerman

Producer/Director/Creative Consultant (1964 to 1972), William Asher (directed 133 episodes)

Producer/Story Editor (1964 to 1965), Danny Arnold (wrote 3 episodes)

Producer/Director/Writer (alternate/1966 to 1967), Jerry Davis (directed 4 episodes/wrote 2)

Producer (1967 to 1968), William Froug

Pilot Creator, Sol Saks

Associate Producers (alternate), Jerry Brisken, Ernest Losso, and Richard Michaels (who also directed 54 episodes)

Directors (alternate), R. Robert Rosenbaum (22 episodes), Richard Kinon (8 episodes), and E. W. Swackhamer (8 episodes)

Assistant Directors (alternate), Marvin Miller, Maxwell Henry, Mark Sandrich, Hal Polaire, Gil Mandolik, Jerome Siegal, Jack Orbison, Michael Dmytryk, Jack R. Berne, and Anthony M. Ray

Story Editor/Writer (1964 to 1966), Bernard Slade (wrote 17 episodes)

Story Editor/Writer (alternate), Ruth Brooks Flippen (wrote 2 episodes)

Story Editor (alternate), Ed Jurist (wrote 52 episodes + 2 as cowriter = 54)

Writers (alternate), James Henerson (10 episodes + 2 as cowriter), Lila Garrett and Bernie Kahn (10), John L. Greene (8 episodes with Paul David, 5 with David V. Robison, and 5 solo), and Barbara Avedon (4 solo, 1 with William Asher)

Special Effects (alternate), Willis Cook (pilot), Richard Albain, Marlow Newkirk, Terry Saunders, and Hal Bigger

Wardrobe (1964 to 1972), Byron Munson (department head) and Vi Alford

Makeup, Ben Lane (department head)

Makeup (1969 to 1972), Rolf Miller

Hairstyles (alternate), Peanuts and Cosmo

Production Supervisor, Seymour Friedman

Music, Warren Barker, Van Alexander, Pete
Carpenter, and Jimmie Haskell

Title Song, Howard Greenfield and Jack Keller

Music Consultant, Don Kirshner

Music Supervisor, Ed Forsyth

Director of Photography, Robert Tobey, Robert
Wyckoff, Frederick Gately, and Lloyd Ahern

Postproduction Supervisor, Lawrence Werner

Art Direction, Ross Bellah, Robert Purcell,
Malcolm C. Bart, and Robert Peterson

Set Decoration, Sidney Clifford, Louis Diage,
Jack Ahern, Milton Stumph, and James M.
Crowe

Film Editors, Aaron Nibley, Jack Ruggiero,
High Chaloupka, Jack Peluso, Asa Clark,
Michael Luciano, and Gerald J. Wilson

Casting Directors, Burt Metcalfe, Ernest Losso,
Al Ornorato, Sally Powers

Opticals Photo, Effex

Sound Effects, Fred J. Brown, Sid Lubow,
Sunset Editorial

Music Effects, Sunset Editorial

Elizabeth Montgomery's Wardrobe, PFC Inc.,
York Town Juniors, Tony Lynn Maternities

Dick York's Wardrobe, Phoenix Clothes,
Michaels-Stern

Dick Sargent's Wardrobe, Botany 500,
Michaels-Stern

Tabitha's (infant) Wardrobe & Furnishings,
Babycrest

Props, George Ballarino

Camera Operator, Val O'Malley

Gaffer, Arthur D. Kaufman

Head Grip, Charles Gibbs

Assistant to the Producer/Production
Secretary, Bobbi Shane

Color by Pathe, Perfect Pathe, Berkey Path

Samantha's Scrolls

The First Season (1964 to 1965)

Scroll 1

I, Darrin, Take This Witch, Samantha
(9-17-64)

Scribe: Sol Saks

Overseer: William Asher

Sojourners: Nancy Kovak, Gene Blakely, Paul
Barselow, Lindsay Workman

Sam-Script: Samantha and Darrin get married
before he discovers her secret. Endora dis-
approves, and Sam begs her not to meddle.
Darrin learns the truth. He makes Sam
promise never to use her powers. His old
girlfriend, Sheila Sommers, invites the
Stephenses to a dinner party and makes
every effort to embarrass Samantha, who
eventually lets Sheila "have it."

Twitch-Bits: The first of four initial episodes
narrated by Jose Ferrer. Sam and Darrin are
living in a furnished rented house. Sam's
spell to get rid of Endora is used again to
make toys disappear in "Toys in Babeland"
and to summon Ophelia (Julie Newmar) in
"The Eight-Year Witch." This episode also
features the most ironic line in the series,
when Samantha says (regarding her witchcraft): "Maybe I can taper off?"

Scroll 2

Be It Ever So Mortgaged
(9-24-64)

Scribe: Barbara Avedon

Overseer: William Asher

Sojourners: (None)

Sam-Script: Endora is still dismayed: Samantha chooses to live the mortal way. Yet, Sam does resort to her witchery when faced with having to bake a cake. Her supernatural wiles also come in handy when she and Endora inspect the house Darrin plans to purchase. Much to the horror of Mrs. Kravitz, the two witches have a good time rearranging the new place.

Twitch-Bits: Endora recites the witches' *Sparkle in a Star* anthem for the first time, and gives the Witches' Honor Sign, right-handed. Also, she's seen reading *Harpee's Bizarre* magazine; and Sam and Darrin's address is introduced as 1164 Morning Glory Circle.

Scroll 3

It Shouldn't Happen to a Dog
(10-1-64)

Scribe: Jerry Davis

Overseer: William Asher

Sojourners: Jack Warden (*Crazy Like A Fox*), Grace Lee Whitney (*Star Trek*), Monroe Arnold, Karl Lukas

Sam-Script: Samantha holds a dinner party to impress Darrin's client Rex Barker, who flirts with her after he has a couple of drinks. Barker becomes too aggressive, Sam changes him into a dog and becomes angry

"Rex Barker" (Jack Warden) grabs Samantha after she returns him to human form from being a dog in "It Shouldn't Happen to a Dog."

with Darrin, who thinks only of losing the account. She eventually retransforms Barker, but the offensive client continues to make passes at her. This time, Darrin knocks him flat.

Twitch-Bits: First Larry and Louise/client show; remade as "A Chance On Love" and "Serena's Richcraft." Mr. Barker was named so by writer Jerry Davis because he would be transformed into a canine (which *barks*).

Scroll 4

Mother Meets What's His Name
(10-8-64)

Scribe: Danny Arnold

Overseer: William Asher

Sojourners: Hollis Irving, Alice Backes, John Copage

Sam-Script: Gladys tries to convince her neighbors of the weird goings-on over at Sam and Darrin's. Endora adds to the mayhem by roping up three neighborhood boys. Gladys struggles to convince the boys' mothers of how impossible it was for them to tie themselves up. Darrin becomes furious with Endora, who threatens to turn him into an artichoke.

Twitch-Bits: The first Darrin/Endora episode. Sam says Endora is 5 feet, 6 inches and 118 pounds.

Scroll 5

Help, Help, Don't Save Me
(10-15-64)

Scribe: Danny Arnold

Overseer: William Asher

Sojourner: Charles Ruggles

Sam-Script: Darrin grapples to produce a campaign for Caldwell Soup. Sam offers her suggestions. He suspects witchery, and presents his own ideas to Philip Caldwell, who rejects them. Darrin accuses Sam of influencing Caldwell's decision, they argue, and Endora's in her glory. After Sam and Darrin make up, he realizes Caldwell sincerely rejected his slogans, and she makes sure her husband still gets the account.

Twitch-Bits: Remade as #252, "A Good Turn Never Goes unpunished."

Scroll 6

Little Pitchers Have Big Fears

Elizabeth, Dick York, June Lockhart, Jimmy Mathers (center), and Joe Brooks from "Little Pitchers Have Big Fears."

(10-22-64)

Scribe: Barbara Avedon

Overseer: William Asher

Sojourners: June Lockhart (*Lost in Space*), Jimmy Mathers (brother of Jerry Mathers, *Leave It to Beaver*), Joe Brooks, Joel Davison, Greger Vigen

Sam-Script: Sam caters to ten-year-old Marshall Burns, whose overprotective widowed mother leaves her son with an inferiority complex. Samantha tries to restore his confidence by convincing him to play Little League baseball. At first, she makes Marshall a star player. She later allows him to succeed on his own merit, much to the delight of his mother, who then finds companionship with her son's coach.

Twitch-Bits: This episode was partially remade as "Soapbox Derby," and includes a scene with Gladys musing over the effect Samantha has had on Marshall: "But then *she* came along (and) he improved one hundred percent. Now what do you think of that, Abner?" Abner: "I think it's entirely possible the same thing would happen to me."

Scroll 7

The Witches Are Out
(10-29-64)

Scribe: Bernard Slade

Overseer: William Asher

Sojourners: Shelley Berman, Reta Shaw, Madge Blake (*Batman*), Jacques Roux

Sam-Script: Darrin is assigned to create a trademark for a new Halloween candy. Sam, Aunt Clara, and witch friends Bertha and Mary grasp the chance to change the popular conception of witches into a more flattering image. Darrin's client wants things to remain status quo, prompting Sam and her friends to haunt him into changing his mind.

Twitch-Bits: This first Halloween segment offers initial insight into Darrin's feelings as he ends up defending the witches' pride. If he really had anything against witches, he would have divorced Samantha long ago. There's a great line of defense from Samantha who says: "I suppose they just can't realize we're like everybody else . . . almost."

Scroll 8

The Girl Reporter
(11-5-64)

Scribes: Paul David, John L. Green

Overseer: William Asher

Sojourners: Cheryl Holdridge, Roger Ewing, Alex Gerry

Sam-Script: Teenager Liz Randell interviews Darrin about his advertising career for a school paper. After he takes her to McMann and Tate, her jealous boyfriend, a football star, sets out to physically attack Darrin. Samantha explains that her husband and Liz's relationship is innocent. Things take a turn for the worse, when Liz's beau develops a crush on Sam.

Twitch-Bits: Partially remade as "The Generation Zap."

Scroll 9

Witch or Wife
(11-12-64)

Scribe: Bernard Slade

Overseer: William Asher

Sojourners: Raquel Welch, Peter Camlin, Rowena Burack

Sam-Script: The Tates fly to Paris for a fashion show. Sam flies to Paris with Endora. They run into Louise and Larry, who phones Darrin. Sam pops home. Darrin declares their marriage a mistake. She returns to Paris. He follows and apologizes.

Twitch-Bits: The Tates meet Endora. Darrin and Sam's phone number is 555-7328 (different from "Nobody but a Frog Knows How

To Live" and "Samantha's Wedding Present"). Sam-to-Darrin's "Especially when you're doing such a good job of it yourself" makes a first appearance. And, Sam: "Darrin, have you been drinking?" Darrin: "Just enough for me to see things in their proper perspective. You can't snatch an eagle out of the sky, tie it to the ground, clip its wings, and expect it to walk around with a smile on its beak." Later, Darrin: "I should have known you can't take a beautiful witch in the prime of her life and expect her to hang up her twitch. It's against nature." (Much of this speech is repeated verbatim in "How Green Was My Grass.")

need for medical assistance; a fact later rebutted when Dr. Bombay was introduced. Maurice and Darrin discuss naming the first male Stephens child; not a concern of York's Darrin (Adam was born in the Dick Sargent years, though Sam became pregnant with Adam in the York era). More: Maurice was identified as *Victor* in an original draft of the script. In the filmed script, the good lines run rampant, as when Darrin tells Larry that he and Sam have a mixed marriage. "I'm English," he says. "She's Norwegian." And Endora, regarding Maurice's mom: "Oh, his mother was a real witch."

Scroll 10

Just One Happy Family
(11-19-64)

Scribes: Fred Freeman, Lawrence J. Cohen
Overseer: William Asher
Sojourners: Thomas Anthony, Charlie Dugdale
Sam-Script: Endora warns Samantha about a visit from Maurice, who will be upset upon learning of Darrin. Maurice arrives. The conversation proceeds nicely until Sam reveals the mortal truth. Maurice then dematerializes Darrin until Sam begs for his return.
Twitch-Bits: The first episode with Maurice. We learn Darrin and Larry sometimes take a commuter train to work, and that Maurice's family did not approve of Endora. Maurice obtains Darrin's birth certificate and makes a conclusion: If Darrin were a warlock, he would not have the

Scroll 11

It Takes One to Know One
(11-26-64)

Scribe: Jack Sher
Overseer: William Asher
Sojourners: Lisa Seagram, Robert Cleaves
Sam-Script: Darrin seeks a Miss Jasmine for a perfume account, while Endora sets out to create doubt in Samantha's mind regarding her husband's fidelity. Larry and Darrin agree that a beautiful model, Janine Fleur, is their "girl." Meanwhile, Sam learns Janine is a witch hired by Endora to cause trouble between her and Darrin.
Twitch-Bits: Remade as "The Eight-Year Witch."

Scroll 12

And Something Makes Three
(12-3-64)

Scribe: Danny Arnold

Overseer: William Asher

Sojourner: Maureen McCormick (*The Brady Bunch*)

Sam-Script: Larry visits his dentist in the same building where Louise (with Sam to keep her company) makes a call to the obstetrician. Larry assumes Sam is expecting and tells Darrin, who imagines his life as the father of supernatural children. That night, the Tates have dinner with Sam and Darrin, and the misunderstanding is cleared up: Louise is the one who's with child.

Twitch-Bits: At one point, Sam zaps up a backyard swimming pool for a quick dip on a hot day, then zaps the pool away. Gladys sees all this from across the street, but Sam and Darrin's backyard was off the rear of their house, and could not be seen from the street.

Scroll 13

Love Is Blind
(12-10-64)

Scribe: Roland Wolpert

Overseer: William Asher

Sojourners: Adam West (*Batman*), Kit Smythe, Chris Noel, Ralph Barnard

Sam-Script: Sam's average-looking friend, Gertrude, expresses envy for her happy marriage. Against the wishes of her husband, Samantha matchmakes Gertrude

Batman himself, Adam West, guested on *Bewitched* in "Love Is Blind," with Chris Noel (center right).

with Darrin's artist pal, Kermit. Suspecting Gertrude may have magical ties, Darrin arranges a date between his former love (Susan) and Kermit. In the end, Kermit ends up with Gertrude, who turns out to be only human after all.

Twitch-Bits: Samantha goes to church.

Scroll 14

Samantha Meets the Folks
(12-17-64)

Scribe: Bernard Slade

Overseer: William Asher

Sojourners: (None)

Sam-Script: Darrin's parents visit for the first time. Phyllis hopes to find Sam lacking in domestic skills. Aunt Clara makes a surprise stop, and the tension builds. Clara wants to help her niece look good, and conjures up an exotic feast for dinner. Phyllis is thrown for a loop. Darrin becomes angry. Clara leaves in a fury. To mend Sam's and Clara's broken hearts, Darrin invites the dysfunctional witch back for dinner.

Twitch-Bits: Recut as Scroll 56 with the same title. Clara and her friend Bertha put a spell on the New York Yankees (that's why they lost two World Series in a row: 1963-1964). Phyllis and Frank talk about her sister Madge who thought she was a lighthouse. Frank says: "You call standing on the garage roof when it rains to warn the ships at sea a *quirk*?" Clara has collected three thousand doorknobs (Marion Lorne collected them in real life).

Scroll 15

A Vision of Sugar Plums
(12-24-64)

Scribe: Herman Groves

Overseer: Alan Rafkin

Sojourners: Sara Seegar (*Dennis, The Menace*), Bill Daily (*I Dream of Jeannie*), Gerry Johnson, Cecil Kellaway, Billy Mumy (*Lost in Space*), Kevin Tate

Sam-Script: Seven-year-old orphan Tommy spends Christmas with Abner and Gladys. Six-year-old Michael, also orphaned, stays with Darrin and Sam. Tommy believes in Santa Claus. Michael doesn't. To inspirit Michael, Sam whisks him and Darrin to the North Pole to meet jolly old St. Nick.

Twitch-Bits: First Christmas show. Recut as Scroll 51 with same title. Michael and Darrin are the first mortals to meet Santa. Darrin meets him again in "Santa Comes To Visit and Stays and Stays," as does Mr. Mortimer in "Humbug Not To Be Spoken Here."

Scroll 16

It's Magic
(1-7-65)

Scribes: Tom Waldman, Frank Waldman

Overseer: Sidney Miller

Sojourners: Walter Burke, Cliff Norton, Virginia Martin, Alice Backes, Hollis Irving

Sam-Script: Samantha is named entertainment chairperson of the Hospital Fund Auxiliary and is allocated only a $50 budget. So she hires Zeno, a has-been magician who drinks. Zeno's luck, however, changes, via Sam, who makes with the magic to revive his career. He's a hit at the fund-raiser, which leads to an appearance on television, which prompts Darrin's client to hire Zeno as well.

Twitch-Bits: Samantha's integrity is confirmed in this episode; she's dealing with money, which she could easily pop up by the truckload. Instead, she chooses to attain it the mortal way, which endears her to the audience.

Scroll 17

A Is for Aardvark
(1-14-65)

Scribe: Earl Barrett

Overseer: Ida Lupino

Sojourners: (None)

Sam-Script: Darrin sprains his ankle and is confined to bed. Samantha gets tired of running up and down the stairs at his beck and call and grants him the gift of magic. He misuses his newfound powers and later realizes the special qualities of being mortal.

Twitch-Bits: Samantha cries real tears in this episode which Bill Asher considers definitive of the series. Yet, according to the big-screen *Bell, Book, and Candle* (1959), witches don't cry. And Darrin always wanted a whistling yo-yo when he was a kid.

Scroll 18

The Cat's Meow
(1-21-65)

Scribes: Richard and Mary Sale

Overseer: David McDearmon

Sojourners: Martha Hyer, Harry Holcombe, George Ives, Clarence Young

Sam-Script: Client Margaret Marshall insists Darrin fly to Chicago for her cosmetic company. Darrin complies, meets Margaret on her yacht and, in the process, sidesteps a six-month wedding anniversary with Sam. He assumes a cat on board may be his wife, prodded by Endora to investigate. Marshall tries to seduce Darrin, who brings the cat home, where he's greeted by Sam.

Twitch-Bits: The client's yacht is called *The True Love.*

Scroll 19

A Nice Little Dinner Party
(1-28-65)

Scribe: Bernard Slade

Overseer: Sherman Marks

Sojourners: Lindsay Workman, David Garner, Hap Holmwood

Sam-Script: Samantha arranges a dinner party for Darrin's parents to meet Endora, who promises not to cause problems. When Darrin's mortal mom and dad arrive, Endora flirts with Frank and is snidely courteous to Phyllis, who becomes upset and boards a train to Arizona. Frank, on the other hand, takes a plane and initiates a world tour. Employing their combined power, Sam and Endora reunite Mr. and Mrs. Stephens in Angel Falls, where he had proposed to her years before.

Twitch-Bits: Salem is revealed as Endora's birthplace in this segment, which features one of only two solo scenes with Endora and Phyllis ever filmed. There's a reference to the Vatican here, and a good line from Darrin, regarding Endora: "Sure! I've seen some of her charms . . . Bang! You're a frog."

Scroll 20

Your Witch Is Showing
(2-4-65)

Scribe: Joanna Lee

Overseer: Joseph Pevney

Sojourners: Jonathan Daly (*Medical Center*), Peggy Lipton (*The Mod Squad*), Alex Gerry

Sam-Script: Endora's upset: Her son-in-law forbids Samantha's journey to Egypt for a cousin's wedding. Instantly, Darrin starts having trouble at work. Larry then enlists an assistant named Gideon, whom Darrin suspects to be a sorcerer hired by Endora to steal his job. Samantha intervenes, and Darrin grasps the truth: The new guy is a mere mortal and proves it by punching him out.

Twitch-Bits: Sam confirms that witches don't bleed (but this was cut from the aired version) and, ironically, refers to a warlock as a witch only to be corrected by Darrin. And: Early on, Larry wonders about the situation and asks if it has anything to do with "Black magic, maybe?" To which Darrin replies: "Would you believe me if I said *yes*?"

Scroll 21

Ling Ling

Samantha and a very sly cat in "Ling Ling."

(2-11-65)

Scribe: Jerry Davis
Overseer: David McDearmon
Sojourners: Jeremy Slate, Greta Chi
Sam-Script: Darrin hopes to find a model for the Jewel of the East campaign so that it may boost the confidence of Wally Ames, a temporary photographer with McMann and Tate. On cue, Sam changes a cat into a beautiful Asian woman named Ling Ling, whom everyone agrees is the perfect Jewel model. Sam and Darrin hold a dinner party to celebrate, Ling Ling and Wally begin to date, and the twitch-witch is forced to tell her mortal husband nothing but the truth.

Twitch-Bits: Cats are known as *familiars* to witches.

Scroll 22

Eye of the Beholder
(2-25-65)

Scribe: Herman Groves
Overseer: William Asher
Sojourners: Gene Blakely, Peter Brocco, Mark Tapscott, Paul Barselow, Lindsay Workman, Carter DeHaven, Georgia Schmidt, Stephen Whittaker, Cindy Eilbacher, Sharon DeBord.
Sam-Script: Endora superimposes Sam's face on an ancient print entitled *Maid of Salem.* Darrin is compelled to purchase it, and later envisions himself as an aged man paired with an ever-youthful witch-wife. Endora reveals that Sam may age with Darrin, who learns Endora is to blame for his doubts.
Twitch-Bits: Sam calls Larry by his first name for the first time. Darrin drives to Westbridge Avenue Park in a 1965 Chevy, license 4R 6558. Sam's unique incantation to call Endora (instead of saying *Mother!*): *"Quadramus—invecta—expedia."*

Scroll 23

Red Light, Green Light
(3-4-65)

Elizabeth and Dick York pose for "Red Light, Green Light."

Scribe: Roland Wolpert

Overseer: David McDearmon

Sojourners: Gene Blakely, Dan Tobin, Vic Tayback (*Alice*), Robert Dorman

Sam-Script: Sam and Darrin become politically involved with constructing a traffic light on their street. Darrin creates an ad for a rally, but the mayor says the light is trivial. After Samantha magically ties up the mayor in traffic, he changes his mind.

Twitch-Bits: The Morning Glory News is mentioned. Abner says there's a missile plant near Morning Glory Circle. Original draft says Sam is attending the meeting at Dave's (then *Joe Harvey*), and Endora cooks for Darrin.

Endora: "I've prepared your dinner, Derwin."

Darrin: "I didn't know you could cook."

Endora: "Oh, yes. Claudius was crazy about my cooking."

Darrin: "Claudius?"

Endora: "The Roman Emperor."

Darrin: "Didn't he die of food poisoning?"

Endora: "Yes—terrible tragedy."

Scroll 24

Which Witch Is Which?
(3-11-65)

Scribe: Earl Barrett

Overseer: William D. Russell

Sojourners: Ron Randell, Monty Margetts, Donald Foster

Sam-Script: Samantha doesn't have time for a dress fitting, so Endora helps out by turning herself into Sam's double. While being fitted, Endora-Samantha captures the heart of author Bob Fraser, who also happens to be Darrin's buddy. Gladys sees the twosome and thinks Sam is having an affair. Meanwhile, Darrin tells his wife to expect a visit from Bob. Endora ends up saving the evening by claiming to be her daughter's exact double.

Twitch-Bits: Gladys calls Samantha by her first name for the first time.

Scroll 25

Pleasure O'Reilly
(3-18-65)

Scribe: Ken Englund

Overseer: William D. Russell

Sojourners: Kipp Hamilton, Norman Burton, William Woodson, Ken Scott

Sam-Script: New neighbor and beautiful model Pleasure O'Reilly is hiding from her jealous boyfriend, an offensive fullback. Darrin helps to shroud Pleasure, while her beau visits Sam, who inadvertently presents the impression that Darrin and Pleasure have a thing going on.

Twitch-Bits: Pleasure's address is 1123 Morning Glory Circle in the house later purchased by Elaine Hanson ("Weep No More My Willow") and Mr. Ferguson ("Return of Darrin, the Bold"). Her kid sister, Dora (also known as Danger; played by Beverly Adams), is house-sitting in "George the Warlock," while Pleasure's on her honeymoon. The headline in *The Star—Dispatch* is *Passion's Plaything.*

Scroll 26

Driving Is the Only Way to Fly
(3-2z5-65)

Scribe: Richard Baer

Overseer: William Asher

Sojourners: Paul Lynde (as Harold Harold), Paul Bryar

Sam-Script: Samantha enrolls in driving school and is guided by an anxiety-ridden driving instructor named Harold Harold. During her test drive, Sam uses magic to avoid accidents, which makes Harold extremely uneasy. Endora makes matters worse by speaking from the backseat while invisible. Harold is fired, and Samantha threatens to switch schools unless he's hired back.

Twitch-Bits: Harold speaks these words extremely fast:

"Carefultheresamovingvanupahead."

Scroll 27

There's No Witch Like an Old Witch
(4-1-65)

Scribe: Ted Sherdeman, Jane Klove

Overseer: William Asher

Sojourners: Gilbert Green, Reta Shaw, Karen Norris, Peg Shirley, Brian Nash, Michael Blake, Vicki Malkin, Nina Roman, Penny Kunard

Sam-Script: Aunt Clara is suffering from a power failure. Samantha and Darrin try to cheer her up by taking her out with the Caldwells, whose baby-sitter fails to appear. Aunt Clara tries to remedy the situation by offering her services as baby-sitter.

Twitch-Bits: We learn that Clara's last name is *Brown.* Remade as "Samantha's Magic Sitter."

Scroll 28

Open the Door Witchcraft
(4-8-65)

Scribe: Ruth Brooks Flippen

Overseer: William Asher

Sojourners: Hal Bokar, Baynes Barron, Eddie Hanley

Sam-Script: Sam is fascinated by electric garage-door openers and creates one of her own. Unhappy about his wife's resorting to magic, Darrin sacrifices new fishing gear to purchase a remote. After radio signals from various aircraft conflict with the doors, Sam and Darrin argue over the use of sorcery. Sam stands firm by her now-reinforced vow not to employ her special abilities as she and Darrin are locked in the garage when a plane flies over.

Twitch-Bits: Sam implies that she will live longer than Darrin. But in "Eye Of the Beholder," she tells him that she will zap herself into aging the mortal way. Sam says: "It's impossible to sniffle and twitch at the same time." A unique conversation takes place between the Kravtizes. Gladys: "I hope you notice. I'm not saying one word about her being strange." Abner: "I hope you're not 'cause she isn't. *He* is."

Scroll 29

Abner Kadabra
(4-15-65)

Scribes: Lawrence J. Cohen, Fred Freeman
Overseer: William Asher
Sojourners: (None)
Sam-Script: Gladys sees moving pictures. Sam convinces her that she has ESP. Sam cautions Gladys, who attempts supernatural feats such as preventing the rain from falling and telling Abner to dry up. On that last command, Sam changes Mr. Kravitz into a pile of dust, which forces Gladys to retire her newfound "abilities."

Twitch-Bits: Abner is retired. From what, we don't know. Sam says her first *Well!* Darrin and Sam call Kravitz, *Abner.* Some good lines:

Gladys: "She said I was a witch?"

Sam: "Isn't that ridiculous?"

Abner: "I don't know? Did you ever see her in the morning?"

Later, Gladys asks Sam, "You're from Venus, aren't you?"

Scroll 30

George, the Warlock
(4-22-65)

Scribe: Ken Englund
Overseer: William Asher
Sojourners: Christopher George (*The Immortal*), Beverly Adams, Lauren Gilbert, Sharon DeBord
Sam-Script: Darrin offers to help D. D. "Danger" O'Reilly, the beautiful younger sister of Pleasure, who's on vacation for a few weeks. Endora seizes another opportunity to break up her daughter's marriage by persuading a Casanova-type warlock named George to romance Samantha.

Twitch-Bits: George turns himself into a raven, and whistles the *Bewitched* theme. In another moment, he turns Darrin into a penguin.

Scroll 31

That Was My Wife
(4-29-65)

Scribe: Bernard Slade
Overseer: William Asher
Sojourner: Warren Ott
Sam-Script: Sam and Darrin decide to take a short vacation and reserve a room at the President's Hotel. Unaware that Larry's in the lobby, Samantha, on a whim, arrives wearing a black wig. She meets to embrace

Darrin. Larry thinks his employee is having an affair, and when Sam goes home to get a book, the usually nonconsoling Mr. Tate comes to comfort her.

Twitch-Bits: Larry is seen reading *Gals Gals* magazine in the bedroom, and refers to Darrin as a *son-of-a-gun* a record seven times. But at one point he just says *son-of-a-gun.*

Scroll 32

Illegal Separation
(5-6-65)

Scribe: Richard Baer

Overseer: William Asher

Sojourner: Dick Balduzzi

Sam-Script: Gladys and Abner have a fight. He stays with Sam and an extremely frustrated Darrin, who encourages his wife to talk Gladys out of a divorce. To reunite her mortal neighbors, Samantha employs a dream conjuration, which projects Abner and Gladys to the day he proposed.

Twitch-Bits: Remade as "Splitsville."

Scroll 33

A Change of Face
(5-13-65)

Scribe: Bernard Slade

Overseer: William Asher

Sojourners: Gene Blakely, Marilyn Hanold, Elisa Ingram, Dick Wilson, Paul Barselow, Henry Hunter

Sam-Script: Darrin's asleep. Endora rearranges his face. At first, Samantha objects but later adds cosmetic changes of her own. Darrin awakes and demands an explanation, of which his wife has none. His confidence suffers, and he grows increasingly concerned about his looks. To boost his ego, Sam transforms herself into a beautiful French woman, who admires Darrin as is.

Twitch-Bits: First Dick Wilson episode.

Scroll 34

Remember the Main
(5-20-65)

Scribe: Mort R. Lewis

Overseer: William D. Russell

Sojourners: Edward Mallory, Byron Morrow, Stuart Nesbit, Justin Smith

Sam-Script: Samantha and Darrin get involved with Ed Wright's campaign for city council. At Darrin's suggestion, Ed faces on television his challenger, John C. Cavenaugh, and they debate illegal fund allocations for a new drainage system. A water main bursts, and Wright looks like the easy winner until Darrin suspects Samantha caused the flood. She didn't, but her mother did.

Twitch-Bits: The local newspaper is *The Gazette.* The debate is on WXIU-TV. When asked about her last name, Endora answers *Waters*, which fits. We also learn that she was at the Lincoln/Douglas debate.

Scroll 35

Eat at Mario's
(5-27-65)

Scribe: Richard Baer

Overseer: William Asher

Sojourners: Vito Scotti, Alan Hewitt, Phil Arnold, Michael Quinn

Sam-Script: Mario's Restaurant is going out of business; he won't sell pizza. Endora and Samantha aren't happy about it. It's their favorite Italian eatery. Samantha conjures up a full page ad for Mario; Endora plugs him on a TV show, which happens to be sponsored by Mr. Baldwin (a client who owns a successful pizza chain). The Baldwin account is in danger, and Sam enlists Endora's help.

Twitch-Bits: Darrin's secretary is named *Alice*.

Scroll 36

Cousin Edgar
(6-3-65)

Scribe: Paul Wayne

Overseer: E. W. Swackhamer

Sojourners: Arte Johnson (*Laugh-In*), Charles Irving, Roy Stuart

Sam-Script: McMann and Tate is struggling to keep the Shelley Shoes account, while Endora summons Sam's cousin Edgar, an elf, in another attempt to foil her daughter's mortal liaison. Edgar makes trouble for Darrin at the office. Sam convinces her cousin that's she's happily attached, which prods Edgar to aggravate Darrin's competitors. Darrin eventually succeeds with the Shelley campaign, which features an elf very similar to Edgar.

Twitch-Bits: There are shades of Alice Ghostley's Esmeralda, as Edgar's body parts fade in and out. Endora says: "Oh, that Darrin" and "I wouldn't go to Darrin's office for any reason." She also says: "A witch who's on the wagon is no match for an elf who's on the warpath."

The Second Season (1965 to 1966)

Scroll 37

Alias Darrin Stephens
(9-16-65)

Sam tells Darrin that he's to be a father in "Alias Darrin Stephens."

Scribe: Richard Baer

Overseer: William Asher

Sojourners: (None)

Sam-Script: With gifts in tow, Aunt Clara celebrates Sam and Darrin's first anniversary. Unfortunately, Clara accidentally transforms

Sam-Script: Ignoring Endora's request that Sam accompany her to a Halloween party, Darrin demands that she remain home for a business dinner. Seething with revenge, Endora impersonates a child in a gypsy costume and turns Darrin into a werewolf. Darrin fears for what might transpire and persuades Sam to lock him away in a closet. Sam confronts her mother, and accuses her of personifying the stereotypical witch she claims to disdain. Endora apologizes to Sam and Darrin, whom she returns to original form.

Twitch-Bits: Endora is surprised that Samantha is throwing a Halloween party in this second Halloween episode. Yet, later in "Twitch or Treat," Endora throws one every year. Endora, as the young girl, says that there are more than seven thousand magic word combinations.

Scroll 44

The Very Informal Dress
(11-4-65)

Scribes: Paul David, John L. Greene

Overseer: William Asher

Sojourners: Max Showaltzer, Dick Wilson, Hardie Albright, Dick Balduzzi, Gene Darfler

Sam-Script: Larry invites Darrin and Sam to a dinner for a prospective client, but they don't have a thing to wear. To remedy the situation, Aunt Clara conjures up a new set of clothes for the couple. Darrin then graciously invites Clara to come along for the evening. He later regrets the decision when Clara removes a fire hydrant when he goes to park the car. The hydrant reappears, and Darrin gets a parking ticket. Things don't get any better when Sam and Darrin's Clara-induced clothing begins to vanish.

Twitch-Bits: One of the more risqué episodes.

Scroll 45

And Then I Wrote
(11-11-65)

Scribe: Paul Wayne

Overseer: E. W. Swackhamer

Sojourners: Chet Stratton, Tom Nardini, Eileen O'Neil, Clan Soule, Joanie Larson, Bill Dungan, Skeets Minton

Sam-Script: A rest-home psychiatrist tells Sam that his patients would like to celebrate the centenary of the Civil War's conclusion with a theatrical performance. Sam tells the doctor that the function could be publicized by Darrin, who assigns his wife to write the script. Later, Darrin tells Sam that she has created wooden characters, and on Endora's advice, Sam literally brings them to life.

Twitch-Bits: Now Darrin calls Mrs. Kravitz *Gladys.*

Scroll 46

Junior Executive
(11-18-65)

Scribe: Bernard Slade

Overseer: Howard Morris

Sojourners: Billy Mumy, Oliver McGowan, Helene Winston, John Reilly, Rory Stevens, Sharon DeBord

Sam-Script: While Darrin is contemplating a model ship for the Harding Toys account, Samantha wonders whether their child will look like Darrin. To help answer her question, Endora turns her son-in-law into an eight-year-old boy. Mr. Harding sees the young Darrin at McMann and Tate and urges Larry to hire the child to create a slogan for his company. Darrin completes the slogan for the Harding account while acting out his childhood in the park.

Twitch-Bits: Remade as "Out of the Mouths of Babes."

Scroll 47

Aunt Clara's Old Flame
(11-25-65)

Scribe: Bernard Slade

Overseer: E. W. Swackhamer

Sojourners: Charles Ruggles

Sam-Script: Hiding from her warlock boyfriend, Hedley Partridge, Aunt Clara pays a visit, fearing Hedley will discover her magic is out of sorts. Endora feels Hedley is the perfect mate for Clara and invites him to meet her at Sam and Darrin's. On the sly, Sam assists Clara with her powers in order to match Hedley trick for trick. Clara's fears are allayed when Hedley admits his magic isn't up to snuff either.

Twitch-Bits: Endora, Clara, and Bertha recently went to a Witches' Convention in London, where Clara lifted a doorknob from Buckingham Palace. And, dialogue early in this show indicates that Clara and Endora are not blood relatives. Also, Hadley and Clara were once known as *The Golden Couple.* More: Remade as "Samantha's Magic Mirror."

Scroll 48

A Strange Little Visitor
(12-2-65)

Scribes: Paul David, John L. Greene

Overseer: E. W. Swackhamer

Sojourners: Craig Hundley, Tim Herbert, James Doohan (*Star Trek*), Ann Sargent, Dick Balduzzi

Sam-Script: While Sam's friends in sorcery attend a convention, she baby-sits for their ten-year-old warlock son, Merel, who promises to keep his powers in check around Darrin. His commitment is tested when a burglar breaks in and overpowers Darrin. Merel abides by his promise only to finally give in and help capture the crook.

Twitch-Bits: Merel is the only young witch/warlock introduced in the series other than Tabitha and Adam.

Scroll 49

My Boss the Teddy Bear
(12-9-65)

Scribe: Bernard Slade

Overseer: William Asher

Sojourners: Jack Collins, Jill Foster, Henry Hunter, Lon Bentley, Lael Jackson

Sam-Script: Larry allows Darrin time to take Sam to a witch wedding. Much obliged,

Endora brings Larry a much-sought-after teddy bear for his son. Darrin, who's working on the Harper's Honey account, is sure Endora has changed Larry into the bear. More confusion abounds as Louise, too, purchases a teddy, and one must be returned to the store. Thinking Larry might be the one she brought back, Darrin buys all the bears at the store, brings them home, and tries to find out which teddy is Larry.

Twitch-Bits: The first time Endora ever did a favor for Larry.

Scroll 50

Speak the Truth
(12-16-65)

Charles Lane

Scribes: Paul David, John L. Greene

Overseer: William Asher

Sojourners: Charles Lane, Elizabeth Fraser, Diana Chesney, Mort Mills, Sharon DeBord

Sam-Script: Endora delivers to Darrin's office a statue that makes people tell the truth. Bad experiences result from too much honesty, yet Darrin establishes a good rapport with a new client. Larry gives his "creative genius" a raise; a consequence of the truth spell. This surprises Endora, who thought only chaos would result from her truth-telling hex.

Twitch-Bits: This episode was remade as "The Truth, Nothing but the Truth, So Help Me Sam," and is also the first segment to feature Charles Lane.

Scroll 51

A Vision of Sugar Plums
(12-23-65)

(A recut version of Scroll 15 with a new opening.)

Scroll 52

The Magic Cabin
(12-30-65)

Scribe: Paul Wayne

Overseer: William Asher

Sojourners: Peter Duryea, Beryl Hammond, Sharon DeBord.

Sam-Script: Larry convinces a fatigued Darrin and Sam to stay at his log cabin, which he hasn't seen in years, and which he's also put up for sale. Upon arrival,

Darrin forbids Sam to use magic to clean up the cabin, which is a shambles. He quickly changes his mind when a storm breaks out. Larry apprehensively sends prospective buyers to inspect the cabin, and he's shocked—Sam's magic cleaning has encouraged a purchase.

Twitch-Bits: Larry's asking price for the cabin is $5,000, but it sells for $1,000.

Scroll 53

Maid to Order
(1-6-66)

Scribe: Richard Baer

Overseer: William Asher

Sojourners: Alice Ghostley (as Naomi), Elvia Allman, Roxanne Arlen

Sam-Script: Bumbling maid Naomi is looking for work: She has to send her son through medical school. She's temporaily hired by Sam and Darrin until the baby is born. When Larry and Louise come to dinner, Sam tries to make a good impression by helping Naomi with her duties. Louise hires Naomi, but without Sam's help she's an incompetent housekeeper. Yet, she displays a mathematical ability: She can calculate the number of dishes she breaks. Sam persuades Darrin to give Naomi a job in the accounting department at McMann and Tate.

Twitch-Bits: When Louise calls Samantha on the telephone, an old *I Love Lucy* laugh track is used and an *uh-oh* from Deedee Ball (Lucy's mom) is plainly audible. Deedee's phrase is also employed in "Follow That Witch," Part 1.

Scroll 54

And Then There Were Three
(1-13-66)

Scribe: Bernard Slade

Overseer: William Asher

Sojourners: Eve Arden (*Our Miss Brooks*), Gene Blakely, Joseph Mell, Bobby Byles, Mason Curry, Celeste Yarnall

Sam-Script: Samantha gives birth to a daughter, whom Endora names *Tabitha*. Darrin doubts the baby will grow up to look like Sam. Endora proposes to transform the infant into adulthood, so he can see differently. Meanwhile, Serena visits Sam in the hospital, and on viewing his witch-cousin for the first time, Darrin thinks Endora's magical threat has been put into action.

Twitch-Bits: Tabitha (spelled with an "A" until Scroll 143) is born; Sam's obstetrician is Dr. Anton played by Mason Curry; William Schallert plays him in "Samantha's Curious Cravings." Also, Serena makes her first appearance here and doesn't appear again until "Double, Double, Toil and Trouble," more than nineteen months later.

Scroll 55

My Baby the Tycoon
(1-20-66)

Scribe: Richard Baer

Overseer: William Asher

Sojourners: Jack Fletcher, William Kendis

Sam-Script: Gladys and Abner give Tabitha a share of their stock, which appreciates exponentially. Tabitha's random pointing at the newspaper stocks causes Darrin to think her witchcraft has developed early and is in full gear. The Kravitzes lose their life savings, and the stock returns to normal. Darrin realizes there was a logical explanation for the stock's behavior.

Twitch-Bits: Abner and Gladys lived in the *Stone* house from *The Donna Reed Show* at this point in the series.

Scroll 56

Samantha Meets the Folks
(1-27-66)

(A recut version of Scroll 14.)

Scroll 57

Fastest Gun on Madison Avenue
(2-3-66)

Scribe: Lee Erwin
Overseer: William Asher
Sojourners: Herbie Faye, Roger Torrey, Rockne Tarkington, Herb Vigran, Dick Wilson
Sam-Script: While dining out, Darrin tries to protect Samantha from heavyweight champion Joe Kovak, who's making passes at her. Darrin tries to defend himself, Sam twitches, and Kovak is knocked out. The newspapers proclaim Darrin as the future champ. He ends up slamming Joe a second time (again with Sam's assistance), and runs into Tommy Carter, another champion, who accidentally clobbers himself cold, indirectly due to Sam's intervention.
Twitch-Bits: Sam orders sixty cans of wax beans from the grocery store (they were on sale), which she does again in "Samantha's Psychic Pslip."

Scroll 58

The Dancing Bear
(2-10-66)

Scribe: James Henerson
Overseer: William Asher
Sojourner: Arthur Jullian
Sam-Script: Darrin's parents come to visit Tabitha and, as usual, Endora and Phyllis don't get along. Adding fuel to the fire, Phyllis brings a toy bear identical to Endora's, except that Endora's bear dances, via wizardry. Frank mistakenly assumes there's money to be made.
Twitch-Bits: Frank's get-rich-quick vending machine idea is discussed again in "Tabitha's Weekend."

Scroll 59

Double Tate
(2-17-66)

Scribe: Paul Wayne
Overseer: William Asher
Sojourners: Irwin Charone, Jill Foster, Kathee Francis
Sam-Script: Endora has granted Darrin three wishes for his birthday, but he doesn't know it. He suddenly receives instant elevator service at McMann and Tate and sees a beautiful girl in a bikini. A prominent client then demands to see Larry, who's in Chicago. Darrin unknowingly wishes he was the boss for "just one day," a desire that leads to trouble between him, Samantha, and the Tates.
Twitch-Bits: We learn that Darrin is the only one who likes Louise's coffee.

Scroll 60

Samantha the Dressmaker
(2-24-66)

Scribe: Lee Erwin

Overseer: William Asher

Sojourners: Dick Gautier (*Get Smart*), Barbara Morrison, Harry Holcombe, Arlen Stuart, Janine Grandel

Sam-Script: Sam fails to make her own dress for client J. T. Glendon's party. Endora flies her to the Paris showroom of Aubert, a designer who has not succeeded in the American market. Back home, Sam magically reproduces an Aubert original and suddenly finds herself a dressmaker for Mrs. Glendon, Mrs. Kravitz, and others. Sam is unaware that Aubert is a client of McMann and Tate's and the artisan threatens to sue the company when he sees the women wearing his creations.

Twitch-Bits: While Samantha works on her dress, Phyllis takes care of Tabitha, which doesn't add up since the senior Mrs. Stephens apparently lives out of state here.

Scroll 61

The Horse's Mouth
(3-3-66)

Scribes: Paul David, John L. Greene

Overseer: William Asher

Sojourners: Patty Regan (not the president's daughter), Robert Sorrells, Sidney Clute

Sam-Script: Samantha transforms an escaped racehorse into a woman named Dolly, who claims she's been coerced into throwing races so her sister horse may be the victor. Dolly tips Darrin's inventor pal, Gus, on how to win races and make money on marketing a new idea. Sam turns Dolly back into a horse. The Stephenses persuade Gus to bet on her; Dolly's a winner, and Gus makes out ahead.

Twitch-Bits: Samantha also transforms a horse into a human in "Three Men and a Witch on a Horse."

Scroll 62

Baby's First Paragraph
(3-10-66)

Scribe: James Henerson

Overseer: William Asher

Sojourners: Clete Roberts, John Newton, Don Hammer, Robert DeCoy

Sam-Script: Sam and Darrin meet an important client. Endora baby-sits with Tabitha and promises to behave. Gladys visits with her nephew Edgar, boasts about his intelligence, and Endora supernaturally induces Tabitha to speak. Tabitha becomes a world sensation. Things then settle down once Endora admits to being a ventriloquist.

Twitch-Bits: The headline in *The Daily Chronicle* is *Infant Talks Sense*; another front-page story: *Face-Lifting Job to Start on City Hall.*

—

Scroll 63

The Leprechaun
(3-17-66)

Parley Baer

Scribes: Paul David, John L. Greene
Overseer: William Asher
Sojourners: Henry Jones (*Phyllis*), Parley Baer, Jess Kirkpatrick
Sam-Script: Sam tells Darrin that visiting leprechaun Brian O'Brian is not one of her relatives but one of his. Brian wishes to reclaim his pot of gold, which is hidden in a fireplace in the States. The gold was delivered here by James Dennis Robinson, whose company would be a very desirable account for McMann and Tate. After a failed solo attempt, Brian is assisted by Sam in recovering his golden treasure, and his powers are restored.

Twitch-Bits: This St. Patrick's Day episode was also the first to feature Parley Baer.

Scroll 64

Double Split
(3-24-66)

Scribe: Howard Leeds
Overseer: Jerry Davis
Sojourners: Julie Gregg, Martin Ashe, Ivan Bonar
Sam-Script: At Darrin's request, Sam tries to be nice to a snobbish daughter of Mr. Ames, a major client. Frustrated by the girl's demeanor, Samantha twitches a canapé in her face, which angers Darrin. Larry criticizes Sam's behavior, Darrin quits McMann and Tate, and Sam and Louise are left to restore their husbands' friendship.
Twitch-Bits: Dick York breaks up during scene in which he sprays Dan Tobin as Mr. Ames with a fire extinguisher.

Scroll 65

Disappearing Samantha
(4-7-66)

Scribes: Paul David, John L. Greene
Overseer: William Asher
Sojourners: Bernard Fox (as Osgood Rightmire), Nina Wayne, Foster Brooks (*The Dean Martin Show*)
Sam-Script: Darrin publicizes Osgood Rightmire, who makes a name for himself by exposing fraudulent witches. The Stephenses and the Tates attend a lecture

John Fiedler made six *Bewitched* episodes.

Years before he played on *The Wonder Years,* David Huddleston quested on *Bewitched.*

Reta Shaw played "Aunt Hagatha" in several Samantha segments.

Ruth McDevitt made several appearances on *Bewitched,* including "Mrs. Parsons," the cat lover in "Mrs. Stephens, Where Are You?"

Marty Ingels was "Dangerous Diaper Dan" in the episode of the same name.

given by Rightmire, who melodramatically presents himself as a witches' scapegoat, an act of which angers Sam. Rightmire recites an incantation causing her to disappear and reappear against her will. When Osgood is at the Stephenses', Endora and Sam make a discovery—his powers exude from an ancient ring he wears, one which Sam destroys and replicates.

Twitch-Bits: One of the more mystic episodes.

Scroll 66

Follow That Witch, Part 1
(4-14-66)

Scribe: Bernard Slade

Overseer: William Asher

Sojourners: Steve Franken, Robert Strauss, Virginia Martin, Jack Collins, Judy Pace

Sam-Script: Darrin is closing a deal with Robbins Baby Food. Mr. Robbins and his assistant, George Barkley, agree that their company must maintain a wholesome image. Darrin's home life comes under inspection, and Sam's secret is discovered.

Twitch-Bits: Mary Grace Canfield's first of three episodes as Miss Kravitz, Abner's sister.

Scroll 67

Follow That Witch, Part 2
(4-21-66)

Scribe: Bernard Slade

Overseer: William Asher

Sojourners: Steve Franken, Robert Strauss, Virginia Martin, Jack Collins, Jill Foster, Renie Riano, Judy Pace

Sam-Script: Private detective Charlie Leach threatens to reveal Sam's true identity unless she makes him rich. Darrin's account is at stake, and she conjures up a new car and a newly remodeled apartment for Leach. Sam later forces Barkley to admit he wants his boss's job. Robbins fires Barkley and hires Darrin, who gives Sam permission to strike back at Leach.

Twitch-Bits: Charlie Leach comes back in "The Catnapper."

Scroll 68

Divided He Falls
(5-5-66)

Scribe: Paul Wayne

Overseer: R. Robert Rosenbaum

Sojourners: Frank Maxwell, Joy Harmon, Jerry Catron, Susan Barrett

Sam-Script: Larry begs Darrin to work on the Stern Chemical Company account, and Sam and Darrin's much-delayed vacation is postponed. Thinking she has the perfect solution, Endora splits Darrin in two: 1, a hard worker and 2, a fun-loving guy. After Endora persuades Samantha to vacation with the second Darrin, she reluctantly reunites the two Darrins.

Twitch-Bits: Remade as "Samantha's Better Halves." Also, this episode eerily foreshadows the show's double Darrin actor scenario.

Scroll 69

A Bum Raps
(4-28-66)

Scribe: Herman Groves

Overseer: Jerry Davis

Sojourners: Cliff Hall, Herbie Faye, Henry Hunter, Ann Prentice

Sam-Script: Darrin's Uncle Albert is about to arrive as two ex-vaudeville performers who are also con artists prowl the neighborhood. One impersonates Uncle Albert and robs the Stephenses' home. Sam realizes what's happened and makes the crooks return with the stolen goods.

Twitch-Bits: Frank and Phyllis baby-sit Tabitha.

Scroll 70

Man's Best Friend
(5-12-66)

Scribe: Bernard Slade

Overseer: Jerry Davis

Sojourners: Richard Dreyfuss, Barbara Morrison

Sam-Script: Darrin's about to celebrate Sam's thirty-day non-use of witchcraft, but a pesky warlock named Rodney begins to cause problems: He wants Sam to run away with him. She refuses, and Rodney turns himself into a shaggy dog to whom Darrin takes a liking. Sam convinces her husband that the canine is Rodney in disguise. Rodney returns to his real form, and Darrin belts him one.

Twitch-Bits: Sam hasn't done the witch deed in the past twenty-nine days, and Endora's been skin diving for a month. Darrin sure hits a lot of people in the first two seasons of the show.

Scroll 71

The Catnapper
(5-19-66)

Scribe: Howard Leeds

Overseer: R. Robert Rosenbaum

Sojourners: Robert Strauss, Virginia Martin, Marion Thompson

Sam-Script: Detective Charlie Leach pays another visit, and this time he discovers the truth about Samantha—and Endora. Meanwhile, Sam and her mother see Darrin with Toni Devlin, an attractive client.

Endora is prompted to change Toni into a cat, which Charlie steals for evidence. He arrives home, and Sam transmutes him into a mouse which, alongside a feline, is not such a great thing. After lessons are learned, Sam and Endora undo their respective hexes.

Twitch-Bits: Sam flies around the world in her flying suit looking for Endora (she finds her in Tibet) in a scene reminiscent of George Reeves in the classic *Superman* TV series.

Scroll 72

What Every Young Man Should Know
(5-26-66)

Scribes: Paul David, John L. Greene
Overseer: Jerry Davis
Sojourners: (None)
Sam-Script: With Samantha's permission, Endora sends the Stephenses to the past to see if Darrin would have married her daughter had he known she was a witch. A first look shows Darrin running when he discovers the truth. He wants another chance, and has Endora continue the test. He thinks she's the one creating problems with his marriage. A second look shows Darrin insisting that Sam give up witchcraft when they get married. The third look, however, offers some real proof of love. No matter what Endora does to him, Darrin still convinces Sam that he loves her despite her supernatural heritage.
Twitch-Bits: The word *bewitched* appears in this script.

Scroll 73

The Girl With the Golden Nose
(6-2-66)

Scribes: Syd Zelinka, Paul Wayne
Overseer: R. Robert Rosenbaum
Sojourners: Oliver McGowan, Gene Blakely, Alice Backes, Owen McGiveney
Sam-Script: Larry has refused Darrin an assignment with a substantial account, and he believes his career is at a dead end. Darrin tells Sam how he feels, and Larry gives him the account. Now Darrin thinks that his wife has somehow used witchcraft to manipulate the situation. Furious that such is not the case, Sam transforms their house into a beautiful mansion with several housekeepers. Darrin protests: He wants to succeed the mortal way. Sam convinces him that he's been doing that all along. The house is restored to its former condition, with their relationship secured.
Twitch-Bits: Endora says that Aunt Agnes was burned at the stake in Salem during the trials. And we learn that Darrin's secretary was born in St. Paul, Minnesota.

Scroll 74

Prodigy
(6-9-66)

Scribes: Fred Freeman, Lawrence J. Cohen
Overseer: Howard Morris
Sojourners: Jack Weston, Lennie Bremen
Sam-Script: As a child, Louis Gruberm, brother of Gladys Kravitz, made an embarrassing violin debut at Carnegie Hall; his knickers

dropped. Abner thinks Louis is still a loser. To boost his confidence, Samantha arranges for Louis to play a hospital benefit and uses her magic to help him utilize his musical ability to the fullest. Louis is unaware of all this and performs wonderfully at the function, which leads to a TV appearance, at which time he loses his pants once again.

Twitch-Bits: This is the last black-and-white episode, and the last to feature Alice Pearce as Gladys.

The Third Season (1966 to 1967)

Scroll 75

Nobody's Perfect
(9-15-66)

Scribe: Douglas Tibbles

Overseer: William Asher

Sojourners: Robert Q. Lewis, David Lewis (no relation), Lindsay Workman

Sam-Script: Endora is ecstatic. Tabitha is a full-blown witch. But Sam stays up all night worrying. How will she break the news to Darrin? While Sam oversleeps, Darrin takes Tabitha to baby photographer Diego Fenman, a man whom Tabitha magically drives up the wall. In the end, Sam still does not reveal Tabitha's truth.

Twitch-Bits: Erin Murphy makes her first appearance as Tabitha in this first color episode. Tab's pediatrician here is Dr. Koblin. In "How Green Was My Grass," it was Dr. McDonald.

Scroll 76

The Moment of Truth
(9-22-66)

Scribes: David V. Robison, John L. Greene

Overseer: William Asher

Sojourners: (None)

Sam-Script: Aunt Clara visits. Sam wonders how to tell Darrin about Tabitha, who makes a magic mess of the living room. The Tates celebrate the Stephenses' anniversary. Sam warns that Tabitha may add a twitch-glitch. Darrin discovers Tabitha's powers. Larry is convinced that he's drunk. He and Louise go home.

Twitch-Bits: First episode with Kasey Rogers as Louise. Great lines:

Sam: "Listen, Tab! Stop fooling around! If Mother wanted to spoil the party, it would be raining in the living room."

Larry's golf story: "It's a birdie. It's plain—I'm Superman."

Darrin realizes: "It's not … not … what's her name?"

Larry regarding Louise's lullabies: "It works like a charm. With her voice, the kids fall asleep in self-defense."

Larry: "Happy Thursday!!" (He celebrates any day of the week with a *Y* in it; *Bewitched* was then seen on Thursdays.)

Sam: "It was Tabitha."

Clara: "Not really."

Darrin: "Sure, really. What isn't really in this house?"

Sam: "Just what's the matter with my family?"

Darrin: "How much time do you have?"

…

Darrin to Tabitha: "Mustn't twitch."

Sam: "That ought to do it."

Darrin: "Think so? That didn't work with her mother."

Larry's Sobriety Test: "Say chrysanthemum."— "Oh, daffodils." His Equilibrium Test: Louise yells "Taxi!" In the walk-a-straight-line part, Darrin says, "Why don't you walk from where you spilled the champagne to where you burned the table?"

Larry: "Is that you, Louise? Are Darrin and Sam still here? Would you say goodnight to them for me, please?"

Scroll 77

Witches and Warlocks Are My Favorite Thing
(9-29-66)

Scribes: David V. Robison, John L. Greene

Overseer: William Asher

Sojourners: Estelle Winwood, Reta Shaw

Sam-Script: Tabitha's powers are put to the test by Aunt Hagatha, Aunt Enchantra, Aunt Clara, and Endora. Just as Darrin arrives home, Tabitha impresses the coven, which decides she's a superior talent who must be enrolled in Hagatha's school for little witches. Outraged, Sam, Darrin, and Aunt Clara side together against the rest, all of whom Maurice whisks to a chilly mountaintop until they reconsider their decision.

Twitch-Bits: Enchantra and Hagatha have been certifying witches for 308 years (since 1558).

Scroll 78

Accidental Twins
(10-6-66)

Scribe: Howard Leeds

Overseer: William Asher

Sojourners: (None)

Sam-Script: Aunt Clara's done it again. Little Jonathan Tate, preschool son of Larry and Louise, is now a set of twins. Somehow, Sam and Darrin persuade the Tates into allowing their offspring to sleep over. The next day, the Stephenses throw two separate birthday parties for two little man Tates. Meanwhile, Aunt Clara is having trouble thinking of how to reverse the spell. Then Sam makes her ten years younger.

Twitch-Bits: Jonathan Tate appeared only once more, in "Mixed Doubles." David White had a real son named Jonathan, who perished in a 1988 airplane mishap.

Scroll 79

A Most Unusual Wood Nymph
(10-13-66)

Scribe: Ed Jurist

Overseer: William Asher

Sojourners: Kathleen Nolan (*The Real McCoys*) Michael Ansara (then married to *I Dream of Jeannie* star Barbara Eden), Henry Corden, Jean Blake

Sam-Script: Endora suspects the visiting Gerri O'Toole to be a witch-hating wood nymph. Sam freezes Darrin and confronts Gerri, who's out to curse Darrin's family. To reverse the curse, Endora sends Sam back to fifteenth-century Ireland to meet with Darrin's ancestor, Darrin the Bold.

Twitch-Bits: The first of fifty-four scripts by Ed Jurist, who penned its sequel, "Return of Darrin The Bold" (now set in the fourteenth century).

Scroll 80

Endora Moves in for a Spell
(10-20-66)

Scribe: Robert Riley Crutcher
Overseer: William Asher
Sojourners: Paul Smith, Sid Clute, Arthur Adams
Sam-Script: Uncle Arthur and Endora clash over Tabitha's powers and debate who's to live across the street. They keep zapping a house there until Sam insists they make up.
Twitch-Bits: First episode with Sandra Gould as Mrs. Kravitz. The same house here was used in *I Dream of Jeannie* ("What House Across the Street?"). Darrin references it before it's zapped away in the next episode. Arthur calls Darrin "my yagazuzie nephew-in-law," a nod to Arthur's phony spell in "The Joker Is a Card."

Good lines abound:

Endora: "You call yourself a brother?"

Arthur: "Only when I'm forced to."

Sam: " … both of you, kiss and make up. Go on, kiss her."

Arthur: "Things aren't that desperate."

Darrin: "What happens if you make the house disappear while the police and Mrs. Kravitz are inside?"

Sam: "Oh, they will too."

Darrin: "They will too what?"

Sam: "Disappear."

Darrin: "Disappear where? Don't answer that."

Scroll 81

Twitch or Treat
(10-27-66)

Scribes: Robert Riley Crutcher, James Henerson
Overseer: William Asher
Sojourners: Joan Huntington, Jeff DeBenning, baseball star Willie Mays, Barry Atwater, Jim Begg
Sam-Script: Endora holds her annual Halloween party at Sam and Darrin's, and remodels the living room in early extravagance. Among the guests: a warlock named Boris, his feline companion, Eva (a catwitch), and Willie Mays, whom Sam assures Darrin is a warlock. Meanwhile, Uncle Arthur and Endora are still battling over the house across the street and continue to confuse Mrs. Kravitz and Councilman Green.
Twitch-Bits: Abner and Gladys's address is shown to be 1168 Morning Glory Circle, but since they live across the street from Sam and Darrin, theirs should be an odd-numbered address.

Scroll 82

Dangerous Diaper Dan
(11-3-66)

Scribes: David Braverman, Bob Marcus
Overseer: William Asher

Sojourners: Marty Ingels (on/off/on-again spouse of Shirley Jones of *The Partridge Family*), Alex Gerry, Jim Begg, Billy Beck

Sam-Script: Diaper Dan, secretly working for A. J. Kimberly Advertising Agency, plants a microphone in a baby rattle that he gives to Tabitha. Sam becomes angry when Darrin tells her she might be responsible for a leak of ideas from McMann and Tate. Endora protests, and Sam finds out about Dan's plan, and she and her mother drive the diaper man up a tree, popping his van wheel and doors, among other things.

Twitch-Bits: Dan's code name is *Dragonfly*. The flowers are from Patterson's Florist. And, after his run-in with Sam and Endora, Dan decides to spend a month at the Country Air Rest Home.

Scroll 83

The Short, Happy Circuit of Aunt Clara
(11-10-66)

Scribe: Lee Erwin

Overseer: William Asher

Sojourners: Reginald Owen, Arthur Julian, Leo DeLyon

Sam-Script: Darrin lets Aunt Clara baby-sit when he and Sam are invited to the Tates to meet Mr. MacElroy, a shoe client. The picture darkens. Aunt Clara accidentally knocks out the lights across the Eastern Seaboard. Desperate for help, she summons Ocky, her old warlock boyfriend. He's able to keep the lights on only by raising his arms. Larry insists that everyone go to the Stephenses'. Darrin opens the closet door, a

pair of shoes walk out; it's Ocky in disguise. MacElroy thinks it's an ad campaign and loves it.

Twitch-Bits: The New York blackout was one year earlier on November 9, 1965. Clara does a "little dance" she learned in Scotland. "It's called the *Wee-kick o' the Kirk*." MacElroy responds: "Bet she knows where the brandy is." Darrin's first slogan for MacElroy Shoes is "There's no business like shoe business."

Scroll 84

I'd Rather Twitch Than Fight
(11-17-66)

Scribe: James Henerson

Overseer: R. Robert Rosenbaum

Sojourners: Bridget Hanley (*Here Come the Brides*, and real-life bride of *Bewitched* director E. W. Swackhamer), Norman Fell (*Three's Company, The Ropers, Dan August*), Parley Baer, James Millhollin, Burt Mustin, Riza Royce

Sam-Script: Darrin is enraged. Sam gave away his favorite sports jacket to Goodwill. They seek marital advice from the Tates. Larry counsels Darrin; Louise comforts Samantha. Shocked by such inferior guidance, Endora conjures up Dr. Sigmund Freud, who settles Sam's conflicts but gets into a free-for-all with the Tates' analyst. To settle this new issue, Sam and Endora return each psychologist to his proper environment.

Twitch-Bits: A perfect mixture of the mortal/supernatural world conflict.

Scroll 85

Oedipus Hex
(11-24-66)

Scribes: David V. Robison, John L. Greene
Overseer: William Asher
Sojourners: Ned Glass, Irwin Charone, Paul Smith, Paul Dooley
Sam-Script: Samantha serves on a fund-raising committee, and Endora casts a spell on a bowl of popcorn, which alters Darrin's work habits and makes him lazy. The milkman and the TV repairman also become afflicted. Sam returns home and finds the house a shambles, with Darrin and the others laughing the day away. Recognizing her mother's handiwork, Sam removes the spell on the carefree kernels and gets the loafers to make a substantial contribution to her committee.
Twitch-Bits: Darrin reads *The Daily Chronicle* at breakfast.

Scroll 86

Sam's Spooky Chair
(12-1-66)

Scribe: Coslough Johnson
Overseer: R. Robert Rosenbaum
Sojourners: J. Pat O'Malley, Anne Seymour, Howard Morton, Roger Garrett
Sam-Script: Samantha purchases a chair that, unbeknownst to her, is bewitched. She prepares dinner for the Tates, client Max Cosgrove and his domineering wife, who wants to purchase the chair. Once a Cosgrove possession, the spooky seat immediately begins making life miserable for them. Endora has an explanation. The misbehaved chair is really Clyde Farnsworth, a warlock who transformed himself years before when Samantha rejected his affections.
Twitch-Bits: The word *bewitched* appears in this episode.

Scroll 87

My Friend Ben
(12-8-66)

Scribe: James Henerson
Overseer: William Asher
Sojourners: Fredd Wayne, Mike Road, Harry Holcomb, Hollis Morrison, Billy Beck, Tim Rooney, Donald Mitchell
Sam-Script: Aunt Clara mistakenly conjures up Benjamin Franklin to fix a lamp, and Darrin finds it difficult to convince Larry that Franklin is not part of an ad campaign. Ben gets lost, and Sam, Darrin, and Clara search him out. Inadvertently, Franklin has started an old fire engine, which he slams into a curb. As a result, he's taken to court.
Twitch-Bits: Part 1 of 2.

Scroll 88

Samantha for the Defense
(12-15-66)

Scribe: James Henerson
Overseer: William Asher
Sojourners: Fredd Wayne, Mike Road, Harry Holcombe, Jonathan Hole, Paul Sand (*Paul Sand* in *Friends and Lovers*), Violet Carlson,

Martin Ashe, The Real Don Steele (playing himself)

Sam-Script: Assistant D.A. Chuck Hawkins feels Ben Franklin's appearance is a publicity stunt by McMann and Tate and tells Darrin that Franklin ("or whoever he is") will be prosecuted to the fullest extent of the law. While in court, Samantha disappears and returns with a plaque from the fire engine Ben was accused of stealing. The inscription bears his name. Case closed.

Twitch-Bits: Part 2 of 2. Fred Wayne, who played Ben, was also the historic consultant for both segments, which are remade as "George Washington Zapped Here," Parts 1 and 2.

Scroll 89

A Gazebo Never Forgets
(12-22-66)

Scribes: Jerry Devine, Izzy Elinson
Overseer: R. Robert Rosenbaum
Sojourners: Paul Reed, Steve Franken
Sam-Script: Aunt Clara baby-sits for Tabitha, and Sam applies for a bank loan to remodel her gazebo into a rumpus room. A bank inspector is sent to review the construction site and sees a large pink elephant that Aunt Clara has created from a Tabitha-desired toy. After a close call with Larry and the bank president, whose brother holds a profitable account with McMann and Tate, Clara returns the elephant to its normal state.

Twitch-Bits: This first of fourteen segments Dick York missed is most similar to "Follow That Witch," Parts 1 and 2.

Scroll 90

Soap Box Derby
(12-29-66)

Scribe: James Henerson
Overseer: Alan Jay Factor
Sojourners: Michael Shea, William Bramley, Arthur Peterson, Peter Dunhill, George Andre
Sam-Script: Sam helps prepare twelve-year-old Johnny Mills for the Soap Box Derby. Gladys brags that her nephew will win the local race and go on to victory in Akron. At the track, both Darrin and Gladys keep an eye on Sam. Neither one wants her to give Johnny any added assistance.

Twitch-Bits: Partial remake of "Little Pitchers Have Big Fears." Robert Ellis Logan, 1965 Derby winner, was credited as this episode's technical adviser.

Scroll 91

Sam in the Moon
(1-5-67)

Scribe: James Henerson
Overseer: R. Robert Rosenbaum
Sojourners: Dort Clark, Tim Herbert, Joseph Mell, Baynes Barron, Bob Okasaki
Sam-Script: Sam baffles Darrin by choosing not to watch a TV newscast about the moon (she's been there; done that). Samantha flies to Tokyo with Endora and buys some unique tea from a Japanese warlock. Back in America, Darrin sees the tea, recalls Sam's earlier remarks about the moon, and takes the mixture to have it analyzed (he thinks

it's moon dust). After some slight confusion involving the pharmacist's brother-in-law (from Nassau County, not NASA), Darrin is almost certain that the tea is genuine.

Twitch-Bits: Part of the story here is based on the fact that "all stores are closed" on Sunday, a nostalgic memory indeed.

Scroll 92

Ho Ho, the Clown
(1-12-67)

Scribe: Richard Baer

Overseer: William Asher

Sojourners: Joey Foreman, Dick Wilson, Charles J. Stewart

Sam-Script: Sam and her mother take Tabitha to a live taping of TV's *Ho Ho, the Clown* show, which is sponsored by Darrin's client, the Solow Toy Company. Endora is angered when her granddaughter is excluded from the program's contest due to her relationship to Darrin. While on the air, Endora makes certain Tabitha wins, Solow finds out Tabitha is Darrin's offspring, and that Darrin feels his career has just ended. Sam saves the day by creating a *Tabitha* doll and claims that her daughter's television appearance was a publicity stunt for the new toy.

Twitch-Bits: Ho Ho's show appears on WXIU-TV; Dick Wilson plays Mr. Solow, a client, not a drunk (which he usually played).

Scroll 93

Super Car
(1-19-67)

Scribe: Ed Jurist

Overseer: William Asher

Sojourners: Irwin Charone, Dave Madden (*The Partridge Family*), Herb Ellis

Sam-Script: Endora gives Darrin a new car. This would be nice except that it's a proto-type she's lifted from its creator in Detroit. Initially unaware of the true deed, Darrin loves the car and makes Sam take a test drive. Client Mr. Sheldrake shows interest in the auto, Darrin learns of its true origins and insists Endora return it. She does so. Problem is, Sheldrake's in the driver's seat.

Twitch-Bits: Dave Madden and Herb Ellis appear together again in "Samantha's Shopping Spree."

Scroll 94

The Corn Is as High as a Guernsey's Eye
(1-26-67)

Scribe: Ruth Brooks Flippen

Overseer: William Asher

Sojourners: Don Penny, Howard Smith, Joseph Perry, Art Lewis, William Thegoe

Sam-Script: Larry tells Darrin to forget the Morton Milk account; another agency plans to promote Morton's famous Guernsey cow in McMann and Tate's office building lobby. Meanwhile, Aunt Clara is despondent and Sam tries to cheer her up by taking her to lunch with Darrin. At McMann and Tate's building, Sam leaves

Clara for a moment and returns to find her dear aunt nowhere in sight. Has the frazzled witch turned herself into a cow? Sam thinks so, and twitches the beast home with her. After a ruckus is raised over the missing beef, Darrin finds Clara and phones Sam to return the meat.

Twitch-Bits: Darrin's office is in the International Building on the 32nd floor.

Scroll 95

The Trial and Error of Aunt Clara
(2-2-67)

Scribe: Ed Jurist

Overseer: William Asher

Sojourners: Nancy Andrews, Arthur Malet (*Easy Street*), Ottola Nesmith

Sam-Script: Aunt Clara's magic is failing (worse than usual), and she's put on trial by the Witches Council (presided over by Judge Bean with Endora). The council plans to "earthbound" Sam's favorite aunt. As court begins session in the Stephenses' living room, Samantha acts as Clara's defense and secretly assists her during a series of magic tests. Sam steps away, Clara gets confused, Darrin arrives, and she makes the judge and all in court disappear. Clara's powers are intact, after all, and she's free.

Twitch-Bits: The court scene in the living room showcases one of the more elaborate witch-in-mortal home sets. First *in color* appearance of Sam's flying suit.

Scroll 96

Three Wishes
(2-9-67)

Scribe: Robert Riley Crutcher

Overseer: William Asher

Sojourners: Linda Gaye Scott, Edythe Sills, Robert Stiles

Sam-Script: Endora once again grants Darrin three wishes to prove his love for Sam. First, he wishes that Larry go on a Hawaiian business trip instead of him because Sam's unable to go. Darrin tells Sam he has to meet with a beautiful model named Buffy. Endora can't wait to hear what she thinks his next wish will be. Darrin and Buffy fly to Boston. Sam phones Darrin's hotel room. Buffy answers. Darrin lets her stay there. There was only one room available at the inn. Sam angrily suspects that Darrin has used up his last wish with Buffy. But he commands Endora to appear, and she does.

Scroll 97

I Remember You ... Sometimes
(2-16-67)

Scribe: David V. Robison, John L. Greene

Overseer: William Asher

Sojourners: Dan Tobin, Grace Albertson, Jill Foster

Sam-Script: Darrin tries to improve his memory for better business maneuvers. Endora casts a spell on his wristwatch to help him out. Now he has total recall whenever he puts it on. The Tates and the braggy client, Mr. Pennybaker and his wife, are invited to Sam and Darrin's for dinner. Darrin monopolizes the conversation with his overactive memory and knowledge, both of which Mr. Pennybaker prides himself with possessing. Sam realizes that the watch is bewitched and zaps it off Darrin and onto Mrs. Pennybaker, who starts reciting her husband's party stories verbatim. Mr. Pennybaker realizes that at times, he, too, is a bore.

Twitch-Bits: A bunch. Darrin celebrates the anniversary of his and Sam's first quarrel, which occurred when Sam waited at the wrong entrance of Darrin's office building, leaving him standing in the rain for an hour. He was at the side entrance because she was shopping at a dress store on the side street where she bought a yellow dress with white polka dots that she later gave to the rummage committee along with a chocolate cake that she "whipped up." They made up by going out to dinner, dancing, and the theater. Every time Darrin brings up the chocolate cake, they have a fight, like now. We learn that Darrin's great-aunt Emma drove a Lexington Minuteman. Al Barabaras (whose famous touchdown catch in the 1934 Rose Bowl provides the ultimate memory test for everyone in this episode) died of cancer in 1988.

Scroll 98

Art for Sam's Sake
(2-23-67)

Scribe: Jack Sher

Overseer: William Asher

Sojourners: Arthur Julian, Tom Palmer, Mickey Deems, Paul Sorenson, John Alonzo

Sam-Script: Endora is disgusted by Samantha's amateurish attempt at painting and replaces her daughter's picture of a fruit bowl with a masterpiece. Unaware of her mom's deed, Sam wins first prize at a charity exhibit. Darrin, the Tates, and perfume client Mr. Cunningham accompany her to the art show. Sam recognizes Endora's handiwork, Mr. Cunningham purchases what he thinks is Sam's masterpiece, trouble brews, and a bargain is made: Sam persuades Mr. Cunningham to use her named-on-the-spot perfume, *I Know You*, for his company.

Twitch-Bits: The paintings used appear courtesy of the Martin Lowitz Gallery.

Scroll 99

Charlie Harper, Winner
(3-2-67)

Scribe: Earl Barrett

Overseer: R. Robert Rosenbaum

Sojourners: Angus Duncan, Joanna Moore (once married to Ryan O'Neal), Henry Hunter, Karl Redcoff, Teresa Tudor

Sam-Script: Sam and Darrin entertain Charlie Harper and his wife, Daphne. Charlie, an old college chum, has surpassed Darrin in every category since school. He's handsome, rich, and the father of triplets. Sam conjures up a fur coat to impress the Harpers, which hurts and angers Darrin. Sam then gives the coat to Daphne, who initially wanted to buy it. Now, she has a hard time understanding how Samantha could give it away, and comes away from the situation with a new set of priorities.

Twitch-Bits: Here Sam tells Charlie that Darrin's campaign for Caldwell Soup upped their sales 27 percent. This is a reference to the account featured in the central premise of "Help, Help, Don't Save Me."

Scroll 100

Aunt Clara's Victoria Victory
(3-9-67)

Scribe: Robert Riley Crutcher
Overseer: William Asher
Sojourners: Jane Connell, Robert H. Harris
Sam-Script: Aunt Clara fondly remembers her days as a lady-in-waiting to Queen Victoria and tries to return to the Victorian Age. Instead, the Queen, with throne and all, appears in Sam and Darrin's living room. Client Mr. Morgan and the Queen hit it off then clash. Sam bewitches Morgan with a dream spell to make him believe that he is Queen Victoria. Sam reveals to the real *Her Highness* that she and Clara are witches. Victoria is furious. Clara herself becomes angry and attempts to zap the queen back to her own time, but Prince Albert appears instead.

Twitch-Bits: Jane Connell makes her first of three "regal" appearances. (She later shows up as Ticheba, high priestess of witches, and then Mother Goose.)

Scroll 101

The Crone of Cawdor
(3-16-67)

Scribe: Ed Jurist
Overseer: R. Robert Rosenbaum
Sojourners: Julie Gregg, Robert P. Lieb, Dorothy Neuman, Heather Woodruff, Del Press
Sam-Script: Sam has to prevent Darrin from kissing beautiful client Terry Warbell who, Endora claims, is the Crone of Cawdor, an old hag who steals the youth from those mortals she smooches. Darrin thinks that's ridiculous, but allegedly, he will age five hundred years if he puckers up to Terry. To spite the curse, Darrin plans to plant one on Terry, the clock strikes 6:00 PM, Warbell transforms into the Crone, and Darrin faints.

Twitch-Bits: Dorothy Neuman, who played the Crone, appeared much earlier with Elizabeth Montgomery as an old hag vampire in an episode of NBC-TV's *Thriller* series, entitled *"Masquerade,"* which aired on October 30, 1961.

Scroll 102

No More Mr. Nice Guy
(3-23-67)

Scribe: Jack Sher
Overseer: William Asher

Sojourners: Larry D. Mann, George Ives, Judy Lang, Judson Pratt, Dick Wilson, Paul Barselow, Heather Woodruff

Sam-Script: Endora casts a spell on Darrin that makes everyone hate him. Upset, Darrin seeks the counsel of a psychiatrist. Sam finds out his job's in jeopardy because of Endora's shenanigans and demands that her mother remove the spell.

Twitch-Bits: Darrin says he voted for Mayor Rocklin.

Scroll 103

It's Wishcraft
(3-30-67)

Scribe: James Henerson
Overseer: Paul Davis (widower of Alice Pearce)
Sojourners: (None)

Sam-Script: Darrin's parents visit. He and Sam try to conceal Tabitha's powers. Sam asks her mother for help. Endora ends up insulting Darrin in front of Phyllis and only adds coal to the fire. Phyllis thinks Sam and Darrin are having a marital rift. To soothe her concerns, Darrin remains happy and chipper as ever in front of his parents. The elder Mr. and Mrs. Stephens never (ever) find out the truth about Tabitha (or Samantha).

Twitch-Bits: Darrin kisses Endora hello; Mrs. Stephens kisses Sam hello; *air kisses* came later.

Scroll 104

How to Fail in Business
with All Kinds of Help
(4-6-67)

Scribe: Ron Friedman
Overseer: Richard Kinon
Sojourners: Lisa Kirk, Henry Beckman, Jill Foster, Myra DeGroot, Ralph Brooks

Sam-Script: Darrin thinks Madame Maruska, a dominating client, is Endora in disguise. He doesn't play what he thinks is Endora's game. Maruska is upset with Darrin's arrogance and refuses to do business with McMann and Tate. Darrin learns that Endora was with Sam at the time in question. He runs to Maruska's office to apologize. Larry's there, too. They both fail to regain the account. Sam takes Darrin's layout and prints it in the newspaper. Maruska is won over, and McMann and Tate seal the account.

Twitch-Bits: Endora recites her famous *Born in the Sparkle of a Star* speech. Madame Maruska pronounces her name *Marooshkaa,* yet says *Steffans* instead of *Stephens.*

Scroll 105

Bewitched, Bothered and Infuriated
(4-13-67)

Scribe: Howard Leeds
Overseer: R. Robert Rosenbaum
Sojourners: George Lymburn, Jack Fletcher

Sam-Script: Aunt Clara pops up a ten-year-old newspaper that reveals how Larry Tate broke his leg on his honeymoon with Louise. Sam and Darrin think it's today's paper. The Tates are off on a second honeymoon; the Stephenses make a nuisance of themselves, as they try to prevent Larry from breaking his limb. Darrin even encourages Sam to use her powers, though she objects to his rude behavior. Upon learning the paper is just another product of Clara's inept magic, Sam and Darrin leave Louise and Larry, with the latter retaining his healthy body part.

Scroll 106

Nobody but a Frog Knows How To Live
(4-27-67)

Scribe: Ruth Brooks Flippen
Overseer: Richard Kinon
Sojourners: Corin Camcho, John Fiedler, Dan Tobin
Sam-Script: A frog has been turned into a man named Fergie by a witch. Samantha learns that a girl frog is waiting for him back at the lily pond. Gladys wonders about this strange frog man. Sam takes pity on him and changes him back into a frog.
Twitch-Bits: Sam and Darrin's phone number here is 555-2134. Saunder's Soups 59th flavor is Sautéed Turtle. The company also makes frozen dinners, chili sauce, and mustard. The episode also includes John Fiedler's first guest appearance.

Scroll 107

There's Gold in Them Thar Pills
(5-4-67)

Scribes: Paul Wayne, Ed Jurist
Overseer: R. Robert Rosenbaum
Sojourners: Milton Frome, Allen Davis, Mark Harris, Stuart Nisbet, Pat McCaffrie
Sam-Script: Darrin catches a cold. Endora calls Dr. Bombay, who prescribes a supernatural pill that cures her son-in-law's flu. But there's a side effect: his voice gets higher. But not before he offers the pills to Larry and a client who both have colds. Their instant return to health prompts Darrin and Larry to think about marketing Bombay's pills, that is, until the side effects surface. Luckily, Sam finds an antidote.
Twitch-Bits: In this first episode with Dr. Bombay, Darrin says he's been with McMann and Tate for three years, but events in "Serena's Youth Pill" indicate that he joined the firm in 1961. In any case, his doctor's name is Dr. Altman, and the pills to be used are called *Dr. Bombay's Cold Bombs.*

The Fourth Season (1967 to 1968)

Scroll 108

Long Live the Queen
(9-7-67)

Scribe: Ed Jurist
Overseer: William Asher

Samantha with old-witch queen (Ruth McDevitt) responds in like manner to her mother's smile of approval after Sam is crowned the new queen of the witches in "Long Live Queen Samantha," a scene signifying Elizabeth's real-life association with Agnes Moorehead.

Sojourners: Ruth McDevitt, J. Edward McKinley, Herb Ellis, Paul Barselow, Carl Princi, Mary Foran, Lal Chand Mehra

Sam-Script: The Witch Queen retires and crowns Sam as her successor. Darrin doesn't mind. The house is invaded by a blackbird, a walking chair, and an assortment of animals, supernatural objects and beings. Now he heads for his favorite bar and speaks with a pathetic drunk and a sympathetic bartender, both of whom influence him to return to Sam.

Twitch-Bits: Samantha was chosen at birth to be queen; the walking chair is the same prop previously employed in "Sam's Spooky Chair".

Scroll 109

Toys in Babeland
(9-14-67)

Scribe: Ed Jurist
Overseer: William Asher
Sojourners: Jim Brooks, Burt Mustin, Dick Wilson, Paul Barselow, William Kendis, Jeri-Lynne Fraser, Joan Petalk

Sam-Script: Endora's expected to party at the Taj Mahal, but she's baby-sitting for Tabitha. What to do? Breathe life into Tabitha's toy soldier and make him the sitter. Tabs later copies her grandmama's spell and brings all of her toys to life. Larry believes he's missed out on a masquerade party and goes out for a drink with a toy soldier and thinks it works for another agency that's trying to hire Darrin.

Twitch-Bits: A spell Sam used in an attempt to get rid of the toys is also used by Sam to summon Ophelia in "The Eight-Year Witch," and in an unsuccessful attempt to force Endora to leave Darrin and Sam's honeymoon in "I, Darrin, Take This Witch, Samantha" (the pilot).

Scroll 110

Business, Italian Style
(9-21-67)

Scribe: Michael Morris
Overseer: William Asher
Sojourners: Renzo Cesana, Fred Roberto

Sam-Script: Darrin tries to learn Italian to please a client of the same national heritage. He struggles with instructive recordings, and Endora zaps him into a native who doesn't understand English. The client, Mr. Rubino, is impressed with Darrin's progress, but he insists that he speak American—an impossibility until Samantha forces Endora to remove the spell.

Twitch-Bits: The phrase *duo volta*, used by Darrin, means *twice*.

Scroll 111

Double, Double, Toil and Trouble
(9-28-67)

Scribe: Ed Jurist

Overseer: William Asher

Sojourners: Stanley Beck

Sam-Script: Queen Samantha holds witch proceedings in the wee hours. Darrin orders her to clear court. Endora is infuriated. Sam attends a church fund-raiser, and Endora and Serena conspire to dispose of Darrin. Serena takes her cousin's place at home and seeks to make a shambles of the marriage. A free-for-all pie fest results between Sam, Endora, Darrin, and Serena, and the situation is cleaned up.

Twitch-Bits: When Darrin and Sam hit each other with pies, Elizabeth Montgomery breaks up so much her lines are dubbed twice. Also, a minstrel sings *The Witches' Anthem*: "Off we go into the wild black yonder, witches all, all in a row, up in the sky … "

Scroll 112

Cheap, Cheap
(10-5-67)

Scribe: Ed Jurist

Overseer: William Asher

Sojourners: Parley Baer, Jill Foster, Mary Lansing

Sam-Script: Darrin makes Sam return an expensive coat, which she thought was a bargain. Endora turns him into a real cheapskate. During a disastrous dinner party with thrifty client Mr. Bigelow, Samantha tries to reverse Endora's stingy spell, and succeeds only in transforming Bigelow into a big spender.

Twitch-Bits: Mr. Bigelow gets his five-cent cigars from Jose Ortega, 1555 Bleeker Street, Apartment 4.

Scroll 113

No Zip in My Zap
(10-12-67)

Scribe: Barbara Avedon

Overseer: Richard Kinon

Sojourners: Mala Powers, Dick Wilson, Paul Barselow, Jerry Margolin

Sam-Script: Samantha loses her powers. Dr. Bombay tells her it's because she doesn't use her magic as much as she should (it's all clogged up). As therapy, Sam must levitate in midair for a time. Darrin phones from a meeting with a client named Mary Jane, who also happens to be someone he used to date. Endora says Sam can't talk right now, she's flying. Darrin now believes his wife has turned herself into a fly who's out to check up on his business encounter with a former love.

Twitch-Bits: With Sam's powers on the blink, she argues for Darrin to "go back to your friendly bartender with your mouth full of olives," and he does (a scene of which was used for original network commercials). Also: Mary Jane wrote "Roses are red, violets are blue, it may take a while, but I'll get you" in Darrin's yearbook.

Scroll 114

Birdies, Bogeys and Baxter
(10-19-67)

When Samantha finds out that even a witch can become a "golf widow," she decides it's time to join Darrin on the green in "Birdies, Bogeys and Baxter."

Scribes: David V. Robison, John L. Greene
Overseer: William Asher
Sojourners: MacDonald Carey (*Days Of Our Lives*), Joan Banks, Frank Alesia
Sam-Script: Larry wants Darrin to impress client Joe Baxter, who prides himself on being an excellent golfer. Darrin wears himself out practicing. Endora gives him a magical boost to better his game. Darrin starts making incredible shots. Larry warns him not to beat Baxter. Mrs. Baxter tells Sam that she wishes her husband would lose just once. Sam complies and contributes to her mother's witchcraft.
Twitch-Bits: In the tag, Sam suggests a movie at the Lyceum, and she wears the coat Darrin bought for her in "Cheap, Cheap."

Scroll 115

The Safe and Sane Halloween
(10-26-67)

Scribe: James Henerson
Overseer: William Asher
Sojourners: Bobby Riha, Monte Margetta, Jerry Maren, Felix Silla, Billy Curtis, Larry Barton
Sam-Script: It's Halloween. Gladys's nephew trades places with one of the goblins Tabitha has brought to life from her storybook. The ghouls cause havoc by playing tricks on Darrin and the Tates. They turn the Kravitz nephew into a goat. Tabitha returns the spirits to their proper places, while Samantha tries to offer a logical explanation.
Twitch-Bits: At this point in the series, Tabitha's name was still spelled in the credits with an *a* (*Tabatha*).

Scroll 116

Out of Sync, Out of Mind
(11-2-67)

Scribe: Ed Jurist

Overseer: Richard Kinon

Sojourners: (None)

Sam-Script: Darrin's parents have a fight. Phyllis comes to stay with him and Sam, who suggests that Darrin show home movies of Tabitha to ease the tension. The audio and the visual are out of sync. Aunt Clara, who's also visiting, casts a spell to splice the movie. Instead, Sam's real voice follows her lip movement off-screen. A call to Dr. Bombay is made. Sam is cured, and Phyllis is delighted when Frank comes to pick her up.

Twitch-Bits: First episode with Roy Roberts as Darrin's dad. Sam makes crêpes suzette for lunch, while the Stephenses' bathroom is shown in the color of orange with green tiles. Also, Clara says that there's a cinder path in front of Dr. Bombay's house.

Scroll 117

That Was No Chick, That Was My Wife
(11-9-67)

Scribe: Rick Mittleman

Overseer: William Asher

Sojourners: Herb Voland, Sara Seegar, William Kendis, Arthur Adams

Sam-Script: Larry asks Darrin to go to Chicago to renew the Springer Pet Food account. Samantha accompanies him, and Aunt Clara baby-sits for Tabitha, who zaps life into a toy monkey. Sam pops home and runs into Louise, who tells Larry she's just seen Samantha. Everyone comes back to Connecticut the normal way, and Sam explains it was Serena who Louise saw at the house. Louise still decides to see a psychiatrist.

Twitch-Bits: In the tag, Darrin recognizes it's Serena posing as Sam. Why not at other times? Late in the episode, there is a sequence on the sidewalk outside Darrin's office building in downtown Manhattan, yet there are mountains clearly visible at the end of the street. These same mountains appear again in "If They Never Met."

Scroll 118

Allergic to Macedonian Dodo Birds
(11-16-67)

Scribe: Richard Baer

Overseer: Richard Kinon

Sojourners: Dick Wilson, Janos Prohaska

Sam-Script: Endora loses her powers. She stays with Sam and Darrin and becomes an irritating presence, especially to her son-in-law. Aunt Clara's witchcraft has improved tenfold. Dr. Bombay is summoned. He says Endora's and Clara's powers have somehow switched hands. The reason: Tabitha had zapped up a Macedonian dodo bird, to which Endora is allergic. The creature is found, and Endora and Clara return to normal (whatever that means).

Twitch-Bits: The spell used by Clara to zap up the food is reused by Serena in "Samantha and the Troll." Tabitha calls the dodo "Bobby the Bird."

Scroll 119

Samantha's Thanksgiving To Remember
(11-23-67)

Scribes: Tom and Helen August

Overseer: Richard Kinon

Sojourners: Jacques Aubuchon, Laurie Main, Richard Bull, Peter Canon

Sam-Script: Aunt Clara zaps the Stephens family, Gladys, and herself back to seventeenth-century Salem for Thanksgiving. Sam asks Darrin to light a fire. He strikes a match and is accused of witchcraft. Samantha defends her husband at his trial. She asks his accuser to ignite the alleged witches' match. He hesitates. Sam twitches the match into a flame. Darrin is proved innocent. Aunt Clara remembers how to get everyone back to the future.

Twitch-Bits: Samantha defends Darrin at the trial, but women were unlikely to appear at such events.

Scroll 120

Solid Gold Mother-In-Law
(11-30-67)

Scribe: Ed Jurist

Overseer: Richard Michaels

Sojourners: Jack Collins, Jill Foster, Peter Dawson

Sam-Script: Client Mr. Grégson has an old-fashioned vision of the American family. Endora pops a picture of herself on Darrin's desk. Mr. Gregson wants to meet Endora, with whom Darrin calls a temporary truce. An evening at the Stephenses'

goes well. Mr. Gregson leaves, though not before asking Darrin to open his own ad firm. Larry accuses Darrin of making him look inferior. Sam submits Darrin's ideas to Mr. Gregson with Larry's signature. Larry and Darrin are friends again.

Twitch-Bits: Late in Act II, Larry promises Darrin a partnership but backs out of it in the next instant—an act which he repeats in "The Warlock in the Gray Flannel Suit." The character of Mr. Gregson, played by Jack Collins, is listed as *Mr. Hudson* in the credits.

Scroll 121

My, What Big Ears You Have
(12-7-67)

Scribe: Ed Jurist

Overseer: Richard Kinon

Sojourners: Joan Hotchkiss, Myra DeGroot, Tom Browne Henry

Sam-Script: Darrin tries to surprise Sam with an antique rocking chair. On hearing Darrin's telephone conversation with a mysterious woman, Endora thinks her son-in-law is fooling around. He's not. The lady's from the antique shop. Is he telling the truth? To find out, Endora makes his ears grow each time he lies. Darrin stretches the truth to keep Sam from finding out about the rocker. His ears expand. Sam is then surprised with the chair, which Darrin has kept concealed in the Kravitz garage. Endora's plans have failed again.

Twitch-Bits: Ear questions:

Gladys: "Mr. Stephens, did you get a haircut?"

Miss Swanton: "Did you ever do any prize-fighting?"

Hazel: "Have you been stung by a bee?"

Scroll 122

I Get Your Nanny, You Get My Goat
(12-14-67)

Scribe: Ron Friedman

Overseer: William Asher

Sojourners: Hermione Baddeley, Reginald Gardiner, Bern Hoffman, Maida Severn, Pauline Dranke

Sam-Script: Darrin's unhappy with Tabitha's new baby-sitter, a witch-maid named Elspeth, who's hired by Endora, and who also took care of Samantha as a child. Lord Montdrako, Elsbeth's former warlock employer, arrives at Sam and Darrin's. He's furious. Darrin has taken his housekeeper. Sam convinces Montdrako that he doesn't need Elspeth, who leaves on her own accord.

Twitch-Bits: Hermione Baddeley's "Elspeth" was to be a semiregular character, but nothing came to fruition. Lord Montdrako, played by Reginald Gardiner, may be a homage to the title of the 1954 omnibus film, *Three Cases of Murder*, in which the role of Montdrago was played by Orson Welles, founder of Mercury Players, of which Agnes Moorehead was a part.

Scroll 123

Humbug Not To Be Spoken Here
(12-21-67)

Scribes: Lila Garrett, Bernie Kahn

Overseer: William Asher

Sojourners: Charles Lane, Don Beddoe, Martin Ashe, Rosalyn Burbage

Sam-Script: Samantha teaches cranky client Mr. Mortimer all about Christmas. She whisks him off to the North Pole to meet Santa and returns him to New York to visit his ex-butler's underprivileged family. Sam brings him home, and he's confused as to whether or not he's been dreaming. The next day is Christmas. Mr. Mortimer arrives at the Stephenses' with gifts and accepts Samantha's invitation to dinner.

Twitch-Bits: Samantha wears her Christmas flying suit and carries her Christmas Broom (with a big red and green bow).

Scroll 124

Samantha's da Vinci Dilemma
(12-28-67)

Scribes: Jerry Mayer, Paul L. Friedman

Overseer: Richard Kinon

Sojourners: John Abbott, Irwin Charone, Willing Thegoe, Vince Howard

Sam-Script: Samantha paints the house. Aunt Clara tries to help out; Leonardo da Vinci shows up. She tries to send him back to the past but fails. Da Vinci becomes angry, especially when he learns his famous Mona Lisa will be used to sell toothpaste in Darrin's campaign. Sam persuades da Vinci to create another campaign involving tooth paint, with Leonardo's likeness on the package. Aunt Clara sends the artist back to his place in history.

Twitch-Bits: Aunt Clara pops in from the annual Witches' Cookout where she made her favorite recipe: sautéed pussy-willow almondine.

Scroll 125

Once in a Vial
(1-4-68)

Scribes: James Henerson, Ed Jurist

Overseer: Bruce Bilson

Sojourners: Henry Beckman, Ron Randell, Arch Johnson, Joan Tompkins, Frederic Downs, Mary Lansing, Jan Arvan, Darlene Enlow

Sam-Script: Endora summons Rollo, a handsome warlock who once dated Samantha. Sam's mom accidentally downs a love potion Rollo had intended for his ex-love. Endora decides to marry the less-than-average Bo Callahan, a client of Darrin's. As Endora is about to say *I do*, the potion wears off.

Twitch-Bits: Bo thinks Endora should be Miss Autumn Flame: "Smart dresser, sophisticated, still pretty good-lookin'."

Scroll 126

Snob in the Grass
(1-11-68)

Scribe: Ed Jurist

Overseer: R. Robert Rosenbaum

Sojourners: Nancy Kovak, Frank Wilcox, Kendrick Huxham, Allan Emerson, Sue Carlton

Sam-Script: Sheila Sommers, Darrin's old flame, pays a visit. Larry seizes the opportunity to acquire her father's account. At a dinner party, Sheila upstages Samantha, monopolizes Darrin's time, and sounds off on wives who are boring. Determined to make an exit, Darrin is derailed by Larry, and Sam gives Sheila a deserved twitch. Larry is angry at losing the Sommers account but is satisfied when Darrin wins the Webley ledger.

Twitch-Bits: A semiremake of the subplot of the pilot, and Part 1 of 2.

Scroll 127

If They Never Met
(1-25-68)

Scribes: William Idelson, Samuel Bobrick

Overseer: R. Robert Rosenbaum

Sojourners: Nancy Kovak, Frank Wilcox, Paul Barselow, Gene Blakely

Sam-Script: Sam maintains that Darrin really loves her, but she accepts Endora's challenge to see what would have happened if they had never met. Back in time, Darrin confides to Al, the bartender, that his girlfriend Sheila is fantastic and the daughter of a millionaire, but he's not sure he loves her. Darrin bumps into Samantha and wonders if he's delaying marrying Sheila and waiting for someone really *fantastic*. Back in the future, Darrin admits for once that Endora was helpful.

Twitch-Bits: Part 2 of 2. Also, in the "might have been" sequence, Larry hints that Darrin will soon become a full partner, and he looks to be sincere.

Scroll 128

Hippie, Hippie, Hooray
(2-1-68)

Scribe: Michael Morris

Overseer: William Asher

Sojourners: Ralph Story, Walter Sands, Jean Blake

Sam-Script: Serena, now the hippest of the hip, sings rock and roll and shakes up the Stephens household by pretending to be Samantha. To convince Larry that Serena is Sam's cousin, Darrin invites the Tates to see the two together. With the table set for five, Darrin admits defeat and is sorry about an earlier confrontation with Serena.

Twitch-Bits: There's no laugh track. A large point in the premise hinges on the fact that the Tates never met Serena, yet Larry met her in "Double, Double, Toil and Trouble, " and Louise met her in "That Was No Chick, That Was My Wife." Larry and Louise have breakfast in the "Tony Nelson" kitchen from *I Dream of Jeannie.* Just before a bridge game, Darrin suggests they all watch the Springer Pet Food commercial on TV. This is a reference to the client they landed in "That Was No Chick, That Was My Wife."

Scroll 129

A Prince of a Guy
(2-8-68)

Scribe: Ed Jurist

Overseer: R. Robert Rosenbaum

Sojourners: William Bassett, Louise Glenn, Stuart Margolin (*The Rockford File*s), Robert P. Lieb, Malda Severn, Steve Woodman, Gerald York

Sam-Script: Tabitha brings Prince Charming to life out of her storybook. Darrin's cousin Helen falls in love with the mythical character, while Ralph, her fiancé, isn't too crazy about the idea. Larry wants to hire Mr. Charming for TV spots. To help return the fictional royalty back to his fake history book, Sam conjures up an alluring Sleeping Beauty. Soon after, Helen and Ralph reunite.

Twitch-Bits: This non-Darrin episode as well as "A Bum Raps" are the only segments to feature Darrin's relatives, other than his parents.

Scroll 130

McTavish
(2-15-68)

Scribe: James Henerson

Overseer: Paul Davis

Sojourners: Reginald Owen, Ronald Long, R. N. Bullard

Sam-Script: Aunt Clara learns her old warlock boyfriend Ocky has opened an old castle in England. McTavish, an ancestral ghost, is ruining business by scaring the guests. Sam reluctantly agrees to help Ocky and suggests that McTavish find a more comfortable place to haunt. He does—her house. Ocky then learns that his castle visitors miss McTavish, who eventually returns to his old haunt.

Twitch-Bits: The ghost's first name is Kevin, and he's the Fifth Earl of Angus who's been haunting Lord Ockham's castle for five hundred years.

Scroll 131

How Green Was My Grass
(2-29-68)

Scribe: Ed Jurist

Overseer: R. Robert Rosenbaum

Sojourners: Richard X. Slattery, Barbara Perry, Joseph Perry, Andy Romano, Robert Lussier, Craig Hundley, Kevin Tate

Sam-Script: Darrin thinks Samantha has conjured up synthetic grass in the front yard. They have a fight. Neighbor Bill MacLane is wondering what happened to the artificial grass he ordered. Before everyone finds out that MacLane's plastic lawn was installed on the Stephenses' property by mistake, the angry neighbor accuses Darrin of pilfering it. MacLane raises his fist only to have Sam twitch it to the fence. She then zaps the proper lawns into position.

Twitch-Bits: Sam and Darrin's address was changed from 1164 Morning Glory Circle to 192. When Darrin slammed the door, the 9 flipped to a 6 and the artificial lawn (supplied by the real-life Monsanto Astro Turf) was delivered by mistake.

Scroll 132

To Twitch or Not to Twitch
(3-14-68)

Scribes: Lila Garrett, Bernie Kahn

Overseer: William Asher

Sojourners: Arthur Julian, Margaret Muse, Jean Blake, Donald Jouneaux

Sam-Script: On the way to a client's dinner party, Sam and Darrin argue about the use

Darrin has a tight fit in "To Twitch or Not to Twitch."

of her powers. It starts to rain. The car gets a flat tire. Sam refuses to help fix it. Darrin gets soaked and wears the client's too-small clothes at the party. Sam and Darrin continue their argument, prompting Sam to leave with Tabitha and go to Cloud Eight. Upon her return, she and Darrin make up.

Twitch-Bits: Writer Lila Garrett was married to partner Bernie Kahn, who went on to write for the *Tabitha* series.

Scroll 133

Playmates
(3-21-68)

....

Scribe: Richard Baer

Overseer: William Asher

Sojourners: Peggy Pope, Teddy Quinn

Sam-Script: Phyllis takes Samantha and Tabitha to visit the Millhowsers. Gretchen, the mother, loves to dabble in child psychology. Michael, the son, wishes he were a dog. Tabitha zaps him that way and turns the Millhowser household upside down. Samantha persuades her daughter to retransform Michael back to his original self.

Twitch-Bits: A non-Darrin segment.

Scroll 134

Tabitha's Cranky Spell
(3-28-68)

....

Scribe: Robert Riley Crutcher

Overseer: William Asher

Sojourners: J. Edward McKinley, Sara Seegar, Nellie Burt, Harry Harvey Sr.

Sam-Script: Louise's Aunt Harriet baby-sits for Tabitha. Larry hopes Sam can help persuade his client, Mr. Baker, to modernize his firm, which was established by Uncle Willie. Tabitha leads Aunt Harriet to believe that she's contacted her dead fiancé, Mr. Henderson. Sam impersonates and then meets the real ghost of Uncle Willie and convinces Mr. Baker to change his company's image. Back at her house, Sam assures Harriet that it was all a dream.

Twitch-Bits: Samantha wears the coat Darrin gave her in "Cheap, Cheap."

Scroll 135

I Confess
(4-4-68)

....

Scribe: Richard Baer

Overseer: Seymour Robbie

Sojourners: Woodrow Parfrey, Herb Ellis, Dick Wilson

Sam-Script: Sam uses witchcraft to fend off a man in the street. Darrin, thinking her only defense in life to be magic, gets angry and decides to end his opposition to her power usage. He's ready to tell the whole world that his wife is a witch. Sam doesn't think he means what he says. She uses a dream spell to show him what life would be like if everyone knew her secret.

Twitch-Bits: Dick Wilson's drunk asks Sam to come to his apartment.

Scroll 136

A Majority of Two
(4-11-68)

....

Scribe: Ed Jurist

Overseer: R. Robert Rosenbaum

Sojourners: Richard Hayden, Helen Funai

Sam-Script: Aunt Clara sets a low table, Japanese style, and pops herself and Samantha into geisha girl costumes to entertain client Kensu Mishimoto, whom Clara charms. She expects him to propose, which prompts Sam to locate Clara's boyfriend Ocky. Mr. Mishimoto feels humiliated and leaves abruptly. Samantha heads him off by allowing herself to lose face, literally. Mishimoto is startled and convinced to stay in Connecticut to finish business with McMann and Tate.

Twitch-Bits: This non-Darrin episode features an American actor (Richard Hayden) as an Asian character.

Scroll 137

Samantha's Secret Saucer
(4-18-68)

Scribes: Jerry Mayer, Paul L. Friedman

Overseer: Richard Michaels

Sojourners: Eldin Quick, Larry D. Mann, Steve Franken, Hamilton Camp

Sam-Script: Aunt Clara zaps a toy spaceship into the real thing, including live spacemen/dogs, Alpha and Orvis. Gladys spots the spacecraft and notifies the air force. Clara pops the aliens back to where they came from right before the air force arrives to inspect a UFO.

Twitch-Bits: In this last episode to feature Aunt Clara, Mrs. Kravitz becomes awfully sweet after a shot from Alpha's *N* Gun. Also, this is the first episode directed by Richard Michaels, and the first to cross fantasy with sci-fi. In a way, however, it doesn't make sense, because Aunt Clara zapped up a toy ship of Tabitha's, not a real ship from space; yet that's what it ended up being.

Scroll 138

The No-Harm Charm
(4-25-68)

Scribe: Ed Jurist

Overseer: Russell B. Mayberry

Sojourners: Vaughn Taylor, Susan Tolsky (*Here Come The Brides*), Paul Smith

Sam-Script: Darrin's brochure for the multi-million dollar Omega Bank mistakenly lists the bank's assets as $100. Larry suggests he take some time off. Darrin thinks he has Uncle Arthur's magic charm for protection. He sets out to salvage the Omega account. Sam learns that Arthur's charm is a fake, and ends up saving Darrin from several blunders. On his own, however, Darrin impresses Omega's Mr. Markham by disarming a robber, and saves the account for McMann and Tate.

Twitch-Bits, Darrin reads about his exploits in *The Daily Chronicle* headline story: "Adman Foils Bank Robber."

Scroll 139

Man of the Year
(5-2-68)

Scribe: John L. Greene

Overseer: R. Robert Rosenbaum

Sojourners: George Ives, Roland Winters (as Mr. McMann), Bill Quinn, Jill Foster, Byron Morrow.

Sam-Script: The Hucksters' Club names Darrin one of the advertising men of the year. Sam claims he won't be affected by such a title. Endora sets out to prove otherwise. She intensifies his likability quota so much that everyone who comes within a few feet of him is charmed. When he envisions himself as the president of another company, Sam realizes that her mother has been up to her old tricks.

Twitch-Bits: Mr. McMann won the first award, back in 1943. "I started the thing and elected myself," he says.

Scroll 140

Splitsville
(5-13-68)

Scribe: Richard Baer

Overseer: William Asher

Sojourners: Arthur Julian, Dort Clark, John J. Fox

Sam-Script: Gladys leaves Abner, and Samantha invites her to stay with her and Darrin. Darrin is not happy about the situation. Sam casts a spell over the butcher, Mr. Hogersdorf, who then falls for Gladys. Abner is jealous, and the Kravitz couple fall back into each other's arms.

Twitch-Bits: Remake of "Illegal Separation."

The Fifth Season (1968 to 1969)

Scroll 141

Samantha's Wedding Present
(9-26-68)

Scribe: Bernard Slade

Overseer: William Asher

Sojourners: Dick Wilson, Jack Griffin, Art Metrano

Sam-Script: Endora offers Sam a belated wedding gift, makes peace with Darrin, then literally shrinks him down to size. He crawls into a liquor bottle that is found by a drunk (who thinks Darrin's a leprechaun). The lush offers to free him for three wishes. The boozer takes him to Sam, who twitches up the requests.

Twitch-Bits: Features excellent special effects, similar to TV's *Land of the Giants*, and includes this revelation from Endora: "If I have to be saddled with a mortal for a son-in-law, I suppose he's as good as any." Yet, when a little Darrin threatens her with, "If you don't listen to me, I'll … ," she replies, "Yes, what will you do? Punch me in the knee?"

Scroll 142

Samantha Goes South for a Spell
(10-3-68)

Scribe: Ed Jurist

Overseer: William Asher

Sojourners: Jack Cassidy, Isabel Sanford (*The Jeffersons*), Clarke Gordon, Barbara Morrison

Sam-Script: Brunhilda, a jealous witch-wife of Serena's boyfriend, thinks Sam is the "other woman," and sends her back to New Orleans of 1868. Aunt Jenny takes Sam (who can't remember her identity) home to Rance, who immediately falls in love. In 1968, Serena sends Darrin back to rescue his wife. When he arrives, Sam doesn't recognize him and refuses a kiss, which Serena said would restore Sam's memory. Darrin duals with Rance, persuades Sam to pucker up, she remembers, and they return home.

Twitch-Bits: Tabitha begins to be spelled with an "I." We learn that Sam has a mole in the middle of her back. Jack Cassidy (father with Shirley Jones of actors David Cassidy and Shaun Cassidy) died in an apartment fire in the mid-1970s.

Scroll 143

Samantha on the Keyboard
(10-10-68)

Scribe: Richard Baer
Overseer: Richard Michaels
Sojourners: Jonathan Harris (*Lost In Space*), Fritz Feld, Arthur Adas, Gerald Edwards
Sam-Script: Endora transforms Tabitha into a virtuoso at the piano. Samantha accepts Darrin's challenge to learn how to play the mortal way. Sam's piano teacher, Mr. Monroe, hears Tabitha playing. He brings a world-famous conductor to hear the little witch play. The maestro becomes upset when, without the benefit of magic, Tabitha produces only noisy random chords. Sam finds a real child prodigy for the maestro and impresses Darrin by learning *Born Free* on the keyboard, minus the magic.
Twitch-Bits: Sam searches for talent Matthew Williams with this spell: "Piano child prodigy, if I am near you … Send vibrations so I can hear you … Youthful genius go on playing … I'm flying now and later paying." She finds him in the music room of University High School, which was erected in 1947. And, Tabitha plays a western swing version of *Turkey in the Straw* on the fiddle.

Scroll 144

Darrin, Gone and Forgotten
(10-17-68)

Scribes: Lila Garrett, Bernie Kahn
Overseer: William Asher
Sojourners: Mercedes McCambridge, Steve Franken
Sam-Script: Witch Carlotta holds Darrin captive. Apparently, eons before, Endora had promised Samantha to Carlotta's Juke. In order to have Darrin returned, Sam tells Carlotta that her marriage is a strain and consents to marry Juke. On the sly, Sam instructs Juke to defy his mother's overprotective ways. Carlotta sees that Juke has sided with Samantha, returns Darrin, and annuls her ancient agreement with Endora.
Twitch-Bits: Mercedes McCambridge, who played Carlotta, was also the voice of the devil in *The Exorcist* (1973).

Scroll 145

It's So Nice To Have a Spouse
Around the House
(10-24-68)

Scribes: Barbara Avedon
Overseer: William Asher
Sojourners: Fifi D'Orsay, Dick Wilson
Sam-Script: Samantha is meeting with the Witches Council. Darrin thinks Serena is Sam and takes her on a second honeymoon. At Moonthatch Inn, Serena is alarmed at Darrin's affectionate mood. Darrin becomes angry; he thinks his wife is a cold fish. Back home, Tabitha mentions

Uncle Arthur (Paul Lynde) jokes around with his favorite niece in "Samantha's French Pastry."

that she saw Serena. Darrin puts two and two together.

Twitch-Bits: We learn that there are eight members of the Witches' Council. Moonthatch Inn is said to be where Sam and Darrin spent their honeymoon, which doesn't match with the hotel suite in the pilot.

Scroll 146

Mirror, Mirror on the Wall
(11-7-68)

Scribes: Lila Garrett, Bernie Kahn
Overseer: Richard Michaels
Sojourners: Herb Voland, Sara Seegar
Sam-Script: Endora zaps Darrin into the most self-centered person in the world, just as Larry deals with the very conservative Hascomb account. At a Tate dinner party, Darrin and Sam arrive in dazzling outfits. Mrs. Hascomb is intrigued. She's won over by Sam's argument that the Hascomb organization should zero in on a younger

market. Endora removes the "vain" spell from Darrin, who Larry insists still dress wildly to attract more clients.

Twitch-Bits: Mrs. Hascomb's red pills are for tension; the white ones are for indigestion; the pink ones for neuritis and neuralgia.

Scroll 147

Samantha's French Pastry
(11-14-68)

Scribe: Richard Baer
Overseer: William Asher
Sojourners: Henry Gibson (*Laugh-In*), Dort Clark, J. Edward McKinley
Sam-Script: Uncle Arthur tries to make napoleons for dessert and instead zaps up Napoleon Bonaparte, whom Larry wants to be in a TV detergent commercial. Sam passes the dignitary off as her cousin from Paris, and later persuades His Eminence to muck up during the spot. Uncle Arthur doesn't know how to send Bonaparte back. Samantha casually utters the correct

incantation, and the Emperor and his clothes are gone.

Twitch-Bits: The boom man's reactions to witchcraft are identical to some of those used in "Bewitched, Bothered and Infuriated" by the hotel manager. Searching in vain for the right spell to send Napoleon back whence he came, Sam mutters, "Bat wings and lizard tails," and the little leader is history.

Scroll 148

Is It Magic or Imagination?
(11-21-68)

Scribe: Arthur Julian

Overseer: Luther James

Sojourners: Dick Wilson

Sam-Script: Darrin is depressed. Barton Industries uses one of Samantha's ideas for its diaper division. Sam leaves Darrin's portfolio, with his slogans enclosed, on Mr. Barton's desk. The Stephenses learn that a computer program has rejected Sam's campaign, which had been entered in a national contest. Darrin's confidence is restored.

Twitch-Bits: Writer Arthur Julian played clients in four episodes, and Hogersdorf the butcher in "Splitsville." Sam and Darrin's birdhouse-style sidewalk mailbox makes its one and only series appearance here.

Scroll 149

Samantha Fights City Hall
(11-28-68)

Scribe: Rick Mittleman

Overseer: Richard Michaels

Sojourners: Arch Johnson, Vic Tayback, Art Metrano, Dodo Denney, Barbara Perry, Jeff Burton, Garland Thompson, Robert Terry, Teddy Quinn

Sam-Script: A neighborhood playground is scheduled for destruction. A supermarket will replace it. Sam and her fellow housewives are upset. Darrin encourages her to organize a protest. He finds out the park is owned by Mr. Mossler, a client. Sam realizes Darrin's job is at stake. She withdraws from a rally to prevent bulldozers from destroying the park. Darrin insists she keep up the fight, even after Larry fires him. Sam brings to life the park's statue, which represents an ancestor of Mr. Mossler's, who decides not to destroy the park. Larry then gives Darrin back his job.

Twitch-Bits: Sam tells Darrin she has an appointment with her councilman on Tuesday, 2:30 P.M., in the year 1997, on April 15th, Elizabeth Montgomery's birthday. Mr. Mossler's shopping center contract is the Tolliver Construction Company. Also, this is the only time Diane Murphy plays Tabitha solely.

Scroll 150

Samantha Loses Her Voice
(12-5-68)

Scribes: Lila Garrett, Bernie Kahn

Overseer: William Asher

Sojourners: (None)

Sam-Script: Samantha comforts Louise, who's had a fight with Larry. Uncle Arthur switches the voices of Sam and Darrin, and they try to keep the Tates from discovering the mishap. After failed attempts, Arthur removes the spell, and Larry and Louise make up.

Twitch-Bits: Similar to "Out of Sync, Out of Mind."

Scroll 151

I Don't Want to Be a Toad,
I Want to Be a Butterfly
(12-12-68)

Scribe: Doug Tibbles

Overseer: Richard Michaels

Sojourners: Maudie Prickett, Maralee Foster, Lola Fisher, Art Metrano, Jean Gillespie, Paul Sorensen, Karl Lukas

Sam-Script: Phyllis enrolls Tabitha in the Delightful Day Nursery School, where she changes classmate Amy into a butterfly. Sam chases Amy, the insect, up a tree and a skyscraper before Tab changes her back. Teacher *Mrs. Burch* is exhausted from what she thinks she sees and ends up taking a long vacation.

Twitch-Bits: Sam tells Darrin of chaos at Tab's school and mixes him a progressively stronger drink until he finally tells her to finish the story after he passes out. The same gag is used in "Samantha's Better Halves," when Sam tries to explain how Darrin was zapped back and forth to Japan. A miniversion of the gag occurs in Act II of "School Days, School Daze," when Sam tells Darrin what happened at school during Tabitha's testing.

Scroll 152

Weep No More My Willow
(12-19-68)

Scribe: Michael Morris

Overseer: William Asher

Sojourners: Paul Sorenson, Sharon Vaughn, Vincent Perry, Jean Blake

Sam-Script: Dr. Bombay chants to restore Sam's ailing willow tree and makes it "weep" with every breeze. Sam gets caught in the fallout, and it's she who starts to cry every time the wind blows. Enough is enough. No more tears. Sam recalls Bombay, who reverses the spell. Darrin finds Sam with Larry (who thinks the Stephenses are having marital difficulties), and they start laughing uncontrollably. Sam's intense giggling is contagious. Bombay comes back again, halts the silliness, and restores the willow tree.

Twitch-Bits: The tree of the title was Sam's "very own Mother's Day present from Darrin, the day Tabitha was born."

Scroll 153

Instant Courtesy
(12-26-68)

Scribe: Arthur Alsberg

Overseer: R. Robert Rosenbaum

Sojourners: Herb Voland, Mala Powers, Jill Foster, Sharon Vaughn, Larry Barton

Sam-Script: Endora transforms Darrin into the perfect gentleman, who ends up impressing client Mrs. Sebastian. She offers to set Darrin up with his own agency, then suspects

Darrin's chivalry was a ploy to trick her into signing with McMann and Tate. Sam zaps her into changing her mind.

Twitch-Bits: As exampled with Mrs. Sebastian, *Bewitched* was one of the first TV programs to showcase a working woman in a position of power.

Scroll 154

Samantha's Super Maid
(1-2-69)

Scribes: Peggy Chantler Dick, Douglas Dick
Overseer: R. Robert Rosenbaum
Sojourners: Nellie Burt, Virginia Gregg, Nora Marlowe
Sam-Script: Phyllis persuades a hesitant Samantha to hire a maid. After many applicants are turned away, the sweet, good-hearted Amelia is chosen. Sam and Darrin know she can't stay, because of the supernatural state of affairs. Neither Sam nor Darrin can find the courage to let her go. Mrs. Otis, a friend of Phyllis's, may hold the answer. She needs a maid and decides to steal Amelia.
Twitch-Bits: Amelia is putting her son through college, which is something Naomi (played by Alice Ghostley) did in "Maid to Order," when Samantha "loaned" her to the Tates.

Scroll 155

Serena Strikes Again, Part 1
(1-9-69)

Scribe: Ed Jurist
Overseer: Richard Michaels
Sojourners: Nancy Kovak

Sam-Script: Sexy client Clio Vanita, who bottles wine, plays up to Darrin. Serena thinks the woman is out to make a fool of Samantha and makes a monkey out of Vanita. Darrin orders Serena to change Clio back and storms out of the house. Serena pops away and leaves the lady a chimp.

Twitch-Bits: One of the many episodes that addressed the world of primates.

Scroll 156

Serena Strikes Again, Part 2
(1-16-69)

Scribe: Ed Jurist
Overseer: Richard Michaels
Sojourners: Nancy Kovak, Cliff Norton, Richard X. Slattery, Bryan O'Byrne, Bobo Lewis, Ezekial Williams, Kathryn Harrow
Sam-Script: Serena returns, but Clio the monkey escapes and has adventures with a boy and his mother, an organgrinder, and the police. After Serena retransforms Clio, Sam presents the organgrinder to Ms. Vanita in Larry's office. There's a campaign in the making: "Don't monkey around with anything but the best. Drink Vino Vanita."
Twitch-Bits: Guest star Nancy Kovak played Darrin's ex-girlfriend, Sheila Sommers, in three previous episodes.

Scroll 157

One Touch of Midas
(1-23-69)

Scribes: Jerry Mayer, Paul Friedman
Overseer: Richard Michaels

Sojourners: Cliff Norton, Meg Wyllie, Jill Foster, Ed McCready, Jerry Rose, Cosmo Sardo, Bob Barr

Sam-Script: Endora's in the mood to do a favor. For Sam's sake, she helps Darrin by creating a foolproof marketing scheme featuring the Fuzz Doll, which automatically charms mortals. The Fuzz becomes amazingly successful. It looks as though Darrin will become a millionaire. He's ecstatic, and in a tender moment, promises Sam everything he was unable to give her before. At Sam's request, Endora removes the spell, and her daughter confirms a previous belief—she already has everything she wants.

Twitch-Bits: Sam and Darrin try to celebrate the sixth anniversary of their first date. Also, Cosmo Sardo, who was Darrin's hairstylist, worked in real life as the show's stylist.

Scroll 158

Samantha the Bard
(1-30-69)

Scribe: Richard Baer

Overseer: Richard Michaels

Sojourners: Larry D. Mann, Dick Wilson, Sara Seegar

Sam-Script: Sam finds herself involuntarily speaking in rhyme, uhm, all the time. She and Darrin are invited to dinner with the Tates, client Mr. Durfee, and his wife. Mr. Durfee has used jingles for years and is reluctant to change. Larry warns Sam to stop rhyming. Sam pages and pages for Dr. Bombay, who finally delivers an antidote. Sam is cured and makes an announcement:

She spoke in rhymes to prove how irritating they can be. Mr. Durfee is won over and requests Larry and Darrin to create a new campaign.

Twitch-Bits: Many of the phrases used by Samantha in this episode are very similar to those used by Mickey Rooney in *Operation Mad Ball*, a 1957 Columbia film which costarred Dick York.

Scroll 159

Samantha the Sculptress
(2-6-69)

Scribe: Doug Tibbles

Overseer: William Asher

Sojourners: Cliff Norton

Sam-Script: Darrin and Larry entertain a client at Morning Glory Circle, where Endora zaps up a couple of living clay busts of the two admen. Darrin and Sam argue over who's to blame for her mother's antics. Despite the lunacy, the client swiftly signs with McMann and Tate. Darrin offers his gratitude to his mother-in-law for helping seal the account. Endora is disgusted.

Twitch-Bits: This episode becomes eerie each time the clay busts speak.

Scroll 160

Mrs. Stephens, Where Are You?
(2-13-69)

Scribes: Peggy Chantler Dick, Douglas Dick

Overseer: Richard Michaels

Sojourners: Ruth McDevitt, Hal England

Sam-Script: Phyllis makes some catty remarks

about Sam and her family. Serena retaliates and turns Darrin's mom into a feline. A dog chases Mrs. Stephens, the cat, up a tree. Next-door neighbor Miss Parsons, a feline-lover, rescues the metamorphed Mrs. Stephens. While Serena entertains Darrin's dad, Sam searches and finds Phyllis, the mom-cat, and commands Serena to redo her thing.

Twitch-Bits: A non-Darrin episode.

Scroll 161

Marriage, Witches' Style
(2-20-69)

Scribe: Michael Morris
Overseer: William Asher
Sojourners: Lloyd Bochner, John Fiedler, Peter Brocco, Robert Terry, Cosmo Sardo
Sam-Script: Serena decides she wants to marry a mortal, and consults a computer dating service. She's matched with Franklyn Blodgett, who, unbeknownst to her, is also a supernatural seeking a mortal love. When both decide to reveal their true identities, a lifetime of wedded bliss is envisioned. That is, until Franklin belittles Serena's style of magic wave and compares it to a windmill.

Twitch-Bits: A non-Darrin episode.

Scroll 162

Going Ape
(2-27-69)

Scribes: Lila Garrett, Bernie Kahn
Overseer: Richard Michaels

Sojourners: Lou Antonio, Paul Smith, Gail Kobe, Gordon De Vol, Judy March, Diki Lerner, Elmer Modlin, Danny Bonaduce (*The Partridge Family*)
Sam-Script: Tabitha turns a chimp into a man named Harry. Client Evelyn Tucker names him as the model for her line of men's cologne. After posing all morning for commercials, Harry decides that being a man isn't any fun. But he's stuck in a contract, and the only way he can break it is to create havoc at the TV studio. No need to worry. Sam says it's all a planned stunt to launch Darrin's campaign based on wild emotions. Tabitha then turns Harry back to his old self.
Twitch-Bits: A non-Darrin episode which features guest star Lou Antonio, who directed Elizabeth Montgomery and Robert Foxworth in *Face to Face* for CBS-TV in 1990.

Scroll 163

Tabitha's Weekend
(3-6-69)

Scribes: Peggy Chantler Dick, Douglas Dick
Overseer: R. Robert Rosenbaum
Sojourners: (None)
Sam-Script: Phyllis is whining—she never gets to spend any time with Tabitha. Frank asks Sam if his granddaughter can spend the weekend with him and his wife. Sam hesitantly allows the visit, but Phyllis is still annoyed: Samantha comes along, as does Endora, who spurns arguments. Tabitha turns herself into a cookie because, as Endora explains it, she feels responsible for the discontent among the

adults. Sam convinces her daughter to de-cookie herself.

Twitch-Bits: In this non-Darrin episode, Mabel Albertson does the voice of Black Bart, the mynah bird owned by Phyllis Stephens.

Scroll 164

The Battle of Burning Oak
(3-13-69)

Scribes: Pauline and Leo Townsend

Overseer: R. Robert Rosenbaum

Sojourners: Harriet MacGibbon, Edward Andrews, Glenda Farrell, June Vincent, Doreen McLean, Mauritz Hugo, Harry Stanton

Sam-Script: Darrin is considered for membership in an exclusive club, he's enthusiastic about the prospect, and Endora changes him into a supersnob. Sam's luncheon with the ladies' screening committee doesn't go well. Endora 'fesses up, and to make up helps Samantha uncover some dirt about some snooty club members. As a result, the club's strict rules are relaxed.

Twitch-Bits: The Burning Oak Country Club dining room is "Tony Nelson's" living room from *I Dream of Jeannie*, totally redressed.

Scroll 165

Samantha's Power Failure
(3-20-69)

Scribes: Lila Garrett, Bernie Kahn

Overseer: William Asher

Sojourners: Ron Masak (*Murder, She Wrote*)

Sam-Script: The Witches' Council demands that Samantha sever her mortal tie to Darrin. She refuses, and her powers are revoked. Uncle Arthur and Serena side with her, and they, too, lose use of their witchcraft. To pass the time, Arthur and Serena get mortal jobs at an ice cream store, and the results are disastrous. Sam pleads before the council: They are just as ignorant as those who condemned the innocent of Old Salem who were accused of witchery. Soon after, Sam, Serena, and Uncle Arthur have their powers restored.

Twitch-Bits: A non-Darrin episode.

Scroll 166

Samantha Twitches for UNICEF
(3-27-69)

Scribe: Ed Jurist

Overseer: William Asher

Herb Voland as "Mr. Haskell" in "Samantha Twitches for UNICEF."

Sojourners: Herb Voland, Bernie Kopell (*The Love Boat*), Sharon Vaughn, Sara Seegar, Rosemary Eilot, Kay Elliot, Judy March, Frank Jamus, Jean Blake, Howard Dayton, Jack Griffin

Sam-Script: Sam spooks Mr. Haskell, a millionaire, into making good on his ten–thousand-dollar pledge to UNICEF. Larry thinks Haskell has problems with his very demanding fiancée, Lila. Sam joins forces with Endora, who bespells Lila into the admission of an affair with another man. Haskell ends his relationship with Lila and coughs up the ten grand.

Twitch-Bits: In this non-Darrin and first Bernie Kopell segment, Sara Seegar plays Mrs. Wehmeyer who refers to events in "Samantha Fights City Hall"; she hasn't seen Sam since she led the fight to save the park, and tells her "We need your help again."

Scroll 167

Daddy Does His Thing
(4-3-69)

Scribe: Michael Morris

Overseer: William Asher

Sojourners: Karl Lukas, Mercedes Moliner, Shiva Rozier, Jack Griffin

Sam-Script: Darrin refuses a magical lighter as a birthday gift from Maurice, who retaliates by turning his human son-in-law into a mule. Maurice flies to Paris, and Sam pops up to meet with him. Upon her return, she finds Darrin has been delivered to an animal shelter. Maurice relents and turns mule back to mortal.

Twitch-Bits: Maurice gifts Dick Sargent's Darrin with a magical amulet in "Daddy Comes for a Visit."

Scroll 168

Samantha's Good News
(4-10-69)

Scribe: Richard Baer

Overseer: Richard Michaels

Sojourners: Murray Natheson, Janine Gray

Sam-Script: Maurice pops in with a beautiful young witch named Miss Beachum who claims to be his secretary. Endora is rabid with jealousy, disappears, and returns with John Van Millwood, a warlock who, like Maurice, is a Shakespearean actor. Maurice and John face off in soliloquies. Endora comforts her husband and declares him the best. But that's nothing. Samantha makes an exciting revelation—she's going to have another baby.

Twitch-Bits: An original draft of this non-Darrin episode was entitled "Samantha and the Secretary." Miss Beacham was named *Lotus La Tourre*. And, Tabitha referred to her grandpapa as Grandpa Maurice. Samantha's pregnancy concurs with Elizabeth Montgomery's delivery of Rebecca Elizabeth on June 17, 1969, Erin and Diane Murphy's fifth birthday.

Scroll 169

Samantha's Shopping Spree
(4-17-69)

Scribe: Richard Baer

Overseer: Richard Michaels

Sojourners: Jack Snow (as himself), Herb Anderson, Steve Franken, Dave Madden, Herb Ellis, Jonathan Daly, Jack Collins, Robert Towers

Sam-Script: Samantha, Endora, Tabitha, and Cousin Henry go shopping. In a department store, Henry takes offense, turns a floor salesman into a mannequin, flies to the moon and refuses to change the dummy back. Endora and Sam attempt to right the wrong, but it's Tabitha who remembers the spell Henry used and reveals it to Endora.

Twitch-Bits: In this non-Darrin episode, we learn that Henry is apparently Uncle Arthur's son. The spell he uses is called the *Transcendental Triple.*

Scroll 170

Samantha and Darrin in Mexico City
(4-24-69)

Scribe: John L. Greene
Overseer: R. Robert Rosenbaum
Sojourners: Thomas Gomez, Victor Millan, Sharon Vaughn, Sandra Caruso
Sam-Script: Sam and Darrin fly to Mexico, where he will work with client Carlos Aragon on introducing his product to the American market. En route on the plane, Endora casts a spell upon Darrin that causes him to disappear every time he speaks Spanish. Sam has her mother remove the hex, but warns Darrin not to utter a Latin word. Endora makes a magic alteration: When he talks English, he vanishes. Sam improvises, and Darrin presents an oration at an ad luncheon with both Spanish and American guests.

Twitch-Bits: Last episode with Dick York.

The Sixth Season (1969 to 1970)

Scroll 171

Samantha and the Beanstalk
(9-18-69)

Scribe: Michael Morris
Overseer: Richard Michaels
Sojourners: Ronald Long, Bobo Lewis, Johnnie Whitaker (*Family Affair*), David "Deacon" Jones
Sam-Script: Tabitha is jealous of the expected new baby and switches places in a storybook with Jack of "Beanstalk" fame. Phyllis is miffed when Jack shows up in Sam and Darrin's living room. Sam zaps into the fairytale and looks for Tabitha who has, among other things, shrunk the fairytale's giant. Sam finds her daughter, whom she orders to return things to normal.

Twitch-Bits: Dick Sargent debuts as Darrin swinging a golf club. The night before, he and Samantha had settled on *James* or *Susan* as names for the baby. The "Romeo if it's a boy, Juliet if it's a girl" line in this scene is taken from similar dialogue in the *I Love Lucy* episode, entitled "Pregnant Women Are Unpredictable."

Scroll 172

Samantha's Yoo-Hoo Maid
(9-25-69)

Scribe: Ed Jurist
Overseer: William Asher
Sojourner: J. Edward McKinley
Sam-Script: Endora thinks Sam needs a maid and introduces her to the nervous-wreck witch, Esmeralda. Against Darrin's objection, Larry brings client Mr. Hampton over to look at some ad layouts. Esmeralda sneezes up a unicorn. Darrin incorporates it into Hampton Motors' new car campaign. Sam says Esmeralda will only visit when called.
Twitch-Bits: First Esmeralda appearance.

Scroll 173

Samantha's Caesar Salad
(10-2-69)

Esmeralda tosses up trouble with the Roman Empire and "Julius Caesar" (Jay Robinson) in "Samantha's Caesar Salad."

Jay Robinson in 1990.

Scribe: Ed Jurist
Overseer: William Asher
Sojourners: Jay Robinson, Herb Ellis, Joyce Easton, John Harmon, John J. Fox, Bart Carpinelli, Elizabeth Thompson
Sam-Script: Larry comes over to discuss ideas for a beauty account. In attempting to make a Caesar salad, Esmeralda instead conjures up Julius Caesar, and she can't send him back to Rome of old. Problem is, he doesn't want to return. On cue, Samantha zaps up Cleopatra as bait. Client Mrs. Charday, who markets beauty products, sees the two historic figures together and approves the slogan, "The Great Romances of History."
Twitch-Bits: Darrin comes up with this slogan: "Top Tiger—the reason why Cleopatra let Julius seize her." Sam's version: "Put a tiger in your toga."

Scroll 174

Samantha's Curious Cravings
(10-9-69)

Scribes: Fred Freeman, Lawrence Cohen

Overseer: Richard Michaels

Sojourners: William Schallert (*The Patty Duke Show*), Tommy Davis, John Lawrence

Sam-Script: Sam develops an unusual food problem: Whatever she thinks of or craves appears. Dr. Bombay offers a treatment, with unusual results: Instead of the food coming to Sam, she goes to it—like when she calls Darrin with a hot dog in her hand from the ballpark to which she's been whisked. Bombay confers with Dr. Anton, Sam's mortal obstetrician; they argue over the diagnosis. Sam soon returns home with a regular appetite.

Twitch-Bits: The first "Witch doctor? I wish you wouldn't call him that" exchange occurs here. Also, Samantha calls Darrin from a telephone at Shea Stadium. On the wall next to the phone is scribbled a heart which is inscribed *B.A. + E.M.* (Bill Asher and Elizabeth Montgomery).

Scroll 175

… And Something Makes Four
(10-16-69)

Scribe: Richard Baer

Overseer: Richard Michaels

Sojourners: Art Metrano, Pat Priest (*The Munsters*), Bobo Lewis, John Hiestand, Marguerite Ray, Kay Elliot, Gordon De Vol, Robert Gros, Stefani Warren

Sam-Script: Sam and Darrin have a boy, around whom Maurice casts a love spell, and everyone takes to the infant. Larry insists the baby is perfect for the Berkley Baby Foods label, and brings a camera crew to the hospital for a screen test. Endora arrives and tells Maurice the publicity will not please the Witches' Council. Maurice removes the hex.

Twitch-Bits: A pretty incantation is recited by Maurice: "Special baby, full of grace; so tiny and so new; whatever mortal sees your face, will fall in love with you." Also, Larry mentions his son, Jonathan.

Scroll 176

Naming Samantha's New Baby
(10-23-69)

Scribe: Ed Jurist

Overseer: William Asher

Sojourners: (None)

Sam-Script: Maurice is upset. His new grandchild will not be named after him. Instead, the baby will be named for his mortal grandfather, Frank Stephens, father to Darrin, whom Maurice then zaps into the Stephenses' hall mirror. Frank and Phyllis are astounded when they see their son's reflection in the looking glass. Sam tells them Maurice has created a new kind of photo mirror that retains images. During a money-making discussion regarding the invention, Frank and Maurice also bring up baby. Darrin offers a solution: He tricks Maurice into naming the baby Adam, a name Darrin says he dislikes but really prefers.

Twitch-Bits: Phyllis and Frank meet Maurice for the first time, though their dialogue upon entering indicates they all know each other.

Scroll 177

To Trick or Treat or Not to Trick or Treat
(10-30-69)

Darrin gets his due in "To Trick or Treat or Not to Trick or Treat."

Scribe: Shirley Gordon
Overseer: William Asher
Sojourners: Larry D. Mann, Paul Sorenson, Judy March, Jean Blake, Jeanne Sorel
Sam-Script: Darrin and Endora argue over the importance of Halloween, and she changes him into the stereotypical image of a witch: an old hag with warts and a big nose. Darrin apologizes to his mother-in-law; she leaves, and removes the spell. To help save an account, Darrin, Sam, and the kids go trick-or-treating for UNICEF, whose local chairperson happens to be a client. In a solemn moment, Endora realizes that millions of hungry children are more important than her magical whims.
Twitch-Bits: Samantha wears her flying suit when dressed as Glinda, the Good Witch from *The Wizard of Oz.*

Scroll 178

A Bunny for Tabitha
(11-6-69)

Scribe: Ed Jurist
Overseer: William Asher
Sojourners: Bernie Kopell, Carol Wayne (*The Tonight Show*), Dick Wilson, Danny Bonaduce, Joan Swift
Sam-Script: Uncle Arthur does a magic trick for Tabitha's birthday party; he conjures up a Playboy bunny instead of a rabbit. Client Mr. Sylvester falls for the bunny lady, and the two secretly exit the festivities. Sam and Uncle Arthur prove the two to be an unlikely couple. The next day, Sylvester is back with an old girlfriend and accepts Darrin's ideas.
Twitch-Bits: Guest star Carol Wayne drowned at forty-two years of age in 1985. Diane Murphy (twin of Erin) plays a party guest.

Scroll 179

Samantha's Secret Spell
(11-13-69)

Scribe: Ed Jurist
Overseer: Richard Michaels

Sojourners: Bernie Kopell, Jerry Rush, Jean Blake

Sam-Script: Darrin and Endora argue, and this time, if he doesn't apologize, she'll turn him into a mouse at midnight. To prevent such a development, Samantha consults with the witch-apothecary, who gives her a prescription she must fill without the assistance of witchcraft.

Twitch-Bits: In this remake of "We're in for a Bad Spell," Bernie Kopell makes his debut as Postlewaite, the Apothecary. And, this is one of three consecutive segments that contain an early scene in which Samantha cracks eggs into a bowl for breakfast.

Scroll 180

Daddy Comes for a Visit
(11-20-69)

Scribe: Rick Mittleman
Overseer: Richard Michaels
Sojourners: John Fiedler, J. Edward McKinley
Sam-Script: Darrin refuses a magic watch with which Maurice gives him in honor of Adam's birth. Maurice is patient and persuades his son-in-law to try the magic life if just for one day. The watch helps Darrin gather data regarding a prospective client. He's hooked on witchcraft, much to Samantha's dismay.

Twitch-Bits: In this first part of a two-part segment, Maurice gives Darrin a watch with magic powers; unlike the magic lighter in "Daddy Does His Thing," Darrin accepts Maurice's gift.

Scroll 181

Darrin, the Warlock
(11-27-69)

Scribes: Rick Mittleman, Ed Jurist
Overseer: Richard Michaels
Sojourners: J. Edward McKinley, John Fiedler, Irene Byatt
Sam-Script: Darrin's newfound powers have Samantha worried: He's enjoying his supernatural ways too much. But there's hope. One day at the office with Larry, he realizes the weakness of easy power, and returns the watch to Maurice. Minus the magic, he creates original ideas for a campaign, and Larry fires him. Darrin knows he'll be hired back, while he, Sam, and Maurice agree how suited he is for the mortal life.

Twitch-Bits: The magic phrase, "Zolda pranken kopek lum," used by Darrin as a warlock in this and the previous connecting segment, is the same one used by Bertha (Reta Shaw) in "The Witches Are Out." Sam's hairstyle changes from scene to scene during the first half of this episode (and in the opening of "How Not to Lose Your Head to Henry VIII," Part1).

Scroll 182

Samantha's Double Mother Trouble
(12-4-69)

Scribes: Peggy Chantler Dick, Douglas Dick
Overseer: David White
Sojourner: Jane Connell
Sam-Script: Esmeralda reads the story of Mother Goose to Tabitha. The manic maid

Samantha, "Mrs. Stephens" (Mabel Anderson), and "Mother Goose" (Jane Connell) in "Samantha's Double Mother Trouble."

sneezes, and out pops the famous fairy-tale mom herself. Phyllis arrives. She's left Frank. He comes to call for her, sees Mother Goose, and is charmed. Samantha is forced to employ the jealous-wife routine. Phyllis and Frank reunite. Esmeralda works on vaporizing Mother Goose, who does a slow fadeout before Mother Stephens's eyes.

Twitch-Bits: Sam's dialogue explaining the presence of Mother Goose to Darrin is almost verbatim to Lucy's explaining her overdrawn checking account to Ricky in the *I Love Lucy* segment, "The Business Manager."

Scroll 183

You're So Agreeable
(12-11-69)

Scribe: Ed Jurist

Overseer: Luther James

Sojourners: Charles Lane, J. Edward McKinley, Morgan Jones, Marion Madden, Sandra Kent, Bernie Kuby

Sam-Script: Darrin tries to be nice to Endora but still gets on her nerves; he's too agreeable. So she casts a spell which makes him overly amicable to everything and with everyone. As a yes-yes-yes man, Darrin loses his job. Endora reverses the spell. Now, he's disagreeable. Just as he's about to accept a new position, Sam makes her mom remove the conjuration.

Twitch-Bits: Spell dialogue abounds including: "A little Darrin or two makes a better Stephens, I always say," spoken by a waiter.

Scroll 184

Santa Comes To Visit and Stays and Stays
(12-18-69)

Scribe: Ed Jurist

Overseer: Richard Michaels

Sojourners: Ronald Long

Sam-Script: Tabitha's friend doesn't believe in Santa. Esmeralda sneezes up the eminent Mr. Claus. Sam succeeds in vamoosing Gladys and Larry and conjures up Santa's elves to help with toy making. What about that sleigh on the front lawn? Sam says it's a Christmas decoration and later convinces a scroogy Larry to purchase a much-desired mink for Louise, proving that Christmas is indeed a time of miracles.

Twitch-Bits: The color of this episode is particularly rich in hue.

Scroll 185

Samantha's Better Halves
(1-1-70)

Scribes: Lila Garrett, Bernie Kahn

Overseer: William Asher

Sojourners: Richard Loo (*Kung Fu*), Frances Fong, Debbie Wong

Sam-Script: Sam and Darrin recall a time when Endora literally split him in half: Darrin 1 takes care of Samantha and attends to her

every need; Darrin 2 talks business in Japan with Mr. Tanaka who, after much confusion, meets the complete Darrin.

Twitch Bits: This remake of "Divided He Falls" is the first episode Dick Sargent filmed and has the longest opening sequence in the series—seven minutes.

Scroll 186

Samantha's Lost Weekend
(1-8-70)

Scribe: Richard Baer

Overseer: Richard Michaels

Sojourners: Bernie Kopell, Pat Priest, Jonathan Hole, Merie Earle, Norman Klar

Sam-Script: Sam can't stop eating. She mistakenly drank a hexed glass of milk intended to assist Tabitha's poor appetite. With Dr. Bombay's help, she breaks the overeating habit but continually falls asleep. Bombay confers with Esmeralda, and the apothecary prescribes the proper antidote.

Twitch-Bits: Funny spell by Dr. Bombay: "By your disease, you won't be bested. Your symptoms are forthwith arrested," and "The results of my treatment shall fade away. Zippidee, do dah, zippidee yea." To which Darrin adds, "My, oh my, what a wonderful day."

Scroll 187

The Phrase Is Familiar
(1-15-70)

Scribe: Jerry Mayer

Overseer: Richard Michaels

Sojourners: Jay Robinson, Cliff Norton, Todd Baron

Sam-Script: Endora offers a triple dose of trouble: She causes Darrin to speak in clichés, and introduces Samantha and Darrin to a warlock tutor, who zaps up the Artful Dodger from *Oliver Twist*. What's worse, Larry threatens to fire Darrin if he doesn't come up with more original ideas for a campaign. After Darrin and client Mr. Sommers appear in New York Mets uniforms, Sam implements the pretend-it-all-never-happened plan.

Twitch-Bits: One of Dick Sargent's most physically animated performances as Darrin.

Scroll 188

Samantha's Secret Is Discovered
(1-22-70)

Scribes: Lila Garrett, Bernie Kahn
Overseer: William Asher
Sojourners: Bernie Kopell, Nydia Westman
Sam-Script: Phyllis thinks she's losing her mind: She sees Samantha and Endora work magic with the living room furniture. Sam decides it's time to tell her mother-in-law the truth. At first Phyllis is calm. When Frank arrives, she can't wait to spill the magic beans. Sam tries to tell her father-in-law, too. The Witches' Council intervenes, and strips Sam of her powers. Phyllis thinks she's gone off the deep end for sure and commits herself to a nursing home. Sam convinces Phyllis that she's been taking the wrong medicine—hallucinogens instead of tranquilizers.

Twitch-Bits: This segment is rarely seen today because of its drug-oriented storyline.

Scroll 189

Tabitha's Very Own Samantha
(1-29-70)

Scribe: Shirley Gordon
Overseer: William Asher
Sojourners: Sara Seegar, Parley Baer, Kay Elliot
Sam-Script: Tabitha is upset; she has to share Samantha with her new baby brother. So she creates her "very own mother"; one who gives her undivided attention. Of course, a disastrous dinner party supervenes with both "Mother Sams" and a client from McMann and Tate. Then Gladys encounters the duplicate Sam with Tabitha at the park. Samantha eventually persuades her daughter to zap away the clone-mommy and professes to Tabitha how equal her love is for both children.

Twitch-Bits: Hagatha takes over for Esmeralda, who "went south for the Galactic Rejuvenation and Dinner Dance." And, no cast credit is offered for the actor who played the Ferris wheel operator.

Scroll 190

Super Arthur
(2-5-70)

Scribe: Ed Jurist
Overseer: Richard Michaels
Sojourners: Paul Smith, Bernie Kuby, Spence Wil-Dee
Sam-Script: Darrin has had it. Uncle Arthur is popping in and out and then breaking every mirror in the house. Sam sees a problem and calls Dr. Bombay. A pill is prescribed, but it

Serena raps with music manager (Art Metrano) about booking Boyce & Hart (playing themselves) to sing at the Cosmos Cotillion in "Serena Stops the Show."

has dreadful side effects: Everything Arthur concentrates upon, comes true—like when he thinks he's Superman. Soon "Super Arthur" begins to fly around the neighborhood. Darrin and Larry drive up, and Sam says it's all a stunt to promote an account.

Twitch-Bits: A *Superman* costume was specifically made for Paul Lynde.

Scroll 191

What Makes Darrin Run
(2-12-70)

Scribes: Lila Garrett, Bernie Kahn
Overseer: William Asher
Sojourners: Leon Ames (as Mr. McMann), Arch

Johnson, Jeanne Sorel, Jerry Rush

Sam-Script: Endora has ambitions. She casts a spell over Darrin, which makes him overly enterprising. So much so, he tries to undermine Larry's position in the firm. Endora reverses her curse, leaving Darrin to restore Mr. McMann's faith in Larry.

Twitch-Bits: The second and last time Mr. McMann appears.

Scroll 192

Serena Stops the Show
(2-19-70)

Scribe: Richard Baer
Overseer: Richard Michaels

Sojourners: Tommy Boyce and Bobby Hart (as themselves), Art Metrano, Jeff Burton, Judy Strangis, Cindy Malone, Pandora Spocks

Sam-Script: Serena is chairperson for the Cosmos Cotillion, a witches' annual dinner dance. She wants to hire the singing duo, Boyce and Hart, who also happen to be clients of McMann and Tate. She approaches the performers, they decline, she makes with the magic, and no one cares about them anymore. Desperate for business, they now comply with Serena's request. After they finish their act, Samantha demands Serena to send them back to Earth, with their success restored.

Twitch-Bits: In this first segment with the "Pandora Spocks" credit listing, the names on the Boyce and Hart backstage pass list include: Jerry Hyams, John Mitchell, Len Goldberg, and Serena. Steve Trainer's name was crossed off the list.

Scroll 193

Just a Kid Again
(2-26-70)

Scribe: Jerry Mayer

Overseer: Richard Michaels

Sojourners: Ron Masak, Richard Powell, Pat Priest, Lindsay Workman

Sam-Script: Irving Bates, a department store salesman, has delusions of childhood. To help him focus on his vision, Tabitha turns him into the nine-year-old version of himself. Sam finds out and orders her daughter to reverse the curse, but she can't: Irving is enjoying his newfound youth, thus the

incantation is useless. Sam finds someone who will make Irving change his mind: his very grown-up girlfriend.

Twitch-Bits: Remake of *Junior Executive.*

Scroll 194

The Generation Zap
(3-5-70)

Scribe: Ed Jurist

Overseer: William Asher

Sojourners: Melodie Johnson, Arch Johnson (no relation)

Sam-Script: Endora makes Dusty Harrison, daughter of a client from McMann and Tate, fall in love with Darrin. Sam becomes jealous and Dusty's father cancels his contract with the firm. Endora removes the spell, and Sam and Darrin learn from a TV newscast that Mr. Harrison has been indicted for embezzlement.

Twitch-Bits: Partial remake of *The Girl Reporter.*

Scroll 195

Okay, Who's the Wise Witch?
(3-12-70)

Scribe: Richard Baer

Overseer: Richard Michaels

Sojourners: (None)

Sam-Script: Sam's non-use of powers is a problem again. A vapor lock seals herself, Darrin, Endora, Esmeralda, and Dr. Bombay in the house. There's a solution, but Bombay must work outdoors. Sam takes his picture, and slides it underneath the front door. Bombay returns to full size, and incants a spell that frees up the house and everyone in it.

Twitch-Bits: Endora references a popular song of the time: "To rescue my daughter, who married a buffoon, up, up and away in my beautiful balloon." Sam transforms her family's doctor: "To make this house again conventional, let Dr. Bombay be three-dimensional." Before that, Bombay says outside: "Heed my solution … to air pollution—obey the doc—vanish vapor lock." In a rare display of affection for Darrin, Endora says: "Samantha, what would your husband do without us?"

Scroll 196

A Chance on Love
(3-19-70)

Scribe: John L. Greene

Overseer: Richard Michaels

Sojourners: Jack Cassidy, Molly Dodd, Pandora Spocks, Bernie Kuby

Sam-Script: Debonair client Mr. Dinsdale falls for Serena. He thinks she's Sam, who tells Serena to come clean. Dinsdale doesn't listen but removes Darrin from his account. Then he sees Sam with Serena, places Darrin back on contract, later sings a little bit of *Fly Me to the Moon*, and actually goes there via "Serena Air."

Twitch-Bits: A mirrored double image of Jack Cassidy prefigures the Sam/Serena mistaken identity plotline, which ultimately sees Cassidy turned into a parrot. In a series oddity, this episode is a remake of "It Shouldn't Happen to a Dog," and was redone itself as "Serena's Richcraft."

Scroll 197

If the Shoe Pinches
(3-26-70)

Scribe: Ed Jurist

Overseer: William Asher

Sojourner: Henry Gibson

Sam-Script: Endora sends a little leprechaun to make big trouble for Darrin, who has his nose grown and is zapped with large, floppy donkey ears. The mean, green tiny man gives Sam's mortal love with a pair of mint shoes that make Darrin lazy. Sam halts the madness by concocting a potion to gain control over small gnomes from Ireland.

Twitch-Bits: Sam's brew: "To one cup of wolfsbane, add two tablespoons of maidenfern, chopped finely, and the beaten yolks of two eggs of a red-eyed kilia bird. Add salt and pepper to taste. Now, zap up one chicken with vegetables and boil in water till tender. This is chicken soup (a favorite of leprechauns). Put potion in soup. Serves four."

Scroll 198

Mona Sammi
(4-2-70)

Scribe: Michael Morris

Overseer: William Asher

Sojourners: (None)

Sam-Script: Larry and Louise see a Mona Lisa–type painting of Sam. The Stephenses claim Darrin to be the artist. The portrait is really a gift from Endora, who says it's a likeness of Sam's grandaunt Cornelia. Louise asks Darrin if he would create an image of her. That night at the Tates, while Sam and Larry play a sordid game of gin, she instills Darrin with artistic talent. He's creating a Louise masterpiece until Endora pops in and counterzaps his hands into rendering an unsightly vision. After many tears and much confusion, Sam and Darrin gift Louise with a more flattering semblance.

Twitch-Bits: The second time Leonardo da Vinci was referenced in the series (the first was in "Samantha's da Vinci Dilemma"); and Mona Lisa was referenced three times (here, in "Dilemma," and in "Eye of the Beholder").

Scroll 199

Turn on the Old Charm
(4-9-70)

Scribe: Richard Baer
Overseer: Richard Michaels
Sojourners: John Fiedler
Sam-Script: Samantha may have something Darrin really could use—a magic amulet to alter Endora courteous in his presence. Endora discovers the charm and punishes her son-in-law and daughter, both of whom she zaps into constant bicker banter. The Stephenses' frequent fury doesn't sit well with Larry or client Mr. Sunshine, who owns a greeting card company. Endora removes the spell, and Sam presents a unique way to market cards: Employ insults instead of poetry.

Twitch-Bits: Sam warns Darrin about Endora finding out about the magic amulet: "*Le'enfer n'a aucune furie comme une sorciere microbee,*" which means, "Hell hath no fury like a bugged witch."

Scroll 200

Make Love, Not Hate
(4-16-70)

Scribe: Ed Jurist
Overseer: William Asher
Sojourners: Sara Seegar, Charles Lane, Cliff Norton
Sam-Script: Dr. Bombay formulates a potion to help Esmeralda find a man. Sam and Darrin throw a dinner party. She accidentally pours the love brew into some clam dip. The results are not pretty. A warlock falls for Sam, a client's wife has eyes for Larry, and the once-shy-around-Darrin Esmeralda can't keep away from Sam's mortal love. After a long night, an antidote is compounded and not soon enough.

Twitch-Bits: Sam asks Darrin to "Tell Larry if I have to make one more dinner for a client, I want to go on the payroll."

The Seventh Season (1970 to 1971)

Scroll 201

To Go or Not To Go, That Is the Question
(9-24-70)

Scribe: Michael Morris
Overseer: William Asher
Sojourners: Jane Connell
Sam-Script: Endora tries to warn her, but Samantha refuses to attend a witches' convention in Salem unless Darrin is allowed to come with her. Hepzibah, high priestess of all witches, is enraged. She pops in and

Samantha and Darrin feel the earth move, courtesy of Hepzibah in "To Go or Not to Go, That Is the Question."

dethrones Darrin in his own home, where the royal sorceress learns to tolerate the mortal's presence. She opts to observe the mixed marriage rather than dissolve it, as she had originally planned.

Twitch-Bits: In this first part of a two-part segment, we would have learned that High Priestess Hepzibah is aunt to Countess Piranha (of "Serena's Richcraft"), but this was deleted from the aired version. Endora displays unusual affection for Darrin when she says to Hepzibah: "He loves my daughter."

Scroll 202

Salem, Here We Come
(10-1-70)

Scribe: Michael Morris
Overseer: William Asher

Sojourners: Jane Connell, Cesar Romero, Ray Young
Sam-Script: While invisible, Hepzibah observes Darrin's every move at McMann and Tate. She takes a liking to client Ernest Hitchcock, who owns an airline. She believes him to be a vastly superior mortal and begins to date him. Employing this development to her advantage, Sam persuades Hepzibah to grant Darrin permission to travel to Salem.
Twitch-Bits: Part 2 of 2.

Scroll 203

Salem Saga
(10-8-70)

Scribe: Ed Jurist
Overseer: William Asher
Sojourners: Jack Griffin, Nancy Priddy, Joan Hotchkiss, Irene Byatt, Maggie Malooley, T. J. Halligan, Etienne Viazie, Dick Wilson, Richard X. Slattery, Ron Masak, Maureen McCurry
Sam-Script: Sam and Darrin tour the House of Seven Gables in Salem. A spooked bed warmer begins to follow them. It takes a particular liking to Sam but despises Darrin. Sam tries to find out more about the haunted antique. She pulls it aside, begins to talk to it, and puzzles the tour guide. The bed warmer follows Sam and Darrin to their hotel room, and Darrin is accused of theft.
Twitch-Bits: We learn that there will be another Witches' Convention in approximately one hundred years.

Scroll 204

Sam's Hot Bed Warmer
(10-15-70)

Scribe: Ed Jurist

Overseer: William Asher

Sojourners: Joan Hotchkiss, Dick Wilson, Noam Pitlik, Richard X. Slattery, Ron Masak, Virginia Hawkins, Jack Wells, Bill Zuckert

Sam-Script: Darrin sits in jail. He and Sam are desperate for answers about the bed warmer. The contraption is really a warlock named Newton who once had the "hots" for Serena (who had transformed him years before). Sam calls upon her cousin to review the steps leading up to the metamorphosis. Serena goes back in time to old Salem where she meets Newton, whom she transforms to protect him from witch-hunters. Upon her return to the present, Serena recalls how to release Newton, while Darrin is sprung from jail.

Twitch-Bits: The Witches' Convention is officially known as *The Centennial Convocation of the Witches of the World.*

Scroll 205

Darrin on a Pedestal
(10-22-70)

Scribe: Bernie Kahn

Overseer: William Asher

Sojourners: Robert Brown, John Gallaudet, Dick Wilson, Pandora Spocks, Wallace Rooney, Jud Strunk, Victoria Thompson

Sam-Script: Serena's aghast with Darrin in Gloucester, Massachusetts, so she turns him to stone; actually, a statue, with which she replaces the image of the famed Helmsman, whom she brings to life. Larry sees too close a similarity between Darrin and the new statue (because Darrin *is* the new statue). Sam persuades Serena to defreeze her husband and resolidify the Helmsman figure, with whom Serena has been gallivanting.

Twitch-Bits: Robert Brown is best known from TV's *Here Come the Brides*, which also featured fellow *Bewitched* guest star Bridget Hanley, who was married to the late E. W. Swackhamer (who directed episodes of *Bewitched* and *Brides*).

Scroll 206

Paul Revere Rides Again
(10-29-70)

Scribes: Philip and Henry Sharp

Overseer: Richard Michaels

Sojourners: Bert Convy, Jonathan Harris, Parley Baer, Ron Masak, Jud Strunk, Jack Naughton, Lew Horn, Dorothy Love

Sam-Script: A classic Paul Revere teapot has mistakenly appeared in Connecticut. Sam asks Esmeralda to return it to Salem. You guessed it, Esmeralda instead zaps up Paul Revere, the historical icon, in the Stephenses' hotel room. Darrin's not too happy, as client Sir Leslie Bancroft will soon pay a visit. Sir Leslie sees Mr. Revere and his horse. Darrin convinces Leslie that the silversmith patriot and his animal friend are party to campaign.

Twitch-Bits: Bert Convy died of brain cancer in 1991.

Scroll 207

Samantha's Bad Day in Salem
(11-5-70)

Scribe: Michael Morris

Overseer: William Asher

Sojourners: Hal England, Anne Seymour, Bernie Kuby

Sam-Script: Sam and Darrin's marriage is threatened by Waldo, a childhood love who still pants for her. Sam rejects his affections. He zaps up a robotlike Sam replica. Larry sees the Sam clone and believes the Stephenses are on the verge of separation. Waldo turns Darrin into a crow and almost does the same to Larry. Sam saves the day by saying the robot was Serena.

Twitch-Bits: Darrin says this is his first vacation in four years, but he and Sam went to the Caribbean in "Samantha's Better Halves," and there was another trip in "What Makes Darrin Run?" We learn that the office of *The Resident Witch of Salem* was established in 1692 by High Priestess Hepzibah.

Scroll 208

Samantha's Old Salem Trip
(11-12-70)

Scribe: Ed Jurist

Overseer: Richard Michaels

Sojourners: Ronald Long, James Westerfield, Maudie Prickett, Joseph Perry, Martin Ashe

Sam-Script: The Stephenses return to Connecticut, but Esmeralda thinks Sam should have stayed in Salem, so she sends her back in time; that is, Sam ends up in sev-enteenth-century Salem. Her only hope is Darrin, whom Endora zaps to the past, where Sam doesn't recognize him (he hasn't been born yet). He writes her a note with a modern ballpoint pen, and he's accused of witchery. He remembers Endora's instruction to restore Sam's memory, and they come back to the future.

Twitch-Bits: The magic phrase, "*Ahmeo talu varsi lupin,*" means "good luck" in ancient Babylonian.

Scroll 209

Samantha's Pet Warlock
(11-19-70)

Scribe: Jerry Mayer

Overseer: Richard Michaels

Sojourners: Edward Andrews, Noam Pitlik, David Huddleston

Sam-Script: Ashley is Sam's egotistical former warlock boyfriend, who tries to persuade her into running away with him. She, of course, rejects his amorous pursuits, and he turns himself into a dog. The warlock/animal initially upsets Darrin—and his chances with Mr. Gibbons, a dog-food client. But Ashley comes around, and helps Darrin win the account.

Twitch-Bits: Ashley says upon meeting Darrin: "You must be Durwood." Darrin: "The name is Darrin." Ashley: "Then why does everybody call you Durwood?"

Scroll 210

Samantha's Old Man
(12-3-70)

Scribe: Michael Morris

Overseer: Richard Michaels

Sojourners: Ruth McDevitt, Edward Platt, Hope Summers, Joe Ross

Sam-Script: Endora won't ever give up. She still thinks Sam's mortal marriage is temporary. So she turns Darrin into a seventy-three-year-old man. Larry and Louise come over, and Darrin is introduced as his grandfather, Grover Stephens. Louise automatically plays matchmaker and sees a perfect couple in Grover and her Aunt Millicent. After a horrendous outing with Darrin/Grover, Samantha, Larry, Louise, and Millicent, Endora restores Darrin's youth. But not before Samantha tells Darrin how she will grow old alongside him, the mortal way.

Twitch-Bits: Makeup artist Rolf Miller was nominated for an Emmy for his work in this episode. Along with guest actor Janos Prohaska (who appeared incognito in many episodes, such as "The Truth, Nothing but the Truth, So Help Me Sam," as the dodo bird), Miller died in a horrific plane crash while en route to film David Wolper's "Primal Man" series.

Scroll 211

The Corsican Cousins
(12-10-71)

Scribe: Ed Jurist

Overseer: Richard Michaels

Sojourners: Barbara Morrison, Ann Doran, Robert Wolders, Jerry Rush

Sam-Script: Sam's so down-to-earth. She has no interest in joining a private club suggested by one of Darrin's clients. Endora thinks she should be more fun-loving; you know, like Serena. Sam vetoes that idea, too. So her mother casts a Corsican Brothers–type spell on the cousins. Sam experiences everything Serena does, and vice versa. That spells trouble, especially when a club member (and client of McMann and Tate's) stops by to inspect the Stephenses' home life and finds Samantha behaving somewhat bizarrely. Endora removes the act-alike hex.

Twitch-Bits: Darrin tells Larry that Sam is a witch, but Larry doesn't believe him. Sam tells the ladies that Tabitha is an international name. Sam tells Darrin that witches don't have psychiatrists. Endora claims that a country club is "just a meeting place for organized mortal snobs," and gives Serena "witches' joy juice."

Scroll 212

Samantha's Magic Potion
(12-17-70)

Scribe: Shirley Gordon

Overseer: William Asher

Sojourners: Charles Lane

Sam-Script: Darrin is experiencing a slump at work. Is it because of Endora? Sam tricks him with a bogus confidence-building potion. After winning over a grouchy client, Darrin realizes that it isn't any fun to be the master of every situation. Sam tells him the

Dr. Bombay assists Sam and Darrin in "Samantha's Magic Potion."

truth. He won the account on his own, without the aid of witchcraft.

Twitch-Bits: Semiremake of "Help, Help, Don't Save Me," which is redone all the way as "A Good Turn Never Goes Unpunished."

Scroll 213

Sisters at Heart
(12-24-70)

Scribes: The Tenth Grade English Class, Thomas Jefferson High School of Los Angeles, 1970; Barbara Avedon, William Asher

Overseer: William Asher

Sojourners: Don Marshall, Janee Michelle, Parley Baer, Venetta Rogers

Sam-Script: It's Christmastime, and Tabitha and her new friend Lisa, who happens to be black, wish they could be sisters. Tabs tries to remedy the problem, but ends up twitching black polka dots on herself and white spots on Lisa. Sam calls Dr. Bombay.

Mr. Brockway, a client, is on his way over to make sure Darrin runs a tight ship. Brockway shows his true colors: He's a bigot, and Sam decides to teach him a lesson. She later convinces Tabitha and Lisa that they don't have to look like each other to be sisters.

Twitch-Bits: This script was the recipient of the Governor's Award at the Emmys in 1971, and was Elizabeth Montgomery's favorite episode. Here are the names of the tenth grade English class of Jefferson High School (1970) who wrote this episode: Sandra Black, Eddie Brown, Burles Cook, Patricia Don, Larry Freeman, Bobby Harris, Carliss Henderson, Harold Henry, James Higdon, Matie Huddleston, Deborah Janise, Angila Thomas, Donnie Wallace, Ronnie Wallace, Glenn Williams, Jo Williams, Bruce Woods, Annette Johnson, Wayman Jones, Orall Joseph Jr., Stephen Kirk, Glenda Petty, Robert Radall, Gail Smith, Carmella Stuckey, Tanya Sweed.

Scroll 214

Mother-In-Law of the Year
(1-14-71)

Scribes: Philip and Henry Sharp

Overseer: William Asher

Sojourners: John McGiver, Jim Lange (*The Dating Game*), Robert Q. Lewis

Sam-Script: Endora, a TV spokesperson? Mother-in-law of the year? Apparently so. She's promoting herself as the ideal candidate for the Bobbins Candy Company in a commercial campaign headed by Darrin.

But when she fails to show up for a shoot, Sam impersonates her. Endora is infuriated and pops up alongside Sam's mother-image during filming. Everyone at the studio is seeing double. Darrin sees red. The answer? The commercial has excellent special effects.

Twitch-Bits: During the Bobbins Bon Bons commercial sequence, Henry Mancini's song, *The Sweetheart Tree,* is heard on the sound track.

Scroll 215

Mary the Good Fairy
(1-21-71)

Scribe: Ed Jurist
Overseer: William Asher
Sojourners: Imogene Coca (*Your Show of Shows*), Ricky Powell
Sam-Script: Tabitha loses a tooth, and Mary, the Good Fairy, an old friend of Sam's, swoops by. Sam and Mary reminisce about past lives as the Good Fairy tries to beat a cold she contracted while flying over a wheat field. To warm up a bit, Mary requests a shot of brandy, sips a little too much, and Sam ends up collecting teeth in Mary's place.
Twitch-Bits: In this first part of a two-part episode, the Reducealator stock number is X13-14Z, Model B. "Stephens will pick up" is written on the carton.

Scroll 216

The Good Fairy Strikes Again
(1-28-71)

Scribe: Ed Jurist
Overseer: William Asher
Sojourners: Imogene Coca, Vic Tayback, Herb Voland, Paul Smith
Sam-Script: "Samantha, the Good Fairy" tires of donning wings and nightly visits to toothless children and persuades Mary to return to the job. Meanwhile, Darrin is working on a slogan for the Reducealator, a contraption that Sam uses to cover her wings. Mary decides this is no way to treat her sacred wardrobe, and returns to her fairy duties, but not before helping Darrin win the account.
Twitch-Bits: Part 2 of 2.

Scroll 217

The Return of Darrin the Bold
(2-4-71)

Scribe: Ed Jurist
Overseer: Richard Michaels
Sojourners: David Huddleston, Gordon Jump (*WKRP in Cincinnati*), Richard X. Slattery, Burt Mustin, Allen Emerson, Nada Rowand, Pandora Spocks
Sam-Script: Endora and Serena decide to transform Darrin into a warlock and retrieve a potion from a wise old supernatural. Serena journeys back to fourteenth-century Ireland, plucks the beard of Darrin's ancestor, and mixes a sample of his hair into the formula. Back in the future, Darrin

Dick Sargent plays Darrin's ancestor when Elizabeth's Serena goes back in time in "Return of Darrin the Bold."

starts wishing things away, including the bush of next-door neighbor Mr. Ferguson. Samantha learns of the Endora/Serena plan, returns to the past, and sets things straight.

Twitch-Bits: In this quasi-sequel to "A Most Unusual Wood Nymph," thinking Sam is Serena in a blonde wig, Darrin the Bold says: "I like what you did to your hair. 'Tis a well-known fact, blondes have more fun."

Scroll 218

The House That Uncle Arthur Built
(2-11-71)

Scribe: Bernie Kahn
Overseer: Richard Michaels
Sojourners: Edward McKinley, Barbara Rhoades, Ysabel MacCloskey, Pandora Spocks
Sam-Script: Uncle Arthur has a new girlfriend named Aretha, and she's one snobby witch who disdains his practical jokes. To retain her affections, Arthur transfers all of his shenanigans into Sam and Darrin's home. The results are extremely annoying, as when a boxing glove, levitating in midair, gives Larry a right hook, or when a bunch of monkeys unsettles a client and his wife in the living room. Sam convinces Uncle Arthur that Aretha is not worth the effort and persuades him to restore the house to normal.
Twitch-Bits: The last episode with Uncle Arthur.

Scroll 219

Samantha and the Troll
(2-18-71)

Scribes: Lila Garrett, Joel Rapp
Overseer: William Asher
Sojourners: Robert Cummings, Nan Martin, Felix Silla, Pandora Spocks, Diane Murphy (as *Raggedy Ann*)
Sam-Script: Sam goes in for a 10,000-zap checkup, and Serena takes her place at home. Darrin fails to derail a party with Larry and hair tonic client Mr. Berkley. Serena brings Tabitha's toys to life. Sam returns and introduces a troll as Harry, whom Berkley assumes to be part of Darrin's campaign.
Twitch-Bits: One of the toys brought to life by Serena is The Fuzz Doll from "One Touch of Midas."

Scroll 220

This Little Piggie
(2-25-71)

Scribe: Ed Jurist

Overseer: Richard Michaels

Sojourners: Herb Edelman, Ysabel MacCloskey, Ann Doran, Allen Jenkins

Sam-Script: Endora thinks Darrin is being pig-headed, so she makes him indecisive and literally gives him the head of a pig—all of which happens at a most inopportune time. Client Colonel Brigham (who specializes in spareribs) is on his way over to the house with Larry. Endora zaps Darrin atop the roof. Samantha has to think quick. She explains that Darrin is modeling a new way to market ribs for Brigham, who goes hog-wild for the idea.

Twitch-Bits: Herb Edelman starred with Bob (*Gilligan's Island*) Denver in *The Good Guys* and later played Bea Arthur's ex-husband on *The Golden Girls*.

Scroll 221

Mixed Doubles
(3-4-71)

Scribe: Richard Baer

Overseer: William Asher

Sojourners: Natalie Core, Mitchell Silberman

Sam-Script: Sam spends a restless night worrying about Louise, who thinks she may be having trouble with Larry. The next day, Sam finds herself in bed with Mr. Tate, while Mrs. Tate is under the covers with Darrin. Larry sees Sam as Louise; Darrin sees Louise as Sam, who's the only one who sees through the confusion. Dr. Bombay is summoned; the real Stephenses invite the disembodied Tates over for a small party. Bombay makes a diagnosis. The quandary has been caused by something called a *dream inversion*, for which he provides a remedy.

Twitch-Bits: Dr. Bombay's antidote incantation goes like this: "Molecules return to their former states, mates return to their former mates, and let Larry and Louise in mortal density, not recall their mistaken identity."

Scroll 222

Darrin Goes Ape
(3-11-71)

Scribes: Leo and Pauline Townsend

Overseer: Richard Michaels

Sojourners: Ysabel MacCloskey, Jack Wells, Pandora Spocks, Paul Smith, Sidney Clute, Herb Vigran, Allen Jenkins, Milton Selzer, Janos Prohaska

Sam-Script: Serena impersonates Samantha and transmutes Darrin into a gorilla who runs amok in the neighborhood. Gladys calls the police, who notifies Johnson's Jungle Isle. Samantha rescues her husband just as a female gorilla named Tillie goes ape for Darrin.

Twitch-Bits: The show's worst episode.

Scroll 223

Money Happy Returns
(3-18-71)

Scribe: Milt Rosen

Overseer: Richard Michaels

Sojourners: Arch Johnson, Allen Jenkins, Karl Lukas, Mitchell Silberman

Sam-Script: Darrin finds in a taxi one thousand dollars, which he thinks Endora has zapped up as a gift. She denies it. He doesn't believe her. He fights with Samantha, who leaves him. Upon her return, Sam finds Darrin in trouble with the thieves who stashed their loot in the cab. Larry comes over, and while he thinks Darrin's negotiating with a rival ad firm, Sam outsmarts the bad guys, whom the police haul away.

Twitch-Bits: Sam and Darrin's abode is mentioned by Endora: "I shall scream and shatter glass all over Westport."

Scroll 224

Out of the Mouths of Babes
(3-25-71)

Scribe: Michael Morris

Overseer: Richard Michaels

Sojourners: David Huddleston, Gene Abdrusco, Eric Scott (*The Waltons*)

Sam-Script: Endora reverts Darrin into a ten-year-old boy. He befriends a youngster named Herbie, who inspires a new campaign for Mother Flanagan's Irish Stew. Endora learns of this development, becomes disgusted, and returns Darrin to adulthood. But Herbie needs Darrin's basketball skills to play against a winning neighborhood team. With her husband's consent, Samantha zaps Darrin back down to size.

Twitch-Bits: In this remake of "Junior Executive," Samantha calls her mom with: "Boil and bubble, toil and trouble; Mother, get here on the double."

Scroll 225

Sam's Psychic Pslip
(4-1-71)

Scribe: John L. Greene

Overseer: William Asher

Sojourners: Irwin Sharone, Irene Byatt, Pandora Spocks

Sam-Script: Darrin gifts Samantha with a bracelet to celebrate thirty days without employing witchcraft. But she feels guilty; every time she hiccups, bikes of all kinds appear. Dr. Bombay offers an apparent cure. Phyllis takes her shopping. They browse past a department-store necklace, and it disappears. Both ladies are accused of shoplifting. Serena helps Darrin recontact Bombay, who helps locate Samantha and finally offers the correct psychic physic.

Twitch-Bits: Dr. Bombay says that Sam's problem is *cycle-logical* and that she has to reverse the curse spell: "Great Leaping Lions of Limbo, what have I done?"

Scroll 226

Samantha's Magic Mirror
(4-8-71)

Scribe: Ed Jurist

Overseer: Richard Michaels

Sojourners: Tom Bosley (*Happy Days*), Richard Rowley, Nancy Priddy, Jack Denton, Ed Deemer, David Manzy

Sam-Script: Esmeralda seeks to marry her boyfriend Ferdy, and asks Samantha for a magic hand. To bolster her confidence, Sam zaps up in the mirror a more attractive reflection for Esmeralda. Ferdy arrives. His powers are as deficient as Esmeralda's, and they find humor and consolation in each other's arms.

Twitch-Bits: Remake of "Aunt Clara's Old Flame."

Scroll 227

Laugh, Clown, Laugh
(4-15-71)

Scribe: Ed Jurist

Overseer: William Asher

Sojourners: Charles Lane, Ysabel MacClosky, Marcia Wallace

Sam-Script: Endora zaps Darrin with an obnoxious sense of humor that forces Larry to send him home. Sam demands that her mother remove the spell. Endora complies, only to replace it with another hex that has Darrin making jokes upon hearing sad news. This does not sit well with the ever-serious Mr. Jameson, an insurance client who takes offense at Darrin's inappropriate comedy. Samantha and Darrin eventually convince Jameson to take a lighter approach at selling insurance.

Twitch-Bits: Darrin's slogans: "Put a little laughter in your disaster" and "Keep your mother-in-law at home, where most accidents happen." Also, Mrs. Kravitz offers the name of a good psychiatrist.

Scroll 228

Samantha and the Antique Doll
(4-22-71)

Scribe: Ed Jurist

Overseer: Richard Michaels

Sojourners: (None)

Sam-Script: Phyllis sees Tabitha and Adam employing their powers. Sam says it's her mother-in-law's subconscious will which allowed the magic mayhem. Frank questions his wife's sanity. Sam makes Phyllis believe she's turned her husband into a mule. During a seance, the younger Mrs. Stephens persuades the elder Mrs. Stephens into forfeiting her "powers," as it's the only way to restore Frank to his original self. Phyllis consents, and Sam retransforms her father-in-law.

Twitch-Bits: The term *familiar* is referenced here when speaking about the doll. Julie Newmar's cat-witch, Ophelia, in "The Eight-Year Witch," is defined as such.

The Eighth Season (1971 to 1972)

Scroll 229

How Not to Lose Your Head to King Henry VIII, Part 1
(9-15-71)

Scribe: Ed Jurist

Overseer: William Asher

Sojourners: Ronald Long, Ivor Barry, Arlene Martel, Laurie Main, Henry Oliver, Victor Rogers, Gerald Peters, Damian London, Mike Howden, Walter Alzman

Sam-Script: Sam and Darrin embark on a European business/pleasure trip. First stop is the Tower of London, where Sam notices a nobleman trapped in a portrait and sets him free. Malvina, the witch who imprisoned him there, zaps Sam back to the court of King Henry VIII, who becomes attracted to the new blonde. Meanwhile, Darrin and Endora believe Sam could literally lose her head, so Endora sends Darrin back to the rescue.

Twitch-Bits: Darrin also went back in time to help Sam in "Samantha Goes South for a Spell" and "Samantha's Old Salem Trip."

Scroll 230

How Not To Lose Your Head to King Henry VIII, Part 2
(9-22-71)

Scribe: Ed Jurist

Overseer: William Asher

Sojourners: Ronald Long, Ivor Barry, Arlene Martel, Laurie Main, Gil Stuart, Henry Oliver, Victor Rogers, John Mitchum, Paul Ryan.

Sam-Script: Darrin arrives just in time at the king's court: Sam is about to be married (and possibly beheaded). Sam doesn't recognize Darrin, but during his wrestling match with the king, she offers a sympathetic kiss. Her memory is restored, the spell is broken, and she, Darrin, and Endora (who came to help) return to the present.

Twitch-Bits: Ronald Long, who plays the king, was the giant in "Samantha and the Beanstalk," and Santa in "Santa Comes for a Visit and Stays and Stays."

Scroll 231

Samantha and the Loch Ness Monster
(9-29-71)

Scribe: Michael Morris

Overseer: William Asher

Sojourners: Steve Franken, Bernie Kopell, Don Knight, Pandora Spocks

Sam-Script: Samantha and Darrin meet up with Scotland's legendary Loch Ness Monster. The creature is really an old warlock friend of Serena's named Bruce whom, ages before, she had transformed into the sea dragon because he was getting on her nerves. All is almost forgiven. Serena restores him to normal, but he makes her a mermaid. Sam leads Bruce to believe that Serena the Mermaid will be more popular than the Loch Ness Monster.

Bruce thinks it over, removes Serena's fins, and returns to the lake as his alter-ego, sea-loving self.

Twitch-Bits: Bruce is at a Warlock Club party for singles over 2100. To find him, Sam says: "Let's see, that's 36.6 degrees north by northwest on the Cosmic Continuum." Serena says: "Jacques Cousteau could drop in anytime," which is a nod to the ABC specials that frequently preempted *Bewitched* at the time.

Scroll 232

Samantha's Not-So-Leaning Tower of Pisa
(10-6-71)

Scribe: Ed Jurist

Overseer: William Asher

Sojourners: John Rico, Robert Casper, Steve Conte, Peter Virgo Sr., Phil Garris

Sam-Script: Sam and Darrin arrive in Pisa, Italy. Esmeralda joins them from home to report some mishaps with the children and reveals that it was she who caused the famous city's tower to lean. Reliving a depressing encounter with Bonano Pisano, the monument's builder, Esmeralda straightens the landmark, and causes havoc in Pisa. To set things crooked again, Samantha and Emeralda travel back to Pisano's time.

Twitch-Bits: One of the more unique episodes in the eighth season and throughout the series.

Scroll 233

Bewitched, Bothered and Baldoni
(10-13-71)

Scribe: Michael Morris

Overseer: William Asher

Sojourners: Francine York, Lou Krugman, Penny Santon (*Life Goes On*), Michael Byron Taylor, Al Molinaro (*Happy Days*), Joe Alfasa, Harriet Gibson

Sam-Script: When in Rome, Endora breathes life into a statue of Venus to test Darrin's love for Samantha once again. The icon, now a woman named Vanessa, persuades Darrin to hire her as his and Sam's villa maid. To counteract her mother's handiwork, Samantha brings to life a graven image of Adonis, who transforms into a man named Alberto. Following a baffling concurrence with a client and his wife, Endora and Samantha return the two lifelike figures to stone (Endora freezes them holding hands), though not before Darrin has proved his love for his one-in-a-million witch-wife.

Twitch-Bits: Upon Sam's negative reaction to the Venus and Adonis clasping palms, Endora retorts, "What's another miracle in the enchanting city of Rome?"

Scroll 234

Paris, Witches' Style
(10-20-71)

Scribe: Michael Morris

Overseer: William Asher

Sojourners: Maurice Marsac, Carl Don

Sam-Script: Samantha and Darrin arrive in Paris, where she fears the wrath of Maurice, who is angered by his daughter's travels through Europe without him. He sets out to punish Darrin, upon whom he places the blame. In a rare display of affection and protection for her son-in-law, Endora zaps up a duplicate Darrin who is charming and pleasing to Maurice. All goes well until the arrival of the real Darrin, whom Maurice, in a fury, sends to the top of the Eiffel Tower. Client Mr. Sagan, of Europa Tours, is convinced a newspaper photo of Darrin is connected to a wonderful campaign.

Twitch-Bits: Darrin says that Maurice once changed him into a pair of galoshes.

Scroll 235

The Ghost Who Made a Spectre of Himself
(10-27-71)

Scribe: Ed Jurist

Overseer: William Asher

Sojourners: Maurice Dallimore, Patrick Horgan, Cicely Walper

Sam-Script: Sam and Darrin spend the weekend with the Tates in a haunted English castle. An amorous ghost causes problems for Samantha. He zaps himself into Darrin's body and refuses to leave. Louise believes the Stephenses are in the midst of an argument and that Darrin is flirting with her. He's not. In reality, Sam is commanding the spectre to vacate her husband's body. He refuses, so she conjures up the spirit's former love, with whom he disappears.

Twitch-Bits: The ghost calls Sam, Louise, and the duchess "Ducky" a total of eighteen times. Cleopatra was conjured up for Caesar in "Samantha's Caesar Salad," Sleeping Beauty for Prince Charming in "A Prince of a Guy," and Martha Washington for George in "George Washington Zapped Here."

Scroll 236

TV Or Not TV
(11-3-71)

Scribe: Bernie Kahn

Overseer: William Asher

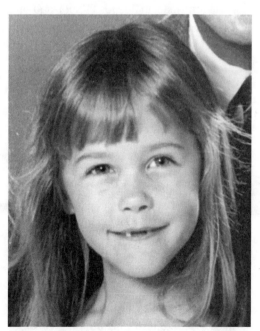

A preteen Erin Murphy took over the role of "Tabitha," minus her twin sister Diane, by the time "TV or Not TV" came around.

Sojourners: John Gallaudet, Robert Q. Lewis, Wanda Hendrix, Ed Call, Kathleen Richards, Barbara Dodd, Bob Baker, Roy R. Etherington

Sam-Script: Sam and Darrin are concerned. Tabitha makes an unexpected appearance on a children's television show, and she may be asked to become a regular. Fortunately, Tabitha tires of the daily TV grind. Samantha tells her to flub her lines and finds a replacement in the daughter of a client, who also happens to be the show's sponsor.

Twitch-Bits: Tabitha asks Sam to define catastrophe: "Something we live with in this house every day." In "Going Ape," Sam tells Harry, the chimp/man, to flub his TV spot, and says the same to Napoleon in "Samantha's French Pastry."

Scroll 237

A Plague on Maurice and Samantha
(11-10-71)

Scribe: Ed Jurist

Overseer: Richard Michaels

Sojourners: Bernie Kopell, J. Edward McKinley, Susan Hathaway

Sam-Script: Because of her frequent mortal contact, Sam once again loses her powers. Dr. Bombay says that any witch or warlock who kisses her will be infected. Maurice arrives, and falls ill to the disease. Bombay finds a cure, but not before Maurice kisses Endora, for whom he saves half the antidote.

Twitch-Bits: Similar to "Allergic to Ancient Macedonian Dodo Birds."

Scroll 238

Hansel and Gretel in Samanthaland
(11-17-71)

Scribe: Michael Morris

Overseer: Richard Michaels

Sojourners: Billie Hayes (*H. R. Pufnstuf*), Richard X. Slattery, Bobo Lewis, Eric Chase, Cindy Henderson, Joel Lawrence

Sam-Script: Tabitha switches places with fairy-tale characters Hansel and Gretel. She goes into their storybook, and they appear in Sam and Darrin's living room, all of which confuses Larry and Louise. Samantha twitches into the storybook and rescues her daughter from the Wicked Witch. Back in *real* life, Tabitha returns Hansel and Gretel to the pages of make-believe.

Twitch-Bits: Great lines between Sam and Old Witch:

Witch: "Scat, Scat."

Sam: "Okay. You old bat."

Witch: "I heard that."

And, back in the real world, Darrin searches the neighborhood for "two little children about so high who answer to the name of Hansel and Gretel?"

Scroll 239

The Warlock in the Gray Flannel Suit
(12-1-71)

Scribe: John L. Greene

Overseer: Richard Michaels

Sojourners: Bernie Kopell, Charles Lane, Samantha Scott

Sam-Script: Darrin won't allow Samantha to attend her cousin Panda's wedding. Endora is at her wit's end and enlists the aid of a hippie warlock named Alonzo. The groovy male-witch poses as a copywriter at McMann and Tate and induces Larry into falling for a bogus slogan for Monticello Carpets. With Sam's help, Darrin opens his own ad agency and persuades Larry to see through Alonzo's lousy ideas.

Twitch-Bits: In the tag, while under a spell, Larry hints at a partnership with Darrin, then reneges on it, a virtual repeat of a scene late in Act II of "Solid Gold Mother-in-Law." Alonzo removes the spell: "Tail of newt and eye of bat, take the spell off this here cat."

Scroll 240

The Eight-Year Witch
(12-8-71)

....

Scribe: Ruth Brooks Flippen

Overseer: Richard Michaels

Sojourners: Julie Newmar (*Batman*), Ron Russell, Parley Baer, Samantha Scott, Roger Lajoie

Sam-Script: Endora summons cat-witch Ophelia and sets out to prove, once and for all, that Darrin has an eye for other women. While Darrin, Larry, and a client are on a business trip, Ophelia manages to become part of the discussed campaign, and later tries to seduce Darrin in his hotel room. Samantha pops in just in time to prevent Ophelia's claws from sinking into Darrin, who has remained faithful to his wife all along.

Julie Newmar was the cat/woman/witch/"Ophelia" in "The Eight Year Itch."

Twitch-Bits: In this remake of "It Takes One To Know One," Sam and Darrin try to celebrate what is apparently the ninth anniversary of their first date.

Scroll 241

Three Men and a Witch on a Horse
(12-15-71)

....

Scribe: Ed Jurist

Overseer: Richard Michaels

Sojourners: John Fiedler, Hoke Howell, Scatman Crothers (*Chico and the Man*)

Sam-Script: In Endora's opinion, Darrin's too conservative. So she endows him with gambling fever, and he wins a bundle at the races. Larry and Mr. Bengler, a client, try their luck with Darrin's strategy, some of which becomes less than great, compliments of Endora. To fix the race would be unethical. Instead, Samantha encourages a losing horse to win and rescues Darrin's reputation.

Twitch-Bits: Darrin's OTB account number is A231, and his code name is *Dog.*

Scroll 242

Adam, Warlock or Washout
(12-29-71)

While Darrin, Endora, and witch-testers "Enchantra" and "Grimalda" (Diana Chesney and Maryesther Denver, right to left in foreground) watch, Adam proves whether he's supernatural or mortal in "Adam, Warlock or Washout."

Scribe: Ed Jurist

Overseer: William Asher

Sojourners: Diana Chesney, Maryesther Denver, Bernie Kuby, Lew Horn

Sam-Script: Grimalda and Enchantra, as representatives of the Witches' Council, visit Samantha and Darrin to test the supernatural expertise of their son Adam. Can he make with the magic or he is only human after all?

Be he mortal, the Stephenses' marriage must be dissolved. Unwilling to subject herself, her husband, or her son to such evaluations, Samantha calls upon her father for help. After all is said and done, Adam proves to have amazing magical ability for his age.

Twitch-Bits: This episode is a remake of "Witches and Warlocks Are My Favorite Things." Also, it's the last segment with Maurice, who's on his way to Petrograd to catch a performance of *Penguin Lake*, an ice ballet for which they couldn't get the skates on the swans. A rerun of this outing on July 1, 1972, was the last time *Bewitched* was broadcast on ABC in prime time, thus formally ending the series' original network run.

Scroll 243

Samantha's Magic Sitter
(1-5-72)

Scribes: Philip and Henry Sharp

Overseer: Richard Michaels

Sojourners: Richard X. Slattery, Jeanne Arnold, Ricky Powell, Christian Juttner

Sam-Script: Esmeralda is having another bad day. But client Mr. Norton and his wife need a baby-sitter. Samantha reluctantly offers the services of Esmeralda, who eventually tells the Norton child that she's a witch. To smooth things over, Sam arranges a party, complete with a magic show and explains what Esmeralda really meant to say.

Twitch-Bits: In the tag to this remake of "No Witch Like an Old Witch," Esmeralda ends up in the refrigerator. Darrin asks: "Does the light really go out when the door closes?"

Scroll 244

Samantha Is Earthbound
(1-15-72)

Scribe: Michael Morris

Overseer: Richard Michaels

Sojourners: Sara Seegar, Jack Collins, Molly Dodd

Sam-Script: Samantha develops a condition that makes her weigh exactly 518 pounds. Dr. Bombay prescribes a potion that makes her lighter than air, and the cure turns out to be worse than the disease, all of which transpires just as she's about to appear as a model at a charity bazaar for client Mr. Prescott. But things work out. Darrin is inspired to create a great slogan: "With Prescott Shoes you don't walk, you float."

Twitch-Bits: In the opening scene, Sam's so heavy that when she rests on the couch, the floor sinks beneath it.

Scroll 245

Serena's Richcraft
(1-22-72)

Scribe: Michael Morris

Overseer: William Asher

Sojourners: Peter Lawford, Ellen Weston, Joe Ross, Bernie Kuby

Sam-Script: Serena is caught fooling around with the fiancé of Contessa Piranha, a powerful witch who, as punishment, subtracts Serena's powers. To amuse herself until her witchcraft returns, Serena hangs out with wealthy client Harrison Woolcott, who sweeps her off her feet. Darrin gets a little nervous: Is he in danger of losing the Woolcott account? When Contessa restores Serena's natural abilities, Darrin's concern disappears, and McMann and Tate's contract with Woolcott is secured.

Twitch-Bits: In this remake of "It Shouldn't Happen to a Dog" and "A Chance on Love," Woolcott says that Serena "can tell you what went on in Alexander Graham Bell's bedroom in 1902." Also, Elizabeth Montgomery's energy in this episode is extremely high, compared to other segments of the eighth season (which she initially did not want to film).

Scroll 246

Samantha on Thin Ice
(1-29-72)

Scribe: Richard Baer

Overseer: William Asher

Sojourners: Alan Oppenheimer (*The Six Million Dollar Man*), former Canadian Olympic skating champ Robert Paul

Sam-Script: Sam and Darrin agree, Tabitha should learn to ice-skate the mortal way. But the little witch performs poorly at the local rink. Endora won't stand for it and makes sure her granddaughter achieves with precision on ice. Tabitha captures the eye of Olympic officials, who schedule a tour. Plans change when Sam persuades her mother to remove the hex from Tabitha's cold feet.

Twitch-Bits: Remake of "Samantha on the Keyboard."

Scroll 247

Serena's Youth Pill
(2-15-72)

Scribe: Michael Morris

Overseer: E. W. Swackhamer

Sojourners: Ted Foulkes, David Hayward, Irene Byatt

Sam-Script: Serena baby-sits for Tabitha and Adam and gives a youth pill to Larry, who starts looking and feeling younger. He wants to market the tablet but regresses to infant status. Sam and Darrin are furious until Serena comes up with a baby balm.

Twitch-Bits: A semiremake of "There's Gold in Them Thar Pills." There's a reference to the New York Mets made by Larry in what he thinks is 1961, but the Mets didn't exist until 1962. There is also a reference to *The Lone Ranger* radio show by Larry as a ten-year-old boy. When Larry was ten, *The Lone Ranger* (which began in 1933) wasn't on the air. Louise says, "We've been married for over twenty years," which matches Larry's statement in "Nice To Have a Spouse Around the House."

Scroll 248

Tabitha's First Day at School
(2-12-72)

Scribe: Ed Jurist

Overseer: Richard Michaels

Sojourners: Nita Talbot, Maudie Prickett, Jeanne Arnold, Michael Hughes, Allen Jenkins

Sam-Script: Tabitha isn't attending school. The authorities find out, and Sam is forced to enroll her daughter in local academia. Will Tabitha employ witchcraft in the classroom? Such fear is well-founded when the school bully turns into a frog. When his mother discovers him missing, she ends up at the Stephenses, where Tabitha restores the frog-boy to normal.

Twitch-Bits: Maudie Prickett played Tabitha's teacher in two other segments. Here she plays Mrs. Peabody, who repeats her Mrs. Burch's archaic philosophy from "I Don't Want To Be a Toad": "No child is essentially different from any other child."

Scroll 249

George Washington Zapped Here, Part 1
(2-19-72)

Scribe: Michael Morris

Overseer: Richard Michaels

Sojourners: Will Geer (*The Waltons*), Jane Connell, Herb Vigran, Dick Wilson, John Garwood, Renee Tetro, Thad Geer

Sam-Script: Tabitha needs help with a school project. What better person to lend a hand than the historic figure, George Washington, whom Esmeralda conjures up by mistake. She makes him disappear, but the president leaves his shoes behind. She tries to return them as well, but George comes back, and this time, he's with his wife, Martha.

Twitch-Bits: Darrin asks: "How come you witches can do anything, but you can't come up with a witch psychiatrist for her (Esmeralda)?" Sam: "Oh, I'll bring that up at the next coven."

Dick Sargent (with glasses), Elizabeth, Will Geer, and Jane Connell rehearse a scene for "George Washington Zapped Here," Part I.

Scroll 250

George Washington Zapped Here, Part 2
(2-26-72)

Scribe: Michael Morris

Overseer: Richard Michaels

Sojourners: Will Geer, Jane Connell, Jack Collins, Herb Vigran, Renee Tetro, Thad Geer, John Garwood, Herb Voland

Sam-Script: Before long, George Washington appears in court to defend his identity. Larry is inspired and envisions Mr. Washington as part of the Whirlaway Washing Machines campaign. George complies, only because he believes it to be a favor to Darrin. The too-honest president meets with the Whirlaway representative and blows the account. His integrity, however, wins him respect in court, and all charges against him are dropped. Esmeralda remembers how to return the Washingtons to the past, and Darrin is sorry to see them go.

Twitch-Bit, The George Washington segments are remakes of "My Friend Ben" and "Samantha for the Defense."

Scroll 251

School Days, School Daze
(3-4-72)

Scribe: Michael Morris

Overseer: Richard Michaels

Sojourners: Maudie Prickett, Charles Lane

Sam-Script: Endora casts a spell on Tabitha which makes her an authority on everything, from Shakespeare to Einstein. School officials take notice, and they discover the truth: Tabitha comes from a long line of witches. Samantha derails that actuality, and explains that she, Darrin, and the children were once a nightclub act called—what else?—*The Witches.*

Twitch-Bits: Samantha gets really furious with an outsider for the only time in the series: the teacher who wants to exploit Tabitha, a classic mother-protects-daughter sequence.

Scroll 252

A Good Turn Never Goes Unpunished
(3-11-72)

Scribe: Bernie Kahn

Overseer: Ernest Losso

Sojourners: J. Edward McKinley

Sam-Script: Sam and Darrin argue over her alleged use of witchcraft to create a slogan for Mr. Benson, a mattress manufacturer. Sam ends up on Cloud Nine with Endora. Darrin realizes his accusations are unfounded, apologizes, and his wife returns home.

Twitch-Bits: In this remake of "Help, Help, Don't Save Me," Sam and Endora have a cool one on Cloud Nine; in "To Twitch or Not To Twitch," they hit Cloud Eight. Sam says: "Just because blondes have more fun doesn't make them brainless, you know."

Scroll 253

Sam's Witchcraft Blows a Fuse
(3-18-72)

Scribe: Leo Townsend

Overseer: Richard Michaels

Sojourners: Bernie Kopell, Reta Shaw, Benson Fong (*Kung Fu*), Richard X. Slattery, Janos Prohaska, Paul Smith, Herb Vigran, Suzanne Little

Sam-Script: Sam has an exotic drink at a Chinese eatery, and her face is crossed with bright red stripes. Dr. Bombay prescribes a cure but leaves out the tail feather of a dodo bird, which Tabitha has zapped up in her room.

Twitch-Bits: A remake of "Take Two Aspirin." Bombay tells how Sam got Bright Red Stripes disease from a drink with a Himalayan cinnamon stick: "Eons ago the Tibetan monks cross-pollinated a rare herb with Himalayan cinnamon and used it to drive the witches out of the Himalayas." Sam: "I didn't know there were any witches in the Himalayas." Bombay: "There aren't. It worked." Bombay fails. Sam asks Aunt Hagatha to "talk to the Witches' Council about replacing that quack," and calls him

a "quackpot." The dodo get-up was also used in "Allergic to Ancient Macedonian Dodo Birds."

Scroll 254

The Truth, Nothing but the Truth, So Help Me, Sam
(3-25-72)

Scribe: Ed Jurist

Overseer: William Asher

Sojourners: Parley Baer, Sara Seegar, Emily Banks, Bernie Kuby

Sam-Script: Endora tests Darrin's devotion for Sam one more time by bewitching a truth-telling pin. Darrin has trouble at the office, then at home, where Larry, a client and his wife pay a visit. Sam latches on to Endora's scheme. The next day, the Stephenses profess their mutual love, without magic assistance.

Twitch-Bits: A remake of "Speak the Truth." The last scene—Darrin: "Honey, you're beautiful, sweet, clever, adorable, and I love you madly. It works." Sam: "Well, it doesn't work on me, but I love you. And that is the truth, the whole truth, and et cetera."

Mortal Account-Ability

Scroll Number	Account	Client
	A TAKE ON MCMANN AND TATE'S CLIENTS	
3	Barker Baby Food	Rex Barker
5	Caldwell Soup	Philip Caldwell
7	Halloween candy	Mr. Brinkman
8		Mr. Austen
11	Jasmine Perfume	
18	Margaret Marshall Cosmetics	Mr. Marshall
20	Woolfe Bros. Department Store	
21	Jewel of the East (jewelry)	Mr. Pickering
23	Slegerhamer's Dairy	
30	Father Touch Typewriters	
35	Perfect Pizza Parlors	Linton Baldwin
36	Shelley's Shoes	
38	Stanwyck Soap	Mr. Martin
41	E Z Open Flush Door	Mr. Foster
42		Howard Norton
43	Party favors	Jack Rogers
44	Mother Jenny's Jam	Charles Barlow
45	Jarvis account; Slater account; Murphy Supermarket	
46	Toy ship models	Mr. Harding
49	Harper's Honey	
50	Hotchkiss Appliance Company	Ed Hotchkiss
52	Kingsley Potato Chips	
53		H. J. Simpson
58	Hockstedder Toy Company	
59		Randolph Turgen
60		J. T. Glendon
61		Aubert of Paris
62	Naisley's Baby Food	
63	Westchester Consolidated Mills	James D. Robinson
64	detergent	J. K. Kabaker
65		Osgood Rightmire
66	Robbins Baby Food Company	

67	Robbins Baby Food Company	
68	Stern Chemical Company	Sanford Stern
71	United Cosmetics	Toni Devlin
73	Waterhouse Thumbtack Company	
75	Robbins Truck Transmissions	
82	Wright Pens	
83	MacElroy Shoes	Mr. MacElroy
85		R. Parkinson Jr.
86		Max Cosgrove
87	Franklin Electronics	Bernie Franklin
89	Super Soapy Soap	Tom Scranton
92	Solow Toy Company	
93	Sheldrake Sausage	Mr. Sheldrake
94	Morton Milk	C. L. Morton
95	Ganzer Garage Doors	
96	Tropical Bathing Suits	
97		Ed Pennybaker
98	Cunningham Perfume	Mr. Cunningham
100		Mr. Morgan
101	Warbell Dresses	Jay/Terry Warbell
102	Baldwin Blankets	Horace Baldwin
103	Mayor Rocklin	Frank Eastwood
104	Madame Maruska Lipstick	Madame Maruska
105		Unnamed client
106	Saunders Soups	
107	Hornbeck Pharmaceutical	
108	Rohrbach Steel Company	
109		Bob Chase
110	Chef Romani Foods	
112	Bigelow Tires	Mr. Bigelow
113	Carter Bros. Industrial Products	
114	Baxter Sporting Goods	Joe Baxter
117	Springer Pet Foods	Alvin Springer
120	Gregson Home Appliances	Mr. Gregson
121		Mr. Grayson
122	Chappell Baby Foods	Roy Chappell
123	Mortimer Instant Soups	Jesse Mortimer

124	Mint Brite Toothpaste	J. P. Pritchfield
125	Autumn Flame Perfume	Bo Callahan
126	Webley Foods	J.P. Summers
127	Prune Valley Retirement Village	Leroy Wendell
128	Giddings Tractors	
129	Abigail Adams Cosmetics	Mr. Blumberg
132		Dwight Sharpe
134	Baker Foods	Edgar Baker
136	Mishimoto TV Sets	Kensu Mishimoto
138	Omega National Bank	R.H. Markham
139	Hercules Tractors	Charles Gilbert
	Slocum Soup	O.J. Slocum
	Angel Coffee	
146	Hascomb Drug Company	Whitney Hascomb
147	Zoom Detergent	H.L. Bradley
148	E Z Way Rent-a-Car	
	Sav-Most Markets	
	Mossler Enterprises	Harlan Mossler
152		Mr. Stewart
153	Adrianne Sebastian Cosmetics	Adrianne Sebastian
155/156	Vino Vanita	Clio Vanita
157	Fuzz Doll/Hanley's Department Store	Jim Hanley
158	Durfee's Dog Food	Oscar Durfee
159	Campbell Sporting Goods	Waldon R. Campbell
160	Struthers account	
162	Brawn Cologne	Evelyn Tucker
164		J. Earl Rockeford
170	Bueno, A.K.A. Zap	Raul Garcia
172	Hampton Motors	Mr. Hampton
173	Top Tiger Cologne	Evelyn Charday
174	a detergent account	Mr. Paxton
175	Berkley Baby Foods	
177	Bartenbach Beauty Products (dental creme, hair tonic, remover)	
178		Alvin J. Sylvester
180	Bliss Pharmaceutical	Silas Bliss Sr. and Jr.
181	Bliss Pharmaceutical	Silas Bliss Sr. and Jr.
183	Shotwell Pharmaceuticals	

185	Tanaka Electronics (a division of Tanaka Enterprises)	Mr. Tanaka
187	Multiple Industries	H. B. Summers
189		Mr. Nickerson
190	Top Pop	
191	Braddock Sporting Goods	Bob Braddock
192	Breeze Shampoo	
194	Harrison Industries	John J. Harrison
195	A housing development	
196	Dinsdale Soups	George Dinsdale
197	Barber Peaches	
199	Sunshine Greeting Card Company	Augustus Sunshine
200		George Meiklejohn
201	Gotham Industries	
202		Ernest Hitchcock
205	Barrows Umbrellas	
206	British Imperial Textile Mills	Sir Leslie Bancroft
207	Blakely account	
209	Gibbons Dog Burgers	Charlie Gibbons
210	Beau Geste Toiletries	Jennings Booker
211	Bigelow Industries	J. J. Langley
212	Harmon Savings and Loan	
213		Mr. Brockway
214	Bobbins Candy Company Bobbins Buttery Bonbons	Bernard Bobbins
216	Reducealater	Mr. Ferber
218	Rockfield Furniture	Lionel Rockfield
219	Berkley Hair Tonic	Roland Berkley
220	Colonel Brigham Spareribs	Colonel Brigham
222	Cushman Cosmetics	
223	Patterson account Bradwell account Cushman's Restaurant	
224	Mother Flanagan's Irish Stew	Sean Flanagan
226	A client in Chicago	
227	Mount Rocky Mutual	Harold Jameson
232	Count Bracini's Olive Oil	
233	House of Baldoni	Ernesto Baldoni
234	Europa Tours	Henri Sagan

235	Regal Silverware	
236	Silverton Toy Company	Lester Silverton
237	Benson's Chili Con Carne	
239	Monticello Carpets	Mr. Cushman
240	Tom Cat Tractors, Inc.	Mr. Buckeholder
241		Mr. Spengler
243		Mr. Norton
244	Prescott Shoes	Wilbur Prescott
245	Woolcott Towers	Harrison Woolcott
250	Whirlaway Washing Machines	Hector Jamison
252	Benson Sleep-Ezy Mattress	Mr. Benson
253	Ah Fong's Restaurant	Mr. Ah Fong
254	Cora May Sportswear	Cora May Franklin

Witch and mortal share a common pastime (baseball) in "Little Pitchers Have Big Fears."

Chapter 12

Magic/Mortal Minutiae

Paranormal Particulars

Samantha is a levelheaded witch who keeps her cool. Except, of course, when Aunt Clara or Esmeralda's spells create havoc. Then she simply says "Oh, my stars!" with the slightest trace of hysteria in her voice. When she sees Mother Goose (Jane Connell) in "Samantha's Double Mother Trouble," she exclaims, "Oh, my goose! It's Mother Stars!"

Other Sam specifics include her first meeting with Darrin in the pilot episode, in a revolving door of the Clark Building in New York City.

Sam moved with Darrin into a furnished rented house in "I, Darrin, Take This Witch, Samantha" and "Be It Ever So Mortgaged" before purchasing their home in "Mortgaged" at 1164 Morning Glory Circle, which is located in Westport, Connecticut (Hopkins Realty is the agent).

Their home phone numbers are 555-7328 ("Witch or Wife; Girl With the Golden Nose"), 555-2134 ("Nobody but a Frog Knows How to Live"), and 555-2368 ("Samantha's Wedding Present").

In the summer of 1968, they have new plumbing installed in the house, or so says Sam in "Snob in the Grass."

Sam had her first date with Darrin on January 23, 1963, at Sorrento's Restaurant ("One Touch of Midas"). On April 2, 1963, they dined at the automat (Darrin forgot to make reservations at The Lobster). Samantha wore a pink wool dress.

People come up to me all the time and quote Bewitched *dialogue, line for line. It's utterly amazing.*

BERNARD FOX
on Bewitched *fan devotion.*

Other Samspecs:

In "Love Is Blind," she says: "All my friends are witches. We're just waiting to swoop down on Morning Glory Circle and claim it in the name of Beelzebub." She's only half serious but is very mad at Darrin.

In "I'd Rather Twitch Than Fight," it's learned that Sam knew she was a witch when she was only nine months old. Endora tells her: "You were very precocious."

"Sam's Spooky Chair" establishes that Sam and Endora lived in Boston (apparently some time in the nineteenth century) on the same block as the Farnsworths. Sam had one date with Clyde Farnsworth, who later asked Sam's aunt Enchantra to transform him into a chair (using the spell without the oxtails) when she rejected him.

In "To Twitch or Not To Twitch," Samantha mentions she knew Shakespeare (who died in 1616); Henry VIII (who died in 1547, and whom she would meet again under the influence of a spell in "How Not To Lose Your Head to Henry VIII," Part 1); and Bluebeard who, as she told Darrin, "was more of a gentleman than you've been tonight."

In "Mirror Mirror on the Wall," Sam explains how Napoleon arrived at the Stephenses' ("It's sorta technical"): "When a witch or a warlock casts a spell involving an object—the name of which may also be used to identify a human being—the kinetic vibrations run the risk of zonking across the atmospheric continuum, and the ectoplasmic manifestations that might not ordinarily occur... "

In "Samantha the Bard," Sam finds herself speaking in rhyme from a witch disease (primary vocabularyitis): "There once was a mommy named Sam, whose speech got her into a jam. Though she tried not to show it, she talked like a poet; if you think I'm unhappy, I am." During dinner with a dog food client: "Who, me? Boop doop de dee" and "Me too. Fiddle de doo" and "I feel groovy. Anyone seen a good movie?" Other rhymes: "I hate to burst your bubble, but I think I'm in trouble"; "In case I'm cured by a last-minute miracle, I have to be ready, don't I, dearicle?" and "There must be a logical answer, or my name is not Samansar." She tests Dr. Bombay's cure with "How now brown horse."

In "Tabitha's Weekend," Sam and Endora have one of their rare disputes, in this case over whether or not Tabitha should be disciplined for turning herself into a raisin cookie:

Endora: "I always tell the truth as I see it."
Sam: "Mother, you are an incorrigible witch."
Endora: "And you are an insensitive, selfish, mortal-marrying child."
Sam: "You don't have to get that huffy about it." (Endora pops out angrily)
Sam: "I guess she does have to get that huffy about it. Oh, well—Mom?"

In "And Something Makes Four," it's noted that Sam was born on the eve of the Galactic Rejuvenation and Dinner Dance (Maurice was on Venus at the time).

In "Sam's Lost Weekend," Samantha thought she had contracted the witch disease called voracious ravenousitus, but she didn't. She was accidentally under Esmeralda's eating spell.

Some of the witch ailments that Sam did acquire include: square green spots disease ("Take Two Aspirins"), primary vocabularyitis ("Samantha the Bard"), metaphysical molecular disturbance ("Mixed Doubles"), gravitutis inflammatitus ("Samantha Is Earthbound"), and bright red stripes disease ("Samantha's Witchcraft Blows a Fuse").

In "Sam's Secret Is Discovered," she imitates Darrin's aunt Madge, who thought she was a lighthouse (mentioned in the pilot and "Samantha Meets the Folks"). The strange behavior of this never-seen relative was one of Sam's defenses against Darrin's tirades about her own unique family.

In "Mona Sammi," we learn that Samantha's grandaunt Cornelia's portrait (which had been cluttering up Endora's attic for centuries) was painted by Leonardo da Vinci. Cornelia looked a great deal like Samantha.

In "Sam's Hot Bed Warmer," it's revealed that when Sam was a little girl, Endora brought Sir Walter Raleigh home for dinner. Since Raleigh died in 1618, that gives us some idea of just how old Samantha really is. (In "Salem Saga," she claims she was just a shield during the Salem witch trials of 1692).

In "Out of the Mouths of Babes," Sam calls Endora with: "Boil and bubble, toil and trouble; Mother, get here on the double." Also, Sam explains the Unicorn Handicap. "It's like the Kentucky Derby, only with unicorns." When Endora asks her what the happiest day of her life was, Sam says: "The day I married Darrin." To which Endora responds, "I didn't say insanely happy."

In "Samantha's Magic Mirror," she explains to Esmeralda: "When you look into the mirror you see the image that you project. Your reflection casts back your inner glow, and your charisma comes to the fore because, after all, beauty is in the eye of the beholder, isn't it? Do you understand?" Esmeralda: "No." In the same segment, Sam explains to Larry: "When you don't respect someone, when you treat him as if he doesn't exist, he just disappears from your consciousness. He fades away. Follow me?" Larry: "No." But her best lines

from "Mirror" are said to Esmeralda again: "What did you have in mind? A little plastic sorcery?" and "I cook by mortal methods."

In "Samantha and the Antique Doll," she says: "Supernatural powers have a tendency to come and go, mostly go. This will probably never happen again." Phyllis, who's listening to this explanation, says: "Samantha, this is one subject you know nothing about."

In "A Plague on Maurice and Samantha," it's learned that she first flew when she was three years old and that when she was a child, she frequently changed herself into a polka-dotted unicorn (a favorite of both Samantha and Elizabeth Montgomery's).

Also, when Sam was a little girl, she turned herself into a postage stamp because Maurice and Uncle Arthur were arguing over who would take her to be introduced at court. She would end up in Istanbul, and as she recalls in "Tabitha's Weekend," "Those Turks are kinda rough."

Samantha is a very intelligent witch. She's fluent in Italian, Spanish, and French, and also speaks very well frog, mule, horse, and goose languages, among others.

Serena's World

Serena likes to sing.

She sings *Iffin* in "Hippie, Hippie Hooray" and *Blow You a Kiss in the Wind*, which was introduced at the Cosmos Cotillion in "Serena Stops the Show."

In "Mrs. Stephens, Where Are You?," she tells Sam's neighbor, Mrs. Parsons, that she came from the cabbage patch. But it's a known fact, she's originally from Babylon ("Eye of the Beholder"). Also, in "Where Are You?," Serena says she's Sam's cousin on her father's side, and tells Phyllis Stephens: "Well, Samantha's always had unusual taste. In people, too. Darrin, for instance, is extremely unusual." She tells her cousin: "Oh, Sammi, you used to be so much fun before you caught mortalitis."

In "A Chance on Love," when Sam tells Serena not to "play innocent with me" regarding Serena's flirtation with a client, Serena replies: "Innocence is not my bag. He's very goodlooking, and I happen to turn him on." Sam: "Well, turn him off!" Serena: "Okay, okay. Don't bust your broom."

In "Darrin on a Pedestal," Sam refers to Serena: "I have a cousin who makes Lucrezia Borgia look like Shirley Temple."

In "Serena's Richcraft," she says: "There's not much difference between witchcraft and richcraft, except maybe you fly a little slower."

In "Serena's Youth Pill," when Sam calls Serena to baby-sit, Serena says: "Do I look like Mary Poppins to you?" and "Do you realize that the French fleet of St. Trapeze was about to crown me Miss Naval?"

Darrin's Double Play

According to the *Bewitched* pilot, Darrin is a vice president of McMann and Tate (rather than account executive), and as noted in "Serena's Youth Pill," he joined the firm in 1961, while "There's Gold in Them Thar Pills" says it was 1964.

Endora's spells turn him into a chimp, a mule, a werewolf, a goose, a pony, a parrot, a goat, a gorilla, a toad, a statue, a crow, a dog, and an invisible man.

Darrin's favorite dishes are beef stew, Irish stew, and corned beef and cabbage. His favorite breakfast is eggs Benedict, but he likes waffles, too. His favorite pie is lemon meringue.

Darrin calls Endora "Mom" in "The Joker Is a Card" and "Speak the Truth."

His office is located in the International Building on the thirty-second floor. Darrin doesn't know how to swim, or so we learn in "Divided He Falls."

In "It's Wishcraft," Darrin kisses Endora upon entering the living room to help convince his parents that he and Samantha are not having an argument. In this segment it is also learned that Darrin was named for his grandfather, a statement later contradicted in "Samantha's Old Man," wherein Grover Stephens (a guise Darrin takes when Endora turns him into an old man) is said to be his grandfather.

Darrin's ancestor, Darrin the Bold, first appears in "A Most Unusual Wood Nymph," and was played by Dick York. He appears again in "Return of Darrin the Bold," portrayed by Dick Sargent.

York's Darrin is zapped into the mirror in "I Get Your Nanny… You Get My Goat," by Lord Montdrako; the same thing happens to Sargent's Darrin by Maurice in "Naming Samantha's New Baby."

York's Darrin is turned into a little boy by Endora in "Junior Executive"; the same thing happens to Sargent's Darrin in "Out of the Mouth of Babes."

York's Darrin says he went to college at Missouri, class of 1950 ("Ling Ling") and Missouri State ("Mouth of Babes"), where he was an all-star forward. Darrin's best time for the 100-yard dash was 10.3 (or so he claims in "What Makes Darrin Run").

Dick York did 156 shows as Darrin; Dick Sargent filmed eighty-four segments. "A Gazebo Never Forgets" was the first episode York missed. He missed a total of fourteen before leaving the show in 1969.

Darrin's Double Talk

In "Be It Ever So Mortgaged," Darrin says, "Welcome, Mother" to Endora. By "What Every Young Man Should Know," he tells her: "This is my house, you're not welcome, and I want you out of here on the next broom." A semitruce is called in "The Joker Is a Card," when he greets her with "Hi, Mom." She replies: "How are you, Darrin?" He's understandably amazed, but she says: "I'll make an agreement with you. I'll try to remember your name if you promise never to call me Mom."

Darrin holds up his end of the bargain, but Endora does not.

Words return to normal in "Nobody's Perfect," when Darrin says: "Hi, Endora. When did you swoop in?" (which he also says in "Samantha's Wedding Present").

In "Twitch or Treat," he says to Sam: "It's been Halloween around here for the past week, what with your mother, Uncle Arthur, houses appearing and disappearing… "

In "Solid Gold Mother-in-Law," Endora gives Tabitha a pony and says: "The pony is on me." Darrin responds: "That, I'd like to see."

In "Snob in the Grass," he says to Sam (regarding her mother): "How is the old war wagon?" In "How Green Was My Grass," he states (about Endora): "Well, that's the last time I try to be nice to her." In "Instant Courtesy," he mutters of Endora: "She never knocks. All of a sudden she's here, like the flu," which he also used in "The Truth, Nothing but the Truth, So Help Me Sam," which is the final episode.

In "Samantha the Sculptress," Darrin greets his mother-in-law: "It's the queen of sick jokes," and later says to her: "We eat at 7:30. You take your broom to a drive-in or something," and, "What can you expect from a crotchety old bat who learned to read from the Dead Sea Scrolls?" And later, he says: "Oh, yes, it's amazing how much help we get around here from Sam's mother."

In "Sam and Darrin in Mexico City," he calls Endora "The Old Lady of the Sea."

Also in "Mexico," York speaks his last lines as Darrin to Sam about Endora: "Yeah, I know your mother. She's every inch a mother-in-law."

Dick Sargent's first line as Darrin appears in "Samantha and the Beanstalk." "Sam, how many times have I told you, never talk in the middle of somebody's backswing." Also in "Beanstalk," Sam wonders if Darrin is sorry he married her: "Between this big witch and the little witch upstairs," she says, "and that witch of a mother of mine, you're really up to your neck in witches." Yet Darrin loves Sam and Tabitha. Sam: "And Mother?" "Well," he replies, "two out of three. That's not bad."

In "Samantha's Yoo-Hoo Maid," Darrin says to Sam: "Show me another mother who sharpens her teeth in the morning."

In "The Phrase Is Familiar," he tells Endora: "If you're able to drop in tomorrow morning, I certainly hope not." Later, during much magic goings-on, he says to Larry: "Crawl in the window? Come on, Larry. What are you trying to do, gaslight me?"

In "What Makes Darrin Run," he's at it again with Endora: "Ah, the cloud in my silver lining." After he asks her if Sam has told her about his "trip," meaning a business trip, Endora replies: "Yes, and I hope you do."

In "The Salem Saga," he asks, after Endora flies on the wing of a plane and the top of the backseat in his convertible: "Must your mother ride on the outside of everything?" Later, after Endora says: "We saw those sights years ago," he responds with: "Let's face it, Endora. Hundreds of years ago you *were* one of the sights."

In "The Corsican Cousins," he offers his best left hook with: "Sam, don't expect your mother to be gracious. She doesn't do imitations." And no matter how rattled Endora may have caused Darrin to become over the years, or how much trouble he finds himself in because of Sam's magic, he still garners the strength to mention lightly to Larry in the same segment: "Don't tell anybody, but I'm married to a witch."

In "Money Happy Returns," he declares to Endora: "Hello, El Moutho," and later, "The *bad fairy* strikes again."

Endora's Open Sesame

In "Long Live the Queen," while Darrin is drowning his sorrows at a bar, Endora says to Sam: "Look, if he comes back, he comes back. If he doesn't, we'll open a bottle of champagne. Well, I thought that was a rather good idea." When Darrin returns, she says: "Samantha, bad news: he's back." After Darrin insults her, she says: "Samantha, I will not stand here and be insulted by something which is 94 percent water," only to have Darrin reply: "Oh, yeah! Well, what about something which is a hundred percent hot air?" When Sam refuses to be queen of the witches, Endora says to Ticheba: "We do our best, but sometimes we fail."

In "Ancient Macedonian Dodo Birds," Endora explains that she always has eggs over-easy for breakfast, while her favorite dish is coq au vin ("Samantha, the Sculptress").

In "Solid Gold Mother-in-Law," she apologizes to Darrin: "I regret my slight transgression of this morning, however deserved." Darrin: "That's an apology?" Sam: "For Mother it is.")

In "My, What Big Ears You Have," when Sam says, "Marriage is a poor excuse for snooping," Endora replies: "Well, if you ask me, this is a poor excuse for a marriage." In "Once in a Vial," Endora gets a taste of her own medicine. She accidentally falls under her own love spell, which she had intended for Samantha, who was to become bewitched by Rollo, an old warlock boyfriend.

In "One Touch of Midas," she gives the witches' honor sign with her mittens on (which probably doesn't count). After Sam asks if she's sure, Endora responds with: "Samantha, have I ever lied to you?"

In "Samantha the Bard," after she catches the rhyme bug from her daughter, Endora says: "This is absolutely outrageous; you must have been contagious." When Darrin gloats over the situation, she says: "Durwood, I do not like the way you gloat, so I'm turning you into a billy goat." When Sam begs her to change him back she says: "I will, I will, but when I'm cured, and not until." Her other rhymes included: "Hello, Darius, the pleasure of seeing you is rather vicarious," and, "That's absurd, I'll not rhyme a single word."

Further noting her witchy wit, in "To Trick or Treat, or Not To Trick or Treat," she says to Samantha: "You took your vows for better or worse, and you certainly are getting the worse." Later, she uncharacteristically retreats with, "You win. I'm bored with all this trivia."

In "Okay, Who's the Wise Witch," when Dr. Bombay says, "Durwood is totally irrelevant," Endora responds with, "I'll buy that." Then Bombay one-ups her with, "It's not for sale."

In "If the Shoe Pinches," Endora explains the leprechaun: "It was a test to see where the breaking point is in this mortal marriage. It was sponsored by the Witches' Council." Sam: "Who suggested it to the Witches' Council?" Endora: "I believe the suggestion came from the floor. All right, I suggested it!"

In "Mona Sammi," when Darrin says Endora "majored in cruelty with the Marquis de Sade," Endora says: "It's not true. He was just a classmate." In "To Go or Not To Go," she tells Darrin: "Aren't we the terrible tiger this morning!" To Sam: "Oh, this room, oh, it's all you."

Her cutest spell occurred in "Man of the Year:" "Edgeful, eyeful, trifle, tree, this removes the spell 'round thee." Her least imaginative spell appeared in "Instant Courtesy": "Disappear courtesy."

In "The Eight-Year Witch," Darrin throws a good-bye kiss, Endora makes a face and says: "Yeucch." Via skywriting in the tag: "I, Endora, promise never, never again to bug what's his name" (also used in "Battle of the Burning Oak"); in "School Days, School Daze," she writes: "Endora promises not to interfere" five hundred times (sort of) on a blackboard.

In "Samantha on Thin Ice," she asks Darrin: "How would you like to be a carrot growing in a field of rabbits?" (also in "Samantha the Sculptress"). Then, after more bickering has given her a headache, she says: "And now that you've made a perfectly marvelous person sick, she's leaving."

Larry's Lunacy

Generally, when Larry (who in "Samantha's French Pastry" says he's forty-seven years old) was at his worst, the Sam and Darrin situation would work out for the best, or they would at least get the best of Larry.

In "Tabitha's Cranky Spell," he states: "I'm the one with a vivid imagination; I can see five hundred thousand dollars flying out the window." At this moment Sam zaps up a winged bag of money that proceeds to float out the window. Larry says to Sam: "If you love Darrin, get him out of the advertising business while there's still time."

All this from a man who, according to "Eat at Mario's," spent seven years in analysis. Maybe a little sympathy is in order as Larry does, on occasion, display his true feelings.

In "Speak the Truth," he admits he can't get along without Darrin, which he also confesses in "The Truth, Nothing but the Truth, So Help Me Sam." Of course, in both cases, he's under a truth spell.

Larry's questionable behavior is also evident in these episodes:

In "How to Fail in Business," he admits his desire for money after Darrin says: "You know, your eyes light up when you talk about money." Larry: "Of course. I'm a greedy person."

In "Hippie, Hippie, Hooray," Larry tells Darrin: "I didn't get to be the head of an advertising agency without stretching the truth now and then. I might honestly say that I'm one of the best truth-stretchers in the business."

In "I Confess," when Larry realizes that Sam's a witch (in a dream sequence), he gets a bit out of hand:

Larry: "Samantha, with my brains and your voodoo, we can control the world… today, the nation, tomorrow, the world!"

Darrin: "Larry, take it easy."

Larry: "I can't. I'm mad with power!"

Sam: "But we're not. We don't want to use my witchcraft to control the world."

Darrin: "Right. And I'm sure when you've had time to think it over you'll decide… "

Larry: "I'll decide I want to rule the world. I've wanted to rule the world ever since I was a little kid."

(Much of this dialogue is repeated almost verbatim in "Darrin the Warlock.")

In "Instant Courtesy," Larry tells Darrin: "I've got radar. I get a ping when something's wrong." He professes his "word of honor, my real word of honor." Only to state later: "I'm going home to celebrate all over again with… " Sam: "Louise." Larry: "… Louise."

In "And Something Makes Four," after Maurice has removed a spell from a just-born Adam, which has made everyone think he's the best baby in the world, Larry, who was all set to use Adam in an ad, is out to look for another baby at the hospital: "You mean to tell me in a place like this we can't borrow a… maybe we could borrow a camera and take a picture in the nursery and then… listen! That's a two-million-dollar account!" Finally, Sam calls it: "Oh, Larry… you son-of-a-gun."

Samantha captures Larry's essence further in "No Harm Charm," where she says: "That's just Larry's way. The hardest thing for him to give is in."

In "A Bunny for Tabitha," after Darrin nearly loses an account, he asks Larry: "What do you want me to do… cut my throat?" Larry: "I'm thinking it over." Later, to his secretary: "Remind me to put Stephens on the *B* list for Christmas."

In "Samantha the Bard," Larry states: "That's not bad character, it's my character."

In "Darrin the Warlock," he says: "Darrin, if I've told you once, I've told you a thousand times, integrity doesn't feed the bulldog."

In "Out of the Mouths of Babes," he offers many moments of insight into his character. On planning to stay with Samantha and Darrin: "It's either here or going home and listening to Louise and her string quartet murder Bach." Later: "I didn't become the president of McMann and Tate without bending my integrity occasionally, and this is one of those occasionallys." To a client: "At McMann and Tate, Sunday is just the day before Monday."

In "Serena's Youth Pill," it's learned that Larry lived at 14532 Elm Street when he was a child. He originally had red hair, played ice hockey for his school team, and served in the navy.

In "That Was My Wife," Larry calls Darrin a *son-of-a-gun* a record seven times. In "Solid Gold Mother-in-Law," Endora calls Darrin a *son-of-a-gun*. In "Samantha's Curious Cravings," Samantha calls Larry a *son-of-a-gun*.

Clara's Heart

Aunt Clara always had the best intentions, but she usually brought about the worst disasters. For example, in "Out of Sync, Out of Mind," she accidentally casts a spell throwing Samantha's speech out of synchronization: She moves her lips, and then her voice is heard later.

Other Clara catastrophes:

In "Samantha's da Vinci Dilemma," she summons legendary artist Leonardo da Vinci to paint Samantha's house.

In "Samantha's Thanksgiving to Remember,"

Esmeralda says she "couldn't have been more than one hundred" when she made the tower lean, and in "Samantha's Yoo-Hoo Maid," she says she was once a lady-in-waiting to a wife of Henry VIII (who ruled from 1509 to 1547, so she's no "spring witchen").

Bombay's A-Way About Him

Dr. Bombay used a bevy of witch-nurses and supernatural medicinal devices to heal the witch-ills of the world. Some of these metaphysical contraptions included the *atmospheric oscillator* (from "Okay, Whose the Wise Witch?"), a *witch-hunter* ("Samantha's Psychic Pslip"), and an *amber corpuscular evaluator* ("Samantha the Bard").

His initial diagnosis of any ailment is usually wrong, as was the case in his first appearance in "There's Gold in Them Thar Pills." Here, Endora threatens to replace him with Dr. Agraphor, as Bombay is reluctant to assist in the matter at hand, which includes treating mortals. Not just any mortal, but Darrin, who has a cold. While Sam's away, Endora has called for the witch doc, who gives Darrin (and later Larry and a client, who also both have colds), pills that have unpleasant side effects in the form of high-pitched voices.

Bombay was first referred to as a *warlock doctor* by Samantha. Later, she tells a doubtful Darrin something like: "He's the only witch doctor we have."

In "Ancient Macedonian Dodo Birds," Sam says Bombay is "just our practitioner; you should see our specialist."

In "Weep No More My Willow," it's learned that Bombay was riding entry number seven in the Ostrich Derby in Sydney, Australia, but he came in last. Yet, the good witch doctor has always remained a very active fellow—witness his escapades with his nurses.

Also, he plants a flag on the summit of Mount Everest, alongside flags of England, Switzerland, and the United States. And he climbs the Matterhorn in "Samantha's Curious Cravings."

In "Samantha the Bard," after Endora misdiagnoses Sam's condition as *Venetian verbal virus*, Bombay also miscalls it as *secondary vocabularyitis*, finally making the proper diagnosis of *primary vocabularyitis*, employing his *amber corpuscular evaluato*r (which, according to Darrin, "no home should be without") and treatment by sound-wave injection. Of his first diagnosis, Bombay says: "Same family as *verbal virus*, but the cure is completely different."

In "Mixed Doubles," Bombay describes the transcendental transplant potion: "Marrow of tooth of saber-toothed tiger, eye of newt, toe of frog, wool of bat, and dietetic cola." His favorite tongue twister is: "Willy Warlock walked away with Wally Walrus."

In "Samantha's Psychic Pslip," there is a wealth of Bombay puns: "I must get back to my nurse, Hazel. Cute little witch. Get it? Witch? Hazel? Witch Hazel?" and "Thursday? So am I. Let's have another drink." During his prognosis of Sam's hiccup-related, various-cycle-appearance disease, he says, "You showed a lack of *wheel* power" and "Your problem is not only logical but *cycle*-logical." Sam comments on his athletic attire: "That's what you wear when you play golf?" He replies: "It is when I'm playing a round with my nurse."

In "Samantha's Witchcraft Blows a Fuse," Bombay's nurse says: "Bomb's away. I call him Bomb." Sam: "What does he call you?" Nurse: "Often. He calls me often." She also says: "I'm his receptionist. I'm very receptive." Later, after

Sam states, "I'm running out of patience," Bombay adds: "You and me both [patients]."

Tabitha's Twitchery

In "Nobody's Perfect," Tabitha levitates all of her toys during a photo session with famous baby photographer Diego Fenman, who is driven out of his tree.

In "How Green Was My Grass," her pediatrician is Dr. McDonald. In "Nobody's Perfect," it's Dr. Koblin.

In "I Don't Want To Be a Toad," she asks: "Is this one of those things called a problem?"

In "Cousin Serena Strikes Again," Part 2, she says: "I want to stay and hear you scream, Daddy."

In "Samantha the Sculptress": "You're a good yeller, Daddy."

In "And Something Makes Four," she says about Adam: "He's very nice. How long is he going to stay here?" Later, she magically gives him a rattle:

Tabitha: "It's my being-born present."
Endora: "Oh, isn't that sweet."
Sam: "Yes… and no."

For her party in "A Bunny for Tabitha," she wears one of the dresses Sam bought her at Hinkley's Department Store in "Samantha's Shopping Spree" (the five-dollar number with the red flowers and blue windowpane checks).

In "Santa Comes to Visit and Stays and Stays": "He kept saying, 'There's no Santa… there's no Santa…' so I turned him into a mushroom."

In "Tabitha's Very Own Samantha," her chin is bandaged, and Sam tells her: "Maybe next time I tell you you're too young to fly, you'll pay attention to me." After Tabitha leaves, Darrin

says: "Women start to get difficult early in life, don't they?"

In "The Corsican Cousins," Sam explains that Tabitha is an international name.

In "Mary the Good Fairy," Tabitha says, "Gee whiz, everything good that happens around here is a secret."

In "Samantha on Thin Ice," she asks her mother: "Is he [Darrin] mad at us?"

In "Tabitha's First Day at School," when Darrin asks her how school went, she replies, "Oh, it's still there."

Tabitha is really just like any other kid; her favorite dessert is chocolate ice cream ("Tabitha's Weekend"), and she wears Poughkeepsie woolen socks ("My Baby the Tycoon"), though Gladys calls them "Kapoopsie."

Adam's Apples and Oranges

Adam was born in "And Something Makes Four," airing on October 16, 1969. David Lawrence made his first appearance as Adam in "The Salem Saga," airing October 8, 1970. He was born at 4:45 A.M. (according to "Makes Four"), and Sam and Darrin originally planned to name him Frank Maurice Stephens ("Naming Samantha's New Baby").

With further regards to Adam's name, Maurice says in "Naming," "That was my great-grandfather's name." Darrin: "*Adam* was your great-grandfather?" Maurice: "Not *that* Adam." Tabitha comments: "I like him the way he is."

In "Salem Here We Come," Adam makes a *no-no* on Hepzibah, prompting Darrin to blurt: "Darn, I wish I'd thought of that."

In "Adam, Warlock or Washout," his powers are revealed, and Darrin makes this comment to the gathered witches and warlocks who have come to find out if his son is mortal or otherwise: "The way you're carrying on [which is very happily], you'd think he'd just taken his first step." Sam: "But... that's exactly what he did."

Maurice's Master Pieces

Samantha's father, Maurice, is a very powerful warlock and is probably the one seriously threatening supernatural force to Darrin (besides the Witches' Council and Endora). Darrin may have been ruffled here and there by Sam's mom, but he is definitely not safe around Maurice, who constantly places his mortal son-in-law at the mercy of some very temperamental mood swings.

Resplendent in top hat and tails (and noted for his eye for the ladies), Maurice has a tendency to quote classic soliloquies in a Shakespearean, if bombastic, fashion.

He resides in London (somewhere), but materializes in his classic Rolls-Royce or has the winds blow at zephyr speeds before making his entry. Like Endora, he arrives at the Stephenses' only to see his daughter and grandchildren, all of whom he loves very much. As to how he feels about Darrin? Well, he refers to him in much the same way as his estranged wife Endora does: hardly at all.

Yet, Maurice is endearing. He loves the theater and has a penchant for the dramatic.

In "Witches and Warlocks Are My Favorite Things," he's on his way to Vienna, and says: "They're doing *Faust* [which includes various devilish references], and I always get a million laughs out of that."

In "Daddy Does His Thing," Maurice mentions that he prefers his martinis made with Spanish gin, Italian vermouth, and a Greek olive. That's exactly how Endora prefers her martinis, but if Maurice knew that, it would be a problem, as he and Endora have a kind of semiseparation. Down deep, however, they truly love each other, and Endora finds it very difficult to resist his charms (some of which are displayed in "And Something Makes Four").

Though Maurice is verbose and, at times, conceited, he's well intentioned, especially where Sam, Tabitha, and Adam are concerned.

Mortal Combats

Abner and Gladys, what a pair. In love but ever at odds.

How long have they been married, anyway? Gladys says in "Illegal Separation" (first shown on May 6, 1965) that she and Abner have been together for thirty years. In "Splitsville" (which aired on May 16, 1969), the Kravitzes' bond has been reduced to twenty-two years. They became engaged while in college, but each would have been too old for college in 1946 (according to calculations). So their earlier date (married in 1935) seems to make more sense.

No matter. Through the years they managed to stay together. By the time Sam and Darrin come to live in the neighborhood, it may have proved more challenging than ever to keep their relationship on an even keel.

Gladys gets very nervous after seeing strange goings-on next door. Abner is never too mystified by his wife's reactions. He's quite the wit when it comes to his reaction to her reactions, which many times have bordered on the maniacal (from his perspective).

Here are some of their interactions:

In "Abner Kadabra":

Gladys: "Guess what I've got!"

Abner: "Heartburn?"

Gladys: "Abner, I've got the power!"

Abner: "Well, take some lemon juice and hot water, that'll knock it out."

Gladys: "It's nothing to joke about."

Abner: "All right, until you get over it, I'll sleep in the den."

In "That Was My Wife," she says to Abner: "You've had your nose stuck in that book all day." Abner: "I want to see how it turns out." Gladys: "It's about the Civil War; the North won" [which is also used in "Weep No More My Willow"].

In "The Joker Is a Card," Abner professes that he "got mugged in the tunnel of love."

In "Take Two Aspirin," Gladys refers to Samantha (who comes down with square green spots disease): "I bet she has some strange disease, and we could catch it. You want to wake up with something strange?" Abner: "I've been doing that for twenty years."

In "Aunt Clara's Old Flame," Gladys says: "Abner, there's a wizard at the Stephenses' house." Abner: "Good for the lawn. It eats the mosquitoes." Gladys: "Not a lizard, a wizard." Abner: "Wizard, lizard, as long as it eats the mosquitoes."

In *Samantha the Dressmaker*, it's made known that Abner and Gladys honeymooned on the S.S. *Sorrento*, and it sank. Abner: "During all the time we were floating around in our life belts, I kept thinking, 'Somebody's trying to tell me something.'"

In "The Short Happy Circuit of Aunt Clara," Abner says to Gladys: "Have you got that buzzing in your head again?" and, "You'll be all right, dear, just as soon as the swelling goes down." Abner: "Gladys, it's dangerous to stand by the window. Somebody might throw a rock at you." Gladys: "Who would do a thing like that?" Abner: "Me, if you don't sit down and shut up."

In "The Crone of Cawdor," Gladys is on the phone to Samantha: "I have a visitor here, and I have a feeling that she's your kind of people." Later, Abner says: "You'll say anything to get me up."

In "Ancient Macedonian Dodo Birds," Gladys says: "Tabitha Stephens just made a newspaper fly through the air like it had wings. Do you know what that proves?" Abner: "Mmm-hmmm. News travels fast."

In "Sam's Secret Saucer," Abner is having a dream. Gladys wakes him up because there are spacemen (whom Aunt Clara accidentally conjured up) next door. Abner to Gladys: "I think your curlers are wound too tight."

In "Splitsville," Gladys ends up staying with Sam and Darrin, which in itself is a very strange development that gets stranger—for Sam and Darrin, that is. Gladys proves to be quite the obnoxious houseguest. She's demanding, selfish, and almost runs the household—so much so, that Darrin almost yearns for a visit from Endora.

Also in "Splitsville," in which there's a Kravitz breakup, Gladys cakes her face with a mud pack, which introduces the Stephenses to her health-oriented lifestyle. As her visit continues, she prepares the following dishes for her host and hostess: alfalfa soup, organic vegetable loaf, kumquat pudding, and soybean brownies. Meanwhile, Abner is as happy as a lark, singing, whistling, and dancing while mowing the lawn.

Contrary to the way he has often been perceived, Abner is not without energy, and his facetiousness is ever rampant and always evident.

In "Samantha the Bard," he witnesses Sam's

(bespelled) rhyming, and says to Gladys (who pushes him out the door): "Don't shove, my love."

In "Santa Comes to Visit and Stays and Stays," he declares: "Gladys, let's play house. You be the door, and I'll shut you."

In "Tabitha's Very Own Samantha," he says: "Great news. Hurricane Gladys is right off your starboard bow."

In "Daddy Does His Thing," Gladys says to Abner: "I tell you it is a jackass, and she is feeding it eggs Benedict for breakfast." Abner: "Lucky jackass, all I ever get is lumpy oatmeal."

In "Tabitha's Very Own Samantha," Gladys shows concern more than curiosity for once when she reacts to what she perceives as strange behavior by Sam, who responds: "There's nothing wrong with me." Gladys: "That's what they all say." Gladys to Darrin: "She keeps insisting she's fine. That's what they all say, you know." Darrin by phone in the tag: "She's fine, Mrs. Kravitz. Of course, that's what they all say." (Sam mouths along from the couch.)

In "Darrin Goes Ape," after Gladys makes a phone call ("Hello, operator, get me the corpse— I mean cops"), Abner sums up what could have been the answer to everybody's problem: "Gladys," he says, "if you had any compassion for your fellow neighbor, you'd move."

Some Little Scenes That Whisper Louise

Larry and Louise each appear for the first time in "It Shouldn't Happen to a Dog," which also happens to be the first episode to feature a McMann and Tate client (Jack Warden's Rex Barker).

Like Samantha, Louise is very supportive of her husband, and she puts up with many business-oriented meetings, luncheons, and dinner parties. Unlike Sam, however, Louise is more prone to talk back to her husband, and speak in a snippy fashion.

In "Double Split," Louise explains how she and Larry got engaged: "One night he blew a smoke ring. I stuck my finger in it and said, "I do."" She spars later with Larry, who says: "I've got news for you, Tinted Top: I run my business the way I see fit, and I don't need any suggestions from the corset crowd." She comes back with: "Be my guest, Snow White."

Overall, Louise (who, according to "Hansel and Gretel in Samanthaland," belongs to the Women's League) is a sensitive soul who goes through some slight badgering.

In "Accidental Twins," Sam creates a double birthday party for the Tates' son, and Louise reacts: "I'm beginning to feel like a yo-yo," and, "Is this a birthday party, or am I training for the Olympics?"

In "Samantha's Magic Mirror," Louise has been on the phone all day. Larry says: "I wonder how Miss AT&T managed to squeeze me into her schedule." Sam then states: "You and Louise should take a little vacation." Larry: "You mean from each other?" However, he later gets on the horn and says: "Hello, Teddy Bear [that's Louise]. How would you like to pack your toothbrush and your chin strap and come to Chicago?"

In "The Ghost Who Made a Spectre of Himself," Larry says his wife "has a pretty tough hide. When it comes to handling ugly moods, Louise is a specialist. She's been handling mine for years."

"Spectre" deals with a sex-starved ghost who possesses Darrin's body. Louise: "He asked me to the gardener's cottage with him." Larry: "What for?"

Louise: "What do you think?"

Larry: "Oh. It's obvious he's having a nervous breakdown."

Darrin is flirting. Louise: "Why is he acting so ridiculous?" Larry: "Because you're old enough to be Darrin's... sister." Larry finally defends his wife and says to Darrin [who is now depossessed]: "The soufflé fell, and you're next." Yet Louise still sniffles about it all: "What you're all saying is that unless somebody's out of his mind, he couldn't possibly be interested in me."

Louise also sheds tears in "Samantha Loses Her Voice," when she and Larry are fighting. He consoles her, though, as he does most every time.

In fact, in "Santa Comes for a Visit and Stays and Stays," Larry wonders if he should buy Louise an expensive mink coat. Filled with the spirit, his *loving* gives in. The audience is led to believe that he truly cares for Louise and that he appreciates all of her support.

Phyllis-Ophical and Frank-Ness

Darrin's parents (Frank and Phyllis) were married thirty-five years as of November 2, 1967 (the air date of "Out of Sync, Out of Mind"). In "A Nice Little Dinner Party", Phyllis says they've been wed for forty. They don't know their daughter-in-law is a witch, so anything supernatural must be kept from them whenever they visit.

Phyllis is convinced she's going crazy more often than not during such visits. She usually begins feeling ill and complains to her husband with: "I'm getting a sick headache."

Frank was named for his grandfather (according to "Naming Samantha's New Baby");

Darrin was named for his grandfather ("It's Wishcraft"); so where did "Grover Stephens" (Darrin's apparent grandfather in "Samantha's Old Man") come from? It's simple. Three episodes, three different writers, three different directors, and a slight vagary of the series.

In "Out of Sync, Out of Mind," Darrin calls his father when his mother says not to. "Darrin Stephens," Phyllis begins, "you do that again and I'll box your ears." Dr. Bombay is called to fix a hex on Sam, but he thinks Phyllis is the patient. "You've got a very sick witch here," the good doctor mistakenly reports. "Oh well, she's not too warm for a mortal."

While talking with Serena in "Mrs. Stephens, Where Are You?," Phyllis mentions that she and Frank have never met Sam's father, whom they finally meet for the first and only time in "Naming Samantha's New Baby."

In "Mrs. Stephens, Where Are You," Phyllis discusses Uncle Arthur at length with Serena, but nowhere in the series do Darrin's parents encounter Sam's practical-joking relative. Also in "Where Are You," due to a mis-spell, Phyllis says: "My, that sherry was strong" (Serena had turned her into a cat). Frank asks: "Phyllis, what is that around your neck?" She replies: "My bell to warn birds."

In "Tabitha's Weekend," Mabel Albertson does the voice of "Black Bart," the mynah bird owned by Phyllis. The bird says: "I'm Black Bart," "Hello there baby," and, "Frank, I'm getting a sick headache." Samantha also tells Endora (about Phyllis): "Most grandparents don't have grandchildren who can turn them into toads." After Phyllis says: "Now that we're all here I have an idea," Endora takes her best shot: "Oh, beginner's luck." (They have been feuding since "A Nice Little Dinner Party.")

In "Samantha and the Antique Doll," Phyllis

thinks she has supernatural powers; one subject which she believes Samantha knows "nothing about." She also scolds Darrin: "This is a private conversation… Out!" And asks Sam: "Do you know what a *familiar* is?" Earlier, Phyllis had shown Frank her childhood doll (which Samantha makes her think has inspirational powers), saying: "It's my familiar." Frank: "Well, it should be familiar, you've had it since you were a child." Phyllis later believes she's turned Frank into a mule during a seance rigged by Samantha. But she really hasn't. It's just all part of Sam's plan to reunite Phyllis and Frank.

Terms of Enchantment

Abner!—The primal scream of Gladys Kravitz, heard anytime after she has witnessed any-thing unusual at Samantha and Darrin's or with regard to the magic mayhem in general.

Bewitched—A general term referring to some-one or something which has been supernat-urally manipulated by a witch or warlock.

Cosmos Cotillion, The—A very hip function held annually for only the coolest of witch-es and warlocks. The affair includes fine intergalactic entertainment, as when Serena employed the mortal rock duo Boyce and Hart to perform a song she composed (*Blow You a Kiss in the Wind*) at the ball.

Cotton Top — Serena's playful nickname for Larry Tate.

Darwin, Durwood, Dagwood, Donald, Dennis, Dumb-Dumb, Dumbo, Derek, Darwood, Durweed, Darius, David,

Dobbin — Names Endora calls Darrin. [Maurice also calls him *Dobbin*, while Serena usually refers to him as *Tall, Dark, and Nothing*.]

Dematerialize/Dematerialization—Terms used whenever a given person, place, or thing disappears because of a spell.

Freeze (also known as *Deep Freeze*)—A spell cast by a witch or warlock that completely halts the physical, verbal, and conscious movement of a particular subject.

Ha ha … ha ha … nothing—Dr. Bombay's self-effacing response to his less-than-funny and often disappointing attempts at humor.

Hiya, Sammi—A greeting to Samantha used by Uncle Arthur and Serena.

Good—A retort spoken by Samantha, express-ing her satisfaction with a particular situa-tion (magic or otherwise).

I have a sick headache—A claim made many times by Darrin's mother, Phyllis, to her husband, Frank, after she witnesses strange goings-on at her son's house.

I love you very much—A response Samantha employs (mostly in the latter years of her marriage) whenever she thinks Darrin is really mad.

I wish you wouldn't call him that;

I wish you wouldn't say that—Phrases used by a semispooked Darrin whenever Samantha tells him that Dr. Bombay is the only witch doctor available.

Larry!—Louise Tate's plea for her husband to act more appropriately.

Louise!—Larry Tate's plea for his wife to act more appropriately.

Materialize/Materialization—Terms employed

whenever something or someone appears because of a spell.

Metaphysical—A locution used in the witch/warlock world that means *beyond physics* and is used to define their existence.

Metaphysical Continuum—The energy field measured by the witches and warlocks. It may be used also when discussing their source or center.

Mother!—Samantha's scream heard around the witch world whenever havoc strikes the Stephens household. Conflict usually created by Endora's interference with Darrin's personality, looks, position, or situation. If Endora fails to appear, Samantha uses a softer voice and shortens the plea to *Mom?*

Oh, my stars!—A phrase Samantha utters whenever the situation at hand seems a little out of hand.

Oh, dear!—An expression employed by Esmeralda just prior to slowly fading out because of her nerves, a condition brought about by either her witchly mistakes or Darrin's arrival.

Oh, Samantha! Really!—A turn of the tongue employed by Endora whenever she seems somewhat disconcerted with Samantha's words or behavior. [And after speaking her mind, Endora usually pops off in a huff.]

One, two, three, four, five—The counting sequence Samantha applies whenever Endora takes longer than usual to appear, used many times between *Mother!* and *Mom!*

Paging Dr. Bombay!
Paging Dr. Bombay!
Emergency! Emergency!
Come right away!—A verbal appeal given by

Samantha whenever she's in need of the warlock medicine man, Dr. Bombay. (Also heard as: *Calling Dr. Bombay! Calling Dr. Bombay!*)

Pop—A colloquial term for casting a spell of transference.

Sam!—A scream usually heard only around the Stephens home whenever Darrin becomes very upset about the magic goings-on in his life.

"Sam, Can I See You?"
"When?"
"Now!"
"Oh!"—Samantha and Darrin's beginning dialogue that takes place either immediately before or shortly after some magical interference in their lives.

Son-of-a-gun—A group of words usually employed by Larry whenever he is impressed with or approves of Darrin's advertising skills, once spoken a record seven times (in "That Was My Wife"), also stated by Samantha ("Samantha's Curious Cravings") and Endora ("Solid Gold Mother-in-Law").

Twitch—A word describing Samantha's magical nose manipulation, allowing her to perform any amount of supernatural feats.

Uh-oh … Uh-oh … Uh-oh!—An extensive exclamation made by Samantha when it looks as if trouble is in the magic-making mode.

Weeelllll!—A phrase Samantha employs whenever trouble really begins and she is unable to think of an answer to Darrin's queries of "What's going on?"

What's going on?—Usually spoken by a suspicious

Darrin when he calls home from the office.

Why did I say that?—Words voiced by various mortals whenever witchcraft makes them say things against their will or things that they cannot have known.

Witchcraft got you into this mess;

I see no reason why witchcraft

shouldn't get you out of it.—A logic Samantha applies to Darrin's predicament in many instances.

Witches' Honor Sign, The—Samantha occasionally makes this galactic gesture to signify the absolute truth; an oath that Samantha usually asks of her mother, though Sam occasionally uses it to assure Darrin things are as she says they are. The correct Witches' Honor Sign: index and middle fingers of the left hand on either side of the nose with fingertips pointing toward the eyes. While giving the sign, the witch intones, "Witches' Honor." It can be done with the right hand as well. (In "Darrin, Gone and Forgotten," Samantha asks Endora for the sign, with the added phrase, "Spiders that crawl, bats that fly, silence my tongue if I'm telling a lie.")

Zap—A colloquial term for casting a spell.

Elizabeth Montgomery in 1991.

Chapter 13

Oh My Stars and Staff Biographies

Starry, Starry Lives

ELIZABETH MONTGOMERY
Samantha/Serena

....

On December 3, 1951, Elizabeth Montgomery made her professional debut in a drama called *Top Secret* on her father's television series, *Robert Montgomery Presents*, in which she played her father's daughter.

Lizzie (as she preferred to be called) became a featured player on *Presents*, and also appeared in a number of other TV anthology shows, including *Studio One, The Twilight Zone, Kraft Theater, GE Theater, Alcoa Presents, One Step Beyond,* and *Armstrong Circle Theater*.

She emerged on Broadway in plays like *The Loud Red Patrick* with Arthur Kennedy and David Wayne, and *Late Love* with Arlene Francis and Cliff Robertson. *Late* was Elizabeth's Broadway debut, for which she received the Theater World Award for *Most Promising Newcomer of the 1953–54* season.

In 1954, she married blue-blooded New Yorker Frederick Gallatin Cammann, a descendent of Albert Gallantin, Thomas Jefferson's secretary of the treasury. The union ended soon afterward.

In 1957, Lizzie married Gig Young (who died in 1978) and semiretired from acting. Her marriage to Young lasted until 1963, when she returned to acting full throttle, making three films in a row, the first being *Johnny Cool* in 1963. Here she met

We all came from different worlds, but ended up at the same wonderful place.

KASEY ROGERS
on the career diversity of the Bewitched *actors and production team.*

•••••••••••••••••••••••••••••

Elizabeth Montgomery at an early age.

and married future *Bewitched* associate William Asher, who directed and produced *Cool.*

She also appeared in *Who's Been Sleeping in My Bed?* (1964), which starred Dean Martin and her good friend Carol Burnett, and *The Court Martial of Billy Mitchell* (1955), which featured Gary Cooper and Robert F. Simon, who would later play one of her father-in-laws on *Bewitched.*

When *Bewitched* ended its original network run in 1972, she took one year off and returned to television in a movie-of-the-week entitled *The Victim*. It was her first dramatic performance since before *Bewitched*. Other television films followed, including *Mrs. Sundance* (1974), during which she met longtime love Robert Foxworth, and the chilling *Legend of Lizzie Borden* (1975).

Her shattering portrayal of a sexually and emotionally abused woman in *A Case of Rape* (1974) earned her an Emmy nomination, while the movie itself received one of the ten highest ratings for a made-for-television film in the medium's history.

Other small-screen movies included *Dark Victory* (1976 remake of the Bette Davis 1939 film classic about a woman with a brain tumor), *A Killing Affair* (a 1977 interracial love story also starring O. J. Simpson), *The Awakening Land* (a 1978 miniseries), *An Act of Violence* (1979), *When the Circus Comes to Town* (a 1981 romantic comedy), *The Rules of Marriage* (a two-part movie from 1982 with Elliot Gould), and *Missing Pieces* (1983).

There were also films like *Second Sight: A Love Story* (1984), *Amos* (with Kirk Douglas, in 1985), *From Darkness 'Til the Dawn* (also in 1985), *Face to Face* (1990; also starring Robert Foxworth), *Sins of the Mother* (1991; based on the true crime book, *Son*). Each of these movies shows Lizzie's talents in a unique way. "They all have different kinds of feels to them," she said. "That's probably one of the reasons why I've done them. I get letters from people saying one of the things they like best about what I've done since *Bewitched* is that they never know what I'm going to do next."

Beyond acting, she had aspirations of becoming a criminal lawyer, a jockey, and an artist for Walt Disney Studios. Of the latter unfulfilled choice, she commented, "But for some reason, I was never asked to be on the payroll. Certainly ruined Walt's career, didn't I?"

Still, her artistic talent remains highly praised.

"One gift I'll always treasure," says *Bewitched* director R. Robert Rosenbaum, "is the painting of a man sitting in a director's chair that Elizabeth created for me."

She remained active on social issues and took every opportunity to make a political statement. "There are times when I know I could still be doing more," she said, "as there are many other things in life that are certainly more important than acting."

She lived in Los Angeles with her husband, actor Robert Foxworth. Besides painting, she also enjoyed tennis, gardening, and cooking. Her children with William Asher are Billy Asher Jr., Robert Asher, and Rebecca Asher.

On Sunday, September 10, 1995, television's top executives, producers, agents, and actors turned out to honor Elizabeth at the Women in Film's Second Annual Lucy Awards.

The award (named for Lucille Ball), also bestowed upon Imogene Coca, Brianne Murphy, Fred Silverman, and Tracey Ullman, is given for innovation in television.

During the three-hour ceremony, which was held at the Beverly Hills Hotel, Robert Foxworth delivered a touching tribute to Elizabeth. Her daughter, Rebecca, accepted the award.

DICK YORK
Darrin

Like Elizabeth Montgomery, Dick York had possessed a strong social awareness and concern for others. In his last years, he was an advocate for the homeless and the less fortunate.

Born September 4, 1928, in Fort Wayne, Indiana, York believed the seeds of his acting career were sown in his Depression-era childhood in Chicago, where his family later moved, and where he began his career in radio in the late 1930s.

Dick York in 1987.

He appeared in many network and local shows, including *Junior Junction* (a children's program), *Jack Armstrong: The All-American Boy* (in 1948), and *That Brewster Boy*.

A student at St. Paul University, York moved to New York in 1950 and began acting on television in many live productions. When TV began the move to California, so did York. He started a commuting routine between New York and the West Coast that ended when he finally transferred his family to Hollywood in 1961.

York met his wife Joan (he was fifteen; she was twelve) when they were acting in a Chicago radio show. He practically ignored her at first, but years later they discovered each other again, courted, and, in 1952, married. Five children followed.

Years before his formal transition to California, York was asked to read for Broadway director Elia Kazan, who cast him in *Tea and Sympathy* in 1953. This brought York a nomination for the Best Supporting Actor Award from the New York Drama Critics. He was also nominated for an Emmy in 1968 for *Bewitched*, as

Outstanding Performance by an Actor in a Leading Role in a Comedy Series.

York appeared in numerous other television shows, including guest spots on *Playhouse 90*, *The Twilight Zone* (two episodes), *Alfred Hitchcock Presents* (as a hired killer), *Route 66*, *Thriller*, *Rawhide*, *Wagon Train*, *Goodyear Playhouse* (*Visit to a Small Planet*, 1955), *The U.S. Steel Hour*, *Father Knows Best*, and *Kraft Theater*.

After *Bewitched*, he appeared on *Simon and Simon*, *Fantasy Island*, and *Our Time*, a mid-1980s NBC summer show hosted by Karen Valentine (of *Room 222* fame), which would be his final on-air acting appearance on August 10, 1985.

Dick Sargent and Lisa Hartman (of the *Tabitha* series) were slated to do a *Bewitched* takeoff in *Time*, but things didn't work. The sketch included Hartman walking into Sam and Darrin's kitchen as Tabitha, seeing York's Darrin, turning away, and having Sargent's Darrin appear in York's place. Tabitha was then to display how confused she was, because her father seemed to be a different person.

York's film credits include *My Sister Eileen* (1955), *Cowboy* (1958), *They Came to Cordura* (1959, when he developed his back ailment), and *Inherit the Wind* (1960).

He lived in Rockford, Michigan, and suffered from a deteriorating spine and emphysema. Despite his physical condition, the actor cared for the homeless. He was a master of his craft, and his heart was filled with compassion for the less fortunate.

Not one for sympathy, York said: "I'm going to keep on doing what I'm doing, no matter what happens. Whether or not *Bewitched* had given me the opportunity to become a known personality or not, I still would have pursued the path I'm on now.

"There are so many young people who cut their teeth on *Bewitched*, that I'm more amazed every day at the show's response. I guess you never know the impact you're going to have."

Dick York passed into spirit on February 20, 1992, at the age of sixty-three.

DICK SARGENT
Darrin

Dick Sargent was born into show business.

His mother, Ruth McNaughton, was an actress who had supporting roles in films such as *Four Horsemen of the Apocalypse* (1961) and *Hearts and Triumphs* (1962). His father, Colonel Elmer Cox, was the business manager of Douglas Fairbanks, among others.

Sargent was enrolled at San Rafael Military School in Menlo Park, California. During his years at Stanford University, he starred in some twenty-five plays with the Stanford Players Theater. He was born Richard Cox, and upon his graduation he won a bit part in MGM's *Prisoner of War* (1954) and changed his name to *Sargent*.

As a struggling actor, he sustained his hopes and needs with a variety of nontheatrical jobs. He even dug ditches. Leaving a position as a department store salesman, he journeyed to the colonial city of San Miguel Allende in Mexico to enter the import-export business. He later began collecting art.

He returned to Hollywood and TV roles in *Medic*, *Playhouse 90*, *Gunsmoke*, *Ripcord*, *West Point*, and *Code 3*.

Dick Sargent

His first major role in a motion picture was as Fo Fo Wilson in 1957's *Bernadine*, for which he received a Laurel Award from the nation's film exhibitors. His other movies include *Operation Petticoat* (1959), *The Great Imposter* (1961), *That Touch of Mink* (1962), *Captain Newman, M.D.* (1963), *For Love or Money* (1964), and T*he Ghost and Mr. Chicken* (1966).

Sargent made dramatic appearances on TV's *The Six Million Dollar Man, Fantasy Island, Vegas, Trapper John M.D.,* among others; in films like *Hardcore* (1979, with George C. Scott), and the witch-spoof, *Teen Witch* (1990). He credited his age and ability to draw upon a larger experience of life as contributory to his expansion as an actor.

His other television appearances included *Family Ties* and an episode of the revived *Columbo* series. In that appearance, Dick played himself sitting in on a poker game with actress Nancy Walker and other celebrities. Peter Falk's character quizzes the game players about a particular mystery. Columbo recognizes Dick from *Bewitched* and says, "I loved that show."

Sargent appeared in twenty-three motion pictures, four made-for-TV movies, and five series of his own. His most recent regular series, *Down to Earth*, was supernaturally premised like *Bewitched*—only instead of having a witch for a wife, he had an angel (Carol Mansell as Ethel) for a maid.

Sargent, like Dick York, was dedicated to ridding the world of hunger and offered hope and support in places where there was little of either.

The Special Olympics were one of the most rewarding experiences of his life. "There are so many of these athletes who can tell me the plots of every *Bewitched* episode. No matter what they're going through, the show seems to be one of the things their minds cling to.

"This makes me happy to know that the power of television has been put to good use, and that the accident of celebrity can be used for something else besides filling up scrapbooks."

About three years before his death by prostate cancer on July 8, 1994, Dick Sargent revealed that he was homosexual. The high rate of suicide among young gays was the reason for his decloaking from the closet. He wanted them to have a role model, to have his message live on.

"Gay and lesbian people," he said, "are just like everybody else."

AGNES MOOREHEAD
Endora

Of Protestant Irish background, Agnes Robertson Moorehead was born on December 6, 1906, in Clinton, Massachusetts, the only child of Reverend John Henderson Moorehead, a minister. Her mother, Mary Mildred MacCauley, had been reared in rural Pennsylvania. Soon after the birth of

Agnes Moorehead

Agnes, the Mooreheads moved to St. Louis, Missouri, where Mr. Moorehead had been assigned to a new pastorate.

At age ten, Agnes spent her summers performing in the theater and also worked with the St. Louis Municipal Opera Company for four years. After completing high school in 1919, she attended Muskingum College in New Concord, Ohio, a coeducational institution founded by an uncle. Agnes majored in biology, performed in the glee club, and was an active member of the Girls Athletic Association and the Student Volunteer Group.

After receiving her bachelor's degree, she remained at Muskingum for an additional year of postgraduate work, majoring in education, speech, and English. The following year she transferred to the University of Wisconsin to be closer to home. There she earned her master's degree in English and public speaking, and later received a doctorate in literature from Bradley University in Illinois.

While attending Wisconsin University, Moorehead began teaching English and public speaking in nearby Soldiers Grove and coached the local drama club. In 1926, she enrolled in the American Academy of Dramatic Arts in New York, where she met John Griffith Lee, whom she married on June 6, 1930. Soon after, she began winning Broadway and radio roles. She became one of radio's most active performers and took part in programs like *The March of Time, Cavalcade of America*, and *Mayor of the Town*. One of her most notable performances was in the radio play, *Sorry, Wrong Number*.

Moorehead's radio comedy credits were *The Fred Allen Show, The Phil Baker Show* (in which she worked with *Bewitched* executive producer Harry Ackerman), and stints with Bob Hope and Jack Benny.

It was her longtime association with Orson Welles and his historic Mercury Theater Company in New York City where she received the most rigorous training. It was an ensemble with a theatrical hierarchy, including Welles and other acting greats such as Joseph Cotten, Everett Sloan, and (director) John Houseman.

In 1941, The Mercury Players made their first film, entitled *Citizen Kane*, in which Agnes made her screen debut (playing Kane's mother). Other movies with the Welles troupe: *The Magnificent Ambersons* (1942, in which she was Oscar-nominated for her role as Aunt Fanny), *Journey Into Fear* (1943), and *Jane Eyre* (1944).

Agnes was also nominated for an Academy Award for roles in *Mrs. Parkington* (1944), *Johnny Belinda* (1948), and *Hush-Hush, Sweet Charlotte* (1964).

Her other films included *Dark Passage* (1947), *The Revolt of Mamie Stover* (1956), and *The Conquerer* (1956), which was filmed in St. George, Utah.

This last motion picture was the subject of controversy.

Moorehead, Dick Powell, John Wayne, and Susan Hayward, all members of *The Conqueror*'s cast, all died of cancer. Many claim their deaths were attributable to the film's location shooting, which was close to a nuclear testing site. Tons of Utah's red oil was brought back to the studio sets for matching purposes.

Agnes Moorehead's numerous TV appearances include *The Twilight Zone*, *Shirley Temple Theater*, *Studio One*, *Night Gallery* (she played an old crone of a witch), and *The Wild, Wild West*. She won an Emmy for *Wild*, in which she played Emma Valentine in an episode entitled "Night of the Vicious Valentine."

In the early 1950s, Agnes toured the United States and Europe in readings of *Don Juan in Hell*.

Moorehead took many stage bows with the Mercury Players, but later, during the filming of *Bewitched*, toured the country with her one-woman show, *An Evening with the Fabulous Red Head*.

Her favorite color, however, was lavender.

She was nicknamed "The Lavender Lady" by one of the maids at her Beverly Hills home. She adored the color purple, drove a lavender 1956 Thunderbird, and decorated both her mansion and *Bewitched* dressing rooms in her pet hue. Of course, she also appeared frequently in purple as Endora.

The great Agnes Moorehead passed away on April 30, 1974.

DAVID WHITE
Larry Tate

David White was born in Denver, Colorado, on April 4, 1916, and received his dramatic training in the 1940s at the Cleveland Playhouse, the Pasadena Playhouse, and Los Angeles City College.

After serving overseas with the Marine Corps for twenty-eight months during World War II, David spent the early postwar era appearing in stage productions of *Home of the Brave*, *Command Decision*, and *State of the Union*. Shortly thereafter, he landed his first major Broadway role in *Leaf and Bough*. He played a small-town drunk with two sons, portrayed by Richard Hart and Charlton Heston, who was only eight years younger than David.

David White in 1989.

The play was a critical failure and ran only two days.

David's performance, however, was impressive, and he went on to more successful Broadway productions, including *The Bird Cage*, *Anniversary Waltz*, and *Romeo and Juliet*.

His film highlights include *Sweet Smell of Success* (1957), *The Apartment* (1960), *Sunrise at Campobello* (1960), *The Great Imposter* (1961), and *Madison Avenue* (1962), the latter two titles of which seemed to foreshadow his role as Darrin's New York boss on *Bewitched*.

White appeared in several TV dramas, including *Studio One*, *Kraft Theater*, *Playhouse 90*, and *The Untouchables*, where he worked with Elizabeth Montgomery in an episode entitled "The Rusty Heller Story."

After *Bewitched*, White made numerous guest appearances in series TV, including *The Rockford Files*, *Rhoda*, *Phyllis*, *The Mary Tyler Moore Show*, *Quincy*, *Remington Steele*, and *Cagney and Lacey*.

His later stage productions included a role in *Savages* at the Mark Taper Forum in Los Angeles, *Enemy of the People* (at the Seattle Repertory), and *Catholics* (at ACT, Seattle).

To pay the rent before his acting career began to flourish, David worked as a farmer, a truck driver, and an executive doorman at the Roxy Theater in New York. He was for a while employed by the J. H. Taylor Management Company, also of New York, and was offered a very prestigious management position.

He responded with a very pleasant, "No thank you, sir, I'm going to be an actor."

And that he was, and a mighty fine one.

White was married to the late actress Mary Welch, who once appeared with her husband on stage in a tour of *Tea and Sympathy*. She also played Charity Hackett in Samuel Fuller's movie version of *Park Row* (1952), and enjoyed a large variety of television credits.

David had one son, Jonathan White (who died in an airline accident in 1988) with Mary Welch, and a daughter, Alexandra White (from a second marriage with Lisa Figus). David White passed away November 26, 1990.

MARION LORNE
Aunt Clara

Before *Bewitched*, television aficionados knew Marion Lorne as Mrs. Gurney on *Mr. Peepers*, starring Wally Cox, and as a stooge on *The Gary Moore Show*. Long before that, Lorne had been the reigning star for many years at the prestigious Whitehall Theater in London.

A very young Marion Lorne in 1935.

She appeared in hit after hit, role after role, each written especially for Lorne by her late husband, Walter Hackett.

"There is no actress on the stage today who can be compared with her," wrote one critic.

Lorne was never a raving beauty, and she knew it. But she also didn't care. Her forte was humor. "In my long, long career," she told *TV Guide* in 1968, "I have played everything, but comedy has always been my favorite."

Most of the characters her husband created for her at Whitehall seemed to have had an Aunt Clara feel. "People seem to like this vague, silly woman," she said.

Alfred Hitchcock directed Lorne in *Strangers on a Train*, in which she appeared with *Bewitched*'s Kasey Rogers.

He was asked which American actress could be compared to Lorne in her London days. Tallulah Bankhead? Helen Hayes? Katherine Cornell?

"All of them put together, and more," Hitchcock replied. "She was more than an actress in England, she was an institution."

Lorne was born in the United States in 1886 in a Pennsylvania mining town called West Pittston, near Wilkes-Barre. Her parents were Scottish and English. She attended the American Academy of Dramatic Arts in New York, played summer stock in Hartford, Connecticut, and made it to Broadway, where she was an instant hit.

"I've been in a complete and absolute panic ever since," she told a reporter. "I've always wanted to retire, but I could never quit."

Lorne did try to retire once, after the sudden death of her husband in 1942. But shortly thereafter she was offered the part of the potty old lady, Veta Louise Simmons, in the road company of *Harvey*.

Marion appeared in several other stage productions and numerous TV shows such as *The Ed Sullivan Show*, *The Dinah Shore Show*, and *The Jack Paar Show*, all prior to her Clara part on *Bewitched*, a role some say she was born to play and for which she posthumously received an Emmy. While the show was in production on May 9, 1968, Marion Lorne passed on at the age of eighty-two.

PAUL LYNDE
Uncle Arthur

Broadway, film, and television audiences began their love affair with Paul Lynde at the Number One Fifth Avenue, where he received his first break: He was a stand-up comedian. Then came *Leonard Sillman's New Faces Of 1952* on Broadway (which also launched the careers of Lynde's *Bewitched* costars Alice Pearce and Alice Ghostley, as well as Eartha Kitt, Carol Lawrence, and oth-

Paul Lynde

ers). A two-year TV run on *The Perry Como Show* followed, as did Broadway and film versions of *Bye Bye Birdie* (1963), which featured Lynde's rousing rendition of the tune *Kids*.

Before his untimely death from a heart attack in January 1982, Paul appeared in summer stock stage productions of *The Impossible Years*, *Don't Drink the Water*, and *Plaza Suite*. He was in the 1954 movie version of *New Faces* (with Alice Ghostley), and in the films *Send Me No Flowers* (1964) and *Rabbit Test* (1978).

Besides bewitching the TV world as Uncle Arthur, Lynde graced the small screen on *The Dean Martin Show*, *The Kraft Music Hall*, *The Donny and Marie Show*, and daytime and prime-time editions of the popular game show *Hollywood Squares*, where for years he occupied the center square (many times co-guesting with Elizabeth Montgomery).

Lynde also starred in two series of his own: *The Paul Lynde Show* and *The New Temperature's Rising Show*, both of which were produced by William Asher, who had directed him in the *Beach Blanket Bingo* feature of 1965 and, of course, *Bewitched*.

The flamboyant performer made several stage appearances before and after his stint as Sam's warlock relation, in which he appeared with Elizabeth Montgomery's mother, Elizabeth Allen (*Mother Is Engaged*), and Alice Ghostley (*Stop, Thief, Stop*).

With tongue in cheek, he handled his success well.

"I always had delusions of grandeur," the actor told an interviewer in 1974. "As far back as I can remember, I was obsessed with being rich and famous."

Lynde was born and raised in Mount Vernon, Ohio, and was a graduate of Northwestern University. He lived his formative years in the Mount Vernon jail, where his father was sheriff for a two-year elective term.

Paul dated his original urge to become an actor from the time he was four or five years old. Shortly after the birth of a younger brother, his mother took him to see the original version of *Ben Hur* in 1926.

As he said in 1974, "I was movie-struck then, and I am movie-struck now."

ALICE GHOSTLEY
Esmeralda

Alice Ghostley was born in Eve, Missouri, and spent part of her childhood in Arkansas and Oklahoma. It was in a small Oklahoma town that her high school teacher inspired her to pursue a dramatic career. Following graduation from the University of Oklahoma (where she minored in drama), Ghostley headed for New Jersey and eventually New York.

"I always wanted to be a movie star like Ruby Keeler," she admits, "and I was just seventeen. I thought the big city was the place to begin."

Alice Ghostley

Alice was also inspired by a cousin who was a tightrope walker for the Ringling Bros. and Barnum and Bailey Circus. She later teamed with her sister, Gladys, and they did an act called *The Ghostley Sisters*.

The actress remembers:

"When I first started out, I had this natural ability to sing. That was another reason why I chose New York, with all the musicals that were happening at the time. But I looked so different from everyone else. I was never what you would call an ingenue. I was having difficulty finding jobs. Get your eyes straightened, they would tell me, and maybe we can work with you."

For a while, nothing happened. To pay for acting lessons, Alice worked in a restaurant, a cosmetics factory, a detective agency, and a motion picture theater.

After some assistance from actor/composer/lyricist G. Wood, Ghostley's big break arrived: She sang *The Boston Beguine* on Broadway with Paul Lynde in *New Faces of 1952*.

Other Broadway appearances included *The Sign in Sidney Brustein's Window*, for which she earned a Tony Award for Best Actress and the Saturday Review Award for Best Performance of the 1964/1965 season. She also received a Tony Award nomination for her role in *The Beauty Part* by S. J. Perelman.

Ghostley recently reemerged on stage as Miss Hannigan in 907 Broadway productions of *Annie*, and in the New York and Vancouver productions of *Nunsense*.

Ghostley's motion picture credits include *To Kill a Mockingbird* (1962), *The Flim Flam Man* (1967), *The Graduate* (1967, with Marion Lorne) *Viva Max* (1969), *Gator* (1976), *Rabbit Test* (with Paul Lynde, 1978), *Grease* (also in 1978), and the blockbuster film *Titanic* (1997).

On television, she was recently Emmy nominated for her role as *Bernice Clifton* in the still-popular, in-syndication "bitch-com," *Designing Women*. She is also remembered fondly for TV parts in such diverse productions as *Twelfth Night*, *The Jackie Gleason Show*, *The Jonathan Winters Show* (1967 to 1969), and her starring role in *Captain Nice* (1966 to 1967).

Ghostley survives her actor/husband Felice Orlandi and lives in Studio City, California.

BERNARD FOX
Dr. Bombay

Born in South Wales, Bernard Fox is the fifth generation of his family to pursue a career in the theater. During the war he served in the Royal Navy. Upon his release he joined the well-known York Repertory Company.

In 1952, he appeared in *Reluctant Heroes*, *Simple Spymen*, and *Dry Rot* for London's Whitehall Farce Players. Upon leaving the troupe, he was seen in other London productions, such as G. B.

Shaw's *Misalliance*, *Saturday Night at the Crown*, and a musical version of *The Bells* at the Irving Theater.

In England, he appeared in films like *Star of India* (1954), *Blue Murder at St. Trinians* (1958), and *The Safecracker* (also 1958, with Ray Milland).

The 1958–59 British television season saw him starring in *Three Live Wires*, a sitcom somewhat similar to America's *Sergeant Bilko* series with Phil Silvers.

Bernard's first Hollywood stint was performed at the Civic Playhouse in a production of *Write Me a Murder*. Numerous televisions followed, including spots on the *Danny Thomas*, *Dick Van Dyke*, and *Andy Griffith* shows. Besides his recurring role as Dr. Bombay on *Bewitched*, Fox was Colonel Crittenden, a semi-regular role on *Hogan's Heroes*.

Bernard Fox

After *Bewitched*, Fox went on to star in the 1972 TV movie, *The Hound of the Baskervilles*, in which he was perfectly cast as the affable *Dr. Watson* to Stewart Granger's *Sherlock Holmes*. Several small-screen movie and program shots followed.

Bernard's motion picture resumé includes *Strange Bedfellows* (1964), *Star!* (1968), *Big Jake* (1971), Walt Disney's *Herbie Goes to Monte Carlo* (1977), and *Private Eyes* (1980).

From 1973 to 1979, Bernard was the Victorian chairman (master of ceremonies) in America's only British music hall, The Mayfair Music Hall in Santa Monica, California, which also once housed the West Coast troupe of Chicago's *Second City* comedians.

The experience and knowledge Fox gained over the years has proved invaluable: his one-man show, *Music Hall Memories*, plays successfully around colleges, conventions, private groups, and in large gatherings, such as the British-American festival in Sante Fe Springs, California.

Fox lives with his wife, Jacqueline, and their two daughters, Amanda and Valerie, in California's San Fernando Valley. He frequently makes television appearances on commercials and in shows like *Murder, She Wrote*.

DIANE MURPHY
Tabitha

Diane Murphy was born five minutes before her twin sister Erin on June 17, 1964, at St. Joseph's Hospital in Burbank, California. Following the double birth, their mother, Stephanie, gave up her job as a teacher to devote herself full-time to the girls. Wherever she took them the twins drew attention.

When a talent agent wanted to sign them up, Stephanie and her husband, Dan, agreed to give it a shot.

Unlike her twin sister, Erin, Diane Murphy was never interested in the acting profession.

Today, she has an M.B.A. in management from Golden Gate University, San Francisco, and a

Diane Murphy

bachelor's degree in psychology and sociology from the University of California, Santa Barbara.

She is the associate executive director of Shelter Services for Women, a nonprofit organization that operates three shelters for battered women and their children in Santa Barbara. Her primary duties are grant writing, contract management, and budgeting.

Diane, who is openly gay, is also a member of the board of directors of the Greater Santa Barbara Community Association, an organization comprised of business, professional, and community members who are gay and lesbian.

Diane served as chairperson of the association's committee, which gives scholarships to gay and lesbian students based upon their grades and community involvement.

"I'm very happy with my life," she says. "I loved working on *Bewitched*, and it gave me some very unique and wonderful experiences, but eventually I wanted to lead a more regular life. So I quit the entertainment business when I was thirteen years old."

Before she left Hollywood, Diane appeared in numerous commercials (including one with Henry Fonda), and television shows such as the *ABC Afterschool Special, The Magical Mystery Trip Through Little Red*.

ERIN MURPHY
Tabitha

After *Bewitched*, Diane and Erin began to live very different lives, as when Erin continued acting (in shows like *Lassie* and *Hawaii Five-O*), and Diane did not.

Erin Murphy

Later, Erin married, gave birth to sons Jason and Grant, divorced, married singer Eric Eden and gave birth to another son named Clark. She now shares domestic duties with real-life husband who is named Darrin.

She has appeared chatting about her career on talk shows such as *The Maury Povich Show*, *Vicki!*, *Faith Daniels*, *Jenny Jones*, *Geraldo*, *Entertainment Tonight*, and *American Journal* (for a tribute to Elizabeth Montgomery), and at a semi-*Bewitched* reunion (with Bernard Fox) at a Cherry Hill, New Jersey, collectibles show.

"I'm hesitant about getting back into the business," she says, "only because it's something that I definitely would like to do when my children are older. But it has to be the right project. If the right thing came along right now, I would only do it if it didn't conflict with their schedules."

DAVID MANDEL-BLOCH
Adam

Like his twin brother Greg, David (Lawrence) is gifted in both art and writing poetry.

One of David's favorite artistic pastimes is painting *Simpsons* characters on denim jackets, such as the one he created for a woman who so admired the one he made for himself that she stopped him on the street and offered to pay him $100 if he would make one for her grandson.

His past acting credits include the TV movie *Victory at Entebbe* (in which he appeared with his brother), and several commercials for Listerine, Southwestern Bell, and Pillsbury (in all of which he appeared with his brother).

"Who knows," he says. "One of these days I may even return to acting, but for now I prefer to kick back and experiment with a lot of different careers."

Those careers included being the head chef and kitchen manager for Italy's Little Kitchen in Manhattan Beach, California. Today, like Darrin Stephens, his TV dad, he works in advertising.

David Lawrence (Mandel-Bloch)

Besides painting, David enjoys other hobbies, such as riding motorcycles, winter skiing, and skateboarding.

What are his favorite contemporary TV shows? *M*A*S*H*, *Absolutely Fabulous*, *COPS*, and *All My Children*. Of the latter, he says, "It's the only soap I can stand."

David is married to Paula Matveld and has a daughter, Phoebe. He joined Erin Murphy at the 2003 TV LAND awards to distribute awards to honorees.

GREG MANDEL
Adam

Greg Lawrence (Mandel)

One of the careers with which Greg Mandel (A.K.A. Greg Lawrence) once experimented was operating a small pizza and pasta restaurant in Simi Valley, California, with his brother David. Though they developed a happy and faithful clientele, they found themselves bored with the restaurant business after two years and decided to sell.

Greg, an avid water and snow skier, is retired and lives in Costa Rica.

Greg is married (his wife's name is Teri). They have no children, but dote on five cats.

Greg and David's mother admits that her sons are typical products of the 1970s and 1980s, and says she's a parent from the fifties who prefers to see them well-educated, with their feet firmly planted on a path toward responsible and lucrative futures. "Not only are they gorgeous, bright, and extremely creative young men," she says, "but they are warm, generous, caring, and beloved by friends and family alike."

MAURICE EVANS
Maurice

Born in the market town of Dorchester, Dorset, England, Maurice Evans was the son of a Welsh druggist and part-time justice of the peace, who also fancied himself a dramatist. Young Maurice (pronounced as *Morris*; different from his *Bewitched* namesake, *Mor-EECE*) began acting in his father's adaptations of Thomas Hardy's novels, making his first appearance onstage in *Hardy's Under the Greenwood Tree*. The boy also had a fair voice and sang in the St. Andrews choir in Stoke Newington after his family moved to London.

Evans then worked in little theater before making his professional debut at Cambridge in 1926. He played Orestes in *The Oresteia*.

But it was his performance as Lieutenant Raleigh in *Journey's End* that made him a London sensation. As a result, he appeared in leading roles in approximately twenty plays between 1930 and 1934.

Maurice Evans in 1989.

After several other stage performances in Shakespearean roles such as *Falstaff, Hamlet,* and *Henry IV,* Evans and wartime friend George Schaefer (former associate dean of theater, film, and television at UCLA) produced *The Teahouse of the August Moon* in 1953.

Moon starred David Wayne and was a satire about a United States Army unit trying to bring democracy to a Pacific island, which ran on Broadway for 1,027 performances and captured the Pulitzer Prize in 1954 for drama, as well as a Tony Award. While *Teahouse* was still thriving, Evans produced (with Evett Rogers) *No Time for Sergeants,* about a hillbilly draftee who nearly brings the army to its knees. It ran for two years and made a star of Andy Griffith, who went on to star in the 1958 film version and the original TV rendition; the latter of which premiered on the *U.S. Steel Hour* on March 15, 1955.

Also in 1955, Evans established a relationship with television's *Hallmark Hall of Fame,* and went on to produce small-screen images of, among others, *Hamlet* (1953), *Macbeth* (1954), *Richard II* (1954), *Dial M for Murder* (1958), *The Tempest* (1960), and *Alice in Wonderland* (1954), for which he also served as narrator.

"It's startling to think," he said in his very prosperous year of 1954, "that the TV audience that will see *Macbeth* probably will be larger than all the combined audiences who have seen the play since Shakespeare wrote it."

The Evans big-screen film library includes *Wedding Rehearsal* (1932), *Scrooge* (1935), *Planet of the Apes* (1968), its first sequel, *Beneath the Planet of the Apes* (1970), and *Rosemary's Baby* (a film both Endora and Uncle Arthur protested on *Bewitched*).

In addition to Sam's classy dad on *Bewitched,* Evans had TV spots on *Batman* (as the *Puzzler* in two episodes), *I Spy, Name of the Game, The Mod Squad,* and *Search.*

After *Bewitched* folded in 1972, he resurfaced in 1980 for a stage tour of *Holiday* (Philip Barry's 1928 comedy glorifying nonconformity), and in small parts on television, including the 1980 syndicated fantasy movie-of-the-week, entitled *The Girl, the Gold Watch and Everything* with Pam Dawber *(Mork and Mindy).*

Maurice Evans passed away in Brighton, England, on March 12, 1989, at the age of eighty-seven.

ALICE PEARCE
Gladys Kravitz

Alice Pearce was born October 16, 1917, the only child of Robert E. Pearce, a National City Bank vice president, and Margaret Clark Pearce. After attending a series of schools in Belgium, France, and Italy, Alice studied drama at Sarah Lawrence College in Bronxville, New York, and graduated in 1940.

She went on to become one of the stars of *New Faces of 1943* on Broadway, which led to her performance in *On the Town* 1944. Other stage hits included *Gentlemen Prefer Blondes, Bells Are Ringing*, and Noel Coward's *Sail Away* in 1961, her final appearance in the theater.

She also had a nightclub act with Mark Lawrence, a friend she met while he was at Princeton and she was at Sarah Lawrence College. The act ran for a record 68 weeks at the Blue Angel in New York City.

Her film history includes *On the Town* (1949) with Gene Kelly, *How to be Very, Very Popular* (with Robert Cummings, 1955), *My Six Loves* (1963), *Kiss Me, Stupid* (1964), *The Disorderly Orderly* (1964), *Dear Bridget* (with James Stewart, 1965) and *The Glass Bottom Boat* (1966), in which she costarred as the wife of fellow *Bewitched* spouse George Tobias.

Alice Pearce in 1950.

Her television appearances include *The Milton Berle Show, The Garry Moore Show, The Ed Sullivan Show, The Jack Paar Show*, and *Hazel*. She starred in her own series in 1948, *The Alice Pearce Show*, which she called "fifteen minutes of songs, topical skits, and me."

Husband John Rox (songwriter of such hits as *It's a Big, Wide, Wonderful World*) died in 1957, and she married Broadway director Paul Davis in 1964.

Pearce played Gladys Kravitz for two years, knowing all the while she was ill with cancer. She was forty-eight when she passed away on March 3, 1966.

To no one's surprise, there was applause the night her husband, Paul, accepted her TV Emmy Award (from Elizabeth Montgomery) for *Best Supporting Actress in a Comedy* in 1966. Members of the television academy and the audience recalled Alice's wonderful, wordless squeals as Gladys, which she had said was her favorite role.

SANDRA GOULD
Gladys Kravitz

Sandra Gould made her radio debut at age nine and appeared on radio's *My Friend Irma, The Danny Thomas Show*, and *The Jack Benny Show* (for fifteen seasons).

She spent five years as Mrs. Duffy on *Duffy's Tavern*.

Gould made her Broadway debut when she was eleven years old in *Fly Away Home* with Montgomery Clift and went on to do other Broadway productions such as *New Faces, Having a Wonderful Time*, and *Detective Story*.

Married and widowed twice (first to broadcasting executive Larry Berns, then director Hollingsworth Morse), Gould made numerous guest appearances on TV shows such as *December Bride, The Joey Bishop Show, I Love Lucy, The Danny Thomas Show, The Joan Davis Show*, and *I Dream of Jeannie*, before her regular stint on *Bewitched*.

Sandra Gould

Gould was also a writer. Her two books, *Always Say Maybe* and *Sexpots and Pans*, were published by Golden Press. *Always* is a guide for women to finding a man; *Pans* is a cookbook on how to cook for forty-six different types of men.

She also worked as a features writer for several magazines, including *Sports Illustrated*, *Los Angeles Magazine*, *Reader's Digest*, and *Cosmopolitan*, and was an accomplished artist, having sold several hundred paintings.

Sandra Gould passed away on July 20, 1999, at the age of 78.

GEORGE TOBIAS
Abner Kravitz

George Tobias began a colorful life on July 14, 1901, on New York's Lower East Side. Coming from a theatrical family, he started his own career at the age of fifteen at the Neighborhood Playhouse in New York. At nineteen, he went into a Provincetown Playhouse production of *The Hairy Ape*, a new Eugene O'Neill play that was destined to become an American classic.

Shortly afterward, he was chosen for the original Broadway cast of *What Price Glory* by Maxwell Anderson and Laurence Stallings. The play was highly successful, and George stayed with it from 1924 to 1926.

He later appeared in such plays as *The Road to Rome*, *The Gray Fox*, and *Elizabeth the Queen*, and went on to work in summer stock with Jose Ferrer. When he returned to New York, he landed in another new production that was to become one of Broadway's all-time hits, *You Can't Take It with You*. From 1937 to 1939, Tobias played the Russian ballet master in the famous George Kaufman-Moss Hart comedy, then he went on to the musical *Leave It to Me!* with Mary Martin (famous as *Peter Pan*, and mother of *I Dream of Jeannie*'s Larry Hagman).

George Tobias

George then came to Hollywood to make movies for MGM, including *Ninotchka* (1939), which years later became a hit on Broadway in a musical version called *Silk Stockings* (1957, with Don Ameche and Hildegard Neff). *Silk* was turned into another MGM film with Fred Astaire and Cyd Charisse. George was in all three versions.

For many years he was under contract to Warner Brothers and appeared in *Yankee Doodle Dandy* (1942) and *Air Force* (1943) for the studios, as well as *Mission to Moscow* (1943) and *My Sister Eileen* (1955), a Columbia release which also featured Dick York.

Tobias made several other movies, including *The Set-Up* (1949), *Ten Tall Men* (1951), *The Glenn Miller Story* (1954), *The*

Seven Little Foys (1955), *Marjorie Morningstar* (1958), and *The Glass Bottom Boat* (with Alice Pearce in 1966).

In addition to his regular role as Abner on *Bewitched*, Tobias made many other TV appearances, including a continuing part in *Adventures in Paradise* from 1959 to 1962, and with former *Bewitched* costar Sandra Gould on the *Bewitched* sequel, *Tabitha*, on which they both reprised their Kravitz roles.

Though Abner may have been a softer role for him to play in any series, Tobias was active and rugged in real life. Tobias was quite the equestrian. He owned and trained many horses, loved to play polo, and was a volunteer mounted policeman.

In fact, according to *Bewitched* costar David White, the off-screen Abner was a sheriff out in Peach Blossom, California, where he lived. "He had a badge and everything," recalled White. "He was told that if he ever saw something suspicious, he should call it in. I mean, he had a two-way radio in his Jeep, and I guess he used to be quite the rambler out there."

He passed away on February 27, 1980.

IRENE VERNON
Louise Tate

Irene Vernon was born in Mishawaka, Indiana, and graduated from Mishawaka High School. From there she traveled to New York to become a dancer, performing in many nightclubs, including Ben Martin's Riviera in Fort Lee, New Jersey.

After doing a few Broadway shows such as the 1943 hit *Artists and Models on Broadway (*which starred Jane Froman and Jackie Gleason), Vernon signed a contract with Metro-Goldwyn-Mayer Studios in California and appeared in bit parts in films, including *'Til the Clouds Roll By* (1946, her first movie) and *The Pirate* (1948), starring Judy Garland and Gene Kelly.

Irene Vernon

"I was very excited," said Vernon, "but very dumb and naive about the business. I was seventeen years old when I left home. Even though I started out as a dancer, acting was really what I wanted to do. I got lucky later because I was pretty and received a lot of publicity because of my contract with MGM."

Vernon came to *Bewitched* through her association with Danny Arnold, whom she had known in New York. "Danny and I knew each other from the forties," she recalled, "and we had studied together with a Russian actress named Batani Schneider and her husband Benno Schneider, who had directed Ingrid Bergman on Broadway in *Liliom*."

Years later, when both Vernon and Arnold resided in Los Angeles, they met again on the Columbia Studios lot. "I was auditioning for some other show," she recalled, "and we had bumped into each other and had coffee. It was then he offered me the part of Louise on *Bewitched*, explaining that it was a very small role but that it would grow. So I said okay."

On leaving *Bewitched*, Vernon ventured into a successful career in real estate and lived in Beverly Hills, California; she later remarried and moved to Florida. She died on April 21, 1998.

KASEY ROGERS
Louise Tate

Kasey Rogers was born in Missouri but lived in California most of her childhood. At two and a half years of age, she began taking elocution lessons, and when she was eight, she was playing the piano at the Hollywood Bowl and the Shrine Auditorium. Kasey went to Burbank High School in Burbank, California, and became interested in acting while doing school plays.

At nineteen she married, and while attending Glendale College, her interest in drama became dominant. She won her first professional job in the entertainment industry as a dancer in an Earl Carrol show. Soon after, she signed with top agency MCA and received her first film lead in the Paramount Pictures release of *Special Agent* (1949).

Kasey's talents were employed in a wide range of roles at Paramount: horse operas with Joel McCrea, heavy drama with the late Robert Walker, comedy with Bob Hope, and adventure with Sterling Hayden. Other Kasey movie credits include Cecil B. DeMille's *Samson and Delilah* (1950), Frank Capra's *Riding High* (also 1950), *Silver City* (1951), George Stevens's *A Place in the Sun* (1951), Alfred Hitchcock's *Strangers on a Train* (1951, costarring Marion Lorne, in which she says she played, "the consummate bitch and loved it,") *Denver and Rio Grande* (1952), and *Jamaica Run* (1953). All of her movie work was done under the stage name of Laura Elliot.

Kasey Rogers

Besides *Bewitched*, Kasey has made more than five hundred television appearances, including guest shots on the classic *Mission Impossible*, *The Lucy Show*, and *Flamingo Road*. She played Julie Anderson for two years on *Peyton Place* prior to *Bewitched*, acted in an episode of *The Lone Ranger*, played a killer on *Perry Mason*, and was in two segments of *Wanted Dead or Alive* in 1959 and 1960.

Now divorced, Kasey has raised four children, teaches acting, and is currently developing a one-woman show and has written (with Mark Wood) *The Bewitched Cookbook* (Kensington, 1996).

MABEL ALBERTSON
Phyllis Stephens

Mabel Albertson in an early publicity photo.

Mabel Albertson was born in 1901. Her career spanned nearly thirty-five years. Mabel appeared in films, including *Mutiny on the Black Hawk* (1938), *My Pal Gus* (1952), *She's Back on Broadway* (1953), *Forever Darling* (1956), *The Long Hot Summer* (1958), *Home Before Dark* (1958), *Don't Give Up the Ship* (1959), *Barefoot in the Park* (1967), and *What's Up, Doc?* (1972).

Besides *Bewitched*, Albertson played similar wise-cracking mothers and mothers-in-law on TV shows such as *That's My Boy*, *The Whiting Girls* (playing grandma to Tom Ewell), and *That Girl*, in which she portrayed another famous mortal man's mom— Ted Bessell's Don Holinger (the one and only love of Marlo Thomas's Ann Marie).

Mabel Albertson, who was mother-in-law in real life of actress Cloris Leachman, died in 1982 of Alzheimer's disease.

ROBERT F. SIMON
Frank Stephens

Robert F. Simon was born on December 2, 1908, in Mansfield, Ohio, where he became an all-state high school basketball star in the 1920s. According to his nephew, Dick Simon, when Bob was in his late forties he would consistently win in one-on-one games between him and his then-teenaged relative.

Before Bob began his career in acting, he aspired to be a traveling salesman.

In fact, he initially ventured into theater to hone his skills as a commercial traveler. "I was shy," he said, "and I thought acting would help me overcome that. Once I stepped on stage, however, performing came easily to me, and it was then I decided to make a career of it."

Simon's first professional job was in the play *No For an Answer* by Marc Blitzstein, in which he had the opportunity to display his song and dance abilities as well. He was also involved with the Cleveland Playhouse, Group Theater, and Actors Studio, which led to an assignment as understudy to Lee J. Cobb for the lead in *Death of a Salesman*.

As he recalled of the latter, "I never expected Lee to fall ill, but at one point he did, and, much to my surprise, I found myself in the production."

From *Salesman* he went on to several other stage performances, as well as many roles in television and film.

Robert F. Simon in the late 1980s.

Beside Darrin's first father on *Bewitched*, his other TV appearances included regular roles on *The Legend of Custer* (as General Alfred Terry), *Nancy* (as Everett Hudson on NBC, 1970-71), and *The Amazing Spider-Man* (as J. Jonah Jameson, a role David White portrayed in the *Spider-Man* pilot).

Simon completed more than fifty films, including *Where the Sidewalk Ends* (1950), *Chief Crazy Horse* (1955), *The Benny Goodman Story* (1955), *The Court Martial of Billy Mitchell* (1955, with Elizabeth Montgomery), *The Last Angry Man* (1959), *Operation Petticoat* (1959) [both *Astronaut* and *Petticoat* also featured Dick Sargent], *Captain Newman, M.D.* (1963), *The Spiral Road* (1962), and *The Reluctant Astronaut* (1967).

Simon died at the age of eighty-three of a massive heart attack in Tarzana, California, on November 29, 1992. He is survived by daughters Barbara Callet and Susan Thompson, and sons Robert L. and James Simon, and several grandchildren and other relatives, including his sister Reni.

ROY ROBERTS
Frank Stephens

Roy Roberts as he appeared in the role of an Indian agent in the 1956 western *The White Squaw*.

Roy Roberts, Darrin's other pop, was born on March 19, 1900, in Tampa, Florida, and passed away on May 28, 1975.

Roberts played John Cushing from 1964 to 1967 on *The Beverly Hillbillies*, Harrison Cheever on *The Lucy Show* from 1965 to 1968, and Mr. Bodine on *Gunsmoke* from 1965 to 1975. Before his appearance on *Bewitched*, he was Captain Huxley on *The Gale Storm Show* from 1956 to 1960 and Norman Curtis on *Petticoat Junction* from 1963 to 1964. Sometime later, on November 2, 1967, Roberts made his first of thirteen appearances as one of Darrin's two dads.

Roberts's film highlights include *The Sullivans* (1944), *It Shouldn't Happen to a Dog* (1946, the title of which was also used for an episode of *Bewitched*), *It's a Mad, Mad, Mad, Mad World* (1963), and *Hotel* (1967).

Behind the Screen Realities

HARRY ACKERMAN
Creative Consultant/Executive Producer

....

Bewitched executive producer Harry Ackerman began his career in radio, working on programs such as *The Phil Baker Show*, where he was assistant director, then he switched to television, where he was a power as executive producer for CBS in New York. He supervised the development writing and cast of all CBS New York-based shows, including *Studio One* and *Suspense,* among others.

As vice president for CBS programs in Hollywood, he supervised the production elements of shows such as *Gunsmoke* (which he personally developed and cast initially for radio, later recasting for television), *The Jack Benny Show, Burns and Allen, Amos 'N' Andy* (the radio series and later the TV series), *Our Miss Brooks, The Edgar Bergen Show,* and *I Love Lucy.*

The late Harry Ackerman in 1988.

Ackerman was instrumental in developing the concept of *I Love Lucy* with Jess Oppenheimer, Lucille Ball, and Desi Arnaz. He personally supervised its production and instituted its technical components.

Martin N. Leeds, once head of business affairs for CBS on the West Coast, wrote in *Emmy Magazine* about Ackerman's contribution to *I Love Lucy*:

"Contrary to popular belief, it was Harry Ackerman—not [Lucille Ball, Desi Arnaz, or cinematographer Karl Freund]—who, on *I Love Lucy,* pioneered the three-camera technique for shows filmed before a live TV audience.

When the series pilot was shot at CBS's Studio A in Hollywood, a kinescope recording was made for sales purposes and sent to the East Coast. Ackerman, then vice president in charge of programming, went with it.

Arthur Lyons, then head of Philip Morris, the show's sponsor, loved the pilot but balked at getting a kinescope recording other than a live program in the east on a regular basis. It was decided to [shoot the show] on film, but Ackerman was afraid the spontaneity created by a live audience would be lost. Lyon remembers:

"Ackerman phoned me and asked, 'Do you know anything about the Fairbanks system [of using multiple cameras locked into a fixed position?]' My answer was, 'No, other than [the camera] took the picture from the same angled position but covered a larger area of activity.'

"Ackerman then asked me to contact Al Simon, who had worked with the Fairbanks technique as a production manager—and [asked him] if it would be feasible to place motion picture cameras on the same type of dollies used for live television in order to film in front of a live audience. Simon thought we could, and we hired him to help implement the system."

Ackerman was offered the presidency of CBS Television by Bill Paley and Frank Stanton after that experiment, but he declined in order to remain in production.

Other television projects that Ackerman produced included the specials *The Day Lincoln Was Shot* (starring Jack Lemmon and Raymond Massey), *Blithe Spirit* (Noel Coward, Lauren Bacall, and Mildred Natwick), and *Twentieth Century* (Orson Welles and Betty Grable).

Besides *Bewitched*, Ackerman produced a wealth of regular TV fare for Screen Gems (of which he was vice president), including *Dennis the Menace*, *The Donna Reed Show*, *Hazel*, *Gidget*, *The Flying Nun*, and three Movies of the Week.

Ackerman also independently produced *Bachelor Father*, and *Leave It to Beaver*, as well as the ninety-minute special *Paramount Presents*, for Paramount Television.

In 1984, Ackerman produced the TV movie *The Sky's No Limit*, starring Sharon Gless (*Cagney and Lacey*), Dee Wallace, Ann Archer, and Barnard Hughes, and *Welcome Home Jelly Bean*, a one-hour *Schoolbreak Special* for CBS starring Dana Hill, and the two-hour pilot for *The New Gidget* series starring Caryn Richman, of which he also produced forty-four episodes for

Harry Ackerman with wife, Elinor Donahue, in 1990.

Columbia Pictures Television (once known as Screen Gems, which produced *Bewitched*, now known as Sony Pictures Television).

In 1991, Ackerman was honored by the membership of the Caucus for Producers, winning one of the organization's top awards as Member of the Year. The award, presented annually to a caucus member for his or her television body of work, was made by producer/writer Gene Reynolds (*M*A*S*H*), the 1989 winner.

Married to actress Elinor Donahue (of *Father Knows Best*, which Ackerman produced, and of *Dr. Quinn, Medicine Woman*), Harry Ackerman (whom Desi Arnaz once called "the finest mind in comedy") died in 1991 of pneumonia contracted while he was in the hospital for cancer treatment.

WILLIAM ASHER
Creative Consultant/Producer/Director

William Asher was born in New York on August 8, 1921, the second child and only son of film producer Ephraim M. Asher and his actress-wife Lillian Bonner. With Universal Pictures head Carl Laemmle Jr., the elder Asher produced the classic 1931 feature film *Frankenstein*. He went on to produce—on his own—more than twenty other motion pictures, including *Magnificent Obsession* (1935, with Agnes Moorehead).

Young Asher's childhood fascination with the movie business was cut short in 1937 by his family's move to New York (following his father's sudden death). Yet it could not be quashed. In his

Bill Asher

teens, Asher made his way back to Hollywood where he began his career in the mailroom at Universal. With the studio now under new management, he was on his own. His classroom: the studio's soundstages. His instructors: the directors, cinematographers, and editors who daily peopled the lot.

His studies interrupted by World War II, Asher served with the U.S. Army Signal Corps in Astoria, New York, and as special unit photographer at Cushing General Hospital. After the war, he returned to Universal and honed his skills as an assistant editor and an assistant cameraman.

With the young film actor Richard Quine (who brought *My Sister Eileen*, with Dick York, to the big screen), he cowrote, coproduced, and codirected his first feature film entitled *Leather Gloves* (1948) for Columbia Pictures.

TV beckoned with directing assignments (*Big Town* and *The Colgate Comedy Hour*). In 1951, Asher married actress Dani Sue Nolan. His work on *Racket Squad* impressed CBS vice president (and future *Bewitched* executive producer) Harry Ackerman. In 1952, Asher was hired to direct the pilot and first ten episodes of *Our Miss Brooks*.

Desi Arnaz was also impressed with the *Brooks* pilot and hired Asher to guide *I Love Lucy* for its second season. (Days before he started *Brooks*, Asher's wife gave birth to their first child, Liane.) Under Asher's direction, *Lucy* displaced Milton Berle and Arthur Godfrey from their top-rated spots, resulting in the first of two Emmy Awards for Ball and the series.

During his first *Lucy* summer hiatus, Asher directed the pilot and most of the first year's episodes of Danny Thomas's *Make Room for Daddy,* for which he was honored with an Emmy (Best New Program), the Sylvania Award, and the *TV Guide* Award.

He followed this same formula with *December Bride, Willy, The Lineup,* and the revised *Ray Bolger Show.* During Asher's third consecutive *Lucy* season, the young director wanted to stretch and took on back-to-back feature film assignments at Columbia: *The Shadow on the Window* and

The Twenty-Seventh Day. The latter was considered by some critics the most important science-fiction film of its time.

Asher next produced and directed a season of NBC's *The Dinah Shore Show,* winning a second Emmy. He returned to direct the last batch of *Lucy* segments.

Asher went on to helm *The Donna Reed Show, Fibber McGee and Molly, The Thin Man,* and the revamped *Shirley Temple Show,* which, as producer, he reinvigorated through the use of two writers and stars, as well as talented young directors (Arthur Miller, David Greene, Robert Ellis Miller).

In 1961, Asher staged and directed President John F. Kennedy's inaugural gala, produced by Frank Sinatra. That spring he did the same for the president's surprise birthday celebration at which Marilyn Monroe sang to the president.

The year 1963 marked the launch of *The Patty Duke Show* (which he produced and directed), *Beach Party* (which created a new and much-imitated big-film genre), his marriage to Elizabeth Montgomery, the release of *Johnny Cool* (he directed, Montgomery starred), and the *Bewitched* pilot.

In 1964, Bill and Liz welcomed their first child, William Jr., and *Bewitched* premiered on ABC (becoming its biggest hit). The following years marked the premiere of *Beach Blanket Bingo, How to Stuff a Wild Bikini,* the new series *Gidget* (with Sally Field), and the arrival of another son, Robert. He completed the groundbreaking teen pictures in 1966 with *Fireball 500.* In June 1969, close to the end of *Bewitched*'s fifth season, the Ashers welcomed their daughter, Rebecca. Two months after *Samantha* left ABC in 1972, Asher was back on the air with *The Paul Lynde Show* and *Temperature's Rising.* Shortly thereafter, he and Elizabeth Montgomery divorced.

In 1976, he began directing TV's *Alice* (with Linda Lavin). That summer, he married actress Joyce Bulifant and adopted her son Jon (who starred in the USA cable series *Weird Science).* In 1980, Asher launched the adventure show, *Here's Boomer.* The following year, his eleventh feature, *Night Warning,* was released.

In 1983, critical acclaim came his way for his lavish TV production of the classic *Charlie's Aunt* (starring Charles Grodin and Bullifant). He next supervised multiple episodes of *Foul Play, Harper Valley PTA, Private Benjamin, Me and Mom,* and *Crazy Like a Fox.* He then directed the MGM/UA feature *Movers and Shakers.* This was followed by the very successful TV movie, *I Dream of Jeannie Fifteen Years Later.* The year 1986 was marked by the appearance of the medical series *Kay O'Brien* (the first of several he developed, produced, and directed for Kushner-Locke Company).

Asher ushered in the 1990s, directing the highly rated TV special *Return to Green Acres* (with Eddie Albert, Eva Gabor, and many of the original *Acres* cast). And he recently served as director of development for Kushner-Locke and completed two original screenplays. He's now at work on his long-anticipated autobiography and continues to be actively involved in many charitable causes.

Asher is the father of Liane, Brian, Billy, Robert, Rebecca, and John; stepfather of Charlie, Mary, Merritt, and David; and grandfather of Alexandra, Megan, Keith, Ruby, Emerald, Elizabeth Anne, and William Robert. Asher lives in Palm Springs with his fourth wife, Meredith.

RICHARD MICHAELS
Associate Producer/Director

Richard Michaels

Richard Michaels began his career as a script clerk during the final season of *Bewitched*. He went on to become an associate producer and finally full-fledged director. Michaels acknowledges Bill Asher's role in advancing his career:

"I owe my career to the show and to Bill Asher. He's the man who gave me my first job. The show has been the central point of my entire life and career, and I'll never forget the time I spent working on it."

After *Bewitched*, Richard Michaels became one of television's most successful directors. Some of the made-for-TV features he directed include *Leave Yesterday Behind* (1978), starring John Ritter as a paralyzed veterinary student; *Berlin Tunnel 21* (1981), starring Richard Thomas; *Love and Betrayal* (1989), featuring Stefanie Powers and David Birney; and *The Leona Helmsley Story* (1990), starring Suzanne Pleshette.

He's directed classic episodes of *The Brady Bunch*, *The Odd Couple*, and *Love, American Style*, is married and divides his time between Los Angeles and Hawaii.

JERRY DAVIS
Producer/Director/Writer

Jerry Davis

Jerry Davis was born in New York City on September 26, 1917, at 33 Riverside Drive. He was educated at George Washington High School and attended Franklin and Marshall College in Lancaster, Pennsylvania. After college, he went into the U.S. Army Signal Corps where he met William Saroyan, Arthur Lawrence, and dozens of other writers and artists who gave him his first taste of show business.

Davis, who passed away in 1991, gathered an impressive list of credits, including MGM musicals starring Mickey Rooney, Judy Garland, Esther Williams, et cetera, and straight films with Ethel Barrymore, Robert Taylor, and Clark Gable, among others.

On film, he wrote the following: *Kind Lady* (1951, starring Maurice Evans), *Duchess of Idaho* (1950), *Pagan Love Song* (1950), *The Devil Makes Three* (1952), *Apache Trail* (1960), and many others.

After *Bewitched*, Davis went on to produce TV's *That Girl* (a position which was later filled by *Bewitched*'s Danny Arnold) and *The Odd Couple* (when he replaced Arnold). In the late 1980s, Davis produced the TV "musi-com," entitled *Throb*, (with *Soap*'s Diana Canova).

He married three times (he met his third wife, actress Beryl Hammond, when she auditioned for a bit on *Bewitched*), and is the father of three children.

Divorced, single, and ever the optimist, Jerry spent the remainder of his life in Beverly Hills. "I believe I can twitch my nose," he said, shortly before he died, "have yet another happy marriage, and a hit TV show" (which he was about to produce with Danny Arnold).

Bernard Slade

Jill Foster, who played Darrin's secretary "Betty" in many *Bewitched* segments, is married to Bernard Slade.

BERNARD SLADE
Story Editor

Bernard Slade, who wrote seventeen segments for *Bewitched*, was born in a little town in Canada called St. Catherines. His family moved to England when he was four years old, only to return to Canada when he was eighteen. At that time, he became interested in acting. Approximately one decade later, he began writing for television.

In 1964, Slade arrived in Los Angeles where, as he recalls, "someone had given me a license to print money. That's how terrific things were for me as a writer."

Slade came to *Bewitched* when the show's first season producer, Danny Arnold, read a play Slade had written entitled *Simon Says Get Married*, and was impressed enough to hire him for the now famous *Samantha* series.

While Slade was writing for *Bewitched*, he also scripted episodes of *My Living Doll* and later went on to create *The Partridge Family* and *The Flying Nun* for ABC. The latter was based on a book called *The Fifteenth Pelican*, written by a Puerto Rican housewife named Marie Teres Versace Rios, who authored her work as *Terry Rios*.

Besides his most well-known stage play, *Same Time Next Year* (which became a successful film of the same name in 1978 with Alan Alda), Slade's other stage credits include *Tribute, Romantic Comedy, Special Occasions, Fatal Attraction,* and *Return Engagements*.

Slade lives in Beverly Hills, California, with his wife, Jill Foster, who played Betty, one of Darrin's secretaries on *Bewitched*. They have two children.

ED JURIST
Story Editor

Bewitched writer and story editor Ed Jurist wrote a total of fifty-one segments for the show (two of which were coauthored) and was its story editor in later seasons.

Born in Newark, New Jersey, Jurist attended the University of Michigan, majored in theater, and had hopes of becoming an actor. When he arrived in Hollywood, his career took a "write" turn into TV.

He became a producer, director, and writer of such early television series as *The Aldrich Family, 77 Sunset Strip, Hawaiian Eye,* and *Colonel Humphrey Flack (The Fabulous Fraud).*

Flack was a situation comedy based on the stories of Everett Rhoades Castle about a modern-day Robin Hood, starred Alan Mownrays from 1957 to 1959, and was broadcast on the Dupont Network.

His other productions included the 1958 game show, *Dotto.*

Jurist also wrote *You're Only Young Twice* and *Room for One More,* which was based on the 1952 Cary Grant feature film of the same name. He classified his *Room* as "a gentle comedy with shades of today's dramedies like *The Wonder Years* and *thirtysomething.*"

Jurist was also a frequent TV contributor to *The Patty Duke Show* (from 1963 to 1966), *M*A*S*H, One Day at a Time, Diff'rent Strokes, Gimme a Break,* and *The Flying Nun (*the latter of which he also produced).

Jurist succumbed to heart failure on March 12, 1993, and is survived by his wife Eleanor and two children.

Ed Jurist

MICHAEL MORRIS
Story Editor

Michael Morris, who scripted twenty-two segments of *Bewitched,* was born in Russia and arrived in America when he was five years old, where he was raised in Brooklyn. His father was a prominent actor, playwright, and scholar in the Yiddish Theater and radio. Morris, who is also an author (*Naked and Alone,* with Larry Lariar, New American Library), was then inspired to become an actor, and became a writer, he says, "quite by accident."

Michael Morris

After producing shows for the army's Special Services division, Morris created a radio game show, entitled *Talk Your Way out of It*, which lasted about six months, and which he says was "a smash hit." While acting, he had also written some commercial copy for his dad at the same radio station which broadcast *Talk* and then decided positively that writing was his forte.

Consequently, Morris completed sixty episodes of a radio show called *Hollywood Stories*, broadcast five days a week, fifteen minutes a day. Then came *Mr. and Mrs. North*, and *The Marriage*, starring Hume Cronin and Jessica Tandy. His lengthy TV credits include story editor positions on *Chico and the Man*, *Gimme a Break*, *The Flying Nun*, *Temperature's Rising*, and *The Paul Lynde Show*. He also filled in as story editor for a year on *Bewitched* when Ed Jurist suffered a mild heart attack. Morris also wrote for such shows as *The Andy Griffith Show* (with Seaman Jacobs), *My Three Sons*, and *Nanny and the Professor*. His feature films include *For Love or Money* (1963, with Kirk Douglas, cowritten by Larry Markes) and *Wild and Wonderful* (1964, also with Markes).

Morris has sold fourteen TV sitcom pilots to ABC, CBS, Desilu Productions, the James Komack Company, Harry Ackerman Productions, and Lucille Ball Productions, eight from all of these with Larry Markes. He also worked on variety shows, including Red Skelton, Arlene Frances, Martha Raye, and *The CBS Morning Show* (with Dick Van Dyke and later, John Henry Falk).

Morris is married and lives in Bel Air, California.

RICHARD BAER
Writer

Richard Baer

Richard Baer wrote twenty-three segments of *Bewitched*, following thirty-eight episodes of TV's *Hennessy* series (starring Jackie Cooper). He began writing when he became interested in propaganda films during World War II, upon thinking such films to be an effective manner for addressing important issues.

Baer went on to write educational films and more commercial ventures in 1954 with TV's *The Life of Riley*, on which he was assistant to the producer.

"One day," he says, "the show was stuck for a script, and I ended up writing an episode, and then another, and yet another. It then occurred to me that writing would be a great way to make a living."

Baer was a psychology major in college, and when he went to write for TV's *Professional Father* in 1955, the producers noted his academic background. In their eyes, this seemed to fit exactly what they needed for *Father*, which featured Steve Dunne as a child psychologist, who handled well the troubles of other people's children but had a problem doing the same for his own offspring.

Father, which also starred Barbara Billingsley (*Leave It to Beaver*) was a semi-forefather to programs such as *The Cosby Show* and *Growing Pains*.

Baer's other TV credits include *Who's the Boss*, *Archie Bunker's Place*, *Barney Miller*, and *Love, Sidney*.

An active member of the Writer's Guild, he recently completed a stage play entitled *Embraceable You*. Baer lives with his wife Louise, and they have three grown children.

LILA GARRETT
Writer

Lila Garrett

Partnered with then-husband Bernie Kahn, Lila Garrett wrote eleven episodes of *Bewitched*, though she started out in the entertainment business as an actress in New York. She attended Yale Drama School, where she directed several theatrical stage productions, including *The Beggar's Opera*.

From there, Garrett went on to write questions for game shows such as *Who Do You Trust?* and cartoons such as *Beetle Bailey*. Shortly thereafter she met Kahn, and they began to collaborate in episodic television.

Following *Bewitched*, she wrote for, produced, and directed many shows and movies for TV, including *Terraces* (the first TV movie directed by a woman).

Other small-screen films she guided include *Bridesmaids* (1989) and *Who Gets the Friends* (1988). TV movies Garrett has written and produced include *Somebody Loves Me* (1986), *The Time of Her Life* (1986), and *The Other Woman* (1985), for which she received a Writer's Guild Award.

Garrett was also nominated for an Emmy three times, winning twice for her efforts in *The Girl Who Couldn't Lose* (1987) and *Mother of the Bride* (1986).

She was also creator and producer of *Baby I'm Back*, a television series starring Damon Wilson and Denise Nichols, from the early 1980s.

Now divorced, Garrett lives happily in a brightly decorated, large condo in Beverly Hills.

BERNIE KAHN
Writer

Bernie Kahn, like other members of the *Bewitched* scribe staff, came to his profession with surprise. Born in Brooklyn, Kahn was, at one time, the second best swimmer in the world. And he has the medals to prove it.

He studied speech at Michigan State University, received his master's degree and went into the army, where he roomed with the men who would become, respectively, president of ABC News, Roone

Bernie Kahn

Arledge, and top NBC publicity official, Bud Rukeyser. After the army, Kahn traveled to Maryland, where he ran a radio station and later landed his first professional writing job on an NBC radio show called *Monitor*, on which Lila Garrett was a production assistant.

Kahn also worked on other radio programs, including *Fibber McGee and Molly*, which featured famed comedians, and *Bob and Ray*. Kahn and Garrett then worked on TV game shows, moved to Los Angeles, and (via a friend) pitched a *Bewitched* story called *The Switch*, which involved Samantha and Darrin becoming one another for a day. Though Kahn says Bill Asher "hated it," the idea was later used in the show's fifth season as "Samantha Loses Her Voice."

This one script led to more for *Bewitched* and more than one hundred other sitcoms, including *Maude, The Addams Family, Get Smart,* and *My World and Welcome To It,* the latter two of which earned Kahn a nomination from The Writer's Guild.

His TV movies include *Twirl* (1981), and *Woman of the Year* (1976), while he also wrote feature films such as Walt Disney's *The Barefoot Executive* (1971).

An avid tennis player, Kahn tries to "play at least once a week," and ends up doing so with fellow former *Bewitched* writer Michael Morris.

In fact, during *Bewitched*, Kahn used to hit the courts with Elizabeth Montgomery and Bill Asher, both of whom were expert players. Kahn remembers telling Asher, "I'll trade you ten *Bewitched* scripts for your backswing."

JOHN L. GREENE
Writer

John L. Greene

Born in Buffalo on November 10, 1912, John L. Greene, who wrote seventeen scripts of *Bewitched* (eight with Paul David and five with David Robison), said his parents "were delighted with my birth."

The family moved to Willamette, Illinois, and once more, to his father's hometown, Fremont, Ohio. The latter move took place because Greene's dad (also a writer) had sold a play to Margaret Anglin, a popular actress in the early part of the century.

In 1930, Greene graduated from Valley Forge Military, was a freshman at Duke University, a sophomore at Ohio State, and a "semitalented" student at the Keane Art Institute in Toledo. He moved on to the University of Iowa, where he graduated from the journalism school in 1935.

Greene's father enjoyed more success as an editor and advertising man than as a writer and was not pleased with his son's chosen vocation. "They'll break his heart," his father told his mother in reference to the literary critics.

Yet after Greene's dad passed away, his mom said, "I guess you better become a writer."

"I did," he recalled, "and they didn't break my heart."

Before he died in 1995, Greene had written for some forty-five different TV shows and created *My Favorite Martian*. He started in radio where he wrote for the *Blondie* show for ten years. He also did a number of segments of *Ozzie and Harriet*. "I never wanted to write a novel or an autobiography," he said. "I just always thought of myself warmly as a pretty good superficial writer."

"The most wonderful thing that ever happened to me," he concluded, "was meeting and marrying the lovely, redheaded Indian girl named Helen Odell."

The couple had been married, he said, "sixty hilarious years."

BARBARA AVEDON
Writer

Barbara Avedon was born in New York at Doctor Loeff's Lying Hospital, which she considered "a mysterious choice," since her family lived in the Bronx at the time, "midpoint, between four candy stores." It was a geographical placement which the writer remembered "thanking God for every day."

Avedon's family made their first upwardly mobile move to Manhattan on Riverside Drive where, as a young artist, she spent four years preparing a portfolio of drawings which helped gain accep-

Barbara Avedon

tance to the High School of Music and Art. In 1946, the Avedon brood moved again, this time to the West Coast where Barbara attended Beverly Hills High in Beverly Hills, California. "I was the only girl who wore Levis," she recalls. "I wore a low-cut peasant blouse with them, sandals without socks, a no-no in the dress code, and discovered I could get the day off just by walking by the office of the dean who would send me home to change. The kids voted me *Biggest Character* and the teachers voted me *Most Likely to Succeed*. They may have meant that sarcastically, as I've always had an authority problem."

Though her son Josh graduated from the University of California at Berkeley with a degree in journalism, Avedon attended UCLA for only six months and dropped out. "It was harder than I thought," she says. Yet, she returned to academia as a teacher at the University of Southern California in late 1989.

Avedon's credits include TV's *The Donna Reed Show*, *Gidget*, *Maude*, *Fish*, and *Trapper John, M.D.*, among others. She cocreated *Cagney and Lacey*, is a playwright and author, and created the musical *Pink Mausoleum*, which is based on her book of the same name. She's "most proud of being one of the women who started the organization Another Mother for Peace, whose motto is 'War is not healthy for children and other living things.' My hope," she says, "is that all of us on earth can evolve into human beings who renounce war as an outmoded, unworkable, barbaric instrument of change."

E. W. SWACKHAMER
Director

Born in Middletown, New Jersey (for which his production company was named), the late E. W. Swackhamer entered the service at age sixteen and was educated at Black Mountain College. He began to act when he was nineteen years old, though he said, "I found out I was a better director than an actor," to which his track record bears testament.

E. W. directed more than one hundred television shows, including several sold pilot episodes which launched *Spider-Man* (with David White), *The Flying Nun, Eight Is Enough, Quincy, Here Come the Brides* (where he met his wife, actress Bridget Hanley, who guested on *Bewitched*), *SWAT, Tenspeed and Brownshoe* (with Ben Vereen and Jeff Goldblum) and *I Dream of Jeannie*.

Swackhamer's other credits include TV movies *The Daine Curse* (for which he received an Emmy nomination), *Terror at London Bridge*, and a two-hour special segment of ABC's *Family* (which was nominated for a Director's Guild Award).

His miniseries credits include *Once an Eagle, Malibu*, and the *Desperado* films. His other series include *LA Law, Murder, She Wrote*, and *Jake and the Fatman*.

Swackhamer enjoyed reading and "was deeply in love with his wife."

E. W. Swackhamer

Bewitched guest star, Bridget Hanley, with her husband, E. W. Swackhamer.

DICK ALBAIN
Special Effects

Dick Albain remains a highly respected wizard of the special effects industry. Born and raised in Los Angeles, Albain went to a school for carpentry, which also allowed him to work with metals and liquids. Yet, it was his supervisory position with Northrup Aircraft in Los Angeles that led him into a career in show business. Northrup was situated next to MGM Studios, where Albain met a car-

Richard Albain

penter who was making more money than he was. Soon after, Albain walked into his local construction union and said, "I'd like to work in the movies."

The union consented and asked him which studio he'd like to work for. Choosing Columbia, Albain continued on to work for all the studio's films during the 1950s and the 1960s, including the 1959 witch feature, *Bell, Book and Candle*, which was his "first big job." *From Here to Eternity* followed in 1952, and the later full-length *Three Stooges* films, including *Three Stooges in Orbit* and *Three Stooges Meet Hercules* (both released in 1962). During production of the *Stooges* films, Albain worked with a staff of eight, "always lending each other a hand whenever we could."

In 1964, a year after Willis Cook did the *Bewitched* pilot, and at the request of Danny Arnold, Albain signed on with Samantha. When producer/creator Sidney Sheldon offered him a hefty raise and requested his presence on *I Dream of Jeannie*, Albain traded in his witches' twitch for a genie blink.

Albain now owns his F/X company (which was once co-owned with Sheldon), continues to work on various TV shows, and designs the effects for several high-profile commercials (i.e., the famous Superbowl 1989 soft drink ad which involved eighty thousand vending machines sliding through the streets of San Francisco and jumping over cars). "You have to be creative in this business," he decides, "and make sure you know a little bit about everything because only a little knowledge about some things is very dangerous."

BEN LANE
Makeup/Hair

Bewitched makeup artist Ben Lane began his career in 1935 at MGM (when the studio was the colossus of the film industry), where he worked on *The Good Earth* and *Annie Oakley* (both released in 1935), *Show Boat* (1936), and several other classics.

Most of the great MGM stars of the era were beneficiaries of Lane's talent (including Ava Gardner, Myrna Loy, Jane Powell, Kathryn Grayson, Judy Garland, Jean Simmons, Greer

Ben Lane

Garson), because his artistry kept pace with the many technical innovations of the cinema. He was able to solve several "facial conflicts" in order for the given actor to appear completely natural and believable.

RKO later lured Lane and his talents away from MGM, where he worked on movies like the original version of *The Hunchback of Notre Dame* and *Gunga Din* (both released in 1939).

In 1955, he was named director of makeup for Columbia Pictures and supervised the techniques for Screen Gems and the TV and movie sectors of Warner Bros. In 1963, he began work on the *Bewitched* screen test and pilot and stayed with the series through its entire eight-year run as makeup executive. Other Columbia TV shows he designed makeup for were *Hazel, Father Knows Best,* and *I Dream of Jeannie.*

In 1941, he received his Masonic degrees at the Mount Olive Lodge in Los Angeles. In 1972, he became a thirty-third-degree Mason (Masonry's highest honor) in recognition of his many contributions to the Masonic Order. He was also the recipient of the DeMolay Legion of Honor in 1975. He is a past president of the Show Business Shrine Club, founder and past president of the Al Malaikah Shrine temple's Masquers, and has served as an officer or board member in four Shrine clubs in Southern California.

Lane moved to Palm Springs in 1979, and in 1981 (after working on the film *Annie)* he retired from Warner/Columbia Studios. In 1983, he started the Scottish Rite in Palm Springs with only a few members and was given Letters of Perfection.

He was then appointed chairman of the Inspector General's Advisory Conference in Palm Springs, where he lives with his wife, Edith. The membership has since increased to more than five hundred.

Byron Munson

BYRON MUNSON
Costumes/Wardrobe

Byron Munson (who passed away in 1990) was born in Illinois and started out in silent movies. But as he once recalled, "I was a lousy actor."

So, eventually, he made his way into the movies via costumes and wardrobe, mainly because he needed the money. "Mostly everything I had," he said, "was burned in a fire."

He was employed at every major Hollywood studio and, as he said, "worked with practically all the major actors. I did all the Bing Crosby and Bob Hope *Road* pictures (*Road to Bali,* 1952, *Road to Denver,* 1955, etc.).

He also worked on films such as *Waterfront* (1944), and *Gidget* on television.

Munson's wife, Doris, was a casting director at Universal Studios for sixteen years and then went on to Filmways (he helped cast TV's *Beverly Hillbillies*) under Will Cowen, who was the head of the short subject films for Universal. (When Cowen moved to Filmways, Doris went with him). Byron's brother, Knox Munson, taught at Northwestern University.

At one time, Byron had one of the "smartest" shops in New York City. His wife said he "always dressed impeccably and improvised when he had to."

He worked on several other films, including *The Pied Piper of Hamelin* (1957, with Van Johnson), and *Kissing Cousins* (1964, with Elvis Presley).

Before *Bewitched* and designing the twin wardrobe for Elizabeth Montgomery's Samantha/Serena scenes, Munson helped a bighearted Presley with similar double duty on *Cousins,* an experience which stood out in Munson's memory.

"I walked past Elvis's car one day," he said, "and I mentioned how much I liked the hubcaps on his Cadillac. The next day, Elvis had purchased an exact set of the wheel covers for my own car. He was a fine human being."

SOL SAKS
Pilot Creator

Born in New York City and raised in Chicago, *Bewitched* pilot creator Sol Saks graduated from the Northwestern University School of Journalism.

Saks arrived in Los Angeles in 1948 and began his career in radio. He had wanted to be a writer since the age of thirteen. Though he is well known for having written the pilot for *Bewitched*, he also gave birth to several other radio and television shows.

Sol Saks

A partial list begins with *Duffy's Tavern* (on radio and featuring Sandra Gould), and *My Favorite Husband*, which was first broadcast on radio (starring Lucille Ball, and later featuring Joan Caufield as a scatterbrained wife to Barry Nelson in the television version). Of the latter, Saks says: "I think that show was the first realistic situation comedy on TV. Both Joan and Barry were actors who did comedy, and not slapstick comedians."

Saks also created *Mr. Adams and Eve*, which starred the legendary actress and *Bewitched* guest director Ida Lupino and Howard Duff. He was once the supervisor of comedy for CBS, as well as a script consultant for the network. Other writing credits include the theatrical feature, *Walk, Don't Run* (1966) starring Cary Grant; the stage plays *The Beginning, Middle and End*, and *Soft Remembrance*; a book, *The Craft of Comedy Writing* (first published in 1985 by Writer's Digest). Saks has also written numerous short stories and articles, such as *The Atlantic Monthly*.

Saks is also an associate professor of script writing for California State University and Pepperdine University and has conducted several successful writing workshops. He's never considered himself a comedy writer, per se, but as he explains, "I write mildly humorous scenes for actors."

Saks's stage play *Soft Remembrance* later opened in Chicago and New York City. He's widowed with two children, Mary Laurie and Daniel, and lives in Sherman Oaks and Malibu.

Parallel Lives

Many *Bewitched* actors, guest performers, supporting players, or central leads worked together in one capacity or another in non-*Bewitched* roles in films, plays, and television.

In the *Bewitched* episode, "Mother-in-Law of the Year," guest star John McGiver played a client who becomes enamored with Endora while under a love spell. McGiver and Agnes Moorehead played husband and wife in the 1963 Jerry Lewis big-screen release, *Who's Minding the Store*. McGiver also worked with William Asher and Elizabeth Montgomery in *Johnny Cool*, also released theatrically in 1963.

Maudie Prickett played Tabitha's teacher in three episodes, two of which featured Dick Sargent. Sargent had costarred with Prickett in the 1966 *Tammy Grimes Show*, whose lead also happened to be ABC's first choice for the *Bewitched* central figure. Prickett's late husband cofounded the Pasadena Playhouse, which was training ground for Prickett and fellow *Bewitched* guest Charles Lane.

Reginald Owen, who played Aunt Clara's boyfriend Ocky in two *Bewitched* segments, appeared with Robert Montgomery, Elizabeth's father, in the 1936 film *Petticoat Fever*.

David White was featured with David Lewis, who played client Mark Robbins in the *Bewitched* episode "Nobody's Perfect," in the 1960 Oscar-winning Best Picture film, *The Apartment*, starring Jack Lemmon.

Samantha visitor Henry Gibson offered his voice work, along with Agnes Moorehead and Paul Lynde, in the animated feature, *Charlotte's Web*, released for the large screen by Hanna-Barbera in 1973. *Bewitched* guest stars Danny Bonaduce, Dave Madden, and Herb Vigran also lent their vocal talents to the film.

Bewitched guest star and writer Arthur Julian appeared with Elizabeth in *How to Stuff a Wild Bikini* (1965), which was directed by William Asher, though only Buster Keaton and Frankie Avalon had a scene with Elizabeth.

Philip Coolidge, who played the witch apothecary on *Bewitched* (before Bernie Kopell came aboard), appeared as *The Mayor* in the 1960s film *Inherit the Wind*, which also featured Dick York and Norman Fell. Fell can also be seen in *The Graduate* (1967) with Marion Lorne and Alice Ghostley.

Bewitched guests Marcia Wallace and Shelley Berman were featured with Dick Sargent in the 1989 movie *Teen Witch*, which also just so happens to be about a young sorceress.

Leon Ames, Edward Andrews, and Maudie Prickett, *Bewitched* guests all, were featured in the 1961 Disney film *The Absent-Minded Professor*, starring Fred MacMurray.

Alice Pearce and George Tobias also played husband and wife in the 1966 Doris Day film *The Glass Bottom Boat*, which was released after Pearce's death (March 1966). Other *Bewitched* alumni in *Boat* were Paul Lynde, Edward Andrews, and John McGiver.

The film *Oceans 11*, released in 1960, starred *Bewitched* guests Norman Fell, Cesar Romero, and Peter Lawford. Lawford's Chrislow Productions financed the Asher/Montgomery film *Johnny Cool* and produced the 1965 film *Billie*, in which Dick Sargent and Charles Lane had featured roles.

Bewitched guest J. Edward McKinley appeared with Elizabeth in her 1975 TV film *The Legend of Lizzie Borden*, and appeared briefly as a murder victim in an episode of TV's *Wild, Wild West*, entitled "Night of the Vicious Valentine." Agnes Moorehead won her only Emmy for "Valentine," which aired on February 2, 1967. Despite a record nine *Bewitched* client performances in ten appearances, McKinley never acted in a sequence with Moorehead.

McKinley, however, was cast in what is probably the all-time *Bewitched* alumni association creation: *The Ghost and Mr. Chicken*, a 1966 theatrical release.

Besides McKinley, *Chicken's* cast included: Dick Sargent, Sandra Gould, Charles Lane, Reta Shaw, and Cliff Norton. The film was directed by Alan Rafkin, who guided two *Bewitched* episodes.

The *Bewitched* alumni record for roles in a regular series may belong to TV's *Mr. Peepers*, which starred Wally Cox. Marion Lorne played Mrs. Guerny on the show, which also featured Ruth McDevitt as Peeper's mother and Reta Shaw as Aunt Lil.

Paul Lynde and Alice Ghostley huddle together (left) in this scene from "New Faces," 1954. Also pictured (from left): Jimmy Russel, Ronny Graham, and Allen Conroy.

Elizabeth magically gazes into *Bewitched* comic book, 1965.

Chapter 14

Necromantic Memorabilia

Bewitched Related Music Releases

Albums

Milton DeLugg and His Orchestra: Music for Monsters, Munsters, Mummies and Other TV Fiends (Epic LN-24125 mono/BN-26125 Stereo) 1965.

Frank Devol: TV Potpourri—Themes From Top Television Shows (Audio Fidelity AFLP 2146 mono/AFSD 6146 Stereo) 1965. [Note: This LP also rereleased through Realistic/Audio Fidelity Boxed Set: *The Wonderful World of Music,* 50-2003, 1968.]

Peggy Lee: Pass Me By (Capitol T-2320 mono/ST-2300 Stereo) [Vocal] 1965.

Jimmy Smith: Monster [Arranged and Conducted by Oliver Nelson] (Verve V-8618 mono/V6-8616 Stereo) 1965.

Lawrence Welk: My First Of 1965 (Dot DLP 3616 mono/DLP 25616 Stereo) 1965.

45 RPM Singles

Billy Costa (Colpix 750) 1965.

Paul and Mimi Evans (Epic 5-9726) [Vocal] 1965.

Steve Lawrence (Columbia 4-43192) [Vocal] 1965.

Peggy Lee (capital 5404 [Vocal/same as album] 1965.

Frankie Randall (RCA 47-8434) [Vocal] 1965.

Foreign (Albums)

The Castle Music Orchestra/Conducted by Eric Cook: Castle Music, Volume 1 *Castle Music LTD* YPRX-1409 (Stereo) [Australia]; no date.

It's very difficult to find original memorabilia on Bewitched.
When you find it, it's rare and incredibly expensive.

STEVE RANDISI
Bewitched *enthusiast and entertainment historian.*

Paperback by Al Hine/Dell.

Samantha posing-doll, by Ideal.

Additions (Albums)

Various Artists: Television's Greatest Hits, Volume II (TeeVEE Toons TVT-1200), 1986. [Note: no artist credited on all these recreations (including *Bewitched* theme).]

Emily Yancy: Yancy (Mainstream 56046 mono/S6046 Stereo) [Vocal] 1965.

Irene Reid: Room for One More [Arranged and conducted by Oliver Nelson] (Verve V-8621 Mono/V6-8621) 1965.

Others

Stymie card game [Milton Bradley, 1964]

Jigsaw Puzzle (painting) with enclosed photo of Samantha [Milton Bradley, 1964]

The Samantha and Endora Board Game [Game Gems, 1965]

Fun and Activity Book [Treasure Books, 1965]

Story Book [Grosset and Dunlap, 1965]

Bewitched (Paperback novel) by Al Hine [Dell, February 1965]

Comic Book Series Nos. 1 through 14 [Dell, April

Bewitched jigsaw puzzle.

1965 to October 1969]

Elizabeth Montgomery Paper Dolls [1966]

Tabitha (spelled *Tab<u>a</u>tha* on box]—*The* Bewitched *Baby Paper Dolls* [Magic Wand Corporation, 1966]

Samantha Doll [1966]

Tabitha Doll [1966]

Plastic Play Dishes for Tabitha *Doll* [1968]

The Opposite Uncle by William Johnston, a hardcover novel [Whitman, 1970]

When *Bewitched* special effects man Richard Albain decided to remodel the patio in his home, he thought it would be a great idea to have the *Bewitched* cast autograph the patio tiles.

Adam (David Ankrum), now a mortal, is easily embarrassed by his sister Tabitha's "nose" for magic in the 1970s *Tabitha* series, starring Lisa Hartman.

Chapter 15

A Tiny TV Tome to Tabitha

*A lot of fans wondered
where I was.*

ERIN MURPHY

••

t was 1977.
Bewitched had ended its original network run merely five
years before.
Miraculously, Tabitha, Samantha, and Darrin's half-sorcer-
ess/half-human daughter, was now twenty-two years old
and starring in a witch-com of her own.

Erin and Diane Murphy, the twin actresses who had originally portrayed the young diviner, were only thirteen years old.

Lisa Hartman (pre-*Knots Landing*) was cast as the immortal
offspring of Elizabeth Montgomery, Dick York, and Dick Sargent.

Apparently, one Samantha and two Darrins added up to three
Tabithas; actually, four if you count the first pilot tabbed as a
Bewitched sequel. The initial outing was entitled *Tabatha*, with
an *a*, and starred Liberty Williams in the lead. Bruce Kimmell
played Adam, and Archie Kahn was her love interest, Cliff.

This Williams-Kimmell-Kahn version was not purchased by
ABC. The second pilot starring Lisa Hartman was made and
sold to the network.

Hartman's Tabitha had powers just like her mom. She was a
lovely, high-spirited witch who could twitch her nose like
Samantha (the finger-to-nose method Tabs used as a kid had
been laid to rest).

Tabitha worked at a Los Angeles television station as a production assistant on a late-night interview program, entitled
The Paul Thurston Show.

Robert Urich played Thurston, who was unaware of
Tabitha's enchanting ways, though he was cast as her

A fresh-faced Liberty Williams glowed in an otherwise uninspiring first *Tabatha* series attempt.

Archie Hahn (left) was boyfriend "Cliff" to Liberty Williams's "Tabatha," while Bruce Himmel played warlock brother Adam in the first pilot.

romantic interest. As the producer and star of his own show, Paul was Tabitha's boss.

Ever under a barrage of ratings, deadlines, and pressures from the top brass and Paul's bullying, Tabitha somehow managed to juggle everything successfully and get the show-with-in-a-show on the air every week.

It was like a magical *Mary Tyler Moore Show.* Well, almost.

Tab's brother Adam (played by twins Greg and David Lawrence on *Bewitched*) was now grown up, too, and played by David Ankrum in the new series. He was also merely mortal and frequently feared the world's possible discovery of his sister's searing personality. As a result, he continually urged Tabs to forget her immortal heredity and live the mortal manner.

You know, just like Mom did.

Or, at least, just like Mom tried to do.

Then there's Aunt Minerva, the Agnes Moorehead equivalent played by Karen

Morrow. Minerva gnaws on Tabitha's nerves as a swinging sorceress (of the intermediate age set), who struggles to persuade her stubborn niece to kick up her heels and use her power for fun and profit, just like any other modern witch, just like Endora tried so insistently with Samantha.

Naturally, this premise set up a constant tug of war between Adam and Minerva, with Tabitha stuck in the middle, just like the relationship between Endora, Darrin, and Samantha on *Bewitched*.

Roger Bennett, Adam's human fraternity brother, was Tabitha's recurrent date and quasirival for Urich's Paul Thurston. Roger was punctual, wholesome, and often the unknowing victim of Tabitha's witchery.

Barry Van Dyke and Lee Stuart costarred in *Tabitha*, while Sandra Gould, George Tobias (Abner and Gladys Kravitz) and Bernard Fox

Producer "Marvin Decker" (Mel Stewart, left), often finds the egocentric TV star "Paul Thurston" (Robert Urich, center) difficult to work with on *Tabitha (now with an "i").*

(Dr. Bombay) from *Bewitched* made periodic guest appearances.

A Lovely Dey

Somewhere in between these consecutive pilots, actress Susan Dey was approached about playing Sam's adult daughter.

Bewitched writer Ed Jurist thought Dey's casting would have been ideal. "She's an exact double for Elizabeth Montgomery," he said.

Yet Dey declined.

Three years before *Tabitha's* premiere, she had completed four seasons as Laurie Partridge on *The Partridge Family*, and she set out to break the sweet daughter mold, a goal she finally reached with her role as Grace Van Owen on NBC's highly acclaimed prime-time hit, *L. A. Law*.

Lisa Hartman also resembled Elizabeth, and even possessed similar body language, but *Tabitha*, any way you spelled it, still did not succeed.

Elizabeth, who had "absolutely zero to do with the show," used to receive mail from people who were outraged that Erin and Diane Murphy were not involved with it. As she recalled, the letters would say, "What in the world is going on here? Tabitha is in her twenties! This doesn't make any sense!" And she responded "to each and every person who was looking for an answer." She said, "I felt an obligation to them. They were annoyed and felt betrayed."

"I wish they had waited a couple of years so I could have done the show," admits Erin Murphy. "I would have loved to do it. But I was only thirteen years old when it came on the air."

Such real-life chronology did not jibe with *Tabitha's* development.

According to Samantha's pilot creator Sol Saks, "*Bewitched* had the feel of success from the beginning. Everyone liked it and enjoyed it while they were making it. *Tabitha* had problems from the get-go."

As Saks remembers, Bill Asher, who had helped to develop *Tabitha* and also directed one of its episodes ("The Arrival of Nancy"), asked him to work on the show.

"I had something totally different in mind from what they finally produced," Saks declares. "With *Tabitha*, they set out to do *Bewitched* without Samantha and the original cast."

Bewitched writer Bernie Kahn was story editor on *Tabitha*, and even he admits, "We were floundering. We didn't understand the character. We really didn't have a fix on the show."

Of winning the *Tabitha* lead in 1977, Lisa Hartman told *The Los Angeles Times* on May 12, 1977:

"It was a real shock to get that. I came out here [L.A. from Texas] to make records and tour. I never really thought about [doing] a series."

Had *Tabitha* not been continually bumped by Christmas specials like *Rudolph the Red-Nosed Reindeer* and *Frosty the Snowman* (great TV shows in their own right), Hartman said the show might have had a better chance.

Tabitha, Again?

Just prior to *Tabitha*'s debut on ABC, an animated Tabitha and Adam appeared in the 1973–1974 Saturday morning special, *Tabitha and Adam and the Clown Family*, featuring the young Stephens children's involvement with a circus. Cindy Eilbacher offered her voice as Tabitha, and Michael Morgan "spoke" for Adam. Other voices included Lennie Weinrib and Paul Winchell (who guest-starred on *Bewitched*).

Tabitha's Testaments

Tab-Title 1

Tabitha (The Pilot)
[No airdate recorded]

Scribe: Jerry Mayer

Overseer: Bruce Bilson

Sojourners: Eric Server, Timothy Blake

Tab-Terse: Tabitha arranges for the debonair and unsettling Professor Andrews Collins, author of a book on fuel frugality, to be a program guest, only to discover that Paul means to supplant Collins with a beauty contestant. Meanwhile, Aunt Minerva pays a visit to discourage Tabitha from dating Adam's fraternity brother.

Tab-Bits: The central Sam/Darrin/Endora conflict from *Bewitched* is employed here. Director Bruce Bilson has recently guided episodes of *Lois and Clark: The New Adventures of Superman.*

Tab-Title 2

Tabitha's Weighty Problem
[11-12-77]

Scribe: Jerry Mayer

Overseer: Charles Dubin

Sojourners: Bernard Fox, Peter Palmer, Robert Clarke

Tab-Terse: Adam is ecstatic: The station has assigned him to oversee an uncommonly prestigious transcontinental weight-lifting athletic event. Tabitha, on the other hand, contracts an uncommon cold, and her magical powers go haywire, causing confusion while she serves as a personal guide to Russian World Champion Vasily Kasseroff during his visit. Aunt Minerva may have the antidote, which has something to do with spiderwebs.

Tab-Bits: Guest star Peter Palmer was *Lil' Abner* on stage and screen. Aunt Minerva conjures up a temporary remedy that includes spiderwebs.

Tab-Title 3

Halloween Show
[No airdate recorded]

Scribe: Jerry Mayer

Overseer: Charles Rondeau

Sojourners: Mary Wickes, Dena Crowder, James Bond III

Tab-Terse: Tabitha clashes with Cassandra, the foremost leader of a potent coven of witches who becomes enraged by Paul's mockery of witchcraft and vows revenge. She tells Minerva that a "hit-witch" will be unleashed upon Paul. Minerva herself faces punishment should she reveal the plan to Tabitha. The plan is executed on Halloween night when Cassandra transforms Paul into a werewolf and the son of Marvin Decker (the station's producer) into a turkey.

Tab-Bits: Guest star Mary Wickes is best known for her role on TV's *Father Dowling Mysteries* and as a nun in *Where Angels Go, Trouble Follows* films of the 1960s, as well as in the *Sister Act* films of the 1990s with Whoopi Goldberg. Wickes died on October 25, 1995. This episode is a semiremake of the *Bewitched* segment entitled "The Witches Are Out."

Tab-Title 4

A Star Is Born
[1-19-77]

Scribes: Roland Wolpert and Bernie Kahn
Overseer: Charles Rondeau
Sojourners: Jeanne Wilson, Montana Smoyer, Fritz Feld
Tab-Terse: A weathergirl named Wanda becomes a friend to Paul and a problem for Tabitha. Aunt Minerva then arranges for her magical niece to become the new weatherperson and makes sure atmospheric conditions perform according to Tabitha's predictions. When Marvin forces Tabitha to wear more revealing outfits on the air, she returns to her old job, which is far from stardom but more in balance with her priorities.

Tab-Bits: Fritz Feld appeared as the maestro in the *Bewitched* episode "Samantha on the Key board."

Tab-Title 5

Minerva Goes Straight
[11-26-77]

Scribe: Jerry Mayer
Overseer: Charles Rondeau
Sojourners: Dick Libertini, Susan Keller, Frank Delfino
Tab-Terse: Trouble erupts when Tabitha suggests that Aunt Minerva try the mortal life. She does so by landing herself a "normal" job at KXLA as Tabitha's coworker. When Paul invites Tabitha for a weekend of skiing, for the sake of Minerva's love life (and her own protection), Tabitha invites her aunt to come along. Upon arrival, Minerva falls madly in love with a philandering French ski instructor, who only has eyes for another (mortal) woman. Tabitha then admits that maybe it wasn't such a good idea for her aunt to take a walk on the mortal side, and Minerva eventually decides to return to her supernatural ways.

Tab-Bits: This premise was also used in the *Bewitched* episode, "Samantha's Power Failure."

Tab-Title 6

Mr. Nice Guy
[12-10-77]

Scribe: Martin Donovan
Overseer: Charles Rondeau
Sojourners: Billie Hayes, Mickey Morton, Richard Branda
Tab-Terse: Minerva's attempts to transform Paul into a good person (any time he looks into

the mirror he becomes "Mr. Nice Guy"), and the ratings for his show take a dive. Tabitha and Adam try to solve the problem by removing all of Paul's mirrors, but to no avail. Paul really seems to go off the deep end when he decides to do missionary work in China with a nun (who appears as a guest on his show).

Tab-Bits: Very similar to the *Bewitched* episode entitled "You're So Agreeable." This episode also employs a nun in one spot who makes a guest appearance on Paul's show.

Tab-Title 7

The Arrival of Nancy
[7-7-78] Rerun

Scribe: George Yanik
Overseer: William Asher
Sojourners: Sandra Gould, George Tobias, Penelope Willis
Tab-Terse: A visit from Tabitha's irresponsible childhood friend, Nancy Kravitz, creates chaos. Nancy, who has a thing for Adam, is the innocent type, and Aunt Minerva sets out to change that. In the end, Nancy becomes a police meter maid, who ends up giving Paul a ticket.
Tab-Bits: Nancy is related to Abner and Gladys Kravitz from *Bewitched*, who also appear in this episode, as well as two other *Tabitha* segments ("Paul Goes to New York"; "Tabitha's Party").

Tab-Title 8

Tabitha's Triangle
[11-12-77]

Scribe: George Yanok
Overseer: Murray Golden
Sojourners: Dack Rambo

Tab-Terse: Ted Bingham, a candidate for state senator, is a guest on Paul's show, where he is questioned with unwarranted hostility. Come to find out, Bingham only decided to do the show because of his attraction to Tabitha, who may indeed have had some kind of infatuation in return. Meanwhile, Aunt Minerva tells her niece that Paul is unsettled by this development. And in the end, Tabitha (who found herself the object of a high-powered campaign to become Bingham's wife) is left to question the quality of sincerity.

Tab-Bits: At one point, a truth spell is employed by Minerva, as were similar hexes by Endora in two *Bewitched* episodes ("Speak the Truth" and "The Truth, Nothing but the Truth, So Help Me Sam"). Guest star Dack Rambo (*Dirty Sally*, *Dallas*) succumbed to AIDS in the early 1990s; he had a twin brother named Dirk, who burned to death in a 1967 car accident.

Tab-Title 9

That New Black Magic
[12-31-77]

Scribe: Robert Stambler
Overseer: Herb Wallerstein
Sojourners: Tracey Reed, Barber Mealy, Frank Delfino
Tab-Terse: Portia, a witch who made Tabitha's high school years unpleasant, returns to create havoc anew. She begins by supernaturally seducing the happily married Marvin Decker (producer of *The Paul Thurston Show*) with a magical red velvet coat. Once he puts on the coat, he turns "hip" and ends up inviting Portia to the "Dirty Disco." With Tabitha's help, Portia's plans backfire, and Marvin falls deeper in love with his wife.

Tab-Bits: Did Tabitha attend a mortal institution or a school for witches?

Tab-Title 10

What's Wrong With Mr. Right?
[No airdate recorded]

Scribe: Jerry Mayer

Overseer: George Tyne

Sojourners: Rod McCary, Fred McCarren, Sydney Lassick

Tab-Terse: Tabitha's encounter with "dreamy" TV director Jeff Baron almost turns into a nightmare due to a jealous and conceited warlock named Monty the Magnificent. The trouble begins when Monty appears in Paul's commercial directed by Jeff. Monty then casts spells giving Jeff the over-romantic qualities of a warlock (which turns Tabitha off) and ruins the commercial (in which Tabitha also appears, singing). Tabitha then decides that she really likes Jeff, and to remedy the situation, she turns back time to work her way.

Tab-Bits: Lisa Hartman, who lent her voice to the opening credits for the series, sings on camera in this episode. Guest star Rod McCary appeared with Barbara Eden in NBC's *Harper Valley PTA* series.

Tab-Title 11

Paul Goes to New York
[1-7-78]

Scribe: Bernie Kahn

Overseer: Charles Rondeau

Sojourners: Penelope Willis, Barbara Sharma, Kenneth Mars

Tab-Terse: Paul leaves KXLA to host a New York City game show called *Make a Pile.* He's replaced by Renee Cummings, who is vicious both to her guests and the backstage crew. Aunt Minerva then suggests to Tabitha that she ask Paul to return. They travel to New York and find out that Paul isn't the star he said he was. Problem is, Renee's contract is for a full year. Tabitha's solution: Paul can be the cohost. But Renee doesn't make things easy. So a good witch then makes a bad woman's true colors seep through when Tabitha makes Renee act like a cat.

Tab-Bits: A similar plot would be employed in future episodes of *Newhart* and *Murphy Brown.*

Tab-Title 12

Tabitha's Party
[1-14-78]

Scribe: Martin Donovan

Overseer: Charles Rondeau

Sojourners: Bernard Fox, Mary Wickes, Penelope Willis

Tab-Terse: KXLA throws a party, and Aunt Minerva crashes it with a love potion that she spikes into the punch and the dip. As a result, Paul and Nancy Kravitz plan to fly to Vegas to get married, Adam and Cassandra fall in love, and Marvin falls for himself in the mirror. Tabitha summons Dr. Bombay, who arrives with one of his sultry nurses—and an antidote. In the end, Cassandra (representing the Witches' Council), learns that Bombay's nurse is nonwitchly, insists that a new decree (to allow supernatural-to-human bonding) be followed, and marries the good doctor and his mortal medic.

Tab-Bits: This plotline was used twice on *Bewitched.* Also, it's established here that the Witches' Council has reversed its position on mixed marriages.

More Mortal Lives

LISA HARTMAN

Lisa Hartman

Lisa Hartman comes from a show business family. Her father was an actor/singer, and her mother is a Houston, Texas, television producer turned publicist.

As a youngster, Lisa began modeling, appearing in television commercials and performing in children's theater productions. She attended Houston High School for the Performing and Visual Arts and appeared in such Houston-based stage productions as *South Pacific* and *Cinderella*.

Lisa's television appearances include two roles on the ever-popular *Knots Landing* and in numerous TV movies and guest shots. One of her major theatrical films was a remake of *Where the Boys Are*, made in 1984.

In addition to acting, Lisa is an accomplished musical vocalist (who sang the opening to *Tabitha*) and has recorded numerous albums.

She's married to country music superstar Clint Black, with whom she resides in Texas.

ROBERT URICH

Two years after initiating his acting career in Chicago, Robert Urich came to Hollywood where he landed his first major role in an episode of the television classic, *Kung Fu*. Since then, he has starred in the television series *SWAT*; as *Bob* in the ahead-of-its-time comedy, *Bob and Carol and Ted and Alice; Soap; Vegas; Spenser for Hire;* and *American Dreamer*.

His big-screen motion pictures have included *Magnum Force* (1973), *Endangered Species* (1982), and *The Ice Pirates* (1984). Production of Urich's new syndicated TV series, *Lazerus Man*, had to be shut down due to his battle with cancer. Urich succumbed in April 2002.

MEL STEWART

Mel Stewart began his career in show business as a musician and got into acting by hanging around his New York neighborhood theaters.

After performing in several off-Broadway plays, he landed a role in the Broadway production of *Simply Heaven*, a play which took him from New York to London and back again. Since then, he has appeared in stage productions such as *Me, My Mother, My father and I*, and *In the Counting House*.

Stewart has guested in several TV series, including *Sanford and Son, Police Story, All in the Family* (where he originated the role of *George Jefferson*), *Good Times*, and *What's Happening?*, and enjoyed a regular role on *Harry O*, with David Jansen.

Stewart made his big-screen debut in *Odds Against Tomorrow* (1959) and went on to do other films, including *The Hustler* (1961), *Serpico* (1973), and *Let's Do It Again* (1975).

DAVID ANKRUM

The son of the late character actor Morris Ankrum, David Ankrum worked with his father in repertory productions when he was a youth.

David continued his acting interest while in high school and college and appeared in several theatrical stage productions.

Ankrum kept acting in workshops and improvisational groups.

He has guested in television shows like *Barnaby Jones, Cannon, The Waltons*, and *Simon and Simon*, and has appeared in numerous commercials.

His feature films include *Zebra Force* (1977).

KAREN MORROW

Karen Morrow

Karen Morrow got her start in show business when she was hired to sing in the chorus at the Equity Theater in Milwaukee, Wisconsin.

After appearing in several Milwaukee stage productions, Karen ventured off to New York where she performed in the off-Broadway production of *Sing, Muse*, and with the National Company of *The Unsinkable Molly Brown*.

Karen made her Broadway debut in *I Had a Ball*, and then became a regular cast member in such television productions as *The Jimmy Dean Show, The Garry Moore Show*, and *The Sid Caesar Hour*. In 1969, she moved to Los Angeles, where she was featured as a regular on TV's *The Jim Nabors Show*.

Karen has since appeared on many TV series and has sung at the White House. She also had a nightclub routine with actress Nancy Dussault, who is best known from television's *Too Close for Comfort*.

BARRY VAN DYKE

Barry Van Dyke broke into acting behind the scenes as a production assistant on his father's comedy series, *The New Dick Van Dyke Show*, in 1971.

After appearing in bit parts on the *New* show, Barry landed roles in such programs as *The Tony Randall Show*, *Wonder Woman*, and *Van Dyke and Company* (a variety show starring his dad), *Lucas Tanner*, *Spencer's Pilots*, and *Gemini Man*.

Recently, he costarred with his father in the short-lived sitcom, *The Van Dyke Show*, and was the featured actor in the cable version of *Airwolf*.

He also starred alongside his father once again in the CBS hit *Diagnosis: Murder*.

JERRY MAYER

Tabitha writer and executive producer Jerry Mayer has served in the television industry as executive story editor on *The Bob Newhart Show*, was the producer of the critically acclaimed, though short-lived, *Fay* sitcom, and has written for such TV fare as *All in the Family*, *M*A*S*H**, and *The Mary Tyler Moore Show*. Mayer has also penned various plays and nightclub acts.

BRUCE BILSON

Tabitha director Bruce Bilson won an Emmy in 1968 for best direction of a segment of TV's *Get Smart*. His other small-screen directing credits include several other *Smart* outings, *Barney Miller*, and numerous movies of the week.

ROBERT STAMBLER

Tabitha producer Robert Stambler has produced television series including *Kate McShane*, *Paper Moon*, and *Hawaii Five-O*. In addition to writing scripts for the classic *Five-O*, Stambler also produced the feature films *Hang 'Em High* (1968) and *The Hawaiians* (1970).

Back in 1963, Stambler became a production assistant on the *Sam Benedict* TV series. Later that year, he began writing scripts for *Benedict* as well as the *Mr. Novak* series. He became *Novak*'s producer in 1964, the year in which *Bewitched* debuted on ABC.

Bewitched Episode Titles in Alphabetical Order

A Is for Aardvark (#17)
Abner Kadabra (#29)
Accidental Twins (#78)
Adam, Warlock or Washout (#242)
Alias Darrin Stephens (#37)
Ancient Macedonian Dodo Birds (#118)
And Something Makes Four (#175)
And Something Makes Three (#12)
And Then I Wrote (#45)
And Then There Were Three (#54)
Art For Sam's Sake (#98)
Aunt Clara's Old Flame (#47)
Aunt Clara's Victoria Victory (#100)
Baby's First Paragraph (#62)
Battle of Burning Oak, The (#164)
Be It Ever So Mortgaged (#2)
Bewitched, Bothered and Baldoni (#233)
Bewitched, Bothered and Infuriated (#105)
Birdies, Bogeys, and Baxters (#114)
Bum Raps, A (#69)
Bunny for Tabitha, A (#178)
Business, Italian Style (#110)
Catnapper, The (#71)
Cat's Meow, The (#18)
Charlie Harper, Winner (#99)
Cheap Cheap (#112)
Corn Is as High as a Guernsey's Eye, The (#94)
Corsican Cousins, The (#211)
Crone of Cawdor, The (#101)
Chance on Love, A (#196)
Change of Face (#33)
Cousin Edgar (#36)

Cousin Serena Strikes Again, Part 1 (#155)
Cousin Serena Strikes Again, Part 2 (#156)
Daddy Does His Thing (#167)
Daddy Comes for a Visit (#180)
Dancing Bear, The (#58)
Dangerous Diaper Dan (#82)
Darrin, Gone and Forgotten (#144)
Darrin Goes Ape (#222)
Darrin on a Pedestal (#205)
Darrin, The Warlock (#181)
Disappearing Samantha (#65)
Divided He Falls (#68)
Double, Double, Toil and Trouble (#111)
Double Split (#64)
Double Tate (#59)
Driving Is the Only Way To Fly (#26)
Eat at Mario's (#35)
Eight-Year Witch, The (#240)
Endora Moves in For a Spell (#80)
Eye of the Beholder (#22)
Fastest Gun on Madison Avenue (#57)
Follow That Witch, Part 1 (#66)
Follow That Witch, Part 2 (#67)
Gazebo Never Forgets, A (#89)
Generation Zap, The (#194)
George, The Warlock (#30)
George Washington Zapped Here, Part 1 (#249)
George Washington Zapped Here, Part 2 (#250)
Ghost Who Made a Spectre of Himself, The (#235)
Girl Reporter, The (#8)
Girl With The Golden Nose, The (#73)

Paris, Witches' Style (#234)
Paul Revere Rides Again (#206)
Phrase Is Familiar, The (#187)
Plague on Maurice and Samantha, A (#237)
Playmates (#133)
Pleasure O'Reilly (#25)
Prince of a Guy (#129)
Prodigy (#74)
Red Light, Green Light (#23)
Remember the Main (#34)
Return of Darrin the Bold (#217)
Safe and Sane Halloween, A (#115)
Salem, Here We Come (#202)
Salem Saga (#203)
Sam and Darrin in Mexico City (#170)
Sam and the Moon (#91)
Sam's Hot Bed Warmer (#204)
Sam's Lost Weekend (#186)
Sam's Pet Warlock (#209)
Sam's Secret Saucer (#137)
Sam's Secret Is Discovered (#188)
Sam's Spooky Chair (#86)
Samantha and the Antique Doll (#228)
Samantha and the Beanstalk (#171)
Samantha and the Loch Ness Monster (#231)
Samantha and the Troll (#219)
Samantha Fights City Hall (#149)
Samantha for the Defense (#88)
Samantha Goes South For A Spell (#142)
Samantha Is Earthbound (#244)
Samantha Loses Her Voice (#150)
Samantha Meets the Folks (#14)
Samantha Meets the Folks (Recut Version, #56)
Samantha on the Keyboard (#143)
Samantha on Thin Ice (#246)
Samantha the Bard (#158)
Samantha the Dressmaker (#60)
Samantha the Sculptress (#159)
Samantha Twitches for UNICEF (#166)
Samantha's Bad Day in Salem (#207)

Samantha's Better Halves (#185)
Samantha's Caesar Salad (#173)
Samantha's Curious Cravings (#174)
Samantha's da Vinci Dilemma (#124)
Samantha's Double Mother Trouble (#182)
Samantha's French Pastry (#147)
Samantha's Good News (#168)
Samantha's Magic Mirror (#226)
Samantha's Magic Potion (#212)
Samantha's Magic Sitter (#243)
Samantha's Not So Leaning Tower of Pisa (#232)
Samantha's Old Man (#210)
Samantha's Old Salem Trip (#208)
Samantha's Power Failure (#165)
Samantha's Psychic Pslip (#225)
Samantha's Secret Spell (#179)
Samantha's Shopping Spree (#169)
Samantha's Super Maid (#154)
Samantha's Thanksgiving to Remember (#119)
Samantha's Yoo-Hoo Maid (#172)
Samantha's Wedding Present (#141)
Samantha's Witchcraft Blows a Fuse (#253)
Santa Comes for a Visit and Stays and Stays (#184)
School Days, School Daze (#251)
Serena Stops the Show (#192)
Serena's Richcraft (#245)
Serena's Youth Pill (#247)
Short Happy Circuit of Aunt Clara (#83)
Sisters at Heart (#213)
Snob in the Grass (#126)
Soapbox Derby (#90)
Solid Gold Mother-in-Law (#120)
Speak the Truth (#50)
Splitsville (#140)
Strange Little Visitor, A (#48)
Super Car, The (#93)
Super Arthur (#190)
Tabitha's Cranky Spell (#134)
Tabitha's First Day at School (#248)

Tabitha Episode Titles in Alphabetical Order

Arrival of Nancy, The (#7)
Halloween Show (#3)
Minerva Goes Straight (#5)
Mr. Nice Guy (#6)
Paul Goes to New York (#11)
Star Is Born, A (#4)
Tabitha (#1 the pilot)
Tabitha's Party (#12)
Tabitha's Triangle (#8)
Tabitha's Weighty Problem (#2)
That New Black Magic (#9)
What's Wrong With Mr. Right? (#10)

Photo Credits

Ackerman, Harry 260
Asher, William 10, 108 top
Baer, Parley 143
Bloch, Vera 251 bot, 252
Brown, Robert 90 top
Canfield, Mary Grace 81
Coblio, Scott 281 top right, middle right, bot right
Cummings, Roy 87 top right
Evatt, Tonya 270
Fiedler, John 144 top left
Foster, Jill 265 bot
Fowler, Tamara – Redhead Photography 110, 266 top, 267, 269 top, 272
Fox, Bernard 249
Franken, Steve 85 bot, 98
Garrett, Lila 268
Ghostley, Alice 248
Gibson, Henry 87 bot left, 262
Gilman, Mark 256, 261, 264 bot, 269 bot, 271
Gould, Sandra 255 top
Grandinetti, Fred 46, 92
Hanley, Bridget 271
Hartman, Jonni – Hartman-Black 290
Huddleston, David 144 top right
Ingels, Marty 145
Jackson, Marty 241, 253
Kopell, Bernie 88
Kovak Mehta, Nancy 33 bot
Lane, Ben 273 TOP

Lane, Charles 139
Levey, Stan 274
Matheson, Gary 280, 281 top left
Michaels, Richard 42, 264 top
Montgomery, Elizabeth 238
Morris, Michael 266 bot
Morrow, Karen 291
Munson, Doris 273 BOT
Noce, Nancy 173, 247, 277
Randisi, Steve 107, 112, 113, 250, 251 top
Regal Collection 23, 24, 111, 240, 258, 259 bot
Robinson, Jay 182 top right
Rogers, Kasey 97 top left, 97 top right, 257
Sargent, Dick 243
Simon, Robert F. 259 top
Slade, Bernard 265 top
Sony Pictures Television xii, 2, 3, 4,7,8, 12, 14, 16, 17, 20, 22, 27, 28, 30, 32, 33 top, 35, 39, 40, 43, 45, 49, 51, 55, 56, 58, 59, 62, 65, 66, 68, 69, 71, 73, 75, 76, 77, 79, 82 bot, 84, 85 top, 87 top left, 90 bot, 93, 95, 96, 97 bot left, 99, 100, 101, 102, 103, 104, 114, 115, 116, 122, 123, 126, 129, 130, 134, 160, 162, 168, 179, 182 bot left, 184, 186, 189, 193, 197, 199, 236, 207, 208, 211, 218, 244, 255 bot, 278, 282, 284, 285, 302
Tucker, Fredrick 144 bot left, 144 bot right, 246
Vernon, Irene 82 top
White, David 245
Wilson, Dick 86
Winner, Craig 108 bot

Abracadabra Acknowledgments

A book is never the result of individual effort. And *Bewitched Forever* is no exception.

First and foremost, I offer my deepest gratitude, love, and prayers to Elizabeth Montgomery, who now shares a magical place in Heaven alongside all of the other gifted souls. Elizabeth contributed a generous amount of time, effort, and recollections, and without her there would not have been a worthy *Bewitched* TV series, let alone any *Bewitched* book.

My sincerest appreciation to the also-passed-on immortal souls of Agnes Moorehead, Dick York, and Dick Sargent (two very special *Darrins*), David White, Alice Pearce, George Tobias, Marion Lorne, Paul Lynde, Mabel Albertson, Robert F. Simon, Roy Roberts, Arthur Julian, Harry Ackerman, Danny Arnold, Jerry Davis, E. W. Swackhamer, Irene Vernon, and Ed Jurist.

My profound thanks for the mammoth contributions from those *Bewitched* cast and crew members who remain in this world, including William Asher (without whose discretion Elizabeth Montgomery never would have consented to conversations for a *Bewitched* literary companion), Alice Ghostley, Bernard Fox, Kasey Rogers, Erin Murphy, Diane Murphy, David Mandel-Bloch, Greg Mandel, Richard Michaels, Nancy Mehta (Kovak), Adam West, Bernie Kopell, Henry Gibson, Steve Franken, Bernard Slade, Michael Morris, Bernie Kahn, Lila Garrett, Barbara Avedon, and Dick Albain.

I would also like to thank Helen Lynde, Alexandra White, Nancy Noce, Joan York, Cloris Leachman, Vera Bloch, Geoff Davis, Milton Davis, M.D., Ph.D., David Mittleman, Franklin B. Robner, and Jim Moorehead (the various relatives of *Bewitched*'s living and nonliving actors and production team, all of whom allowed various facts, quotes, and photos of and/or about their family members to be included in this publication).

An extremely large thank-you must go out to top-notch entertainment historian David Keil for his incredible amount of *Bewitched* support, knowledge, facts, trivia, and quotations, all of which are an integral part of this book.

A very special thank-you also to Gary Matheson for his astounding efforts in attaining and categorizing various *Bewitched* photos and memorabilia. And to artist/author Fred Grandinetti for his brilliant contributions.

Also thanks to photographers/artists Tamara Fowler, Mark Gilman, Marty Jackson, Scott Coblio, Dawn Rocha, Mauricio Lopez, and Sam Campanaro.

Big-time gratitude to the following TV-movie memorabilia collectors: Larry Edmunds, Eddie Brandt's Saturday Matinee (and Claire), The Memory Shop, Milton T. Moore Jr., E. Ben Emerson, and Jim and Melody Rondeau.

More acknowledgments to my fellow authors who offered immeasurable advice and assistance through the years: Steve Cox, Laurie Klobas, Bart Andrews, Richard Lamparski, Professor Arthur Asa Berger, and Mark Wood.

I wish also to thank the *Bewitched* Brigade of Fans, headed by Steve Randisi (whose devotion to *Bewitched* is immeasurable, thus matching his humanitarianism), Dan Weaver, Fredrick Tucker, George Gallucci, Carmen Grunke, Jim Pierson, and Nerida Claudio. A special thanks also to Paul Kreft for his dazzling visions of this book's front and back covers.

For unending support in a variety of ways, thank you Robert Foxworth, Robert "Skip" Montgomery Jr., Barry Krost, Dan Levy and Betsy Bundschuh (who helped to edit material for this book); Nancy Spellman, Michael Lipton, Peggy Egan, Ray Biswanger, Helen Gurley, Laurie Britton, and Peter Abel; Michael Silverman, and Douglas Galloway; Harry Medved, George Schaeffer, Julie Franken, Lillian Roberts-Risdon, Peter Todd of the British Film Institute of London, Molden Philips (of PRS. Ltd, also in London); radio show host/producer Neil L. Midman (of WRC in Boston), Lisa Hartman, Jonni Hartman, and Marcella Saunders and the 1970 graduating class of Jefferson High School of Los Angeles.

Special thanks also to Barbara A. Cyprus, Joseph Janowics, the Santa Monica Library; the Rundell, Charlotte, and Paddy Hill Libraries of Rochester, New York; Kathleen O'Brien and David Hamblin; Bob and Bonnie Marinetti, Ethel Levert, Arnold Patent, Rev. G. Arthur Hammons, Bob Greg, Ken Crosby, Mike Nannini (A.K.A. Opie Cunningham), Shirley DiRisio, Rosetta Mundt, Bobby Leaf, Ellen Carter, Ellen Kelley, Bob Jacobs, Debbie Keil, Gloria Delano, Turie Kontianen, Doug and Margie Staheli, Nancy Becker, Marcella Lee, Michael Hyler, Robin Lippincott, Mario and Linda Bosio, John and Denise McNulty, Carol Munshi; Giovanna Curatalo, Clarence Raymer, Howard Raymer, Sharon Petersheim, Theresa Cacia, Laurie Cacia, and Diane Zaborowski (all from Greenleaf Meadows); to Patti, Brenda, Judi, Sue, Gloria, Steve, the boss at the Rochester/Greece Post Office, and Andy Marvel.

Appreciative accolades to everyone at Tapestry Press, including Jill Bertolet, Bill Scott, and David Sims; Catherine Bitran, Mark Caplan Grace Ressler, and Cindy Irwin at Sony Pictures Consumer Products; and Don de Mesqitas, Terence McClusky, Lisa Krone, Lamont Blake, Allan Press, and Linda Kazynski.

A cherished concession to my mom, Frances Mary (who is a living angel); my sister Pam, brother-in-law Sam, and nephew Sammy (who remains a constant inspiration); cousins Rita, Bill, Fred, and Dani Valerie; Jay and Wendy Mann; Marie Turri and her beautiful son Nicolas, Aunt Antoinette, The D'Agostino/Berardi family, Joe, Joanne and Vincent Profetta; Uncle Vincent and Rita, Jimmy, and Carl; David and Eva Leaf; Aunt Elva, Aunt Amelia, Aunt Anna, Aunt Sue, Mary Sue, Jimmy B., Guy, George, Mark, Mike, Gerald, Donny, Rose Alice, Paul (and all of their families); Barney Masters; and Joe, Mary Ann, Joey and Janine Pizzo, Carlos Rivera, and lastly, Melanie and Bob of www.harpiesbizarre.com.

A much-beloved thanks to my divinely departed dad Herbie P. (St. Pompeii), whom I know is helping me now, more than ever. Thanks also to the invisible-but-ever-close family members, including: Aunt Mary, Uncle Albert, Uncle Carl, Aunt Alice and Uncle Ange, Uncle Joe, Uncle Adolph and Aunt Gerdie, Sonny, Uncle Val; Aunt Alice A. and Uncle Frank; Aunt Fay and Uncle Jerry; Grandma and Grandpa Pilato; Nonna and Pappa Turri, Mary Masters, Aunt

Rita, and Boo Boo the best "man's best friend" any man could have; I send out all of my love to you, knowing that you have received it.

Superior spiritual gratitude goes out to Jesus the Christ, The Blessed Mother, St. Joseph, St. Theresa, St. Peter, St. Paul, St. Augustine, St. Anthony of Padua, St. Thomas Aquinas, Buddha, Paramahansa Yogananda, my Guardian Angel Andre, and, most of all, to the Supreme Being of the Universe who is with us *all* the time, in *every* dimension. As such, I say:

Thank you God, for life and light; abundant, full and free; for perfect, boundless, health, wealth, peace, and the power of love and forgiveness, unhampered liberty.

About the Author

Herbie J Pilato graduated in 1983 from Nazareth College of Rochester with a bachelor's degree in Theater Arts. Soon after, he moved to Los Angeles and began his career in the entertainment industry as an actor. He went on to appear on such TV programs as *The Bold and the Beautiful*, *General Hospital*, *The Golden Girls*, and *Highway to Heaven*, as well as in films such as *Fatal Beauty* (with Whoopi Goldberg).

In 1984, he became more interested in the technical end of how Hollywood works and was contracted for eighteen months with NBC Television in Burbank, serving as a page, public relations figure, and production liaison on such popular TV programs as *The Tonight Show* (starring Johnny Carson), *Family Ties*, *Wheel of Fortune*, and the Bob Hope specials.

While with NBC, Herbie J also helped coordinate *An All-Star Salute to President Dutch Reagan*, an affiliates' convention, two publicity tours, *The 1984 Emmy Awards*, the 1984 Democratic presidential debates, and several other television programs and industry-related events.

As author of *The Kung Fu Book of Wisdom* (Tuttle 1995) and *The Kung Fu Book of Caine* (Tuttle 1993), Herbie J believes popular television programs to be an untapped resource for positive social reform. As he told *US* magazine regarding *Bewitched*, "The show has lasted so long [it debuted in 1964] because it's about prejudice. Samantha and Darrin loved each other irrespective of the fact that she was a witch."

Herbie J employs his books with *TV & Self-Esteem Seminars*: the first lecture series to bridge the gap between popular culture and education, advocating against violence on television, and promoting the medium's more emphatic aspects.

Herbie J has also written for *The Gannett Newspapers*, *Sci-Fi Entertainment and Starlog*, *Remember*, *Full-Time Dads*, *Sci-Fi Universe and Classic TV* magazines. For the latter he penned a monthly column about TV's social circuitry. He has appeared on several local and national radio/TV shows such as *The Maury Povich Show*, where he discusses ethnocentrism as the pivotal theme of his tomes and the television shows they profile.

He has also served as a producer and consultant for the E! *True Hollywood Story*, the Screen Gems Network, the Sci-Fi Channel, The Learning Channel, Bravo, and *Entertainment Tonight*, and has worked as a website editor/writer for TV-Now.com, and PAXTV.com. He is working on a combined book about *The Six Million Dollar Man* and *The Bionic Woman*, as well as a guide-book to *Life Goes On*—each of which will address TV heroes of the human spirit.

He will be seen in TV Land's new reality show, *Chasing Farrah*, and Bravo's five part documentary, *The Greatest TV Characters of All Times*. Currrently, Herbie J is serving as a consultant on the forthcoming feature film, *Bewitched*, which will be released in 2005 and stars Nicole Kidman, Will Ferrel, Shirley MacLaine, and Michael Caine.